CHILD ABUSE
AND
NEGLECT
SHARING RESPONSIBILITY

CHILD ABUSE AND NEGLECT
SHARING RESPONSIBILITY

Pamela D. Mayhall
Pima Community College

Katherine Eastlack Norgard
Arizona State University

Illustrations by:
Travis L. Mayhall

JOHN WILEY & SONS
New York   Chichester   Brisbane   Toronto   Singapore

ISBN 0-471-09929-5

Printed in the United States of America

10 9 8 7 6 5 4 3 2

Dedication

To The Children

Preface

As authors of this book, we want to confess our underlying assumptions at the beginning. They will come as no great surprise to most people who grapple with problems of child abuse and neglect daily:

—Child maltreatment does not occur as an isolated event; it is an integral part of the family and social system in which it takes place.

—Both the child and the family need to be understood and treated if prevention and protection are to occur.

—Child maltreatment exists on a continuum; at some time everyone has been abusive and has been abused.

—The history of the family and the law has great bearing on prevention and intervention in child abuse and neglect situations, especially in the difficult questions of rights of the child versus rights of the parents.

The most effective prevention, protection, and intervention options available occur not because we have an organized formal response system, although its importance should not be discounted. In our view it is committed, informed, individuals who work with and care about other individuals, both within and outside the formal system, who offer the most effective options.

This book offers readers an opportunity to study maltreatment in an organized generic way. Abuse and neglect are presented in the context of time and culture, the family system, human development, impact, and formal response systems. The prevention, intervention, and treatment roles of professionals, paraprofessionals, volunteers, friends, neighbors, relatives, and the family are discussed in relationship to each other.

In writing the book we have drawn on our own experience of more than 20 years as practitioners in the juvenile justice and social welfare systems, as educators, and as consultants to human service agencies. We have also had a lot of help. The most positive part of writing this book has been an exchange with the people (many not individually acknowledged), who have contributed ideas, inspiration, resources, specific content, criticism, and support to this project. Even though they do not all share a common position on the many issues of child abuse and neglect, they actively share responsibility for prevention, intervention, and treatment. They include professionals, paraprofessionals, volunteers working in and outside the formal response system, scholars, parents (birth, adoptive, and foster), and children from every part of the United States.

Pamela D. Mayhall
Katherine Eastlack Norgard

Acknowledgments

We wish to thank the following people who reviewed drafts of the manuscript: Richard Bourne, Robert J. Conklin, Lawrence Kobilinsky, Mary Rutherford, Peggy Anderson Smith, Linda L. Stabile, and Jane Penton White.

Several people assisted us by reviewing individual chapters. They were Irene August, Early Childhood Education Programs, Pima College; Jean Baker, Ph.D., Practicing Clinical Psychologist, Tucson; DeAnn Barber, ACSW, Independent Professional Review Team, Tucson; Joan Kaye Beigel, M.A., M.S., Founder and Director, Center For Family and Individual Counseling, Tucson; David K. Bruce, Administration of Justice Programs, Pima College; John R. Evans, Esq., Tucson; Joseph Ferlanto, Chief Referee, Pima County Juvenile Court, Tucson; Reba Grubb, Education Department, Tucson Medical Center; Jorge Iglesias, Chairman, Social Services Program, Pima College; James Kluger, Ph.D., Human Sciences Division, Pima College; Moses A. Leon, Chairman, Administration of Justice Programs, Pima College; Jo Dile, Tucson; Arnie Fuller, Cochise College, Douglas, Arizona; Myra Levenson, M.A., Family Counseling Agency, Tucson; Helena Orlinsky, ACSW, Mental Health Clinician, St. Mary's Hospital, Tucson; Jan Pearson, Permanent Home Planning Unit, D.E.S., Division II; Carmen Preciado, ACSW, Sexual Abuse Unit, Child Protective Services, Tucson; Billie Underwood, Ph.D., Early Childhood Education, Pima College; Ruth Unger, ACSW, Sexual Abuse Unit, Child

Protective Services, Tucson; Georgia Vancza, child advocate, Tucson; Stephen T. Whitman, ACSW, Family Mental Health Services, Veterans Administration Hospital, Tucson; Alayne Yates, M.D. Chief, Child Psychiatry, Arizona Health Sciences Center, Tucson.

Many people have been invaluable in helping us to gain a better understanding of the response network, its programs, problems, resources, and directions for the future. We thank Richard Arthur, San Francisco Department of Social Services; Ken Bergdorf, Ph.D., Westat, Inc., Rockville, Maryland; Douglas Besharov, Visiting Scholar, Brookings Institute, Washington, D.C.; Jeanne Cyriaque, Illinois Department of Corrections, Juvenile Management Information Systems, Springfield, Illinois; Scott Christenson, Director, School of Criminal Justice, Minority Studies, Albany, New York; Gay Deitrich, National Center for Prevention and Treatment of Child Abuse and Neglect, Denver, Colorado; Lorraine Fox, College of St. Francis, Child Programs, Joliet, Illinois; Lt. Brit A. Goodroe, Head, Juvenile Squad, Memphis Police Department, Memphis, Tennessee; Jane Goggins, Director, N.E. Mississippi Emergency Shelter, Corinth, Mississippi; Bob and Diana Grubb, San Francisco; Annie Guerin, Probation Officer, McDowell County, West Virginia; Karen Hanas, Executive Director, Crisis Homes, Inc., Chicago; Les Hendricks, National American Indian Court Judges Association, Reno, Nevada; Hunter Hurst, National Center for Juvenile Justice, Pennsylvania; Aeolian Jackson, NCCAN, Washington, D.C.; Rose Marie Joseph, Placement Officer, Iberia Paris School Board, New Iberia, Louisiana; Barbara Kenny, Corinth, Mississippi.

Charles V. Lanza, Visiting Teacher, Iberia Parish School Board, New Iberia; Beth Lennon, Child Protective Service Liaison, Special Abuse Unit, San Diego Police Department, San Diego; Linda Lewis, Memphis; Merwin Lynch, Navajo Children's Rights Service, Guardian Ad Litem Program, Fort Defiance Agency, Arizona; Jim Mead, Executive Director, For Kid's Sake, Brea, California; Nancy Murphy, Arthur D. Little, Inc., San Francisco; Parents Anonymous, Torrance, California; Ann Pastore, Criminal Justice Research Center, Albany; Maureen Schlenker, American Humane Association, Denver; Cathy Schmitz, Sexual Assault Center, Harborview Medical Center, Seattle; Julius Segal, Ph.D., NIMH, Washington, D.C.; Mike Strozik, counselor, Anderson Street Junior High, New Iberia; Jo Tiger, National Indian Child Abuse and Neglect Center, Tulsa, Oklahoma; Janenne H. Trahan, Child Protective Services, Iberia Parish, OHD/DES, New Iberia; Florence Tritt, R.N., P.T., Association for Retarded Citizens, Pensacola, Florida; Nancy Tuthill, Deputy Director, American Indian Law Center, University of New Mexico, Albuquerque; Lydia Eileen Vigil, Education Commission of the States, Denver; Joseph Wechsler, NCCAN, Washington, D.C.; Gerald Wittman, former Training Director of the National Council of Juvenile Court and Family Judges, Reno; Susan Zimmerman, Registered Speech Therapist, Olsburg, Kansas.

We are grateful for the ongoing professional help of the West Campus Pima Community College Library Staff, especially Peggy Holleman, Coordinator, Cathy Stanley, Kathy Curley, and for the assistance of our typists, Pat Finnegan and Edelmira Gastelum.

Special thanks to 'Carol Luitjens, Editor, and Pamela Bellet-Cassell, Administrative Assistant, from Wiley for their support and assistance, and to our families, who somehow managed to walk patiently with us through this project: Travis, Stacey, David, Don, Sonda, and John.

P.D.M.
K.E.N.

Contents

CHAPTER 1

In The Context Of Time And Culture

What is best for children is never their own choice, but the choice of adults. It is a choice based on what adults believe their children should grow up to be. (Blanchard and Barsh, p. 356.)

THE CHILD'S PLACE

What is the value of a child? Where do children fit into the structure of the society and the family? There is no single answer to either of these questions. Any answer always (1) relates to time and culture; (2) is influenced by the priorities of the society in which it is offered; and (3) is influenced by the unique interactions of a given child, family, and environment.[1] In a very basic sense, children are necessary if a culture is to survive. As a group they represent its future. As individuals, at least some of the children represent its hope, if it is to have a future.

A child is a person who is going to carry on what you have started. He is going to sit where you are sitting, and when you are gone, attend to those things which you think are important. You may adopt all the policies you please, but how they are carried out depends on him. He will assume control of your cities,

[1]See Chapter 2 for more detailed discussion of this concept.

1

states, and nations. He is going to move in and take over your churches, schools, universities, and corporations . . . the fate of humanity is in his hands.

Source. Abraham Lincoln quoted in Grubb, Reba Douglas, *Historical File,* West Virginia Parent–Teacher Association Conference Speeches.

In different times and cultures, children have been valued as hands to do work, as property to be used, bought, and sold, as economic assets, and as valued commodities. Children have been counted as treasures, gifts from the Deity to be cared for, trained, and returned to their source (sometimes by sacrifice). They have existed as nonessentials and even as entertainment for adults. Children have been viewed as evil and as the result of sin. They have been seen as economic liabilities and burdens to individuals and society.

Today, all of these values no doubt exist and add, in their pluralism, confusion to questions relating to the value of children and where they fit or should fit in the structure of our society. Dr. Joseph Jacob strikes a solemn note, one that is shared by several observers, in his concern that a child may be an economic liability today for many families, competing very poorly with other values. As he sees it, "Marked increases in the cost of raising a child cause individual parents, and the economy generally, to view child bearing and child rearing as an economic liability in competition with other values." (Bolton, p. 1.)

Certain characteristics of children have an impact on the value of an individual child. First-born, healthy males have consistently held a high value in society. Girls, often have not fared as well. Children found to be mentally retarded, physically handicapped, born as a twin, conceived out of wedlock, or in some cases, merely born into a poor family have been in most jeopardy throughout history. Seen as economic liabilities, as "evil," or as the result of sin, these children often have been treated cruelly when they have been allowed to survive.

"What is the value of a child?" is an important question in any society. Determination of that value has helped to define a child's right to exist and the conditions and rules under which a child exists. What a society decides is damaging or harmful to a child, as well as what is critical to a child's development exists in this context.

James Garbarino argues that ". . . the maltreatment of children and youth is a prime social indicator of the overall quality of life for families." He suggests that the problem has cultural origins and that maltreatment, in order to exist, ". . . requires a social context that will permit it, specifically one which offers support in law and custom for violence against children . . ." (Garbarino, p. 206). Children throughout time and in most cultures have lived in a world that has supported in law and custom some level of violence against children. The rationale for that violence has often "made sense" within the context of that culture or time and has not been defined as harm to the child. It is instructive to study the precarious and changing position of children throughout history. This experience will assist our understanding and defining the standards by which we judge harm today.

HARM TO THE CHILD

Child maltreatment is as new as tomorrow and as old as human existence. Although it is defined and redefined in every time and culture, it always means harm to a child. Harm is, of necessity, defined within a cultural context in terms of human values, human goals, and available information. What one person may define as harm, another may define as character building. What is generally defined as harm in our culture, may be defined in a different culture as necessary for survival, either of the child or of the social group. As William Lecky (1838–1903), a historian of the nineteenth century observed, "There is no line of conduct which has not, at some time and place been condemned, and which has not at some other time and place, been enjoined as a duty."

Jill Korbin suggests that there are three levels at which we can observe child treatment in a given culture: (1) child rearing accepted in one culture and not accepted in another; (2) harm to the child as a departure from the culturally and socially acceptable standard in one's own society; (3) social conditions or the "society which is sick" and that sick society's impact on treatment of children. (Korbin, p. 22–23.) In a multicultured society, harm becomes particularly difficult to commonly define.

Overall, the critical issues that must be solved do not seem to change very much from culture to culture and time to time. Families in early societies had to solve the issue of how to define right to life, which child rearing rules to follow (including whether or not to use corporal punishment), and how best to help children "fit," that is, become socialized into their culture and their family. They had to decide what is damaging to a child. How these issues are solved has changed constantly, as have community decisions regarding who, that is, which of society's agents, should solve them. Power and responsibility to decide has moved from the father and the family to the state, church, societal and community institutions to a tentative balancing of power and responsibility among all of these.

THE RIGHT TO ABUSE

The Child as Property

As violence against children is viewed in an historical context, it becomes clear that the right to abuse a child may be vested in part in two important rights: the right to property and the right to own a child. Aristotle stated, "The justice of a master or a father is a different thing from that of a citizen, for a son or slave is property, and there can be no injustice to one's own property." (*Child Abuse: The Problem and Its Management* V. 2.) Although this right to own a child was most pronounced in antiquity, children as property was a tradition that the English colonists brought with them from the mother country. It was not until 1967 that children were assigned rights in the juvenile justice process in the United States. The issue of a parent's right to decide for children versus children's rights to decide for themselves is far from resolved today. Presently, in the United States, the state may, in the interest of protecting a child, act *in loco parentis* (in the place of the parent) and make a decision to remove a child from the parents' custody. The child can be placed in a variety of and sometimes a sequence of alternative settings.

Fitness to Live

In many cultures, infants were born without even the right to exist. Usually the child's fitness to live was determined by the father of the child. In ancient Rome, a man had the freedom to sell, abandon, or kill his child. He had the power of *patria potestas* (the power of life and death) over the child. When a man entered his father's house he moved from a position of power to one of property (Thomas, p. 295.)

Once a child was acknowledged by his father, he was assured a place in the home and in the community. In some cultures, however, this was not enough. Children were not recognized as persons until they were formally named or baptized. The ancient Greeks had both customs.

> On the fifth or seventh day the infant went through the ceremony of purification; the midwife holding him in her arms, walked several times around a burning altar. A festive meal on this day was given to the family. The door was decorated with an olive crown for a boy, with wool for a girl. On the tenth day after its birth the child was named and another feast took place. This ceremony implies the acknowledgment, on the part of the father, of the child's legitimacy. Friends and relatives presented the infant with toys of metal or clay, while the mother received painted vases. (Eicher, p. 618.)

In many Christian faiths today children do not receive spiritual recognition until they are christened.

The child born out of wedlock was considered to be born in sin. This child had no place and often no nourishment or nurturing. He received no protection under its legal codes.

Fitness to live was sometimes defined in terms of ability to survive. It might be confirmed by survival of a specific period of time (as an hour, half hour, or day.) Earthly nourishment was apparently the key to life in some cultures. Rites specified placing liquid (milk, honey, or water) on the child's lips and having the child accept nourishment in order to be bestowed with life. In British New Guinea, if water placed on the infant's lips was not accepted by the infant, the baby was thrown away. (Radbill, p.4.) Germans threw infants into an icy river and saved them if they cried; the North American Indians threw children into a pool. If they rose and cried, they were saved. (Radbill, p.4–5.) Girls were more likely to be left exposed to die or to be killed than were boys. Children who were weak, premature, deformed, or retarded were declared not fit to survive. Twins were often included in this group. Such children were believed to be evil or possessed. Greek, Roman, Chinese, Indian, and many other cultures shared this belief. In several countries, such as China, Peru, Mexico, and India, children were cast into rivers in order to ensure good fortune and good harvest. (Smith, p. 4–6.) Children were buried alive under the foundations of buildings and dikes in India, China, Germany, and Canaan to assure the durability of the structures. The Bible discusses several incidents of real or implied infanticide: Abraham was willing to sacrifice his son, Isaac; Herod's massacre of male infants; King Ahaz burning his children in a fire. "Infanticide has, from time immemorial, been the accepted procedure for disposing not only of deformed or sickly infants, but of all such newborns who might strain the resources of the individual family or larger comunity." (Langer, pp. 353–362.) The most frequently recorded methods of infanticide were drowning, and lay over or "roll over," (suffocation of a child sleeping in bed with an adult, accomplished by the adult rolling or laying over the child. (Death of the child was often claimed to be accidental.) Exposure to the elements and human sacrifice were also employed. Favorite disposal sites included cisterns and privies (Radbill, p.6.)

To summarize the most commonly noted reasons for the practice of infanticide are:

1. As a way of limiting family size, that is, a form of birth control.
2. As a means of avoiding the certain dishonor and financial problems of illegitimacy.
3. As a way of gaining power.
4. As a way of disposing of a retarded or deformed child.
5. As a way to please the gods and expel evil spirits, or more generally, to serve religious beliefs.
6. As a means of insuring financial security.

Child Rearing Issues

Cultures in antiquity seemed to have a high level of consensus within their societies as to how a child should be reared. Conversely in modern society, there is some disagreement on child rearing issues even within a single family. Differences become more pronounced as cross cultural aspects are considered.

XSince there is no universal norm or standard for child rearing, it becomes very difficult to determine what is and is not an appropriate approach especially as we attempt to impose our personal standards on other cultures. If we judge their behavior in the context of our culture rather than their own, we may even increase rather than decrease harm to children. For example, although initiation rites in some cultures may seem harsh, the child who does not paticipate in them becomes an outsider to the group. Sometimes these rites include scarification, hazing, no food for an extended period, an ordeal to demonstrate courage, cranial deformation, or bodily mutilation. Which is more harmful: to have the child be an outcast in his society or to be scarred, as are his friends, for life? Is there some middle ground?

Some of the difficulties experienced by American Indian families today have been created by well meaning people who have had legitimate concerns for the welfare of Indian children, but who have lacked understanding and appreciation of American Indian culture. Authorities who have intervened to improve the circumstances of Indian children have sometimes contributed to weakening the Indian family and isolating the child. Recent surveys (1977 and 1979) indicate that ". . . between one-fourth and one-third of all Indian children are separated from their families and placed in foster homes, adoptive homes, or institutions. Indian children are placed in foster homes at per capita rates of up to 25 times greater than non-Indian families."

("Implementing the Indian child Welfare Act of 1978," p. 1.) Rather than operating to strengthen the family and increase safety and nurturing for the child, this process has sometimes weakened family bonds and placed both the child and the family more at risk. (Blanchard and Barsh, p. 351.) Positive intervention and treatment must be based on an understanding and appreciation of a family's culture.

Appropriate Discipline

Acceptable standards and approaches to discipline are affected by time and culture. In many cultures corporal punishment, in the form of spankings, whippings and floggings by parents and schoolmasters is and has been acceptable and expected. In other cultures corporal punishment has been and is viewed as inappropriate, disrespectful to the child, and a violent and abusive act.

No matter what the dominant view regarding corporal punishment has been, a dissenting view seems to have existed also. An interesting comment is found in a 1753 essay regarding discipline of English children of the upper middle classes.

> Severe and frequent Whipping is I think a very bad Practice; it inflames the Skin, it puts the Blood into a Ferment, and there is besides, a Meanness, a Degree of Ignominy attending it, which makes it very unbecoming: still there may be Occasions which will render it necessary: but I earnestly advise that all the milder Methods be first try'd. A coarse clamorous manner of enforcing Obedience is also to be avoided; it is vulgar, and nothing vulgar should be seen in the Behaviour of Parents to the Children, because through the Eyes and Ears it taints their tender Minds: still, let Parents make their Children later see and feel the Power they have over them.
>
> Source. James Nelson, "An Essay on the Government of Children, Under Three General Heads: viz. Health, Manners, and Education, (London, 1753) as quoted in Simonsen and Gordon, p. 16).

Sweden, in 1979, outlawed corporal punishment of children as abusive. In the United Sates much discussion continues regarding the same issue but with little resolution. The findings of a national survey of family violence conducted by Gelles and Straus (1979) are of interest on this subject. The definition of violence used in the survey was ". . . an act carried out with the intention or perceived intention of physically hurting another person." This definition includes spanking a child since, as the researchers point out, the act of spanking is intended to cause physical pain and, if a spanking were administered to someone outside the family the action would be legally defined as assault. (Gelles and Straus, p. 20.) Although they found that 58% of the respondents in their survey had used some form of violence within the twelve months prior to the survey and that 71% had done so at some time, they suggest that this finding is an underestimate since other studies show that probably "90% or more of American children have been hit at leat once by their parents." (Gelles and Straus, p. 23.)

Discipline and independent thinking were considered important in a traditional Navajo culture. The life that Navajo children needed to be prepared for was seen as a continuing struggle to survive. It was believed that a child would have many problems to face in life: old age, poverty, sickness, death. Children, therefore, needed to be strong and self disciplined. Wilson offers some examples of the teaching of discipline.

> At the break of dawn, the parents threw the young ones out of their sleeping places; they whipped some of them; some awoke on their own will, knowing the

consequences if they did not. They were told that if they slept, they would find themselves killed by the enemy; they would be weak; their mind would not respond with alertness, and they would not survive the cruelness of life. (Wilson, p. 9.)

Older children were ". . . sent out in the rain and snow without clothing." Training to specific responsibilities was accomplished through encouraging older siblings to care for younger siblings. When harsh discipline was used, its purpose was explained to the children and followed by reassurances of caring. (Wilson p. 9.)

Emphasis in the Navajo traditional culture and in most other traditional American Indian cultures seemed to be on the context in which discipline was administered, as well as on the discipline itself. That context, in early American Indian life, appears to have been one of respect and high regard for children. As Blanchard and Barsh state, "The lessons children learn make sense because they are directly related to the life of the tribal community and children's place in that life." (p. 351.) Lewis elaborates further.

Respect lies at the very center of a person's relationship with all others, starting with the child's relationship with the parents. It lies at the center of a person's relationship to nature and to the creator; respect for the elders, respect for the child, respect for all living creatures and life. Respect is really the foundation of discipline and authority—it is basic to every kind of learning as well as to the enjoyment of life." (Lewis, p. 3.)

In some early societies the punishments that appear to have been imposed on children seem very extreme by today's standards. Children were locked in isolation for several days. They were dipped in hot baths, had excrement smeared in their faces, and their palms cut with a knife. The Code of Hammurabi (2270 B.C.) provided that ". . . if a son strike his father, one shall cut off his hands." (Quoted in Simonsen and Gordon, p. 4.) During this period of history, punishment was handled by the father, as the authority in family matters. Even more recently, in the New England colonies, (1641 – 1672):

If any child, or children, above sixteen years old, and of sufficient understanding, shall CURSE, or SMITE their natural FATHER, or MOTHER: he or they shall be put to death: unles it can be sufficiently testified that the Parents have been very unchristianly negligent in the education of such children; or so provoked them by extreme, and cruel correction; that they have been forced thereunto to preserve themselves from death or maiming.

Source. Exod. 21. 17. Lev. 20.9 Exod. 21. 15. From Mass. Records III, (1854); see also Sanders, Wiley B., pp. 317–18; and other references.

In this instance the mother is also mentioned in the code, and although the child continues to be responsible to his/her parents and within their control, there appear to be some boundaries to the degree of punishment that a child is required to endure. There is an inference in this code as to what conduct is appropriate for the parents.

An elderly black woman, being interviewed for the Arizona Foster Parent Education Video Series production entitled "Cultural Childhoods: Three Visits" (1980), described her youth as a time of hard work in the fields and her father as a stern disciplinarian. Any variance from her father's rules resulted in a "killin' " for her. For example, if she was not home by dark, a beating with a strap was forthcoming, and, as she stated, she often "raced with the sun" to avoid a "whooping." As an adult, she reflected on the time and her father's wisdom, "I used to think that he was the meanest man in the world. I found out later t'was better that way."

Today, we do not require some of the ordeals that were demanded of children in other times and cultures, but we do have our own child rearing issues and high expectations of children. Compared to other cultures, parents in Western nations tend to be low in infant indulgence, to initiate child-training practices at an earlier developmental stage, and to be harsher in their expectations of compliance from young children." (Korbin, p. 29–30.)

We may underwrite child abuse by the very nature of our lifestyle. The industrial revolution changed our predominantly agrarian society in which work and living were family centered to an industrial society with separate work and living functions. Skills needed to compete in the marketplace change quickly in our society. Today, father and sometimes mother work outside the home. Many families are single-parent households. Compared to other societies and our own history, we raise children in isolation from an extended family support system. The mother is often the person who has to make most decisions regarding the issues of child rearing. Often she decides these issues alone and from a widely expanded number of choices than were available in the past. We are a migratory, mobile society with fewer family members and friends to act as support and information resources. Our cultural rules are sometimes vague and our values less consistent and less universally accepted and therefore, more confusing than were the rules and values of many cultures. We are, according to Korbin, at risk in ways that most cultures have never been. As our expectations and anxieties increase, the probability of child abuse increases. Research has shown this to be the case surrounding the issue of soiling. For example, if parents expect that a child should be toilet trained by the time the child is two years old, and soiling "accidents" continue to occur, the soiling may become a crisis that precipitates abuse. In fact, soiling has been demonstrated to be a key precipitating incident in child abuse. (Korbin, p. 30.)

Returning to Korbin's suggestion of the three levels at which we can observe child rearing issues in a given culture, it is possible that idiosyncratic abuse, that is, abuse that deviates from the cultural and socially acceptable standard in one's own society may be occurring with greater frequency in our society than ever before. Again, this statement in part depends on the standard that we use to define "acceptable." Its meaning is very unclear. If spanking is accepted in a particular society and that society is not a "sick society," then spanking does not constitute abuse in that society even though it may be considered abuse elsewhere. If, however, in that society, spanking is not accepted and the society is not a "sick society," then if spanking were to occur, it would be a deviation from the accepted standard. In our society, is the increased deviation a sign that we are in the midst of transition to new standards? Is it possibly a statement that our society is a very heterogeneous, rather than a homogeneous culture, with many different and sometimes conflicting standards? Or is it perhaps a symptom statement about stresses and problems existing in our society?

Mutilation of Children

Initiation rites as a reason for mutilating children was discussed earlier in this chapter. Mutilation also occurs and has occurred throughout history as a means of curing or warding off some illness. Cosmetic mutilation, a type which our society is more familiar with, is done most often in the name of beauty. Beauty, like so many other concepts, is culturally relative. Mutilation has also been practiced with religious purpose, to appease or gain station with the Deity.

Parents, caretakers, and states have mutilated children for economic gain. Some boys have been castrated so that they would make better eunuchs for harems; others, so that they would retain their young voices. Many children have been mained and disfigured in order to be more appealing as beggars on the streets. (Geiser, p. 142.) Mutilation for economic reasons was not generally supported and, in fact, was outlawed in the seventeenth century by China, frowned upon and finally prohibited by Pope Clement XIV (1769–74), and eventually, similarly prohibited in England.

Sexual Exploitation of Children

Every society has rules regarding sex. Some sexual behavior that is considered inappropriate in present day U.S. society fit within the cultural framework of the society in which it was commonly practiced, for example, defloration rites at puberty or in preparation for marriage (many times publicly enforced); and the hospitable loaning of daughters and wives to guests.

Many societies have accepted as proper and have even encouraged treating children as marketable commodities and selling them into slavery, apprenticeships, and other similar fates. Some societies have encouraged selling children into prostitution. Children were used in Babylonia as temple prostitutes. In ancient Egypt the "... most beautiful and highest-born Egyptian maidens were forced into prostitution as a religious practice, and they continued as prostitutes until their first menstruation." (Benjamin and Masters, p. 161.) In the Rome of the Caesars child prostitution was encouraged, even during one period to the point of introducing cradling infants into brothels. In China and India children were often sold by their parents into prostitution. Persia was known for centuries for its boy-brothels. (Benjamin and Masters, p. 162; see also Moll, 1913.) Pederasty (boy-loving) existed and, in some periods, was encouraged in ancient Rome. In Greece, however, it was strongly discouraged. Superstition was an important reason for having sexual intercourse with children. It was believed, for example, in some societies that venereal disease could be cured by having intercourse with children. (Radbill, p. 9.)

Sexual violence has consistently been a part of human history. Rape is especially prevalent during times of war. Rape has not been generally approved, but it is represented in the literature and historical documents as a fact of life.

A study by Jeanne Giovannoni and Rosina Becerra sought to determine how various groups in our society differ in the degree of seriousness they ascribe to specific kinds of mistreatment. They examined the opinions of professionals and of community members from several ethnic groups. They also reviewed the identification and disposition of several hundred cases. Although they noted variations in some areas, they found, regarding the subject of sexual abuse, "Among all the groups studied, there was greater consensus about the extreme seriousness of this kind of child mistreatment than about any other." (Giovannoni and Becerra, p. 242.) Sexual abuse is a taboo in our society. Although it has been present in societies throughout history, "... sexual abuse of children has always been considered a very serious kind of mistreatment." (Giovannoni and Becerra, p. 242.)

Exploitation of Children: Child Labor

Child labor has existed throughout history. It was controlled to some extent during the Middle Ages through indenturing children to their masters for a period of seven years. Under this system, children were actually slaves of their masters. This system prevented the children from competing (at a lower wage) in the general labor market. Indenturing of children lasted into the nineteenth century (Figure 1-1.) (Radbill, p. 7;) (Geiser, pp. 142–143.)

We often relate the terms "industrialization" and "urbanization" to the

Figure 1-1 Cosette, a character in Victor Hugo's (1802–1885), *Les Miserables,* was, at age 8, a servant to "... a fierce and cruel master."

nineteenth and twentieth centuries, but it was the same phenomenon in the 1600s that led to a major increase in the use of child labor. Child labor was encouraged by England and the American colonies. Children were found in apprenticeships, workhouses, orphanage placements, mills, factories, mines, and other industries. Children were sometimes apprenticed out of their homes or orphanages when they were very young, even as infants in some cases. Often they were held in apprenticeship until the age of 21 and set free with sometimes as little as a small sum of money and the clothes they wore. In England, it was not rare to find five-year-old children in chains and leg irons working sixteen-hour days in factories. (Geiser, pp. 139–153.) Such practices continued into the nineteenth century. Reform tracts illustrating and condemning some of these practices helped to encourage public outcry against them. (See Figure 1-2.) In the 1830s and 1840s Parliament responded by passing laws (the so-called "factory acts") which prohibited boys under the age of 10 from going into underground mines and limiting the work day of children to 10 hours. (Beach, p. 386.)

Figure 1-2 This nineteenth century illustration from the reform tract, *The White Slaves of England*, depicts children being lowered into a mine shaft to work.

Transportation was used in many European countries as a means of reducing overcrowding in institutions of all types and as a means of settling colonies. England transported thousands of children and adults to the American colonies to work in the New World. When the American Revolution prevented further transportation to America in 1776, England increased transportation to Australia until 1875 when the system was abandoned. (Allen and Simonsen, p. 23–24.) Transportation was considered an appropriate punishment for children who had committed crimes. A seventeenth century court record states that Charles Atlee, ". . . a little boy," was sentenced to be transported for stealing. Transcripts from seventeenth century court records indicate that John Lynch, age 9 and John Johnson, age 9, who stole ". . . a till containing upwards of £1 (one pound)," were sentenced to seven years transportation for their crimes. (Simonsen and Gordon, p. 10.) Transportation was also considered by many to be a proper means of caring for dependent and neglected children; it gave them an opportunity to learn a trade and live a responsible life.

Transportation, apprenticeships, and other work opportunities, sometimes offered at least the hope of improvement over life in orphanages and
other institutions. Mortality of infants in institutions was, according to some
figures, as high as 97%. (Warner et. al., p. 124.) For those children who
survived infancy to work in mills and mines at young ages, beatings,
starvation, and sometimes suicide, awaited them. Even these may have been
the lucky children, however, since the majority of those who remained in
institutions died before reaching adulthood.

In the nineteenth century, child labor laws began to initiate reforms, but
as recently as 1866, a Massachusetts legislative report viewed child labor as
". . . a boon to society." (Radbill, p. 6–8; Geiser, 137–153). At the turn of
the century Louise Bowen comments that a number of children were
employed in 40 nut factories in Chicago, cracking nuts with hammers from
4 p.m. until midnight. (Bowen, p. 132.)

On Behalf Of Children

Child welfare did not begin with the social charities of the 1800s, even
though much of the available material regarding the history of child welfare
centers is from this period. If, as Radbill suggests, the gods ". . . reflect a
mirror image of mankind," then very possibly protection of orphans and
children may have occurred since the beginnings of civilization. Radbill
notes a patron goddess in Mesopotamia 6000 years ago, who looked after
orphans. Another deity among the ancient Hindus rescued exposed children
and endowed them with legal rights. (Radbill, p. 11.)

Generally, the children who have been candidates for protection have
been labeled using Homer Folks' terms: destitute, neglected, or delinquent.
(Folks, 1902.) Removal from home, however, was more often accomplished
because of community interest rather than for the protection of the child.
Many children were removed from the homes of their parents because of the
economic dependency of the parents. With the English experience of the
Elizabethan Poor Laws (1601) as a precedent, American citizens equated
being poor with not meeting parental obligations. (Giovannoni and Becerra,
p. 37.)

Giovannoni and Becerra note that in Massachusetts in the 1670s, a
tithingman (again based on English custom) was assigned to supervise 10 to
12 families in his neighborhood. This person had power equivalent to arrest
and was able to intervene in family affairs if parents were not fulfilling their
appropriate duty and keeping their family members behaving in an orderly
and socially acceptable manner. Justification for this power was not so much
in the interest of protecting the child but protecting the community.
(Giovannoni and Becerra, pp. 39–40.) Both seemed to be the concern of the

Juvenile Protection Association. In Chicago in the early 1900s the association paid officers to supervise defined "blocks" of their city ". . . to keep children out of disreputable ice cream parlors, candy stores, and pool rooms, and to try in every way to protect and safeguard the children and young people," and to investigate reports ". . . concerning children who were ill-used or who were exposed to temptation." (Bowen, pp. 119–120.)

Generally, protection of children has meant placement of destitute, neglected, and delinquent children in institutions or in foster care. Geiser states that there were three dominant categories of early protective care of children in the American colonies prior to 1800: indenture and apprenticeship; institutionalization, predominately in almshouses; outdoor (home) relief.

Indenture and apprenticeship were not only the means of saving their lives, but also a means of providing for their welfare and teaching them a trade. Where masters were benevolent, the system worked as it was intended to work. The difficulty, of course, was that it was dependent totally upon the master for success. The child had little, if any, recourse if the system failed.

Almshouses were originally, in concept, poorhouses. However, they were usually a combination of the functions of poorhouses, workhouses, and houses of correction.

Poorhouses were developed for people who were unable to work; Workhouses were developed for people who were poor, but able-bodied and willing to work; houses of correction were developed for people who were not willing to work, even though they were able-bodied, or for those people who had committed misdemeanors and had been sentenced to a house of correction. These three separate houses were first developed to perform three separate functions. In many locales, however, a common building mixed all three, either because of lack of funding or because of a confusion in designated function. Adults and children were housed together. There was no classification system to separate persons by age, sex, or reason for being institutionalized. As a consequence children, the most dependent group, suffered most. Disease and abuse were commonplace. Overcrowding was often an issue. Many times, children were placed out, transported, and/or indentured or apprenticed from the almshouse in order to ease the overcrowding problems as well as to provide training for the children. Other institutions included foundling homes and orphanages. Although these date back to antiquity, they were less prevalent in the American colonies until the nineteenth century when they were championed as the means of saving children from almshouses and indenture.

Outdoor (home) relief took many forms. Generally, it included relief in the child's home (sometimes putting the parent to work) or placing out, a type of foster care that could be arranged by an institution, a parent, or by the state with and without compensation.

The first child to be "placed out" by public authority in Massachusetts was Benjamin Eaton, a seven-year-old, who was placed with a widow in 1636 for a period of fourteen years or until he was twenty-one years of age. (Geiser, p. 146–147.) Some of these homes were no doubt excellent ones. Certainly, it could be argued that such care was cheaper than institutional care and provided "family life" for the child. Considering the nature of institutional care and the other options available for these children, it may have been the least detrimental alternative for most. However, it was a virtually unmonitored system. Many children were treated as if they were indentured in this system. Nineteenth century English and German records indicate that a high percentage of children, particularly illegitimate children, died when placed out to nurse and into foster care. Some were killed or maimed by nurses in whose care they were placed. The Germans called nurses who had a reputation as baby killers, "angel makers." (Radbill, p. 13.)

In the American colonies, child welfare institutions came about chiefly as a reaction to placing children in almshouses and the devastating results of such practice. Although the first such institution in American was founded in New Orleans by an order of Ursuline nuns in 1729, most child care institutions in this country originated after 1850, when the need for homes for Civil War orphans was high (Geiser, p. 155.) Still, high death rates for infants and the dangers of disease and abuse persisted, even in these child care facilities.

> In a great majority of cases, it can matter but little to the individual infant whether it is murdered outright or is placed in a foundling hospital—death comes only a little sooner in one case than in the other. This fact, that foundling hospitals are, for the most part, places where infants die, is not sufficiently appreciated by the public. A death-rate of 97 per cent per annum for children under three years of age is not uncommon. (Warner, p. 124.)

Women were a particularly important part of the "child saver" movement and the charitable groups that came to the "rescue" of children in the late nineteenth and early twentieth centuries. Among these were Julia Lathrop, Louise de Koven Bowen, and Jane Addams. In her book, *The Spirit of Youth and the City Streets,* Jane Addams sounded a call to the citizens of her day.

> It is as if we ignored a wistful, over-confident creature who walked through out city streets calling out, "I am the spirit of Youth! With me, all things are

possible!'' We fail to understand what he wants or even to see his doings, although his acts are pregnant with meaning, and we may either translate them into a sordid chronicle of petty vice or turn them into a solemn school for civic righteousness.

She concludes with:

We may either smother the divine fire of youth or we may feed it. We may either stand stupidly staring as it sinks into a murky fire of crime and flare into the intermittent blaze of folly or we may tend it into a lambent flame with power to make clean and bright our dingy city streets. (Addams, p. 161–162.)

AN ACCENT ON CHILDREN'S RIGHTS

It is possible throughout history to trace a thread of increasing esteem for the child as a person. (See Appendix 1, Intervention and Protection of Children.) Reform movements have helped to improve the circumstances of children and provide such protections as child labor laws, child welfare benefits, and educational opportunities. These movements, however, did not provide children with rights, and therefore power. Instead, children were provided with privileges. They were not permitted to choose for themselves. Choices on their behalf were increasingly monitored by law. They were not considered participants in the process of growing and living, but were recognized to be deserving of humane and just treatment. Even when the first juvenile court was established in 1899, initiating the separation of juvenile from adult court functions, the philosophical goal it sought was the protection of children, in the sense of fatherly concern. Due process for children was ''. . . in the best interest of the child'' and ''. . . in a sense of fair play.'' Certainly such a standard would seem to be ideal. It had one fatal flaw. There was no consistent criteria established to determine what might constitute ''best interest'' or ''fair play.'' As a result, criteria varied widely from court to court and child to child and sometimes appeared to be frivolous, if not actually harmful in itself to the child.

Even during the period of 1838–1900 several people initiated legal challenges to the actions of private and public organizations and the courts in their application of the doctrine of *parens patriae*. Their concern was with the balance between the authority of parents and the authority of the state relating to children rather than with the rights of children. Most of the outcomes of these cases supported the doctrine and its application. (See *Ex parte Crouse*, 4 Wharton (9 (Pa. 1838) and *People* v. *Turner*, 55 Ill., 280 [1870] for an example of both positions regarding *parens patriae*.)

People who have been involved in the most recent movement on behalf of children have sought something more than fatherly concern. They are distrustful of the benevolence of the court, its agents, and social welfare agents. Patricia Wald calls it ``. . . sharing power with the next generation,'' (Wald, p. 11.) Perhaps, more precisely, it is giving children the right to participate in decision-making, to provide children with rights and responsibilities rather than privileges.

Certainly this is a more explicitly powerful position for a child to hold, but it is also a frightening one.[2] Giving children explicit power requires that our society rethink tradition and the alignment of the roles of parents and children. Where is the proper balance between the rights of parents and child? What is the responsibility of the parent and of the child in a family relationship? What is abuse? Neglect? How can children be taught to exercise their responsibilities as well as their rights?

Out of balance, the practice of some of these rights appears to threaten the family. In many states, children now have the right to purchase contraceptives, to participate in abortion decisions, to decide whether or not they will participate in their parents' religion, to have a decision-making role in adoption and custody proceedings, the right to drug and venereal disease treatment without parental knowledge or consent, the right to privacy of records, and the right to see records relating to them. Removing status offenses from the statutes or changing procedural requirements relating to such offenses in many states has removed some of the power of the court over unruly children, resulting in the loss of one of the powerful authorities parents depended upon to provide external controls when they could not. Some parents complain that they are given the responsibility for the rearing of their children but are not given the authority to carry out that responsibility.

Efforts now seem to be moving toward striking a balance that will preserve the family and still protect its members so that none are defined as property. The U.S. Supreme Court, in *J. L.* v. *Parham*, for example, seems to seek such balance. In this decision the Court appears to give parents the right to make decisions regarding child placement so long as they consult an independent physician or psychologist who concurs that the placement would be in the child's best interest.

In the final analysis adults decide and interpret the parameters of choice for children based on what they believe to be best. Advocacy for children in its best intentions may still operate from the values of the advocator which may or may not be in the best interest of the child.[3]

---

[2] In the view of the authors, children, as a part of family and social systems, have impact on the behavior of others, in the sense of transactional reciprocity as defined in Chapter Two. This is a subtly shared power with others in the system. Shared power, in the sense of legal right to participate in decision making is a more explicit power, and could be exercised in a child's behalf as well as through the child's interaction with others in the system.

[3] See also the discussion of family integrity in chapter 9.

Summary

The value of children and how children fit into the structure of the society and family in which they live relate to time and culture; are influenced by the priorities of the society in which they live; and are influenced by the unique interactions of a given child, family, and environment.

Overall, the critical issues that must be solved regarding children do not seem to change very much from culture to culture and time to time. How these issues are solved has changed constantly, as have community decisions as to which of society's agents should solve them. Power and responsibility to decide has moved from the father and the family of the child, to the state, to the church, to societal and community institutions, and now, it seems, to a tentative balancing of power and responsibility among all of these and the child.

Whether or not we observe the child's position in his/her society and family within the context of that time and culture or from the perspective of our own time and culture, it is clear that the position of children has been a precarious one throughout history. We tend to believe that we are more humane in our treatment of children today than has been true in the past. In fact, however, we may violate our own standards of treatment more than any other culture not considered to be a "sick society" has done. Perhaps that is because our standards are higher or because we have less agreement regarding the standards. Whatever the reason, it is still precarious to be a child in some families, some neighborhoods, and at some times.

BIBLIOGRAPHY

Addams, Jane, *The Spirit of Youth and the City Streets*. Macmillan Co., New York, 1909.

Allen, Harry E., and Simonsen, Clifford, *Corrections in America: An Introduction*. 3rd Ed. Macmillan Co., New York, 1981.

Beach, Chandler B., Ed., *Student's Reference Work for Teachers, Students and Families*. Vol. I, F. E. Compton and Co., Chicago, 1909.

Benjamin, Harry, and Masters, R. E. L., *Prostitution and Morality*. Julian Press, Inc., New York, 1964.

Blanchard, Evelyn Lance, and Barsh, Russel Lawrence, "What is Best for Tribal Children?" *Social Work*, 0037-8046/80/2505-0350, N.A.S.W. Inc, Sept. 1980.

Bolton, F. G., Jr, Arizona Community Development for Abuse and Neglect, No Date, Grant Publication NCCAN.

Bowen, Louise de Koven, *Growing up With a City*. Macmillan Co., New York, 1926.

Child Abuse and Neglect U.S. Department of Justice, National Institute of Justice, February, 1980.

Child Abuse: The Problem and Its Management. Vol. 1, U.S. Department H.E.W., OHD 75-30073, 1977.

DeMause, Lloyd, "Our Forebearers Made Childhood A Nightmare," *Psychology Today, 8;* April, 1975, pp. 85–98.

Eicher, Lillian, *The Customs of Mankind* Nelson–Doubleday, New York, 1925.

Ex parte Crouse, 4 Wharton 9 (Pa. 1838).

Folks, Homer, *The Care of Destitute, Neglected and Delinquent Children*. Macmillan Co, London, 1902; (NASW Classics Series Edition, Washington, D.C., 1978.)

Garbarino, James, "The Role of the School in the Human Ecology of Child Maltreatment." *School Review*, University of Chicago Press, Chicago, Feb. 1979.

In re Gault, 387 U.S., 1428 (1967).

Geiser, Robert L., *The Illusion of Caring*. Beacon Press, Boston, 1973.

Gelles, Richard J., and Straus, Murray A., "Violence in the American Family." *Journal of Social Issues*, *35*, 2, 1979, pp. 15–39.

Giovannoni, Jeanne M., and Becerra, Rosina M., *Defining Child Abuse*. The Free Press, New York, 1979.

Grubb, Reba Douglass, *Historical File*. West Virginia Parent-Teacher Association Conference Speeches.

"Implementing the Indian Child Welfare Act of 1978." National Indian Child Abuse and Neglect Resource Center, Tulsa, Okla. Spring 1980.

J. L. v. *Parham*, 99 S. Ct. 2493 (1979)

Juvenile Justice and Delinquency Prevention Act of 1974, 88 Stat. 1109 year as amended by 91 Stat. 1048 (1977)

Korbin, Jill E., "The Cross-Cultural Context of Child Abuse and Neglect." In Kempe, C. Henry and Helfer, Ray E., *The Battered Child*. 3rd Ed., University of Chicago Press, Chicago, 1980, pp. 21–35.

Langer, L., "Infanticide: A Historical Survey." *History of Childhood Quarterly, 1*, 1974, pp. 353–362.

Lewis, Ron, "Strengths of the American Indian Family", National Indian Child Abuse and Neglect Resource Center, Tulsa, Okla., (90-C-1744(02).

Mayhall, Pamela D. and Norgard, Katherine E., "Cultural Childhoods: Three Visits." Arizona Foster Parent Education Series, 1980.

Moll, Albert, *Sexual Life of the Child*. Trans. by Eden, Paul. Macmillan, New York, 1913.

People v. *Turner*, 55 Ill. 280 [1870]

President's Commission on Law Enforcement and the Administration of Justice, Task Force Report on Juvenile Delinquency and Youth Crime (1967), Ch. 1.

Radbill, Samuel X., "Children in a World of Violence." In Kempe, C. Henry and Helfer, Ray E., *The Battered Child*. 3rd Ed. University of Chicago Press, Chicago, 1980.

Sanders, Wiley B., Ed., *Juvenile Offenders for a Thousand Years*. University of North Carolina Press, Chapel Hill, 1970.

Smith, Charles P., Berkman, David J., and Fraser, Warren M., "A Preliminary National Assessment of Child Abuse and Neglect and The Juvenile Justice System: The Shadows of Distress." *Reports of the National Juvenile Justice Assessment Centers*. U.S. Dept of Justice, April, 1980. (© 1979 by American Justice Institute.)

Simonsen, Clifford E., and Gordon, Marshall S., III, *Juvenile Justice in America*. Glencoe Publishing, California, 1979.

Smith, Selwyn M., *The Battered Child Syndrome*. Butterworth and Co., England, 1975, pp. 3–34.

Stanley v. *Illinois,* 405 U.S. 645 (1972).

Straus, M.A., Gelles, R.J., and Steinmetz, S.K. *Behind Closed Doors: Violence in the American Family.* Doubleday/Anchor, Garden City, N.Y., 1979.

ten Bensel, Robert, and Watson, Jane, "Historical Aspects of Child Abuse", HV 715 .T46x.

Thomas, Mason P., Jr., "Child Abuse and Neglect, Part I: Historical Overview, Legal Matrix, and Social Perspectives," *North Carolina Law Review,* 50, (1972) 293–349.

Wald, Patricia M., "Introduction to the Juvenile Justice Process: The Rights of Children and the Rights of Passage," *Child Psychiatry and the Law.* Brumner/ Mazel, Publishers, N.Y., 1980, pp. 9–20.

Warner, Amos G., Queen, Stuart A., and Harper, Ernest B., *American Charities and Social Work.* 4th Ed. Thomas Y. Crowell Co. New York, 1919 and 1930.

Wilson, Marilyn, "Child Abuse and Neglect, A Navajo Perspective." for Bi-State, Summer, 1978, in *Foster Parenting the Abused and Neglected Child: Advanced Foster Parent Education,* Pima College, Tucson Arizona, 1980.

397 U.S., 358 (1970) *In Re Winship,* 397 U.S. 358 (1970)

CHAPTER 2

In The Context Of The Family

DEFINING THE FAMILY

Traditionally, the family has been defined as a group of people related by blood or marriage living under the same roof and depending upon one another in certain emotional and physical ways for survival. The family, throughout history, has had legal status within the larger society. Ogden suggests that a family also includes the elements of trust (actively developed and maintained), commitment of the members of the family group to one another and to the notion of holding together as a family unit, expectations of mutual satisfaction of needs, communication, and a shared living space. (Ogden, p. 1.)

Today, perhaps more than any time in the past, families are held together and stay together by choice. The increase in the number of divorces is evidence that no legal or moral sanctions influence people as much as their own choices. Jane Howard states this as a central theme in her book, *Families*, which she researched by visiting and living with many different families across the United States. She states that families are "connections" of choice and of change. In this context "connections" means being joined for a common goal. These connections sometimes bless and other times cripple the lives of the people within the family unit. For better and for worse, Ms. Howard unequivocally believes that families are enduring; they are not disappearing as some modern thinkers might question. (Howard, p. 15.)

The family can also be defined as . . . "a collection of individuals differing in roles, ages, and biological attributes, but nevertheless having the same fundamental needs and wants. Every individual has a need for Survival, and in addition, has wants for Productivity, Intimacy, Making Sense and Order and Uniqueness. They distinguish survival need from wants. In times of stress, the wants may be experienced as needs, as though necessary for survival." (Sorrells and Ford, p. 150.)

"Family" need not be limited by legal definition. Many varied and creative forms of families exist today: people living together united by the bonds of marriage, with or without children; people with or without children living together without the bonds of legal marriage; single parent families; extended families; communal families; homosexual families. These and many other combinations live together and exercise many of the functions said to be family functions.

FUNCTIONS OF THE FAMILY

Encyclopedia Britannica states that seven roles and activities occur throughout the family life cycle: (1) sexual aspects, (2) economic aspects, (3) household tasks and their distribution, (4) patterns of power distribution, (5) social activities, (6) educational aspects, and (7) community aspects. (Encyclopedia Britannica, p. 160–162.) Robert Bell, who researched and authored a text on marriage and the family, states that the family is an economic unit which exists traditionally for production, consumption, and the pooling of workloads. He states that this traditional definition may clash with the current function of the family. (Bell, p. 4–8.) In fact, the modern family still produces together but not necessarily in traditional ways. In this broader context, production is not simply the pooling of labor to produce a single product. The single product in the past might have been a crop or a family line of furniture. In current times, family members may pool earnings from their individual labors. Each person's needs and wants may be expressed quite independently of one another. Bell also notes four other major functions of the family that include division of labor, protection and care of family members, provision of social standing, and reproductive functions. (Bell, p. 4–8.)

Countries around the world have been experimenting over the years with varying some of the functions generally performed by the family. Israel, China, and Cuba have found options outside the family to deal with child rearing, financial, and medical responsibilities that were previously functions of the family. Individuals are experimenting with alternative family lifestyles in the United States with respect to child rearing. Federal and state government also have impact on child rearing practices through the regulations and standards that accompany the funding that contributes to the support of day care centers.

All of these family forms and functions, traditional, modern and those forms yet to be discovered, have more in common than they do in differences. As Sorrells and Ford elaborate, each individual living in any kind of family form has a basic need for survival, a desire to make sense and order out of the world, a want to be productive and the need for intimacy. (Sorrells and Ford, p. 150–151.)

Virginia Satir, a well-known author and teacher on the subject of families, sees the family as a peoplemaking factory. No matter what other options are available, the family still has the primary task of raising children. Within the family each of us learns about our own and the family's self esteem, the emotional rules for living, how to communicate, and how to make connections outside the family group. These four important functions of the family and the outcomes of the process stay with most of us for our lifetime unless or until the outcome is called into question. The family has a very powerful shaping influence over the lives of its members. (Satir, p. 3.)

The family has been described and dreamed about as a place of safety and a place of protection from the stress and strain of life. The family at its best is a haven for its members. Within this framework, the family provides safety from external dangers, both physical and emotional. Shaeffer describes the family as an ecologically balanced environment, the birthplace of creativity, a formation center for human relationships, a shelter in time of storm, an economic unit, an educational control, blended balances, and a museum of memories. (Shaeffer, p. 7.)

Even though the family has many constructive, creative forms and offers people many advantages over solitary life, it is within the family that physical and emotional violence most often takes place. Child abuse and neglect occur most commonly within the context of the family. As family members each seek to carry out their lives, they each get a view of what survival together is like. Family relationships are quite intense since group goals often compete with individual needs and wants. Blaming, scapegoating, or forcing one another to do things in a specific way may escalate into violence.

To better understand violence against children as well as the other types of violence discussed in this chapter, it is important to understand the concept of the family as a system. Simply stated, this means that each family is influenced by certain principles affecting a family system.

UNDERSTANDING THE FAMILY AS A SYSTEM

The principles of transformation, homeostasis, information flow, and transactional reciprocity influence the family unit at every moment in time.

Transformation

Transformation means change. It is impossible for a family to stay the same, to be static, just as it is impossible for the individuals within the family not to age and grow older. Change is always occurring within a family and within individual family members.

Homeostasis

Homeostasis implies balancing. Family groups attempt to maintain an equilibrium through the process of balancing. The position each family member takes to maintain the group's equilibrium is his/her part in the homeostatic process.

Families are not only influenced by events and people within the family but also by outside events, that is, the state of the economy, floods, or changes in government. These continuous changes influence the process of homeostasis. One such change is aging. Everyone alive is aging. As everyone in a family ages s/he makes some subtle daily changes with respect to the aging process. There are certain periods in the life of a family, illustrated by Figure 2-1, that reflect the normal developmental changes that many families experience. Every family is unique. Every family has its own family life cycle which is not exactly like, although in some ways is similar to the life cycles of other families. The principle of homeostasis or balancing is a continuous process. Since the only part of life that is constant is change, families and individuals are always responding to changes.

Information Flow

Information flow is communication in its most complete definition. Information is continually flowing between and among the family members. It is impossible for such communication not to exist. It is possible, however, for that communication to be fuzzy, garbled, misleading, and misunderstood. Information in a family flows verbally and nonverbally in all the many ways that messages can be sent and received.

Transactional Reciprocity

Transactional reciprocity means mutual influence. If you throw a rock into a pond, you effect a change in the pond. Notice the ripples that generate from the point where the rock entered the pond. If you watch long enough and closely enough, you will see the widening ripples eventually reach all points on the pond. The same rippling effect occurs in families. One person's behavior, attitudes, and ideas affects everyone else's behavior, attitudes,

FAMILY LIFE CYCLE

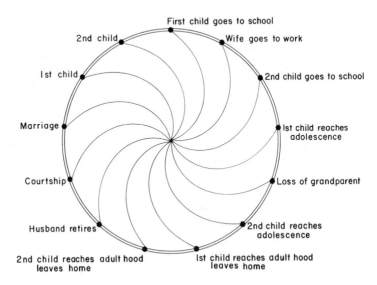

Figure 2-1 The family life cycle.

and ideas. A mother's loss of her job may affect her son's ability to take music lessons. Her daughter may have to contribute her income from a part-time job to the family. The father may feel irritable at the increased financial pressure. All of these effects influence one another. This is an example of transactional reciprocity.

Working Together

The four principles of a system work together in their application to a family and must be understood and assessed in relationship to each other. None of the principles applies in isolation from the other three. It is important to understand these principles, how they function together, and the three-level definition of a family in order to understand child abuse and neglect within the context of the family.

Three Level Definition of A Family

A family is defined at three levels: (1) in its members' relationships with one another; (2) in its internal structural variables; (3) in its relationship to impinging systems and processes outside the family.

The First Level. Since families are groups by choice, the members have some degree of choice in respect to where they stand with one another. How close will each family member be emotionally and geographically to each other family member? How close and intimate will husband and wife be with one another? Each of these choices and ways of being and standing together affects the family as a whole, since one part affects everything else within the family.

The Second Level. Understanding the family at this level requires understanding the internal parts of the family. Every family has common internal workings. The husband and the wife are usually the originators of the family and as such have some architectural functions as to how the blueprint and design of the family will be laid out. The structure must make sense and must include how the family will deal with power, autonomy, communication patterns, self-esteem issues, emotional rules for operating, change, and risk-taking within the family.

Some of the design of the second level of the family comes with each of the architects from their families of origin. These architects do not automatically repeat patterns from the past (from their family of origin), but they design their family structure in relationship to their experience of their family of origin and its definitions. Some individuals may select marital partners who fit some of the same patterns of the family of origin. None of the internal workings of this second level stand independently from one another. They mutually influence one another.

These questions may be helpful in defining a family through its internal parts.

1. What are the emotional rules in this family? Are they vague or clear?
2. What is the process of communication in the family? Is the communication clear, open, and spontaneous or vague/confusing, closed, and stiff?
3. How is power handled within this family?
4. How do individuals feel about themselves and how do they feel about their membership in the family?

The Third Level. At this level, the family is defined in relationship to those forces that exist outside the family unit that affect the family at a given point in time. Most families are affected by the economic system. Families are also affected by the educational system, the health care system, and religious systems, to name only a few. Since the family does not live in a vacuum, these other systems continually impact on the family system. These outside systems add stress and strain to the family. The family must face these strains and deal with them.

Understanding a family as a system in its three-level definition enables us to appreciate the circumstances of a family at any given point in time and to deal with the individual or group problems within the family. (Norgard and Whitman.)

The family, just like any other group of people, is continually faced with the need to deal with conflict, stress, and change. The universal problem faced by individuals in families is how to deal creatively with change that influences us from outside the family and change that influences us from within the family.

FUNCTIONING FAMILIES

Functioning families coexist as family groups and meet the basic needs of their members (closeness, food and shelter, economic aspects, etc.). Three commonalities seem to exist for families that function in a nonviolent way. These families (1) accept change and stress as a part of life, (2) have an overt or covert rule that violence is not permitted within the family structure, and (3) seem to have the working parts working for rather than against the family. In other words, communication tends to be clear; self esteem for the individuals and for the family as a whole tends to be high and family members seem to have the skills to negotiate, compromise, give and take, and get their individual needs met within the family unit.

Most of us are confronted with a great deal of emotional if not physical violence on a daily basis. Place yourself in the following situation: The office where you work is, at least in your view, a very unpleasant place. No one trusts anyone else. Your boss frequently has temper tantrums in the office, directing his fury at whoever happens to be handy. When you walk through the door at the end of the working day, you are exhausted mentally and physically. You go home to your family. Is your family strong enough in the three levels of definition to rebuff and deal with pressures and influences from that outside world of work so that you can regain your sense of personal worth? Or does your family negatively influence your already sagging self esteem?

Families who function without violence find creative ways of meeting the needs of the individual family members so that each family member is given the opportunity to survive in a safe atmosphere, make sense out of the world, be productive, experience intimacy, and live out his/her respective uniqueness. One of the most exciting aspects of working with and understanding families has to do with the principle of transformation discussed earlier in this chapter. Families are not static and cast in concrete. The possibility for change always exists.

DYSFUNCTIONAL FAMILIES

F. G. Bolton, a psychologist who has worked with many abusing families, cites the following factors which in the context of this chapter might relate to family dysfunction. (Bolton, p. 16.)

1. *Environmental chance factors,* in which pure chance will alter a life situation from a commonplace event to a tragic outcome.
2. *Environmental stress factors,* in which the pressure of today's world with its complex demands force a crisis situation.
3. *Deviance and Pathology,* in which a person at a loss to deal with life's responsibilities manifests an inability to function through social, intellectual, or emotional dysfunction which results in harm to a child.
4. *Dysfunctional intrafamilial behavior styles,* in which the behavioral alternatives selected by the parental figures in the family are maladaptive for the children in their care.
5. Some combination of the above factors.

Case Example One

A Family Isolated from an External Network

Tony was transferred to Montana from New Jersey, where all his and his wife's family lived. Semi, Tony's wife, had strong family ties; Semi's family was so close that she never had time for friends. Semi's parents were Italian immigrants. Semi was also very active in the Catholic Italian church.

Semi and Tony arrived in Montana in the middle of a snowstorm and their lodging reservations were confused. Housing was difficult to find. Semi discovered she was pregnant. The other children were one, three, and four years old. Semi was suddenly without help with the three young children and early in the pregnancy she was very sick. Tony and Semi had not planned to have another child for at least two more years.

The Catholic church in the new town was very informal. The liturgies were less traditional. Semi and Tony felt uncomfortable with some of the liberal attitudes of the members of the church. From all they could determine, there was not another Italian family in town. Tony's bad temper seemed worse than it had ever been when the family lived in New Jersey.

Key Questions

1. What factors contribute to the isolation of this family?
2. What other factors might be contributing to the family dysfunction in addition to the family's isolation?

These factors include a lack of a known religious support group, a lack of family support, a new doctor, a new neighborhood, no Italian–American community, stress, change, pregnancy, conflict over Tony's temper, and perhaps his job demands.

Semi and Tony have a potential for the eruption of violence. Some of the dynamics that could lead to a violent outburst include (1) Tony's temperament; (2) The strain of the unplanned pregnancy; (3) The change to a new location; (4) Isolation from religious, family, health care, and neighborhood support; (5) Stress created by housing problems; (6) Conflict over the pregnancy; (7) Demands presented by three preschool-aged children.

It is clear from this example that isolation is just one stress factor. How the family copes with these strains depends upon their patterns of operating as a family and all the features of the three levels of defining a family discussed in this Chapter.

Case Example Two

Fragmented Internal Family Structure With Excessive External Integration

Willie was seen as one of the most influential members in the community. Her name appeared on many of the community's social agencies board of director lists. Willie served on food drives to collect and distribute food to the town's needy and as a volunteer to the Red Cross. She also was the store manager for a busy store with twenty employees. Willie and Tom's children were active with tennis lessons and tournaments, music lessons and recitals, and normal school activities. Willie could always be counted on to help with any of these activities any of the time. Tom golfed three times a week and often went on weekend hunting trips with his friends from the office. Tom rarely ate meals with the family except on special holidays or birthdays.

Key Questions

1. What features in this family are examples of energy directed outside the family?

2. What guesses would you make as to how satisfying Tom and Willie's marriage is to both partners?

Answers to the first question might include Willie's abundance of outside activities and overinvolvement with her children's activities. As to the second question, it would seem that Willie and Tom do not spend much time together. The level of satisfaction in their marriage for both partners seems low. They have not taken care of their emotional relationship. Instead they have invested their energies in outside events to the exclusion of the needs of their marriage.

Tom and Willie's family structure may have evolved without their awareness. Many times a spouse may derive major satisfaction from work or community activities and minor satisfaction from the marriage and the family. Sometimes both spouses are simultaneously veering off in different directions. Other times, one spouse is overly invested outside the family over the objection of the other spouse.

The case of Willie and Tom focused largely on Willie's outside activities and on the investments both have made outside the marriage. Another common situation and perhaps more likely to lead to violence is that the husband or sometimes the wife is ambitious and wants to rise to the top of the corporate ladder. S/he works hard at work and even at home. The couple have children. The other spouse becomes the primary caretaker and parent. As time passes, the division between the two becomes greater and they no longer share interests in common. At some point, one of the spouses may be able to recognize the changes that are occurring but may not know how to reverse the trend. These family dynamics can be fertile ground for family violence which erupts in the midst of the frustration and seeming impotence of one or both adults to maintain a marriage and balance the demands from the outside world which may be proving to be more satisfactory at least to one member of the family than the marriage. Because of their greater vulnerability, the children may become the targets of the violence.

Case Example Three

Internally Unintegrated Families

Marge and Will have been married for 13 years. Seven-year-old Peter and Marge are inseparable. They play games together, shop together, often take separate vacations together, and are very close. Will developed a drinking problem when Peter was three years old.

Key Questions

1. Where are the bonds in this family unit?
2. Which bonds are missing?

The answers might include Marge and her son, Peter, seem to have strong emotional bonds but Marge and Will do not.

Will may eventually feel so alienated that he will resort to violence. Marge may intentionally or unintentionally be pitting Peter against his father, partially out of her own dissatisfaction and emotional pain with the lack of satisfaction in her marriage.

The dynamics of this family group may be such that the bonds between family members have not been firmly cemented. It is important that there be an emotional bond between the husband and the wife as architects of the family unit. It is equally important that a bond exist between the parents and the children. A lack of these necessary bondings may weaken the family's ability to deal with change and stress.

Case Example Four

Mark is a high school freshman. He is on the basketball team and is very popular at school. His little sister, Mary, is 11 years old. She has a learning disability and attends special classes in her sixth grade. Marvin, the father, works in the office of a local bank. Because of new laws affecting banking and income tax, the bank has increased its service hours during the week and on Saturdays. Marvin likes to watch Saturday basketball games but has been unable to do so since the bank has been open on Saturdays all during the season. Dorothy works at an all-night doughnut establishment. She makes meals for her family in the morning when she gets home from work before she goes to sleep for that day. The family heats them up when they get home at night. Dorothy likes to watch soap operas on television, but has been too tired to do so since taking the job at the doughnut store to help with the family's income.

Marvin is notified that he has been laid off during a one-month construction project at the bank. He will receive half of his monthly salary. While spending daytimes at home, Marvin and Dorothy become increasingly hostile toward one another. The tension escalates when the parents discover that Mark drinks beer with his friends after basketball games. This example illustrates two of the following factors relating to dysfunction: (1) environmental chance (Marvin's job lay off); (2) environmental stress factors (the economic pressures on Dorothy and Marvin's family budget necessitating that Dorothy work.)

Families may exhibit dysfunction in many ways. Among these are:

1. *External isolation.* Family members are isolated from relationships and networks outside the family.

2. *Fragmented internal structure with an overabundance of external integration.* Family members do not have clear boundaries within membership subgroups, but are individually very involved with groups and endeavors outside the family.

3. *Internal unintegration.* The family group does not have sufficient emotional and physical connections within its membership.

4. *Unintended family group* where the adults are the only important people in the family and the children's rights and needs are subordinate to those of the adults.

5. *Immature family group.* The family group does not adequately meet the needs of the family members.

6. *Deviant family group.* One or more of the family members (adults) is engaged in drug or alcohol abuse or illegal activities.

Families may or may not function for the mutual benefit of the family members. When violence occurs within the family, the family system is not working. In order to understand violence in the family, we need to first have an understanding of violence as a concept.

UNDERSTANDING VIOLENCE

The term "violence" does not have an objective meaning or definition. What is violence to one person may not be violence to another. Webster defines violence as ". . . physical force used so as to injure or damage; roughness in action." The words used in the definition are subjective at best and are difficult to operationally define. Many definitions also include emotional injury, physical injury, and refusal to act as well as to act. The common theme in most definitions of violence, however, is the imposing of harm. (See also Chapters One and Four.)

Interpersonal violence, whether between nations or people, is paradoxical in that it reaches its greatest intensity at opposite extremes: conditions of close intimacy and cold, impersonal, stranger-to-stranger situations. During World War II, at the moment the bomb exploded on Hiroshima, there was undoubtedly very little intimate contact between the victims of this human violence on a massive scale and the pilots of the Enola Gay. Rapes, burglaries, and other violent acts generally occur between strangers. At the other extreme, police statistics show that victims of murder and assault are often friends or loved ones of the offender. The family is one of the most intimate social groups to which any of us belong, yet the highest percentage of violence occurs in this context.

EXPLAINING VIOLENCE

Conflict Theory

Several theories attempt to explain violence. Conflict theory, for instance, maintains that when groups are faced with a problem, they do not seek consensus or compromise. Instead, each person seeks self-serving solutions. Violence is a natural outcome of such a position since it is the most persuasive way of advancing one's self-interest when all other modes of influence fail.

Resource Theory

Resource theory states that violence and threats of violence are fundamental to the organization of all social systems. Violence is used as a resource only when other resources fail. This theory implies that the more resources people have, the less likely they will be to employ violence as a means to an end. Logically, the "underdog" is more likely to employ violence as a tactic than the "top dog."

Instinctual Theory

Instinctual theory (Freud and others) holds that humans have strong instinctual drives. From this theory, it is argued that the frustration of these drives increases aggression and gratification reduces aggression.

Learning Theory

Learning theory suggests that humans are innately neutral—neither violent or nonviolent. Rather, we learn through observation, imitation, and rein-forcement. One of the societal conditions listed as producing violence is the feeling of being trapped, without choice, or hemmed in by the boundaries of society. (Haynie, p. 289.)

Cultural Impact Theory

Cultural explanations for violence result from cross-cultural studies. One study found that societies that use physical punishment on infants also tend to neglect them in terms of physical affection. This combination results in a high violence rate among adults.

> The statistics associated with the relationship are extraordinary: the percent likelihood of a society being physically violent if it is physically affectionate

toward its infants and tolerant of premarital sexual behavior is 2% (1/49). The probability of this relationship occurring by chance is 125,000 to one. (Haynie, p. 292.)

A culturally related explanation of violence states that violence is rooted in the structure of a society. (Gil, p. 357.) Societal violence is defined as that violence that is a part of the core of society, a normal, ongoing condition reflected in socially sanctioned practices. Many people believe that this structural violence or violence that is an integral part of society must be overcome before personal violence can be dealt with as a problem. "To overcome structural violence in the United States and in similarly organized societies, prevailing policies concerning resources, work, production and rights need to be adjusted." (Gil, p. 380.) This philosophy holds that there is a need for humanistic, equalitarian, libertarian, democratic, cooperative, and collective values within a society before the structural violence can be overcome.

Julius Segal suggests that the seeds of violence can be successfully planted in the lives of children who may never be physically battered. "It does not require fractures, burns, or bruises to learn the lessons of violence—only a pervasive acceptance of aggression as a style of life." (Segal, p. 187.) This point of view maintains that when violence is a given in the larger social structures and families, children learn their lessons whether or not they are ever direct targets of violent acts. In this way, the tradition of violence is carried through generations.

VIOLENCE IN THE FAMILY

An old English proverb suggests that violence within the family has a long history:

A spaniel, a woman and a walnut tree, the more they're beaten the better they be. (St. Bernadine of Siena—Fifteenth Century)

More recently, based on their study findings regarding violence in the American family, Gelles and Straus observe:

With the exception of the police and the military, the family is perhaps the most violent social group, and the home the most violent social setting, in our society. A person is more likely to be hit or killed in his or her own home by another family member than anywhere else or by anyone else. (Gelles and Straus, p. 15.)

For the purposes of this section, family violence is defined as that behavior within a family which leads to foreseeable and avoidable physical or emotional injury or damage to a family member. All types of child maltreatment are violent by this definition. Neglect, which constitutes a major part of child maltreatment, is violent behavior because it is an act or omission which, if not purposive, is at least marked inattention to the child's basic needs. Harm which results from neglect is avoidable and foreseeable particularly in the sense that it is often the worsening of an existing condition. (See also Chapter Four; National Incidence Study, p. 4.)

Types of Intrafamilial Violence

Violence by parents or caretakers toward children, violence by children toward parents or caretakers, and violence between children are all types of intrafamilial violence. In this sense of intrafamilial, we include, in the broader definition of family, a living unit which exercises many of the functions of a family. This definition includes foster families, group homes, and other alternative settings.

Specific statistics about family violence are difficult to find. Reported data is unreliable. Family members have difficulty admitting to problems of family violence at any level. A stigma is attached to such admissions. Problems of family violence are easy to hide. A battered wife can go to great lengths to hide bruises or explain them away without ever telling anyone that her injuries were the result of a physical fight with her husband. Family violence is embarrassing to most people who are a part of it.

Since the family is often thought of as a place of protection and safety, this protection often acts against the members of the family. A child may believe, for example, that it is important to protect the parent by not reporting sexual abuse. What "good" child would start a process that could mean that the parent would end up in prison? Children and other family members often take this position. Telling someone outside the family about problems within the family unit may also be acting against an unwritten family rule, such as "family business is private business and nobody else's business." Family members may suffer much pain and anguish in support of such rules and in fear of possible changes beyond their control.

VIOLENCE BETWEEN HUSBANDS AND WIVES

The situation of spouse abuse is painfully familiar to people working in the law enforcement sector. The most common form of spouse abuse (perhaps only because it comes to public notice more often than other forms) is of the female being assaulted by the male. There is some indication that 20% of those families in which physical child abuse occurs are also involved in spouse abuse. (King, p. 7.) Scott reported that in England 25% of child battering fathers also batter their wives. (Scott, p. 441.)

Violence between spouses usually occurs within the home, behind closed doors. Unless there is a report to the police, an attorney, or a mental health agency, much of this type of family violence goes unreported and unnoticed.

Spouse abuse affects everyone. Most directly, spouse abuse affects the children in the family emotionally if not physically. "Research postulates that children living in violent families are emotionally and psychologically vulnerable as adults to enacting the role of either the victim or abuser which they observed or experienced during their childhoods." (King, p. 7.)[1]

Violence between spouses has a potentially profound impact on children. Not only can children receive emotional scars from this experience but, if family ties are weakened, children may experience a loss of supportive loving contact. It is within the family that we all first learn how to talk to one another about what we feel, think, and believe. Such communication may be squelched in situations of spouse abuse. Children living through this experience may have a reduced opportunity to observe and practice effective, clear communication processes. Perhaps the most important potential loss to a child living in a family with spouse abuse is that the child may fail to experience the joy of family life. As a result, the child may have lowered feelings of self esteem, poor abilities to solve problems, and vulnerability to feelings of loss.

VIOLENCE BETWEEN CHILDREN OR BY CHILDREN TOWARD ADULTS

Carol Warren, who conducted a study of fifteen adolescents who were hospitalized in a psychiatric setting, concluded that there are three major explanations for children's violence against parents: (1) violence as a response to alcohol use by the victim; (2) violence as described in frustration—aggression theory (an individual resorts to violence when his or her goals are blocked); (3) violence as a resource to be used in much the same way as money or status might be used. This theory assumes that violence will be used when other resources fail. (Warren, p. 3—5.)

Children, like adults, are subject to stress. They have disagreements with one another, with their parents, and with other adults. The family is the arena where children first learn to deal with inside and outside pressures and

---

[1]Findings thus far have been inconclusive. See Chapter Four for further comments on the topic of violence transmitted across generations. See also Srinika Jayaratne in Child Abusers as Parents and Children: A Review, *Social Work*, May 1977, for a review of the literature on intergenerational transmission of child maltreatment.

disagreements with others. It is within the family that children learn how to represent themselves in relationships between two or more people. Children watch their parents and older brothers and sisters to learn how to deal with difficulties. Violence between children and violence directed against parents by children might be understood in relationship to:

1. Parental modeling of brutality (physical and emotional).
2. Parental subtle or overt encouragement of aggression.
3. The build-up of emotions over a period of time with no appropriate way to release or work out these pent-up emotions.

In most families a great deal of child-raising energy is spent settling fights between children and in trying to teach children to get along together. Rudolf Dreikurs suggested that, unless there are some very severe underlying issues within the family or within the individual person, children fight for the purpose of getting their parent's attention. In some cases, the children know of no other way to get attention. (Dreikurs, p. 201.) Dreikurs was a child psychiatrist who worked with hundreds of children, families, and pediatricians. He believed that children given encouragement and supportive parenting will not become involved in violence with one another or their parents.

The real issue with violence by children is the issue of violence and unsettledness among adults. Annually, hundreds of thousands of children are beaten, kicked, punched, threatened with a gun or knife, or actually have a gun or knife used on them by their parents. If the family is the setting where children are taught how to fit into society, then the lessons the children in these families learn are lessons in violence.

Children may also see their parents physically and emotionally abuse their grandparents. Grandparent abuse is not a phenomenon that is limited to poor emotional and physical care within the confines of nursing homes. More and more adult protective agencies are coming into existence across the nation expressly to deal with this kind of family violence.

VIOLENCE AGAINST CHILDREN

Violence against children is what is generally referred to as child maltreatment. Just like other types of family violence, the nature and extent of child maltreatment is difficult to absolutely define and identify. Current findings suggest that at least a million children are abused and neglected in this country every year. (See also Chapter Four.)

Research indicates consistent differences among familial correlates of abuse and neglect. Giovannoni (1971) found that compared to neglecting families, abusive families had higher incomes, higher educational levels for males in the family, and members in higher status positions. The National Study of the Incidence and Severity of Abuse and Neglect (1981)[2] found similar contrasts.

Findings of a recent study of familial correlates of selected types of child abuse and neglect are particularly interesting.

Type of Maltreatment	Most Reliably Associated With
Abandonment	Promiscuousness and/or alcoholism of the mother
Physical Abuse	Parent/child conflict; biological/nonbiological relationship to the child
Emotional Abuse	Emotional/psychological problems of the child; intellecutal inadequacies of the child
Neglect	Intellectual status of the parents
Sexual Abuse	Father promiscuous/alcoholic

Source. M. Martin and J. Walters, Familial Correlates of Selected Types of Child Abuse and Neglect, Journal of Marriage and Family, May 1982, 44 (12). Reprinted by permission.

This study suggests that types of family circumstances may be predictive of different types of maltreatment. Both abusive and neglectful families show a higher level of social disorganization, marital problems, alcoholism, and mental illness than functional families. Understanding the difference, however, has implications for prevention, intervention, and treatment efforts with families and individuals.

CHILDREN'S INTERACTIONAL PATTERNS IN THE CONTEXT OF THE FAMILY

As social beings, each of us seeks to find a place in our primary groups. For most people, the family is the most important such group. For young children, the family may be the only primary group where belonging can occur. Children who have experienced abuse or neglect within their primary group often develop particular styles of interactional relationships within the family that they generalize to other groups.

Four of the interactional patterns that children often develop within the context of an abusive or neglectful family situation are caretaking, hiding, becoming the scapegoat, and provoking.

[2]The National Study of the Incidence and Severity of Abuse and Neglect (1981) will be referred to as NIS in this text.

The Caretaker

The caretaker is the child who avoids abuse or neglect by excessive caretaking of adults or other children within the family. This child has learned to be extra sensitive and alert to the needs of others and works hard to take care of other's needs to the exclusion of the child's normal emotional growth and development. This child may be missing out on age-appropriate opportunities for growth and development. The caretaking child may not be experiencing important developmental milestones that are important to him/her chronological and physical/emotional age.

Sara

My mother was sick in bed a lot of the time. Often I had to stay home from school to take care of her and to keep the house clean. My father always told me that if it weren't for me my mother wouldn't be so sick because she got sick when she was pregnant with me. Sometimes at the end of the day I was so tired that I just dropped into bed. When my father got home from work around 11:00 P.M. (he worked the night shift), he would wake me up to cook his supper or do some house chores that he wanted done. When I forgot to do things, my dad would hit me with my belt very hard. One time I had to go to the hospital after he beat me.

Caretaking is a pattern that may help a child survive in an unsafe setting. Children should not be encouraged to give up these patterns unless the family situation is safe.

The Hider

This child is one who has learned that it is sometimes important to physically as well as emotionally hide as a way of avoiding assault from adults. He has learned that it is often better to leave or hide when trouble seems to be in the air. If mother comes home drunk, if mom and dad are arguing, if mom's boyfriend is there, or if danger seems to exist for some other reason, this child may hide. Hiding provides emotional as well as physical safety.

Mark

When I came home from school, I never knew what to expect. Sometimes my mother and one of her boyfriends would be drinking wine and not have their clothes on. One time when I came home from school, my mother's boyfriend forced me to take off my clothes and do nasty things with him. After a while, I learned to come home quietly without making a sound so that my mother wouldn't know that I was there. If my mother had a boyfriend in the house when I got home, I would just hide or go to the shopping center until he left.

As with caretaking, hiding may be important to the physical and emotional well-being of the child and should not be discouraged until the family situation is safe.

The Scapegoat

This child may assume or be given the blame for events that occur in the family that are anger-arousing for the adults. Over time, with repetition of family patterns, everyone in the family can come to believe that this child is at fault for any problem that occurs. This child soon assigns blame to him/herself and finds a place in the family system as the family scapegoat. This child must find another place within the family if the dynamics of the abusive situation are to change.

Alice

Whenever anything bad happened at my house, I knew it was my fault. One day my dad came home from work and he had been fired from his job. He told me that if I had been a better kid it wouldn't have happened. My mom would get real mad at me when she burned things on the stove. I knew I was a bad person because everything that ever went wrong at our house, I was the cause of it.

The Provoker

The provoker is a child who provokes others within the context of the family. Provokers may intentionally start fights with adults or with their brothers and sisters, even though they may be aware that there will be consequences. Provokers may unconsciously believe that the only way that they can find a place in the family is to be a trouble-maker. Learning the troublemaking skills well within the context of a family, children may become trouble-makers at school or in other social situations which heap reprisals against them. Since this can be a very devastating pattern for the child as well as for his/her family and within other contexts in society, it is vitally important that the child be assisted through a treatment process or foster care in order to change this pattern. (McFadden)

Steve

My counselor tells me that I "set myself up for trouble." I don't know exactly what she means but I know that I end up getting people mad at me a lot and that sometimes I even end up getting hurt.

Interactional patterns are usually acquired by children early in life, largely through a process of trial and error within the family system. A child learns patterns of behavior that allow for his/her survival and place within the family. The reasons why a child picks a certain interactional pattern in an abusive family are endless. It is important that the child be helped to find his/her place in the family and other groups in more positive and productive ways which do not rob the child of childhood and/or contribute to his/her abuse or neglect.

FROM A SYSTEMS POINT OF VIEW

It is vital to remember as we consider family violence and family dynamics that functioning and dysfunctioning exist on a continuum. Each of us has had violent thoughts and committed violent actions. Every family is, as it constantly changes, functional and dysfunctional. Few families are never functional or never dysfunctional in some way. From a systems point of view, the commonalities shared by other families with abusing families become resources. It is not possible in this view to take a we–they position. It is possible, however to effect change in families.

The Question of Fault

When we hear about a dramatic case of child abuse or neglect, we are appalled. Often we feel angry at the people involved for hurting an innocent child. Understanding child abuse within the context of the family system is the first step to erasing blame and replacing it with understanding. When we stop to consider that building a system requires cooperation from people within the family and people and events outside the family, who is at fault becomes a nonsense question since its answer may be everyone and no one.

When a family is not functioning to the benefit of its members, it is easy to recognize that no one person designed the family to be that way. No one gets married and starts a family to create pain and suffering. Family members do not hope for dysfunctioning outcomes in their families. On the contrary, when people marry and join together in a committed relationship, it is with the understanding and implied hope that their lives will improve from what they were before. People join together for the express purpose of fulfilling hopes and dreams, not to create nightmares and newspaper headlines that distress us all. People come together to create families in the hope of creating a safe haven from the stresses and strains of life.

Likewise, institutions are not created for expressing negative influences. Schools, neighborhoods, social welfare agencies, and health care facilities are created to support and help people and families. Yet, sometimes they become the outside influences that work against a family functioning at its best.

Salvador Minuchin, a well-known family therapist who has worked with child abuse treatment in the context of the family states, "Joining with a child abuse family presents a particularly difficult problem. The therapist's immediate response may well be to side with the battered child, communicating his sense of outrage to the adults responsible." (Minuchin, p. 41.) Minuchin goes on to explain that in order to facilitate change within the context of the family system, the parents must feel the therapist's support so that the therapist can gain their support to work with the entire family in creating changes within the system. It is also important for the family therapist to understand and look carefully at the role that the injured member plays in the maintenance of the family system.

If the therapist views child abuse and neglect as symptoms of dysfunctioning within the family system, family members may be more willing to cooperate to make changes. Considered from this light and adding the possibility of chance factors, it is possible to see that child maltreatment in its multitude of dynamics is not a simple issue of fault.

ACHIEVING A FUNCTIONAL FAMILY

Approaching abuse and neglect from the understanding of the family as a system does not mean that an identified abuser should or should not be brought to trial and incarcerated. Nor does it mean that a child should or should not be removed from the home. Although the opposite result might seem to be anticipated, it can be shown that sometimes, for example, in incest situations, the bringing of criminal charges against the father or stepfather who committed the acts of incest can help to motivate the positive change within the family system and bring power to the child and mother. (See Chapters 9–13.) In any case, if the dysfunction is such that the child is not safe in the environment, then the child's safety must be assured through whatever means are deemed most appropriate in the given circumstances.

Other chapters discuss in detail the criteria for assessing risk and weighing of alternative dispositions and placements. The important point to be made in this context is that actions taken do not exist in a vacuum. The system principles of transformation, homeostasis, information flow, and transactional reciprocity influence each family member and the family as a whole. Simply removing a family member, although effecting change, will not necessarily effect positive change. Understanding the family as a system, however, will help in making such decisions and in assisting individual family members in making changes that will help them fit in more functional ways in other family groups as well as in their own. Such understanding may even help to prevent problems in other environments for family members.

A SHARED RESPONSIBILITY

If it is true that cooperation within a family structure and within a societal structure is required for violence to take place and that system principles apply to families, each of us certainly shares in the responsibility for change and has the power to effect change.

Summary

The family has been variously defined in form and function throughout history. Generally, the family has been seen as a group of people who are related by blood or marriage living under the same roof and depending upon one another in certain emotional and physical ways for survival. Today, the defined family group may or may not be related by blood or marriage. The family at its best is a haven for its members. Within this framework, the family provides safety from external physical and emotional dangers. It is "a people-making factory," where each of us learns about our own and the family's self-esteem, emotional rules for living, how to communicate, and how to make connections outside the family group. The family is one of the most intimate social groups to which any of us belong during our lifetimes. The level of vulnerability and intensity of relationships is high. Violence, including child abuse and neglect, occur most commonly within the context of the family.

Systems theory maintains that a family is a group of mutual influence. As a system, the family is always affected by the principles of transformation, homeostasis, information flow, and transactional reciprocity and their interaction. A family is defined at three levels: (1) in its members' relationships with one another; (2) in its internal structural variables; (3) in its relationship to impinging systems and processes outside the family. Understanding a family as a system in its three-level definition enables us to appreciate the circumstances of a family at any given point in time and to deal with individual or group problems within the family.

Functioning families are those that coexist as a family group and meet the basic needs of their membership. These families accept change and stress as a part of life, have an overt or covert rule that violence is not permitted within the family structure, and seem to have the working parts working for rather than against the family. When violence occurs within the family, the family system is working to the detriment of the group and in dysfunctional ways.

Violence is difficult to define objectively. The common theme in most definitions of violence, however variously defined, is the imposing of harm. Several theories have been proposed in the effort to explain violence. These include but are not limited to conflict theory, resource theory, instinctual theory, learning theory, and cultural impact theory.

Family violence is defined for the purposes of this chapter as that behavior within a family that leads to foreseeable and avoidable physical or emotional injury or damage to a family member. All types of child maltreatment are violent according to this definition. Family violence also includes violence between adults within the family and violence against adults by children. New studies indicate that different types of family circumstances are predictive of different types of maltreatment.

As social beings, each of us seeks to find a place in our primary groups. Children in abusive homes, in their effort to find a place, sometimes develop one of the four interactional patterns of caretaking, hiding, provoking, or becoming the scapegoat.

Understanding child abuse and neglect within the context of the family system is the first step to erasing blame and replacing it with understanding new possibilities for change. Child maltreatment was not the hope of the people who joined together as a family. Understanding that function and dysfunction exist on a continuum and that all families share some commonalities as well as differences permits functioning families to act as resources for those that are not functioning in the best interest of their members.

Actions do not exist in a vacuum. Decisions made by those who intervene in situations of child maltreatment regarding one family member have an impact on the rest of the family system. Understanding the concept of the family as a system can help those persons to encourage positive change in efforts of prevention, intervention, and treatment. The concept of the family as a system of mutual influence has broader implications. Each of us shares in the responsibility for change and each of us has the power to effect it.

BIBLIOGRAPHY

Bell, Robert R., *Marriage and Family Interaction.* Dorsey Press, Homewood, IL, 1979.

Bolton, F.G., Director of Human Resource Services, Arizona Community Development for Abuse and Neglect. D.E.S. 5027 (4-76), Phoenix, AZ.

Corfman, E. (Ed), *Families Today.* Vol. I. U.S. Department of Health, Education and Welfare, Rockville, MD, 1979.

———, *Families Today.* Vol. II. A Research Sampler on Families and Children. National Institute of Mental Health, Washington, DC, 1979

Dreikurs, Rudolf and Saltz, Vicki, *Children: The Challenge.* Hawthorne Books, New York, 1964.

Encyclopedia Britannica, *Macropedia, Knowledge in Depth.,* Vol. 7, Chicago, IL, 1978.

Fischhoff J., "Abused Children: A Psychiatrist Examines Violence in the Family." In *The American Family.* Smithkline Corp., Philadelphia, 1978.

Freeman, D.S., *Techniques of Family Therapy.* Jason Aronson, New York, 1981.

Gil, D.G., *Child Abuse and Violence.* AMS Press, Inc., New York, 1979.

Gil, Eliana, and Baxter, K., "Abuse of Children in Institutions." San Francisco Child Abuse Council, (an undated unpublished paper).

Haynie, Roena L., "Deprivation of Body Pleasure: Origin of Violent Behavior? A Survey of the LIterature." In *Child Welfare.* LIX:5, May 1980, pp. 287–297.

Howard, J., *Families.* Simon and Schuster, New York, 1978.

King, Linda Silverman, "Responding to Spouse Abuse: The Mental Health Profession." In *Response to Family Violence.* 4,5, May/June 1981, pp. 7–9.

Knopf, I.J., *Child Psychopathology*. Prentice–Hall, Inc., New Jersey, 1979.

Lerman, Lisa G., Landis, Leslie, and Galdzwerg, Sharon, "State Legislation on Domestic Violence." Response to *Violence in the Family. 4,7*, September/October 1981, pp. 1–18.

McKechnie J.L., *Webster's New Twentieth Century Dictionary of the English Language*. William Collins Publishers, Inc., Cleveland, OH, 1980.

Minuchin, S. and Fishman, H.C., *Family Therapy Techniques*. Harvard University Press, Cambridge, MA, 1981.

Newman, G., *Understanding Violence*. J.B. Lippincott Co., New York, 1979.

Norgard, K.E. and Whitman S.T., Understanding the Family as a System—SW 131A. A project sponsored by The Arizona Department of Economic Security and funded by Title XX, Phoenix, AZ, March 1980.

Ogden, G. and Zevin, A., *When a Family Needs Therapy*. Beacon Press, Boston, MA, 1976.

Satir V., *Peoplemaking*. Science and Behavior Books, Inc., Palo Alto, 1972.

Schaeffer, E., *What is a Family?* Fleming H. Revell Co., New Jersey, 1975.

Scott, P.D., "Battered Wives," *British Journal of Psychiatry. 125,* 1975, pp. 433–441.

Segal, J. and Yahraes, H., *A Child's Journey: Forces That Shape the Lives of our Young*. McGraw Hill, Inc., New York, 1979.

Sorrells, J.M. and Ford, F.R., "Toward an integrated theory of families and family therapy." *Psychotherapy: Theory, Research and Practice 6,3*, Summer 1969, pp. 150–160.

Stein, T., *Social Work Practice in Child Welfare*. Prentice-Hall, Inc., New Jersey, 1981.

Steinmetz, Suzanne K. and Straus, Murray A., (Eds.) *Violence in the Family*. Dodd, Mead and Co., New York, 1975.

Thomas, H.E., (Ed.) *Medical, Legal, and Psychosocial Aspects on Violence in Families*. American Academy of Psychiatry and Law, Philadelphia Symposium, 1976.

Turner, Willie M. and Westt, Lois A., "Violence in Military Families." Response to *Violence in the Family. 4,5*, May/June 1981, pp. 1–5.

Warren, Carol A.B., "Parent Batterers": Adolescent Violence and the Family." Paper presented at the annual meeting Pacific Sociological Assn., Anaheim, CA, April 1978.

Webster, Noah, Webster's New 20th Century Dictionary of the English Language. (Unabridged) William Collins, Cleveland, OH, 1980.

3

In The Context Of Development

IN THE BEGINNING

Controversy exists about when human life actually begins. Does life begin at the moment of conception, sometime during the gestation process, or at the moment of birth? Whenever human life begins, so does human development. This process of human development and what influences it in positive and negative ways is critical to the survival and quality of mankind.

Human development is defined as physical, emotional, and social development. "Development can be defined as the changes in the structure, thought, or behavior of a person which occur as a function of both biological and environmental influences." (Craig, p. 11.)

Whether we are as we are because of our basic nature or because of the nurturance that we have received from others is a basic question in theories of human development. At any point in time, are we a product of our genetic heritage which evolves with maturation or are we a product of the environment and our learning about the world through this influence? The position taken by most people in the field of human development is that it is a combination of both nature and nurture that explains who we are.

Child abuse and neglect occurs within the context of human development. Every time a child is maltreated, that child is somewhere en route along his life cycle. Child abuse and neglect interferes with and interrupts human development. It is our position that child abuse has a shared impact, both on the child and on others in relationship to the child.

THEORIES OF HUMAN DEVELOPMENT

Four major theoretical explanations of human development will be discussed. Each of these theories is important in explaining human development, but each is incomplete in and of itself.

Learning Theory

Learning theory states that there is a process by which humans acquire or change patterns of behavior. Environment, planned or happenstance, creates circumstances (stimuli) to which people respond (response). A child grows and changes in response to the environmental stimuli.

Learning theory asserts that learning occurs within the context of a person's development and genetic heritage. Developmental and genetic factors predispose a person's learning at any given point in time. Learning theory makes the basic assumption that people are reactive and are shaped and molded by experiences within the environment. Ivan Pavlov, Edward Thorndike, B. F. Skinner, and John B. Watson are some of the well-known names connected with the learning theory school of thought.

Learning theory is most useful in testing empirical areas. It is not particularly helpful in dealing with the area of moral development, creativity, love, or other broad contexts of human behavior.

Cognitive Theory

Cognitive theory is popularly linked to the psychology of thinking including problem solving, memory development, creativity, and the capacity for logical and abstract thinking. Prior to 1930, children were thought to be miniature adults. The only difference between adults and children was thought to be in quantity of knowledge. Since adults have a greater number of years and life experiences than a child, their quantity of knowledge was considered to be greater. Against this backdrop, Jean Piaget and Heins Werner made a major contribution to the understanding of human development. Their research found that the way children think is related to their age and is quite different from the ways that adults think. (Ambron, p. 12.)

Jean Piaget, a well-known Swiss psychologist, and J. S. Bruner, an American, were key figures in the area of cognitive theory. Unlike some of his colleagues, Piaget believed that the human mind is not a blank slate waiting for the imprinting of knowledge. Young children make judgments based upon perceptual instead of logical processes. Piaget's famous experiment has been repeated around the world. He first asked children under six years of age which glass had the most liquid when actually the amounts in the glasses were equal. Then he would show the child two identical glasses with the same amount of liquid in each glass. Finally he would transfer the liquid from one of the glasses into a taller glass and ask the child which glass had the larger amount of liquid. Children perceived the amount in the taller glass to have the larger amount of liquid even though they saw Piaget pour the liquid from the glass containing an equal amount of liquid to the other glass. From this base, Piaget adopted his stages of mental development which state that as the human grows and develops, his/her structural abilities for organizing new information becomes more complex.

The cognitive theory of human development has been widely used in the field of education. The human being is seen as creative and able to plan and problem-solve. The shortcoming of this theory is that it is concerned mainly with intellectual development and has little explanation for emotional development.

Psychoanalytic Theory

Sigmund Freud is credited as the founder of the psychoanalytic theory whose purpose is to explain emotional development. Many believe Freud's theory to be outdated since it was developed at the turn of the twentieth century. However, it is still one of the most popular explanations of human emotional behavior. Freud stated that at birth each of us has a collection of strong drives and motivations which are largely sexually oriented. At different chronological ages during growth, different parts of the body become the primary focus of gratification.

Freud can be considered to be a developmentalist in respect to his study of personality. He hypothesized that a personality grows and develops in a way similar to the human physical structure. People pass through stages in both physical and emotional growth. "From his adult patients Freud learned that a failure to develop in one stage inhibited later development, often causing maladjustment. He concluded that adult personality was profoundly affected by early experience." (Ambron, p.9.)

Neo-Freudians added to Freud's original ideas. One of the neo-Freudians, Erik Erikson, expanded and modified Freud's theory by focusing more on cultural and social aspects of influence and less on instinctual and biological aspects of human nature. Erikson theorized eight stages of development that span the lifetime of a human being. During each one of these stages, the human has certain issues that must be solved. Erikson believed that our conflicts center more around our family members and other important social groups and less around the internal conflicts that were Freud's focus of attention. These eight stages of human development were derived from Freud's base as well as Erikson's ideas that there are emotional tasks, central people, and certain needs at different stages in the life cycle. The five stages that relate to child development are explained in Table 3-1.

Table 3-1   Erik Erikson's Stages of Childhood

Stage/Age	Emotional Task	Significant Person(s)	Needs from Caretakers or Others
Infancy Birth–1 year	Sense of trust	Primary caretaker or parent (which can be a male or a female)	Infants need to receive consistent, predictable care from familiar, loving caretakers to be able to accept the world as a trustworthy place where they can get their basic needs met. Caretakers must respond to the baby's physical (feeding, diapering, shelter) and emotional (cuddling, holding, and talking to) needs.
Toddler 1½–3 years	Sense of automomy (development of self-awareness)	Primary caretaker and larger family	The child needs to be able to make choices and be allowed to do things independently that are within his/her capability to be able to develop a mind and will of her own. The child is learning to experience control over the world during this time.
Preschool age 3–6 years	Initiative	Primary caretaker, larger family, and significant people outside the family group.	The child needs to be allowed to continue to take risks. The child of this age has a normal curosity, imagination, and need to experiment. The child is eager to find out what kind of a person he/she is. The child observes and imitates others and invents fantasies. The child is beginning to make sex role identification during this period.

Middle childhood 7–11 years	Industry	Primary caretaker, family, neighborhood, and school	This stage builds on the previous three. Basically, the child learns industry through a relationship with school but the same needs carry over into the home. As with all the stages, the child self-esteem level is associated with accomplishing the task of this stage of development.
Adolescence 12–17 years	Identity	Peer group and adult models	This is a period when the individual needs to be allowed to question. It is by this questioning that gender identity and career choices can occur. This stage requires a great deal of patience, love, and understanding on the part of adults as the adolescent struggles to find their own appropriate roles, values and behaviors. It is important to affirm the adolescent's uniqueness as an individual so that he or she can develop a solid sense of self worth.

Source. Derived from Erik Erikson, *Childhood and Society.*

Humanistic Theory

Abraham Maslow, who is identified with the humanistic school of thought, is credited with a term called "self-actualization." Maslow builds his theory of human development with self-actualization as a cornerstone. He believed that people move toward the ultimate goal of self-actualization, which simply stated means reaching their full potential. It is difficult to operationally define "potential" and this may be one of the weakest links in Maslow's theory. Maslow stated that people have basic needs and that there is an hierarchy of needs, each one building and dependent upon the one before. To reach full potential, each need on the scale must be satisfied, first the basic needs and then the metaneeds. If the basic needs are not first satisfied, the individual has deficiencies that get in the way of attaining self-actualization.

The following are Maslow's steps on the hierarchy ladder.

Sustenance. Satisfying hunger and thirst. If people do not have enough to eat or drink, they are not concerned about anything else. They have no morality, friends, nor loved ones which can substitute for having this basic need fulfilled.

Security. Satisfying safety needs. Once people have secured enough to eat and drink, they begin to create security. They find a way to insure that they will have enough to eat and drink at all times. If they are not secure, if their access to food and drink is blocked, they continue to stay at this level until they have achieved some measure of security. This rung on the hierarchy also pertains to security of person. People at this level take fewer risks than they were willing to take when they were constantly hungry. They protect themselves more carefully.

Socialization. Satisfying the need to belong. Once people have achieved a measure of security, they can begin to work on reaching out to others for love, affection, and affiliation. They begin to act in a more social way. They do things to please others even when it might bring somewhat of a hardship to them personally. They usually will not risk their security, nor their food supply, but they will act unselfishly for the benefit of others more and more often.

Another humanist, Rudolf Dreikurs, authors of *Children: The Challenge* and numerous other books, expanded on Alfred Adler's ideas about social interest and theorized that the basic part of our personal identity is how we find our place in the primary groups in which we participate. He believed that the basic need that each of us has is to belong and every other need is secondary to this one. Certainly, this idea is similar to Maslow's notion of socialization.

Self esteem—gaining approval from others and self-recognition, feeling competent. This need can only be sought after and accomplished when the previous basic needs are satisfied.

Self-actualization. The gaining of one's full potential. This is the ultimate of a person's needs. Figure 3.1 illustrates the building block nature of Maslow's theory.

Humanistic psychology has had more impact in the counseling area than it has in the area of explaining or predicting human development. As with some of the other theories, there is little empirical data to support some of the ideas. This is a major shortcoming.

Each of these four theories plays a major role in understanding and dealing with human development. There is much more to learn from each of these areas than has been covered in this thumbnail sketch. Each of the theories is useful in explaining and dealing with the development of the child.

A Transactional Model of Development

Sameroff and Chandler (1975) proposed a model of development that draws from and is congruent with theories conceived by Piaget (1971), Werner (1948), Reese and Overton (1970), White (1976), and Sroufe (1979). This model accents a systems approach to development. It is particularly useful

Drawing by Travis L. Mayhall
February, 1982

Figure 3-1 Maslow's building blocks of development. (*Source:* From Abraham Maslow, *The Farther Reaches of Human Nature.* Viking Press, New York, 1971.)

when attempting to understand the interaction of abuse and neglect and development.

The Sameroff and Chandler model applies the principle of transactional reciprocity discussed in Chapter Two. The many transactions among environmental forces, parent/caretaker characteristics, and child characteristics are seen as mutually influencing. They make dynamic reciprocal contributions to both the events and the outcome of child development.

From a transactional perspective it is possible to see that the behavior of a sixteen-year-old youth who was physically abused at the age of five reflects not only the quality of that youth's adaptation to the abuse at the time but also what transactions among environmental forces, parent/ caretaker characteristics, and child characteristics came before, during, and since. As the child developed, the match between parent and child and parent and child characteristics may have changed. How the child met each developmental task along the way influenced with many other factors how other tasks have been and will be met. In the context of this model, a child is an active participant in development. As Cicchetti and Rizley state, "The maladapted child in ways creates its own environment and may contribute to its own developmental anomalies." (1981, p. 51.)

IN THE CONTEXT OF GROWING

Child abuse and neglect occur within the context of human growth and development and as such, interact with the child's development emotionally, socially, and physically. Children grow within the context of their families (or other caretaking arrangements) just as plants grow within the context of their containers. Children need nurturing and nourishment at each stage in their development in order to be able to reach adulthood. There are special requirements of nurturing and nourishment for each stage of human growth and development. Growing a human is like building a house. Each step in the process is vital and is a link to the next step. Each stage builds upon and counts upon the preceding one.

Prenatal Development

Abuse and neglect can occur at the prenatal stage in human development. The fetus has certain physical (perhaps even emotional) needs that can best be supplied by the mother during pregnancy.

Pregnancy is not a neutral phenomenon in people's lives. Everyone involved (fathers, mothers, grandparents, friends, *et al.*) has feelings— positive, negative, and mixed—about pregnancy. It is possible that the feelings of the mother and those she interacts with (the father and others) affect the growth and development of the fetus. Negative feelings not only affect the mother but it is possible that these feelings can be transmitted to the unborn child. The care that a pregnant woman requires, accepts, and receives, coupled with her emotional state, affects the well-being of the mother and therefore the child.

Certainly a pregnant woman who is poorly nourished, is involved in drug or alcohol abuse, or who smokes tobacco may cause harm to the unborn child. Questions of intent may be raised. Is it possible that some of these mothers are intentionally abusing themselves in an effort to abuse the fetus? Does a woman addicted to heroin who must have her baby detoxed from heroin shortly after birth intentionally abuse and neglect her child? In a broader sense the question may be: What responsibilities, legally and morally, should the mother have to the unborn child? There is no question that child abuse and neglect can occur almost from the moment of birth, but can abuse and neglect also occur before birth?

Infancy

Scientists are beginning to recognize that ". . . new-borns come highly equipped for their first intense meeting with their parents, and in particular their mothers." (Marano, p. 9.) Babies seem to orient themselves toward sound and sight. They seem to require this as a part of their emotional attachment or bonding with their primary caretaker (usually their mother). "Unable to cling to the fur of a highly mobile mother (as do monkeys), the human infant depends for all of its early needs on the strength of its mother's emotional attachment." (Marano, p. 9.)

There is widespread agreement that the most critical aspect of infancy is the parent–child bonding process.[1] (Fischoff, p. 7; Steele, p. 55; Wilson, p. 402.) Without effective bonding, there is evidence that the infant may be more vulnerable both in infancy and in later life to abuse and neglect. (Marano, p. 9.) Klaus and Kennell have been conducting research at Rainbow Babies and Children's Hospital in Cleveland on the special problems of premature babies in attaching to mothers. Lack of infant responsiveness may reflect lack of parental stimulation (Klaus and Kennell.) Klaus and Kennell found that in spite of medical efforts to save the lives of these premature babies, a disproportionate number of these premature babies came to the hospital emergency rooms battered and abused. This finding again suggests the possibility of a correlation between early bonding and the future relationship between parent and child. The validity and reliability of such findings are still in question and more research is needed in this area.

---

[1]Bonding is the process of emotional attachment between a parent and his/her infant.

How does this bonding or emotional attachment process occur? Most mothers want to see, touch, and talk to their newborns. Pregnancy may be the beginning of bonding between mother and child since there is a physical closeness between the two and the mother has feelings about her pregnancy. It is also possible that nursing a baby can bring a close (or distant) feeling between the two. Most mothers seem to rely on some response from their infant as one part of reaching out so that the bonding can begin to take place.

A Repertoire of Competencies. There are some observable and predictable factors that will either facilitate or inhibit attachment during infancy. First, the infant has a repertoire of competencies. These competencies include responsiveness to social overtures on the part of the parent. Auditory, visual, and tactile sensory responses are the usual ways the infant responds to others. If the infant does not respond to the caretaker in all or some of these ways, the caretaker can misinterpret this lack of responsiveness as rejection or an inability on the caretaker's part to make a connection with the infant.

Temperament. A second factor that may influence the attachment between the infant and the caretaker has to do with the infant's temperament. Babies are individuals even from the moment of birth. Some infants are active while others are docile. Some infants are cuddly, others cry. Premature babies, by that fact alone, are fighting for their lives. Some babies seem to be naturally happy, cuddly, and easy to care for while others are just the opposite. Some babies' temperament and needs for special care and attention are a result of their being premature or having some physical handicap, brain damage, chronic illness, or severe congenital anomalies. Infants have been described as the easy child, the difficult child, and the slow-to-warm up child. (Chess, p. 92.) Continuing with this line of thinking, it is possible to conclude that there may also be a "goodness of fit" concept that influences how well the parent and the child adjust and match to one another. The goodness of fit theory suggests that if parents are more active, they will match better with infants who are more active than would parents who are less active. The literature holds that infants who are classified as "easy infants" have a better chance for successful bonding and attachment during the early days and months than do the infants who fall into the other two categories. (Gross, p. 23.) "The new arrival introduces a stress which often tests the limits of a parent's capacity to protect and care for a child." (Segal, p. 597, *Families.*) Whether it is the child's temperament or unfulfilled expectations, either can be a prelude to physical abuse or neglect. This new child can add a stress that may push the parents' limits to protect and care for the child beyond their limits, particularly if their commitment was weak in the beginning.

Physical Characteristics. Some infants are born physically unattractive as a result of a difficult birth process or genetic factors. Other infants are born into a family where the mother and father are separated and the mother has bitter, angry, hurt feelings directed toward the father. An infant who is born resembling his father physically may make it difficult for the mother to feel drawn to this infant and attachment difficulties may result. It is also possible that the mother or father may have wished for a boy (or a girl), and have difficulty getting past the initial disappointment that the infant is not the "right" sex. The size of the infant may also be important to the parent. The fact that the infant is too large or too small (which may have influenced the birth process for the mother), may influence bonding.

Segal notes that a further compounding factor for the infant who fails to meet the parents' expectations as to appearance and who is abused as a result, may be that the infant will develop behavior patterns that are unattractive and therefore, invite further harm. In other words, if abused children are unlovable to begin with, they may become more unlovable as they become ugly in behavior. "The victim, it would seem, begins early to contribute to his own disastrous fate." (Segal, p. 597, *Families*.)

Support Systems. Everyone needs a support system or network. This group may be composed of extended family members, neighbors, or close friends. Since stresses are inherent in parenting a new infant, whether the child be the first or later child, a support system is vital to the parents at this particularly vulnerable time.

Parent Education. One other factor that may have some influence on the success of the emotional attachment process between infant and caretaker is parent education. Gordon has written about parent effectiveness training. Dreikurs has written about children as a challenge and Haim Ginott has also written several books on the subject of parent education. They all discuss that it is important for parents to be realistic in their expectations of their children. These authors do not directly encourage the parent to be as aware of developmental stages of children as Erikson, but they do encourage a humanistic, loving approach to parenthood. Parent education is important from the moment of birth, but it is equally important that parents not become robotlike in applying "techniques" of parent education to their children.

Postpartum Syndrome. Kathleen Gilliam describes the postpartum syndrome as any psychiatric disorder in which childbirth is one of the interacting causal agents. (Gilliam, p. 484.) She notes that over one-half of women who bear children experience a marked degree of emotional upset after the birth of their baby. Profound confusion about what it means to be a mother coupled with uncertainty about child rearing procedures may be the basis for this syndrome. This information underscores the need for support and education of new parents.

Failure to Thrive

The failure to thrive (FTT) syndrome is characterized by chronic undernutrition of the infant or young child. Twenty-five % of these problems are believed to have an organic cause, twenty-five percent of the children have a mother who is not feeding them properly, and it is believed that fifty percent of the FTT infants and young children are being subjected to extreme neglect and grossly distorted mothering. (Fischhoff, p. 7.) FTT children are below the third percentile for their age in height and weight and have feeding and other associated difficulties. Chess and Hassibi note three explanations for this syndrome: maternal neglect and poverty, inadequate and immature mothers, or maternal emotional disorder or outright rejection of the infant. (Chess, p. 88.) This type of child abuse, which occurs during infancy or early childhood, is often difficult to detect until it is at a critical point. If left unattended it can result in permanent damage to the infant or child. Mental or physical retardation can be a permanent result of the FTT syndrome. It is also possible that this condition early in the infant's life can lead to later chronic states of dissatisfaction and unhappiness with the self and the environment.

Parents of infants who are less than six pounds at birth may need special help and support since statistics indicate that one-fourth of the victims of battered child syndrome are infants with less than a six pound birth weight. (Segal, p. 598.) Explanations for this fact range from parents' difficulties in relating to babies who are more irritable or have feeding/eating problems. Babies who are slower in muscular and speech development and socialization during the first two years of life may contribute to increased parental distress, resulting in isolation between the parent and the child.

Parents in our society are not encouraged or even given the opportunity to express negative feelings about their newborns and infants. There seems to be a pervasive cultural attitude that babies are intrinsically good and should be seen that way by all concerned. What happens for the parent who may have questioned being pregnant and now that the baby has actually arrived is still puzzled by those questions compounded by further doubts and resentments about the baby? Every infant's very survival is dependent upon the caretaker's expression of love and caring and providing for the infant's physical needs. If parents are either unwilling or unable to provide for the basic needs of the infant, child abuse or neglect may result. Without having his/her early needs met, the infant may fail to develop trust, a sense of security, and/or a sense of belonging that is vital to the infant's growth and development.

The child whose needs have not been met in infancy may enter the next stage of development less equipped to handle the challenge of that period. There appears to be a relationship in this period between emotional and physical deprivation and learning delays, hearing difficulties, difficulty in forming emotional attachments, etc. (See also Chapter Four.)

Toddler

The basic task of a child this age is to become autonomous. The toddler should be allowed and encouraged to do things over and over until s/he masters the task. Will power is an important part of autonomy. Once a toddler sets his/her mind to doing something, s/he will keep on going until s/he has accomplished the task. The task may be climbing a chair, pulling over a tablecloth, or becoming toilet trained. The toddler needs approval and freedom. The parent must encourage this exploration while setting protective limits at the same time. As the parent sets limits for the child's safety and protection, it is important for the parent to make good judgments about what the child can and cannot do and not unduly frustrate the child during this process. The parent must understand that this period in a child's life is a normal part of growing up.

During his/her second year, the toddler has a dramatic increase in language skills. Along with language development comes the child's ability to say "no." This is a part of the child's quest for autonomy and independence. Self-centeredness is also normal for this period of development.

Even though the research indicates that premature babies appear to have a higher risk of abuse and neglect than other infants, abuse and neglect are no more prevalent among the very, very young than among older children. Major physical injury occurs most frequently to children under the age of two and 15- to 17-year-old children. (A.H.A., 1981.) Some data suggest that the young male is more likely to be abused than the young female, as well as more likely to be the recipient of a greater degree of violence. Younger females, in general, may be less punished than their male counterparts. (Lefrancois, p. 303.)[2]

One subtle form of neglect is the failure of the parents to "childproof" their house. Parents need to put attractive, but dangerous objects out of the reach of the exploring toddler. This can be a stressful time for parents because their toddler may be in perpetual motion and in need of continual supervision. This strain coupled with whatever strains (economic, marital, or emotional) already exist within the family unit can be the stage for possible child abuse or neglect.

[2]For a discussion of some of the major limitations of this type of date, see Chapter 4.

If a child suffers from abuse or neglect during this period in his/her life, the child may have difficulty in developing autonomy. An abused or neglected toddler might feel excessively doubtful of his/her own autonomy or even feel ashamed about him/herself. Some possible behavior that might be observed in a child who has been abused or neglected during this period include:

1. Daydreaming as an escape.
2. A calm, unemotional attitude that may be a repression of fear or true emotion.
3. Withdrawal or lack of communication.
4. Intentional seeking of punishment which can become a provoking interactional pattern with parents and other adults.
5. Regression to an earlier level of development out of fear (a child who is toilet trained may begin wetting again, etc.)

Preschool Age

The child's task during this stage of development is to develop initiative. Initiative is the desire to think and/or carry out one's own ideas. This desire is part of the child's growing independence. Many times during this period, the child will start something without asking or telling his/her parents. This may be distressful for the parents, particularly if they are not aware that this is normal behavior. Even though the preschool age child is striving toward increased independence, the child still requires a great deal of supervision from adults. The adult is still responsible in a major way for the health and safety of this age child.

Sometimes in his/her striving for independence and coupled with his/her self-centeredness, the child may physically or verbally strike out at the parent. It is common for children to say "I hate you" in a fit of anger. A parent needs to be aware that this is just another way that the child tests his/her independence. If the parent is overly invested emotionally in the child, he/she might feel very disappointed and frustrated during this stage. The parent might feel that the child is ungrateful for all the sacrifices made on his/her behalf. If the parents lack other social supports and connections for themselves, they may rely too heavily on the child for these needs and this reliance may be unrealistic.

During this stage, a child's peers and play become important. Children learn about relationships with people their own age and about people outside their immediate families through play. They learn about give and take and cooperation through this process. Parents need to facilitate the learning of these skills by allowing their children to play with other children.

At about age three, children learn to differentiate between male and female. Children begin to become aware of behaviors expected of males and females. They begin to form a sex identification during this time. Positive experiences with adult males and females are critical during this period to enhance this process for the child.

Children need love and affection from both parents. Preschool children who are sexually abused may have difficulty developing their sexual identification. Sexually abused children are ahead of their years in development since sexual experiences are not expected or overtly permitted at this developmental stage. Problems may occur for children who have had pleasurable experiences in being sexually abused. They may want to continue this behavior with other people. It is sometimes difficult to help children learn about age-appropriate sexual behavior when they have been sexually abused and have experienced pleasure either physically or emotionally from this experience, because relearning risks interfering with the child's normal sexual development during this period of his or her life.

During this period, parents need to encourage children to test their abilities. It is usually during this period that children learn to control their bladder and bowels. This can be a difficult task. This control requires judgment, initiative, and awareness on the part of the child. Anxiety or tension may interfere with this process. Children who are anxious or tense may be retarded in this developmental area.

Children develop an imagination during this time. Fantasies can sometimes be difficult to distinguish from reality. A child who has had severe experiences may focus on his/her fantasies to the extent that s/he retreats from the too painful real world.

This period in the development of a child may be more difficult than infancy for the parent because the child is more mobile, and is practicing decision-making without the benefit of experience. In addition, the child is learning how to say "no," something which may be threatening to even the most assured adult. These factors may contribute particularly to physical and emotional abuse during this age period.

One of the geratest psychological costs to children who experience abuse or neglect during the preschool period is that their initiative may suffer. They may not learn how to feel competent enough to assert themselves and to trust their own judgment and awareness of the world around them. Children who have been exposed to neglect or abuse during this stage of development may develop difficulties in the following areas:

1. *Excessive self-centeredness.* The child who has experienced sexual abuse may begin to think of him/herself as the most important person in the world and certainly of equal importance (or superior to) the other parent in the family who would normally be involved in the sexual activity.

2. *Regression to a behavior that may have been appropriate at an earlier stage of development.*

3. *Withdrawal, lack of initiative, and guilt over the goals contemplated but not completed during this stage.* Children who have experienced severe neglect or abuse may withdraw rather than continue to try to assert their initiative.

4. *Refusal to associate or play with other children.* An extreme form of this behavior is the child who has lost interest in most forms of individual play.

5. *Excessive physical aggression of destructiveness.* This may be exhibited by the child who has experienced extreme physical punishment by a parent or has been neglected to the extent that the parent permits any kind of behavior on the part of the child and does not set limits for the child's safety or health. (Adapted from Thompson, p. 25–27.)

Middle Childhood

In this period, a child's basic task is to learn industry. Industry means diligence, doing something that is worthwhile, figuring out how something works, and making a contribution either to self or to others. School, friends, and the immediate family form the most common arena for the child in middle childhood to learn and practice industry. Other tasks of this period include continuing to form an identity and gender role, and continuing the process of physical and social development. Learning to problem-solve is also a task of middle childhood.

Commonly this stage in development is referred to as "latency." Latency means that a quality or power may be hidden or dormant. Freud thought that this time period in the life of a human being was dormant in sexuality, drive, and power.

Children start school during this period and begin to get out into the larger world away from their families. Children bring information into the family from the outside world. A child's territory is enlarged greatly during this time. This is a time of "belonging." S/he may join a club or associate with other groups of children. A child this age is comparing his/her own family values to those of others. This may also be a time when prejudices and preferences are developing. Most importantly, the child is learning to relate to work.

Sexual development begins at this age. Toward the end of this period, girls' breasts begin to enlarge, boys' genitals enlarge, and both boys and girls begin to get pubic hair. Sometimes parents have difficulty coping with this developing sexuality.

As this period draws to a close and adolescence approaches, a child's interest in family activities decreases and increases in the activities of his/her peers. Self-centeredness seems to decrease. A child's main focus during this time is school, peers, and on establishing his/her own competency in the midst of his/her world and family.

If a child is abused or neglected during this period, some or all of the following difficulties might arise:

1. Regression to an earlier level of development.
2. Withdrawal and lack of attempting to master the task of industry.
3. Excessive physical aggression or destructiveness that may take the form of juvenile delinquency.
4. Difficulties in school, with the extreme being a school drop out.

The cost certainly could be in the area of industry to a child who is abused during this life period. If a child does not believe in his/her ability, he may act, instead out of a sense of inferiority.

Adolescence

This is the final stage before adulthood in human development. During this time a youth must master a sense of identity versus role diffusion. It is during this stage that a youth must also move more and more toward independence from his/her parents. The youth must assimilate and establish his/her own set of values and ways of behaving in the world.

R. J. Havighurst (1972) is credited with outlining the developmental tasks of the adolescent:

1. Achievement of new and mature relations with age mates of both sexes.
2. Achievement of masculine or feminine social roles.
3. Acceptance and use of one's body effectively.
4. Achievement of emotional independence from parents and other adults.
5. Preparation for marriage and family life.
6. Preparation for a career.
7. Acquisition of a set of values and ethical system.
8. Acquisition and utilization of socially responsible behavior.

The adolescent years are a time of experimentation. We all experiment to some degree during our lifetime, but the adolescent is more conspicuous and experimentation goes on both privately and publicly. During this time, youths are searching for new and different levels of interdependence with the family and with others. Ultimately, adolescents must reach a balance between their own self-reliance and their reliance on others.

Adolescence is also a time of rapid physical changes. Puberty involves both physical and emotional changing. This body growth is accompanied by sexual and intellectual maturation and by the onset of a host of intense and often conflicting feelings. Often an adolescent is not sure how to cope with these feelings and his/her ultimate decision is a part of the experimentation process. The adolescent's search for identity is characterized by concerns about how one feels, behaves and what one believes. It is a time of soul searching and contemplation.

The facets of growth that are going on at this time are very individualized. It is possible to be "too" tall, "too" short, "too" big-breasted, "too" flat-chested and "too this" and "too that." Sometimes this period is also characterized by mood swings from loneliness and vulnerability to feelings of bravado.

"In short, much of what is normal, healthy, and necessary to successful adolescent development is expressed in behavior that is not very pleasant for adults to be around. Adolescent behavior can be annoying, disconcerting and even frightening." (Fisher, p. 33.) Even parents who are fully educated in the developmental facets of this time period have a difficult time living with an adolescent. Perhaps this is as it should be because both the youth and the parent must prepare to separate during this period. Parents have difficult times setting limits for the youth during this time because there are no clear rules for health and safety. At this point in time, the adolescent can set many of his/her own rules for health and safety and most of the enforcing of rules is out of the control of the parents anyway.

Many of us have images of what a victim of child abuse or neglect is like. Fisher suggests the following characteristics portray the perpetrator in cases of child abuse: the perpetrator is larger and more powerful than the abused; the perpetrator is more responsible for his action than the abused; the perpetrator's power is increased by the fact that the abused is more isolated from potential help or sources of support; the perpetrator should be more responsible for himself and more in control even though the abused behavior may have been inappropriate. (Fisher, p. 33–36.) However, the maltreated adolescent may be as big or bigger than the perpetrator, is usually assumed to be capable of impulse control, and has access to other resources.

It seems that adolescents should not be victims of abuse as frequently as other age groups and yet available data does not support this thought. Why are these youth vulnerable to maltreatment? One explanation is that adolescents are still dependent upon their parents to a large degree. Because of this dependence, the youth may not believe that there are any alternatives other than the abuse. The youth is not ready to be self-sufficient, may have no other place to live, and may be too embarrassed to discuss the experiences with other adults or peers. Therefore, even though they are physically able to defend themselves, they may not choose to do so.

Three patterns of adolescent maltreatment are most common: (1) The maltreatment may just be a continuation of a pattern; (2) During adolescence, the parent may increase and intensify the type of physical punishment normally used. For example, instead of just spanking the youth, the parent may now hit the youth with a fist; (3) Abuse and/or neglect, (particularly abuse) may originate in the adolescent period. This pattern may be a result of the parent's increased frustration and feelings of impotency in trying to influence and control the adolescent. Sexual abuse during adolescence seems to follow the same three patterns. (Fisher, p. 5.) The most common form of sexual abuse reported is between father and stepdaughter. The sex play becomes more sophisticated over time and finally progresses to intercourse during puberty. (Brady.)

Most people agree that adolescence is a difficult time for both parent and youth. The problems of adolescence are often compounded by the fact that the parents of adolescents are also in a difficult stage and time in their own lives, middle-age. Combining these two difficult times in growth and development may increase tension in the family and the possibility of abuse.

When adolescents are experiencing abuse or neglect, their reactions may be more drastic than when younger children experience similar life events, for example,

Runaway behavior.

Delinquent behavior.

Aggressive or other acting out behavior.

Future abusive behavior as parents.

Sexual promiscuity and maladjustment.

School drop out or difficulties in school.

Difficulties in peer relationships.

The youth who experiences maltreatment may have great difficulty with the formation of identity, and with attainment of the balance between interdependence and dependence. Confusion about feelings, beliefs, and behavior may occur as well as difficulty in sorting out a value system.

Young Adulthood

"The strength acquired at any stage is tested by the necessity to transcend it in such a way that the individual can take chances in the next stage with what was most vulnerably precious in the previous one.'' (Erikson, p. 263.) The task of adulthood is to be able to establish intimacy and to be able to make commitments to a partnership even in the face of sacrifice and compromise. This task is seen as a natural outgrowth of one having an identity—a wish to fuse that identity with the identity of another.

The counterpart of intimacy is isolation. Much of the literature reviewed in this and later chapters mentions isolation as a major risk factor. It would seem, then, if an individual reaches adulthood and has not established him/herself clearly in each of the developmental areas, many of the tools s/he will require to be a competent adult and to form positive, meaningful relationships will not be in his/her repertoire of competencies.

The Adult

Certainly human development does not stop when a person becomes an adult. In fact, the process of developing through the several steps to adulthood is one that has received much attention in the literature in recent years. As adults, we carry with us our adaptations and a well-tested approach to continuing developmental tasks. Emotional rules are learned, for the most part, within the family but are then transferred and translated into the families that we create as adults. We pass on today with what we have learned in the transactions of the past.

Since caretaker child maltreatment is the primary focus of this book, we need to consider the adult as abuser in the context of development. Certainly parents/caretakers of children are not always adults. They may be less than 15 years of age. In fact, A.H.A. (1980), found female perpetrators under age 15 were associated with a greater frequency of major and minor physical injury and sexual maltreatment than other perpetrators. Their very youth may contribute to some of the problems they experience in parent/caretaker roles.

Little research is available to provide guidance on this topic. We suggest that the same process that operates in the transactional model continues to operate for this individual as an adult, both influencing his/her potential function and dysfunction.

Understanding the manner in which information flows through the family and between family members is critical to understanding child abuse from the standpoint of the abuser. What is the communication process in the family of the abuser? Are family members able to be open and direct with one another in expressing their wants, needs, and fears or is communication stifled and unclear? The way in which information is shared within the family has a direct bearing on the explanation of child abuse. If an adult, one of the architects of the family, does not know how to communicate his/her wants, needs, and fears, the family is at risk.

HUMAN DEVELOPMENT IS FROM BIRTH TO DEATH

For each of us, life is a collection of experiences and decisions. We have a shared responsibility in the process of human development. When individuals are not given the opportunity to establish emotional rules of nonviolence, share power, learn effective means of communicating with one another, build and maintain positive self-esteem, and find satisfying links with the world outside the family, we all reap the consequences of these stumbling blocks in the form of social problems, not the least of which is child maltreatment.

Life is a process that ultimately ends in death. A normal lifespan, moves through infancy, childhood, adolescence, and adulthood. Child abuse and neglect affect every aspect of human development, sometimes only slightly, and other times dramatically and tragically. Child abuse touches the emotional, physical, and intellectual functioning of the abused, the abuser, the family, and society.

Summary

Human development is defined as physical, emotional, and social changes in structure, thought, or behavior which are functions of biological and environmental influences. Four major theories of human development discussed in this chapter include learning, cognitive, psychoanalytic, and humanistic theory. A transactional model of development that accents a systems approach to development is also described.

Child abuse and neglect occur in the context of growing through many stages: prenatal development, infancy, toddler, preschool, middle childhood, adolescence, young adulthood, and adulthood. Maltreatment can have impact on development and may interact with the developmental tasks of each of these periods in different ways. Possible indicators or symptoms of abuse and neglect as they related to development are outlined.

When abuse or neglect occurs during any phase of human development, interruption of the individual's emotional, physical, and/or intellecutal development and functioning may result. As in other contexts of child maltreatment, we share in the responsibility for assuring that the process of development for our children is positive and not interrupted by abuse or neglect.

BIBLIOGRAPHY

Ambron, Sveann Robinson, *Child Development.* Holt, Rinehart and Winston, New York, 1981.

American Humane Association, Child Protective Division, *Annual Report, 1980 National Analysis of Official Child Neglect and Abuse Reporting.* American Humane Association, Denver, Colorado, 1981.

Bijou, Sidney W., and Baer, Donald M. *Child Development I.* Appleton–Century–Crofts, New York, 1961.

Bijou, Sidney W., and Baer, Donald M. *Child Development II. Universal Stage of Infancy.* Vol. II. Appleton–Century–Crofts, New York, 1965.

Brady, Katheryn. *Father's Day.* Seaview Books, New York, 1979.

Chess, Stella and Hassibi, Machin. *Principles and Practice of Child Psychiatry.* Plenum Press, New York, 1978.

Cicchetti, Dante, and Rizley, Ross. Developmental Perspectives on the Etiology, Intergenerational Transmission and Sequelae of Child Maltreatment. *New Directions for Child Development, 11,* 1981.

Craig, Grace J. *Human Development.* Prentice-Hall, Inc., Englewood Cliffs, New Jersey, 1976.

Dreikurs, Rudolf and Soltz, Vicki. *Children: The Challenge.* Hawthorn Books, Inc., New York, 1964.

Erikson, Erik. *Childhood and Society.* Norton, New York, 1950.

Fischhoff, Joseph, M.D. Abused Children—A Psychiatrist Examines Violence in the Family. Report Number 1. *The American Family.* A Continuing Education Service from Smith Kline and French Laboratories. Philadelphia, Pennsylvania, October 1978.

Fisher, Bruce, Berdie, Jane, Cook, JoAnn, and Day, Noel. *Adolescent Abuse and Neglect: Intervention Strategies.* U.S. Dept. of Health and Human Services, DHHS Publication No. (OHDS) 80-30266, 1980.

Gilliam, Kathleen. Parents Ambivalence Toward Their Newborn Baby: A Problem in Community and Professional Denial. *Child Welfare. LX,*7, July/August 1981, pp. 483–489.

Ginott, Hiam. *Between Parent and Child.* Avon, New York, 1969.

Gordon, Thomas, P.E.T. *Parent Effectiveness Training.* Peter H. Wyden, Inc., New York, 1972.

Gross, Barbara Danzger and Shuman, Bernard J. *The Essentials of Parenting in the First Years of Life.* Child Welfare League of America, Inc., New York, 1979.

Havighurst, R.J., *Developmental Tasks and Education.* 3rd Ed. David McKay, New York, 1972.

Hindelang, Michael J., Gattfredson, Michael R., and Flanagan, Truialtey J. *Sourcebook of Criminal Statistics—1980.* U.S. Dept. of Justice Criminal Justice Research Center, Albany, NY, 1981.

Klaus, M. and Kennell, J. *Maternal–Infant Bonding.* Mosby, St. Louis, 1976.

Lefrancois, Guy R. *Of Children.* Wadsworth Publishing Co., Belmont, CA, 1980.

Marano (Smithsonian) Hara Estroff. The Bonding of Mothers and their Babies. In *Family Therapy Network Newsletter* September 1981, pp. 9–10.

Maslow, Abraham. *The Farther Reaches of Human Nature.* Viking Press, New York, 1971.

Mayhall, Pamela D. and Norgard, Katherine Eastlack. *Independent Studies in Advanced Foster Parent Education–Child Development.* Arizona Department of Economic Security, Phoenix, AZ, 1980.

McFadden, E.J. (Ryan, Patricia, Series Editor), *Fostering the Battered and Abused Child.* Foster Parent Training Project, Eastern Michigan University, 1978.

Murphy, Lois Barclay and Moriarty, Alice E. *Vulnerability, Coping and Growth.* Yale University Press, New Haven, 1976.

Newman, Barbara M. and Newman, Philip R. *An Introduction to the Psychology of Adolescence*. Dorsey Press, Homewood, IL, 1979.

Richards, Martin. *Infancy*. Harper and Row, New York, 1980.

Segal, Julius. Child Abuse: A Review of Research. In *Families Today*. Vol. II, U.S. Dept. of H.E.W., Rockville, MD, undated.

Sameroff, A., and Chandler, M. Reproductive Risk and the Continuum of Caretaking Casualty. In F. Horowitz (Ed.), *Review of Child Development Research*. Vol. 4. University of Chicago Press, Chicago, 1975.

Sroufe, L. Alan. Attachment and the Roots of Competence. *Personal Growth and Adjustment*. Dushkin Publishing Group, Inc., Ginlford, CT, 80/81, pp. 17–21.

Steele, Brandt. Psychodynamic Factors in Child Abuse. In *The Battered Child*. 3rd Ed. C Henry Kempe, and Ray E. Helfer, Eds. The University of Chicago Press, Chicago, 1980.

Strommen, Ellen A., McKinney, John Paul, and Fitzgerald, Hiram E. *Developmental Psychology*. Dorsey Press, Homewood, IL, 1977.

Thompson, Betty. *Social and Psychological Development of Children 3 to 5*. Kansas State University, Manhattan, KS, 1976.

Wilson, Ann L. Promoting a Routine Parent–Baby Relationship. In The Battered Child. 3rd Ed. C. Henry Kempe and Ray E. Helfer, Eds. The University of Chicago Press, Chicago, 1980.

4

The Nature and Impact of Child Abuse and Neglect

INTRODUCTION TO CONTROVERSY

Child maltreatment, child abuse and neglect, is a serious and tragic problem. There is nothing controversial about this statement. This is almost the only statement about this subject that can be made without controversy. Myths, half-truths, and general confusion continue to complicate even the simplest questions relating to child maltreatment. Even the process of sorting through the questions and determining which ones to ask and how to ask them is a challenge.

Several key questions about the nature and impact of child abuse and neglect can be answered if we can detemine two elements: (1) the rate at which child abuse and neglect occurs in the United States during a specific period of time, that is, its incidence and (2) how much child abuse exists in the population or put another way, how much of the population is affected by child abuse at a given time, that is, its prevalence. A profile of abusers and abused could be developed from such data. The characteristics of each could then be studied in relationship to many other factors such as psychological, sociological, socio-economic, age, geographic location, special population characteristics, etc. Valid research studies on specific, related topics could be made using such data as a part of a reliable data base.

Every step of child abuse and neglect research is complicated. Almost every difficulty that can distort and muddy research findings plague the efforts of those who attempt to answer the key questions of child maltreatment. Although research methods have improved and progress in understanding the nature and impact of child abuse and neglect has been made, many extremely elusive problems continue to exist. Child maltreatment is rarely a neutral topic. Many of the variables or factors that interact with maltreatment are not identified or are not easily controlled in a research study. Yet the need for research is critical. In some situations, practitioners are able to use their best intuition. With child abuse and neglect, however, that approach seems very much like an educated game of Russian roulette. Potentially life and death decisions are made this way such as whether a child should be removed from or later returned to a previously abusive home situation. A better understanding of the nature and impact of child abuse and neglect increases the "educated edge" and the possibility of primary prevention.

This chapter begins with an exploration of the problems encountered in defining the terms of child maltreatment, and continues with an exploration of some of the research that has been done on the nature of child abuse and neglect and the limitations of that work. It concludes with a discussion of the possible impact of maltreatment on the child, the persons directly involved in that child's life, the community, and our society as a whole.

THE PROBLEM OF DEFINITION

One of the basic struggles in understanding child abuse and neglect is in adequately defining the terms. Lack of common, clear, and concise definitions affect our ability to both study and deal with the problem. It even affects our ability to communicate effectively with other people about this subject.

In our society, the law and its interpretation provide the parameters of minimum acceptable behavior. The law on child maltreatment varies widely from state to state and jurisdiction to jurisdiction. Laws and interpretations of laws regarding child abuse and neglect determine:

What is legally considered to be harmful to a child.

When and what must be reported.

When is intervention appropriate and/or required.

Who is to intervene.

How is intervention to proceed.

When a child is legally in imminent danger of being harmed.

When the court is justified in interfering in the privacy of the family, overriding the authority of the parents and their wishes, and possibly severing their parental rights, in order to protect the child.

It is no wonder that proposed and tested definitions of child abuse and neglect have been criticized as being both too broad and too narrow. State and federal legislatures have discovered that it is very difficult to draft legislation that is specific enough to provide protection of the integrity of the family and to prevent overzealous intervention, and, yet, at the same time, provide a high level of protection to the child.

In an effort to provide an operational definition of abuse and neglect, researchers have been equally frustrated. In the absence of a common, clear, and concise definition, each researcher has found it necessary to define child maltreatment in relation to the needs of an individual project. Thus there are many definitions of child abuse, originating in many different disciplines and approaching abuse from many different perspectives.

Until a clear and common definition is found and accepted, an accurate assessment of the nature and impact of child maltreatment cannot be made. Even then, it will be difficult to make comparative studies to earlier periods of history. As Chapter 1 indicates, abuse and neglect are now and have always been defined in the context of time and culture. Ten years ago, the scarcity of data on aspects of child abuse was a major concern. In response to that concern, the total body of literature on this subject has increased tremendously in the last few years. This literature reflects the findings of studies, the experience of practitioners, the confusion and ambiguity of definition, and practical and theoretical problems experienced by researchers.

COMMON, CLEAR, CONCISE, AND CONSISTENT

For a definition to be common, clear, concise, and consistent, it must be:

Common   Generally shared and agreed upon.
Clear   Not ambiguous and vague.
Concise   Without unnecessary words and phrases, brief, to the point.
Consistent   Coherent, without variation or contradiction.

The definition should be:

1. Stated in such a way that the terms are not vague and ambiguous. The terms should have common, objective meaning.
2. Agreed upon as definitive, reliable, and able to be consistently utilized by researchers and practitioners in many different disciplines.

The many and varied definitions of abuse share some common characteristics. They all see the child as victim and most see the caretaker, who is usually within the family, as the perpetrator of the abuse. Abuse has generally meant nonaccidental threat or harm to the child. It is the measure of the threat or harm that has varied most dramatically from definition to definition. Often, child abuse is assumed to incorporate neglect and is used synonymously with child maltreatment. Recently, the trend has been to separate abuse and neglect more distinctly, narrowing both definitions. Child maltreatment then becomes an encompassing term.

Henry C. Kempe and his associates, in introducing what he called "the battered child syndrome," defined abuse as ". . . a clinical condition in young children who have received serious physical abuse, generally from a parent or foster parent." (Kempe et al., p. 4.) This definition is very narrow and is actually a medical diagnosis. Vincent Fontana's definition of the syndrome broadens the scope of abuse to include emotional and nutritional deprivation, neglect, and abuse. (Fontana, pp. 14–16.) David Gil seems to focus on the intent of the perpetrator in his definition. In "Unraveling Child Abuse," he appears to interpret abuse as any force that compromises a child's capacity to achieve his physical and psychological potential. This definition is broader than Fontana's. (Gil, pp. 346–356.) R.J. Gelles states that child abuse ". . . is as much a political concept, designed to draw attention to a social problem, as it is a scientific concept which can be used to measure a specific phenomenon." (Gelles, p. 13.) Kempe and Ray Helfer, in the third edition of their book, *The Battered Child,* discuss the prevention of abuse, defining the phenomenon in that context as ". . . any interaction or lack of interactions between caretaker and child, which results in nonaccidental harm to the child's physical and/or developmental state." (p. 369.)

It is possible to find definitions of child abuse in these examples that include neglect and others that only include physical maltreatment. Since incidences of neglect make up at least half of the total reported maltreatment statistics, compared to approximately 30% for abuse (AHA, 1981), this variance in definition, alone, has a major impact on the answers given to the key questions that are asked about child maltreatment.

According to the National Juvenile Justice System Assessment Center studies, there are three theoretical orientations that dominate literature on child maltreatment, each focusing on a different dimension of a multidimensional problem

Outcome for the child.

Intent of the perpetrator. (Was the act against the child nonaccidental?)

Perception of the observer, including biases of discipline, experience, and culture. (Smith, p. 6–7.)

Perception, in a larger sense, may be the most pervasive, encompassing viewfinder we have. It even determines for individuals and groups which dimension(s) will be focused upon. Perception influences the type of definition used and the discipline in which it originates (legal, sociological, medical, psychological, etc.) It also affects the theoretical frame of reference within which data is collected and processed, conclusions are drawn, interpretations are made, and actions are taken.

Were we to separate all the different perspectives available on a basis of discipline and individual experience and consider them one at a time, child maltreatment would be easily understood. In order to illustrate this point, the following examples are grossly oversimplified.

- Child maltreatment as a medical problem needs to be diagnosed and treated by a medical doctor. The language might include such words and phrases as perceptual motor disorders, fractures, trauma, failure to thrive, battered child syndrome, etc.
- Child maltreatment as criminal conduct needs to be halted and prosecuted to the full extent of the law. The language might include crime, arrest, allegation, evidence, sentencing, and incarceration.
- Child maltreatment as a social problem needs to be studied and dissected as a social phenomenon. The language might include family constellation, correlates of maltreatment, an ecological model, social indicators, and statistical significance.
- Child maltreatment as a problem of protecting the child needs to be solved through the intervention of child protective services. The language might include shelter care, substantiated abuse, placement, dependency, custody, and petition.
- Child maltreatment as a family problem needs to be understood in the context of the family. The language becomes centered on emotional connections and includes the expression of fear, anger, frustration, apathy, and sadness.

Each perspective is clear, but none takes into account the perspectives of others. The complexities of child abuse and neglect require that all sides be considered. It is in this step that much confusion and contradiction lie.

Child maltreatment is a personal experience, even when it is a professional one. Personal rules and fears, cultural issues, and issues relating to traditions are difficult to set aside. Opinions. often strong ones, about rights and responsibilities of children and parents make remaining neutral a very difficult task. Child abuse and neglect permeate the armor of even those who would prefer to deny its existence.

Protection of children, defined broadly enough, infringes on a family's right to privacy, right to choose how a child will be reared, what standards constitute an ''adequate'' home environment, and how or if a parent may spank or otherwise discipline a child. Protection of children may also interfere with what parents believe to be the practice of their religious beliefs. Protection of children also changes as social values change over time. Both child abuse and child rearing are culturally relative and may vary in many segments of a single society as well as over time.

Few of us feel neutral about these issues. We do not agree on what is proper child rearing, proper discipline, and an "adequate" home. The challenge presented to legislatures and to federal, state, and local advisory groups (whose task it is to define standards for child abuse and neglect prevention and treatment) is to set aside their personal feelings and define the standards in a meaningful way. Certainly this is no simple task; it is one which never seems to be finished. As this book goes to press, the U.S. Congress, very much involved in the defining of abuse and neglect and in the support of prevention and intervention efforts, is once again being asked to redefine abuse. The group that supports this legislation would like abuse to be defined in very restricted terms. If this legislation or legislation like it, were to pass, child abuse would not include anything considered to be discipline by the parents. The effect of the legislation would be to make the child property of the parents.

The question, "What is child abuse?" becomes many questions. How would you know abuse or its results if you saw them? Given some clear way of knowing, what would you or should you do about your awareness? What protection should be available to the chiild? What penalty and/or treatment should be available for the perpetrator?

LEGAL DEFINITIONS OF CHILD ABUSE AND NEGLECT

Congress has legally defined child abuse and neglect with the 1974 Federal Child Abuse Prevention and Treatment Act (P.L. 93-247) and the 1978 amendments (see P.L. 95-266) as:

> . . . the phyical or mental injury, sexual abuse or exploitation, negligent treatment, or maltreatment of a child under the age of eighteen, by a person who is responsible for the child's welfare under circumstances which indicate the child's health or welfare is harmed or threatened thereby.

All 50 states have enacted statutes requiring mandatory reporting of abuse and/or neglect. However, less than half have defined abuse so that reportable conditions are clear. (Eskin, p. 10.)

Formal, legal definitions of child abuse and neglect can be found in state statutes in at least three major areas.

1. *Criminal Laws.* Definitions in this area focus upon the offense and its punishment, not upon the child. These statutes define acts or

omissions that may cause harm to a child and that are punishable as criminal offenses. The behavior of the perpetrator is considered outside or deviant from the standard set by the society in which he/she lives.

2. *Juvenile Statutes.* These statutes attempt to define what, legally, is to be viewed as harm or damage to a child and under what circumstances intervention is appropriate. They also assign responsibility and authority for the application of child protective services to appropriate agencies under the legal jurisdiction of the juvenile (or family) court. Usually, they also define the limits of that responsibility and authority. The major focus of these juvenile statutes is the welfare of the child. The difficulty encountered, both by those persons formulating these statutes and those developing policies and procedures from them, is to adequately protect the child while still safeguarding the rights of the parents and the integrity of the family.

3. *Reporting Laws.* These laws define who must report suspicion of abuse, to whom the report is to be made, and under what circumstances reporting is required. They also define penalties for not reporting and protections to persons who do report.

Policies and procedures of the various agencies given authority and responsibility in child abuse matters are affected by these formal definitions. They vary as the law varies.

Specificity in definition continues to change from jurisdiction to jurisdiction and state to state. Recently, Arizona revised its law relating to child abuse. The change is illustrative of the problems discussed in this chapter and provides an opportunity to review some of the difficulties with definitions. Table 4-1 shows a sample portion of the original document in regular type. The new text is indicated in capitals.

Legislators have attempted to make the law more specific, especially in relation to the definition of mental or emotional injury. Although the change in the law is so new that interpretations have not yet been made, some observations and inferences may be made based on the statements as they exist.

1. More precise evidence will be needed before a child can be removed from the home.

2. A child who is suffering from neglect cannot be removed from the home unless physical or emotional damage can be proven.

3. Evidence of abuse will be defined in medical terms and will be diagnosed only by physicians and psychologists.

Table 4-1 Amended Juvenile Statutes, ARS 8-201; 8-222 (1981)

Be it enacted by the Legislature of the State of Arizona:

Section 1. Section 8-201, Arizona Revised Statutes, as amended by Laws 1980, chapter 47, section 1, is amended to read:

8-201. *Definitions*

In this chapter, unless the context otherwise requires:

1. "Abandoned" means the failure of the parent to provide reasonable support and to maintain regular contact with the child, including the providing of normal supervision. Failure to maintain a normal parental relationship with the child without just cause for a period of six months shall constitute prima facie evidence of abandonment.

2. "Abuse" means the infliction of physical injury, IMPAIRMENT OF BODILY FUNCTION OR DISFIGUREMENT OR THE INFLICTION OF SERIOUS EMOTIONAL DAMAGE AS EVIDENCED BY SEVERE ANXIETY, DEPRESSION, WITHDRAWAL OR UNTOWARD AGGRESSIVE BEHAVIOR AND WHICH EMOTIONAL DAMAGE IS DIAGNOSED BY A MEDICAL DOCTOR OR PSYCHOLOGIST AS PROVIDED IN SECTION 8-223 and shall include INFLICTING OR ALLOWING SEXUAL ABUSE AS PROVIDED IN SECTION 13-1404, SEXUAL CONDUCT WITH A MINOR AS PROVIDED IN SECTION 13-1405, SEXUAL ASSAULT AS PROVIDED IN SECTION 13-1406, MOLESTATION OF A CHILD AS PROVIDED IN SECTION 13-1410, SEXUAL EXPLOITATION OF A MINOR AS PROVIDED IN SECTION 13-3552, COMMERCIAL SEXUAL EXPLOITATION OF A MINOR AS PROVIDED IN SECTION 13-3553 OR INCEST AS PROVIDED IN SECTION 13-3608.

Sec. 2. Section 8-223, Arizona Revised Statutes, is amended to read:

8-223. *Taking into temporary custody; interference; release*

A. A child SHALL be taken into temporary custody:

1. PURSUANT TO AN ORDER OF THE JUVENILE COURT.

2. PURSUANT TO A WARRANT ISSUED ACCORDING TO THE LAWS OF ARREST.

3. IN PROCEEDINGS TO DECLARE A CHILD A TEMPORARY WARD OF THE COURT TO PROTECT THE CHILD, pursuant to an order of the juvenile court UPON A PETITION BY A PEACE OFFICER OR A CHILD PROTECTIVE SERVICES SPECIALIST UNDER OATH THAT REASONABLE GROUNDS EXIST TO BELIEVE THAT TEMPORARY CUSTODY IS CLEARLY NECESSARY TO PROTECT THE CHILD FROM SUFFERING ABUSE.

B. A CHILD MAY BE TAKEN INTO TEMPORARY CUSTODY:

1. BY A PEACE OFFICER pursuant to the laws of arrest, without a warrant, IF there are reasonable grounds to believe that he has committed a delinquent act or is incorrigible.

2. By a PEACE officer or a child protective services specialist of the state department of economic security if TEMPORARY CUSTODY IS CLEARLY NECESSARY TO PROTECT THE CHILD BECAUSE THE CHILD IS EITHER:

(a) SUFFERING OR WILL IMMINENTLY SUFFER ABUSE.

(b) SUFFERING SERIOUS PHYSICAL OR EMOTIONAL DAMAGE WHICH CAN ONLY BE DIAGNOSED BY A MEDICAL DOCTOR OR PSYCHOLOGIST.

Table 4-1 *(Continued)*

THE PERSON TAKING A CHILD INTO CUSTODY PURSUANT TO THIS
SUBDIVISION SHALL IMMEDIATELY HAVE THE CHILD EXAMINED BY A
MEDICAL DOCTOR OR PSYCHOLOGIST AND AFTER THE EXAMINATION
THE PERSON SHALL RELEASE THE CHILD TO THE CUSTODY OF THE
PARENT, GUARDIAN OR CUSTODIAN OF THE CHILD UNLESS THE
EXAMINATION REVEALS ABUSE. TEMPORARY CUSTODY OF A CHILD
TAKEN INTO CUSTODY PURSUANT TO THIS SUBDIVISION SHALL NOT
EXCEED TWELVE HOURS.

3. By a PEACE officer if there are reasonable grounds to believe that the child has
run away from his parents, guardian or other custodian.

4. BY A PRIVATE PERSON AS PROVIDED BY SECTION 13-3884.

C. IF A CHILD IS TAKEN INTO TEMPORARY CUSTODY AS PROVIDED
IN SUBSECTION A, PARAGRAPH 1 OR PARAGRAPH 3 OF THIS SECTION,
THE LAW ENFORCEMENT OFFICER OR CHILD PROTECTIVE SERVICES
SPECIALIST OF THE DEPARTMENT OF ECONOMIC SECURITY TAKING
THE CHILD INTO CUSTODY SHALL PROVIDE WRITTEN NOTICE WITHIN
SIX HOURS TO THE PARENT, GUARDIAN OR CUSTODIAN OF THE CHILD,
UNLESS:

1. THE PARENT, GUARDIAN OR CUSTODIAN IS PRESENT WHEN THE
CHILD IS TAKEN INTO CUSTODY, THEN WRITTEN NOTICE SHALL BE
PROVIDED IMMEDIATELY.

2. THE RESIDENCE OF THE PARENT, GUARDIAN OR CUSTODIAN IS
OUT-OF-STATE AND NOTICE CANNOT BE PROVIDED WITHIN SIX
HOURS, THEN WRITTEN NOTICE SHALL BE PROVIDED WITHIN
TWENTY-FOUR HOURS.

3. THE RESIDENCE OF THE PARENT, GUARDIAN OR CUSTODIAN IS
NOT ASCERTAINABLE, THEN REASONABLE EFFORTS SHALL BE MADE
TO LOCATE AND NOTIFY AS SOON AS POSSIBLE THE PARENT,
GUARDIAN OR CUSTODIAN OF THE CHILD.

D. THE WRITTEN NOTICE SHALL CONTAIN THE NAME OF THE
PERSON AND AGENCY TAKING THE CHILD INTO CUSTODY AND THE
LOCATION FROM WHICH THE CHILD WAS TAKEN AND ALL THE
FOLLOWING INFORMATION:

(a) THE DATE AND TIME OF THE TAKING INTO CUSTODY.

(b) THE NAME AND PHONE NUMBER OF THE AGENCY RESPONSIBLE
FOR THE CHILD.

(c) A STATEMENT OF THE REASONS FOR TEMPORARY CUSTODY OF
THE CHILD.

(d) A STATEMENT THAT THE CHILD MUST BE RETURNED WITHIN
FORTY-EIGHT HOURS EXCLUDING SATURDAYS, SUNDAYS AND
HOLIDAYS UNLESS A DEPENDENCY PETITION IS FILED AND A
STATEMENT THAT A CHILD IN TEMPORARY CUSTODY FOR
EXAMINATION PURSUANT TO SUBSECTION B, PARAGRAPH 2,
SUBDIVISION (b) OF THIS SECTION MUST BE RETURNED WITHIN
TWELVE HOURS UNLESS ABUSE IS DIAGNOSED.

Table 4-1 *(Continued)*

(e) A STATEMENT THAT IF A DEPENDENCY PETITION IS FILED AND CHILD IS DECLARED A TEMPORARY WARD OF THE COURT:

(i) THE PARENT, GUARDIAN OR CUSTODIAN OF THE CHILD MAY FILE A WRITTEN REQUEST WITH THE JUVENILE COURT FOR A HEARING TO REVIEW THE TEMPORARY CUSTODY PURSUANT TO SECTION 8-546.06.

(ii) THE HEARING ON THE DEPENDENCY PETITION SHALL BE SET NOT LATER THAN TWENTY-ONE DAYS FROM THE FILING OF THE PETITION.

(iii) THE PARENT, GUARDIAN OR CUSTODIAN OF THE CHILD MAY REQUIRE APPOINTMENT OF COUNSEL PURSUANT TO SECTION 8-225 THROUGH THE JUVENILE COURT.

---

4. Sexual abuse reports may increase because of the additional categories of sexual abuse specifically added in the law.

A major impact of the law will be to decrease the number of children removed from homes and to limit the definition of abuse to more severe cases. The advantage of such a law is that it provides protection to families and leaves little room for misinterpretation. Discretion is limited. On the other hand, it may take out of the discretion of the court and the child protective services the option of intervening to prevent abuse, leaving them only the option of acting after the fact.

Statutes vary from state to state. Figure 4-1 provides a comparison of child protection statutes. Some of these statutes are currently in the process of being changed.

The Draft Model Child Protection Act developed by the National Center on Child Abuse and Neglect suggests the following definitions:

(a) *Child* means a person under the age of 18.

(b) An *abused or neglected child* means a child whose physical or mental health or welfare is harmed or threatened with harm by the acts or omissions of his/her parent or other person responsible for the child's welfare.

(c) *Harm* to a child's health or welfare can occur when the parent or other person responsible for his/her welfare.

    (i) Inflicts or allows to be inflicted upon the child physical or mental injury, including injuries sustained as a result of excessive corporal punishment.

    (ii) Commits or allows to be committed against the child a sexual offense, as defined by state law.

    (iii) Fails to supply the child with adequate food, clothing, shelter, education (as defined by state law), or health care, though

Figure 4-1

State Action on Child Protection

	Alabama	Alaska	Arizona	Arkansas	California	Colorado	Connecticut	Delaware	Florida	Georgia	Hawaii	Idaho	Illinois	Indiana	Iowa	Kansas	Kentucky	Louisiana	Maine	Maryland	Massachusetts	Michigan	Minnesota	Mississippi	Missouri	Montana	Nebraska
What Elements of Child Abuse Must Be Reported																											
nonaccidental	X	X	X	X	X	X	X	X	X	X	X	X	X	X	X	X	X	X	X	X	X	X	X	X	X	X	X
neglect	X	X	X	X	X	X	X	X	X	X	X	1	X	X	X	X	X	X	X	X	X	X	X	X	X	X	X
sexual abuse	X	X	X	X	X	X	X	X	X	X	X	X	X	X	X	X	X	X	X	X	X	X	X	X	X	X	X
emotional abuse	X			X	X		X		X		X		X			X	X		X	X	X	X		X	X	X	X
Who Must Report																											
doctors	X	X	X	X	X	X	X	X	X	X	X	X	X	2	X	X	X	X	X	X	X	X	X	X	X	X	X
social workers	X	X	X	X	X	X	X	X	X	X	X	X	X	2	X	X	X	X	X	X	X	X	X	X	X	X	X
teachers	X	X	X	X	X	X	X	X	X	X	X	X	X	2	X	X	X	X	X	X	X	X	X	X	X	X	X
law enforcement	X	X	X	X	X	X	X			X			X	2	X	X	X		X	X	X	X	X	X	X	X	
When Must Report Be Made (I = Immediately, P = Promptly, S = Soon, L = Longer)	I	I	I	I	L	I	I	I		I	P	L	I	I	L	P	I	I	I	S	I	I	I	I	I	P	3
To Whom Must Report Be Made (SS = Social Services, C = Court, PO = Law Enforcement)	SS/PO	SS/SS	SS/PO	SS	SS/PO	SS/PO	SS/PO	SS	SS	SS	SS	PO	SS	SS/PO	SS	SS/C	SS	SS/PO	SS	SS/SS	SS	SS	SS/PO	SS	SS	SS	PO
Immunity for Good Faith Report	X	X	X	X	X	X	X	X	X	X	X	X	X		X	X	X	X	X	X	X	X		X	X	X	X
Penalty for Not Making Report (CR = Criminal, CI = Civil)	CR		CR	CR/CI	CR	CR/CI	CR	CR	CR	CR				CR	CR/CI	CR	CR	CR	CI		CR	CI	CR	CR	CR		CR
Abrogation of Privileged Communication																											
husband																											
doctor		X	X	X		X	X							X	X					X		X			X		
all but attorney/client	X				X	X		X	X							X	X	X	X								X
Photographs and X-rays			PX	PX	PX	PX			PX				PX	PX	PX		PX		PX			PX			PX		
Temporary Protective Custody – Emergency Removal	X	X	X	X	X	X	X		X		X	X	X	X	X	X	X	X		X	X	X	X	X	X	X	X
Central Registry	X	X	X	X	X	X	X		X	5		X	X	5			5	X			6	6	5		6	X	
Child Protection Team	X				X	X					X	X		X	X			X			X	X			X	X	X
Guardian ad Litem/Counsel	X	X	X	X	X	X	X	X	X	X		X	X	X	X	X		X				X			X	X	
Public Education					X	X			X					X	X	X		X	X		X	X	X	X	X	X	X

80

Comparative table of state child abuse reporting statutes (rotated table). Columns are states; rows are statute elements.

	Nevada	New Hampshire	New Jersey	New Mexico	New York	North Carolina	North Dakota	Ohio	Oklahoma	Oregon	Pennsylvania	Rhode Island	South Carolina	South Dakota	Tennessee	Texas	Utah	Vermont	Virginia	Washington	West Virginia	Wisconsin	Wyoming	Washington, D.C.	Total
What Elements of Child Abuse Must Be Reported																									
nonaccidental	x	x	x	x	x	x	x	x	x	x	x	x	x	x	x	x	x	x	x	x	x	x	x	x	51
neglect	x	x	x	x	x	x	x	x	x	x	x	x	x	x		x	x	x	x	x	x	x	x	x	50
sexual abuse	x	x	x	x	x		x	x	x	x	x	x	x		x	x	x	x	x	x	x	x	x	x	46
emotional abuse	x	x	x		x		x	x	x		x	x	x				x		x		x		x	x	37
Who Must Report																									
doctors	x	x	2	x	x	x	x	x	x	x	x	2	x	x	2	2	2	x	x	x	x	x	2	x	51
social workers	x	x	2	x	x	x	x	x	x	x	x	2	x	x	2	2	2	x	x	x	x	x	2	x	51
teachers	x	x	2	x	x	x	x	x	x	x	x	2	x	x	2	2	2	x	x	x	x	x	2	x	51
law enforcement			2	x	x	x	x		x	x	x	2	x	x	2	2	2	x	x	x	x	x	2	x	42
When Must Report Be Made (I = Immediately, P = Promptly, S = Soon, L = Longer)	P	I	P	I	I	3	I	I	P	I	I	L	3	I	I	I	2 X	3	I	I	I	I	I	I	I=36, P=6, L=4, S=1
To Whom Must Report Be Made (SS = Social Services, C = Court, PO = Law Enforcement)	SS/PO	SS	SS	4/SS	SS	SS	SS	SS/PO	SS	SS/PO	SS	SS	SS/PO	4/SS	all	SS/PO	SS/PO	SS	SS	SS/PO	SS	SS/PO	SS/PO	SS/PO	SS=28, SS/PO=19, PO=2, SS/CI=1, all=1
Immunity for Good Faith Report	x	x	x	x	x	x	x	x	x	x	x	x	x	x		x	x	x	x	x	x	x	x		51
Penalty for Not Making Report (CR = Criminal, CI = Civil)	CR	CR	CR	CR	CR/CI	CR	CR	CR	CR	CR	CR		CR/CI	CR	CR	CR	CR	CR	CR	CR	CR	CR		CR	CR=33, CI=2, CR/CI=5
Abrogation of Privileged Communication																									
husband					x						x								x						
doctor					x					x	x								x					x	19
all but attorney/client	x	x		x		x	x		x	x			x	x	x	x	x	x	x	x	x	x	x	x	22
Photographs and X-rays		PX	PX	PX			PX	PX		P	PX	PX	PX			x	PX		PX	P	PX		PX		PX=21, P=2, X=1
Temporary Protective Custody – Emergency Removal		x	x	x	x	x	x	x	x	x	x	x	x	x	x	x	x	x	x	x	x	x	x	x	20
Central Registry	x	x	x	x	x	x	x	x	x	x	x	x	x	x	x	x	x	x	x	x	5	x	x	5	38
Child Protection Team											x		x						x	x			x		41
Guardian ad Litem/Counsel											6	6	6												6
Public Education	x	x	x	x	x	x	x	x	x	x	x	x	x	x	x	x	x	x	x	x	x	x	x	x	46

1 "Neglected child" is defined but not included in the required reporting statute.
2 Require reporting by "any person."
3 Do not indicate when the report of suspected child abuse must be made.
4 New Mexico: Reports can be made to state district attorney or probation office.
  South Dakota: Reports can be made to state district attorney or social services.
5 Via administrative fiat, not by statute.
6 Have child consultation and advisory boards.

financially able to do so or offered financial or other reasonable means to do so. For the purposes of this Act, *adequate health care* includes any medical or nonmedical health care permitted or authorized under state law.

(iv) Abandons the child, as defined by state law.

(v) Fails to provide the child with adequate care, supervision, or guardianship by specific acts or omissions of a similarly serious nature requiring the intervention of the child protective service or a court.

(d) *Threatened harm* means a substantial risk of harm.

(e) A *person responsible for a child's welfare* includes the child's parent; guardian; foster parent; an employee of a public or private residential home, institution, or agency; or other person responsible for the child's welfare.

(f) *Physical injury* means death, disfigurement, or the impairment of any organ.

(g) *Mental injury* means an injury to the intellectual or psychological capacity of a child as evidenced by an observable and substantial impairment in his ability to function within a normal range of performance and behavior, with due regard to his culture.[1]

OPERATIONALIZING TERMS

One major attempt to operationalize the definition of child abuse and neglect and associated legal and social implications on a national basis was developed by the Juvenile Justice Advisory Committee. The results of their efforts are published in a report of recommended standards. The committee was concerned with delineating between actual and potential physical harm to the child. Intervention is defined as ". . . the moment the public official makes contact with the youth or family." Intervention, as it is defined in the standards, may be coercive, noncoercive or somewhere on the continuum between the two extremes. Noncoercive intervention is voluntary on the part of the family. Coercive intervention is involuntary or imposed. Coercive intervention is suggested only in situations of greatest identifiable actual harm to the child in the standards.

These Federal Standards for juvenile courts and other courts of juvenile jurisdiction specifically address: the areas of confidentiality of records, the circumstances in which intervention should take place, criteria and procedures for referral to intake and taking into emergency protective custody

---

[1]Information based on the draft Federal Standards for Child Abuse and Neglect Prevention and Treatment Programs and Projects.

(with guidelines for police and other governmental agencies), jurisdictional issues, criteria and procedures for intake and imposition of protective measures, preadjudication procedures, appointment and role of *guardian ad litem,* adjudication procedures, dispositional alternatives and criteria, criteria for termination of parental rights, and the review and enforcement of dispositional orders. Abuse and neglect situations are considered in the standards for prevention and supervision, but with less specificity. The committee suggests that since local problems and practices differ, implementation of the proposed standards will need to be accompanied by "vigorous evaluation."

The committee's definition of neglect and abuse for jurisdictional purposes is ". . . intended to focus attention on specific harms to the child rather than on broadly drawn descriptions of parental behavior." No "parental fault" has to be shown. In fact, "intervention should be a nonpunitive act." It follows, then, that intervention based solely on the parent's lifestyle, values, or morals is inappropriate. The court is seen as a last resort. Its jurisdiction should not be exercised unless (1) available noncoercive alternatives cannot adequately protect the child or (2) the child has been placed in emergency custody. They do recommend, however, that the jurisdiction of the court extend over the public agencies who provide services to the juveniles and their families as well as over the family members specifically involved in the complaint or petition. (See Table 4-2).

The standards specifying circumstances in which intervention is appropriate take a broader definition of protection, but only in a voluntary, noncoercive context. Provision of services is suggested on a voluntary basis unless ". . . the harm or risk of harm to the juvenile is cognizable under the jurisdiction of the family court described in Standard 3.113 and there is no other measure which will provide adequate protection." (See Table 4-3).

Perhaps abuse and neglect should be defined only in terms of absolute minimum standards of care. Protection from harm, on the other hand, should be defined more broadly and should encourage prevention through noncoercive means. Ideally, the latter would not be legally defined in the negative context of child maltreatment but in the more positive context of strengthening families.

Although there continues to be no single accepted definition of child abuse and neglect among researchers, just as there is none among states and jurisdictions, clarity, consistency, and conciseness have improved. As more and more evidence indicates differences among different forms of maltreatment, the need for operational criteria for each form becomes more apparent. Such criteria would help to resolve some of the problems that frustrate research efforts. Since we have traditionally focused on physical abuse and generalized from that point, such specific criteria would help us be

Table 4-2   3.113 Jurisdiction Over Neglect and Abuse

The jurisdiction of the family court over neglect and abuse should include:
  a. Juveniles who are unable to provide for themselves and who have no parent, guardian, relative, or other adult with whom they have substantial ties willing and able to provide supervision and care;
  b. Juveniles who have suffered or are likely to suffer physical injury inflicted nonaccidentally by their parent, guardian, or primary caretaker, which causes or creates a substantial risk of death, disfigurement, impairment of bodily function, or bodily harm;
  c. Juveniles who have been sexually abused by their parents, guardian, primary caretaker, or a member of the household;
  d. Juveniles whose physical health is seriously impaired or is likely to be seriously impaired as a result of conditions created by their parents, guardian, or primary caretaker, or by the failure of such persons to provide adequate supervision and protection;
  e. Juveniles whose emotional health is seriously impaired and whose parents, guardian, or primary caretaker fail to provide or cooperate with treatment;
  f. Juveniles whose physical health is seriously impaired because of the failure of their parents, guardian, or primary caretaker to supply them with adequate food, clothing, shelter or health care, although financially able or offered the means to do so;
  g. Juveniles whose physical health has been seriously impaired or is likely to be seriously impaired or whose emotional health has been seriously impaired because their parents have placed them for care or adoption, in violation of the law, with an agency, an institution, a nonrelative, or a person with whom they have no substantial ties;
  h. Juveniles who are committing acts of delinquency as a result of pressure from or with the approval of their parents, guardian, or primary caretaker; and
  i. Juveniles whose parents, guardian, or primary caretaker prevent them from obtaining the education required by law.

Jurisdiction over neglect and abuse should extend to the juvenile, his/her parents, guardian or primary caretaker, and any agency or institution with a legal responsibility to provide needed services to those persons.

Source. Standards for Juvenile Justice Administration, The National Advisory Council.

more specific in prevention, intervention, and treatment. Recent articles by Michael Martin and James Walters (1982) and Dante Cicchetti and Ross Rizley (1981) emphasize this need.

Definitions used in the *National Study of the Incidence and Severity of Child Abuse and Neglect* (commonly referred to as the National Incidence Study) were geared toward such a goal. This study was carried out by Westat, Inc. and Development Associates, Inc. and was supported by the

Table 4-3   2.13 Intervention to Protect Against Harm

It is appropriate for society to intervene in the life of a juvenile and/or family when the juvenile has no parent, guardian, relative, or other adult with whom he/she has substantial ties, who is willing to provide supervision and care, and:

    a. The juvenile's physical health is seriously impaired, or is likely to be so impaired;

    b. The juvenile's emotional health is seriously impaired;

    c. The juvenile has been sexually abused; or

    d. The juvenile's parent, guardian, or primary caretaker is preventing him/her from obtaining the education required by law.

Except when immediate medical care is required, intervention in such circumstances should not include removal of juveniles from their homes, or the provision of services on other than a voluntary basis unless the harm or risk of harm to the juvenile is cognizable under the jurisdiction of the family court described in Standard 3.113 and there is no other measure which will provide adequate protection.

Source. Standards for Juvenile Justice Administration, The National Advisory Committee.

National Center on Child Abuse and Neglect. Data was collected between May 1979 and April 1980. The study was completed in December 1980. The definitions of child abuse and neglect that were used required that a child suffer "demonstrable" physical or emotional harm in order to be included in the "in-scope" group. (See Table 4-4 for forms of maltreatment as defined by the National Incidence Study.) Certainly these parameters provide a narrow umbrella, no doubt excluding many situations of probable abuse and neglect. This effort has the distinction of being the first national study of child abuse and neglect that has used common, clear, concise, and consistent definitions at all sites where data has been collected. The data is reliable enough to provide the basis for several secondary analysis studies.

Beginning in 1973, under a grant from the Children's Bureau (part of the then Department of Health, Education, and Welfare), the Child Protection Division of the American Humane Association (AHA) was given the responsibility to determine the feasibility of establishing and then of establishing a clearinghouse for child abuse and neglect reports. AHA's efforts through the National Analysis of Official Child Neglect and Abuse Reporting, have been to record all reported cases of child abuse and neglect in the United States, the District of Columbia, and U.S. territories. The challenge was to find a basis for comparison that took into account the variations of jurisdictional reporting standards and definitions of terms. The American Humane Association is currently working, with funding provided by NCCAN (National Center for Child Abuse and Neglect), to improve the

Table 4-4   Forms of Maltreatment Encompassed by the National Incidence Study

Physical Abuse
1. Assault with implement (e.g., knife, strap, cigarette)
2. Assault without implement (e.g., hit with fist, bit, or means of assault unknown)

Sexual Abuse
3. Intrusion (acts involving penile penetration—oral, anal, or genital; e.g., rape, incest)
4. Molestation with genital contact
5. Other or unknown

Emotional Abuse
6. Verbal or emotional assault, (e.g., threatening, belittling)
7. Close confinement (e.g., tying, locking in closet)
8. Other or unknown (e.g., attempted physical or sexual assault)

Physical Neglect
9. Abandonment
10. Other refusal of custody (e.g., expulsion, refusal to accept custody of runaway)
11. Refusal to allow or provide needed care for diagnosed illness, health condition, or impairment
12. Unwarranted delay or failure to seek needed remedial health care
13. Inadequate physical supervision
14. Disregard of avoidable hazards in home (e.g., exposed wiring, broken glass)
15. Inadequate nutrition, clothing, or hygiene
16. Other (e.g., reckless disregard of child's safety such as driving while intoxicated)

Educational Neglect
17. Knowingly "permitted" chronic truancy
18. Other (e.g., repeatedly kept child home, failed to enroll)

Emotional Neglect
19. Inadequate nurturance/affection, (e.g., failure-to-thrive)
20. Knowingly "permitted" maladaptive behavior (e.g., delinquency, serious drug/alcohol abuse)
21. Other (e.g., refusal to allow needed remedial care for diagnosed emotional problem)

Source. Executive Summary: National Incidence Study, Westat, Inc. (NCCAN), 1981.

quality of the official reporting of child abuse and neglect by helping state agencies to better manage data through improved data collection. If all states collect a comparable minimal data set for all reported cases of child abuse and neglect, this set can act as a baseline for comparison from state to state and year to year. AHA is also attempting to assist states in enhancing their capability to collect and use reporting data.

THOSE ELUSIVE VARIABLES

In any research, the researchers hope to control as many variables as possible. The more control over the variables, the better the quality of the results. Control of variables is particularly elusive relating to topics of child maltreatment. The following summarizes some of the key areas of concern.

1. Variance in legal definitions of child abuse from state to state and jurisdiction to jurisdiction.
2. Variance in reporting laws and their application from state to state and jurisdiction to jurisdiction.
3. Variance in the methods used to collect data regarding child abuse including variations in sampling methods, problems in acquiring a true random sample, and the difficulty of defining matched groups, so that one can be used as a control group.
4. Unreliability of the statistical measures applied to data in order to determine the incidence of child abuse.
5. Major changes in law, public awareness, and professional awareness have altered reporting of cases dramatically in individual jurisdictions. As reporting fluctuates owing to unknown factors, trend analysis becomes increasingly more difficult.
6. Differential intervention and enforcement.
7. The privacy of the family, which increases the difficulty of detection and the development of clear proof of child abuse. Abusive actions are private actions, not generally witnessed by outsiders, and often not easily admitted to by the abused or the abuser.
8. The issue of what is meant by validation or substantiation of reports of child abuse. (In some instances, it means adjudication, i.e., formal court action on the basis of a petition. In other instances, it means that a child protective services worker has determined that a file has been created for the family. In some cases, it simply means that the reported incident did take place.)
9. Reporting biases. For example, situations of abuse in middle-class families may be less likely to be reported than situations in lower socio-economic groups. In middle-class situations, some agencies are less likely to intervene. Sources of information may be biased in many other ways.
10. Availability of resources. For example, if there are few resources in a community, such as foster homes, counseling services in home services, fewer cases are likely to be reported and the standards for intervention will be higher.

11. Reluctance of people to report to authorities (distrust issues, wish to avoid getting involved, fear, etc.)
12. Abuses as a multifactored condition. The difficulty of sorting out the other factors in personality and environment that might have a major impact on the child and the family.
13. Lack of central reporting in an area and the inability to effectively track cases.
14. Funding issues. The availability of funding and the limitations stipulated by funding sources have impact on the nature, the quality, and the quantity of research projects.

Major strides have been taken in recent years to overcome some of these problems. Research methodology has improved. Public awareness has increased. Professional training has become better and more available. Information has been shared at national and international conferences on child abuse and neglect. Federal funding for many prevention, intervention, treatment, and research projects has been made available, chiefly through the Office of Juvenile Justice and Delinquency Prevention (OJJDP) and the National Center for Child Abuse and Neglect (NCCAN).

NCCAN now serves as the center for federal activities relating to child abuse and neglect, including the funding of regional resource centers and several research and service projects in all areas of child abuse and neglect. Although funding resources are greatly curtailed, NCCAN currently supports several secondary analyses of data projects relating to the National Incidence Study. A variety of other projects are also supported, for example, in adolescent maltreatment, neglect, improvement of quality of reporting, upgrading the quality of child protective services in public agencies, diagnosis and referral of developmentally disabled abused and neglected children, services to children in battered women's shelters, improved screening and tracking of child protective service children in courts, improvement of child protective services through cultural and ethnic minority group involvement, improved *guardian ad litem* services, voluntary or legal advocacy for child-protective-service-supervised improvement of health-based services to prevent child abuse and neglect, improved mental health services for diagnosis and treatment, and minority professional resource centers.

THE NATIONAL PICTURE OF CHILD ABUSE AND NEGLECT

Estimates of the incidence of child abuse and neglect in the United States using nationwide data have varied from thousands to millions. Generally, data is gathered either through official reports of child abuse and neglect or through surveys relating to victimization. Victimization surveys question such areas as: Have you ever been a victim? Do you know of victims? Similar surveys might also collect self reports of abuse, for example, Have you or any other person responsible for your child's care ever hit, beat, bitten, etc. that child?

Certainly, many issues exist about the use of report data, particularly in relation to its true estimate of incidence. Some of these are discussed earlier in this chapter. If findings of the survey and report data are reviewed within the limitations of the study, they provide useful and interesting information. Estimates from survey data are generally higher than those from official reports. A parallel can be drawn here to efforts to collect national crime data through the Uniform Crime Reports and the National Crime Survey. The first is a collection of official reports of specific categories of crime to police agencies. The second is a victimization survey that includes both reported and unreported crime. The first victimization survey was completed in 1965. A comparison of the data from the two sources indicates that from one-half to two-thirds of crime is not reported. (National Crime Survey, 1965–1980.)

Comparison of the findings of studies relating to child abuse and neglect is difficult in part because the definition of terms has varied, sometimes dramatically. Generally, however, studies that have utilized a survey approach have consistently indicated much higher estimates of abuse and neglect. This is true even when the studies utilized self reports by abusers, a group of reports who might be hesitant to report and therefore, admit to such behavior.

In 1965, Gil conducted the first national incidence study of abuse working with the National Opinion Research Center. He used a self reporting approach and surveyed 1520 people. Respondents were asked if they knew of families involved in incidents of child abuse that resulted in physical injury (in the 12 months prior to the survey) and if they had physically injured a child (not limited to the 12 month period.) His estimates of child abuse based on this definition and this survey are high. They ranged from a minimum of 2,500,000 to 4,070,000. Gil was criticized at the time as overestimating the problem. Light, who recalculated Gil's findings, arrived at the lower figure of 500,000. (Light, 1973.) Recent data suggests, however, that Gil's original estimate may be more realistic than originally believed.

Figures 4-5 and 4-6 present a comparison of national estimates of the extent of abuse and neglect from 1962–1981. They are of particular interest because they describe the measurement criteria utilized by these studies, the estimate of incidence of child abuse, the origin of the data and the reference. Even with just a superficial glance, the reader should note both the wide variance of criteria and results as well as the wide range of origins of data utilized in the study.

Table 4-5 Comparison of National Estimates of the Extent of Abuse (1962–1980)

	Reference	Measurement Criteria	Estimate of Incidence	Origin of Data
1.	DeFrancis, V. (1963) (CD-01511)	Abuse, not further specified	662	Newspaper accounts, 1962 data
2.	Kempe, C.H. et al. (1962) (Reported in CD-00560)	Abuse, not further specified	302	71 hospitals, 1962 data
3.	Kempe, C.H. et al. (1962) (Reported in CD-00560)	Abuse, not further specified	447	77 district attorneys, 1962 data
4.	Gil, D.G. (1970) (Reported in CD-01187)	Abuse that resulted in some degree of injury	2,500,000–4,070,000	National survey, 1965 data
5.	Light, R.J. (1973) (CD-00613)	Abuse that resulted in some degree of injury	200,000–500,000	Reanalysis of Gil's 1965 data
6.	Helfer, R.E.; Pollock, C.B. (1968) (CD-00463)	Serious injury by nonaccidental means	10,000–15,000	1966 data, no source given
7.	Gil, D.G. (1970) (Reported in CD-01187)	Abuse that resulted in some degree of injury	6,617	Central registries, nationwide, 1968 data
8.	Kempe, C.H.; Helfer, R.E. (1972) (CD-00559)	Reported abuse	60,000	Additive estimate, based on cases reported in Denver and New York City, 1972 data
9.	Cohen, S.J.; Sussman, A. (1975) (CD-01136)	Reported abuse	41,104	Official reporting systems from 10 largest states, 1973 data
10.	Nagi, S.Z. (1975) (CD-00704)	Reported abuse Abuse, not reported	167,000 91,000 Total 258,000	Agency survey, 1972–1973 data Difference between projections from rate of reports in Florida and rate from agency survey, 1972–1973 data
11.	Gelles, R.J. (1977) (CD-02079)	Estimate of children at risk of physical injury from parental violence	1,400,000–1,900,000	Household survey, 1975 data

No.	Reference	Definition	Number	Description
12.	American Humane Association (1978) (CD-02538)	Abuse officially reported to state departments of social services[1]	111,072	National study of officially reported cases, 1976 data
13.	American Humane Association (1979) (D-03743)	Abuse officially reported to state departments of social services[1]	68,337[2]	National study of officially reported cases, 1977 data
14.	American Humane Association (1980) (*National Analysis of Official Child Neglect Reporting, 1978*, Washington DC: National Center on Child Abuse and Neglect, (OHDS-80-30271), September 1980).	Abuse officially reported to state departments of social services[3]	30,310	National study of officially reported cases, 1978 data
15.	Sarafino, E.P. (1979) (CD-02717)	Reported sexual abuse	74,725	Published data on incidence of child molestation at various times in 4 different areas in the country
16.	Straus, M.A. (1978) (CD-02720)	Physical abuse	More than 14 of every 100 American children, 3–17	Interviews with parents in 1,146 nationally representative families
17.	Burgdorf, K.; Romashko, T. (1981) *Recognition and Reporting of Child Maltreatment: Summary Findings from the National Study of the Incidence and Severity of Child Abuse and Neglect. Draft.* 1981 (Mimeo.)	Abuse reported to and substantiated by CPS agencies, known to some official agency, or identifiable from other official	351,000	National survey of child protective service agencies and front-line professionals, in selected communities, 1979/1980 data

Table 4-5 Comparison of National Estimates of the Extent of Abuse (1962–1980)

Reference	Measurement Criteria	Estimate of Incidence	Origin of Data
18. American Humane Association (1981) *National Analysis of Official Child Neglect & Abuse Reporting, 1979.* In conjunction with Denver Research Institute and the National Center on Child Abuse and Neglect. (NCCD: 105-80-067)	Abuse officially reported to state departments of Social Services[4]	101,630	National study of officially reported cases, 1979 data
19. American Humane Association (1982) *National Analysis of Official Child Neglect & Abuse Reporting, 1980.*	Abuse officially reported to state departments of social services.[5]	180,909	National study of officially reported cases, 1980 data

[1] Includes abuse categories and abuse and neglect categories from all 50 states. Excludes 54,170 reports in the "unspecified" category.
[2] Less than one-third of the total reports were categorized into abuse or neglect categories.
[3] Includes substantiated abuse and substantiated abuse/neglect categories from individual case data of 33 states. 60% of the total cases in the database were unsubstantiated.
[4] Introduction of National Analysis use of minimal data set. Includes abuse and neglect/abuse categories from individual case data from 33 states.
[5] Includes abuse and neglect/abuse categories from individual case data of 36 states.
Source. Adapted from *Review of Child Abuse and Neglect Research 1979–81.* Prepared for the National Center on Child Abuse and Neglect by the Herner Co., Arlington, Va. 1981.

Three major studies that have provided perhaps the most accurate picture to date of child abuse and neglect in the United States are included in Figures 4-6 and 4-7 have been mentioned briefly in the discussion of the operationalization of a definition of child maltreatment.

One is the Yearly National Analysis of Official Child Neglect and Abuse Reporting, conducted by the American Humane Association, beginning with the study in 1976 when data from all 50 states was included. The other study is the National Incidence Study, which provides data from child protective services agencies and other community institutions in sample counties. A third study, somewhat different in context and purpose than the other two, deserves special mention. It is the work of Straus et al. (1979) in which a nationally representative sample of 2143 American couples were interviewed. Of these couples, 1146 had one or more children aged 3 to 17 years old living at home at the time of the interview. This study provides a perspective on violence in the American family.

The Yearly Analysis of Official Reports

The American Humane Association data is limited to that which is voluntarily reported from various states and jurisdictions, not necessarily using the same definition of abuse and neglect. Summary data is not figured from the total reports from all states, but only from those states that submit individual case data, (33 states in 1978 and 1979 and 39 states in 1980.) In 1978, from this sample, the data base was developed only from substantiated cases, which represented less than 40% of the reported cases from the states providing individual case data. In 1979 and 1980, however, a more complete base was used and a minimal data set was established. (See Table 4-7.) Based on individual case data, 30% of the 1980 reports were for Abuse, 48% for Neglect, and 18% for both Abuse and Neglect. Some states still do not differentiate the reports into Abuse, Neglect, and Abuse and Neglect. As a result, the "Other" category becomes a very important one. For 1980, Michigan, for example, reported over 15,000 cases in this category. Florida and Texas used this category to report all of their cases. The total for these two states is 95,790 (Florida, 56,998; Texas 38,792). In the 1979 report, the "Other" category made up 9.1% of the total reports from the 33 states that reported individual case data and 4% of those reports from 39 states in 1980. This includes reports in which the type was not specified (as abuse, neglect, or abuse and neglect), or where the child may be considered "at risk" but no clear evidence of maltreatment exists.

With the qualifications noted and since the individual case data represents, roughly, only about one-third of the total number of reported cases in

Table 4-6 Comparison of National Estimates of the Extent of Neglect, (1962–1980)

Reference	Measurement Criteria	Estimate of Incidence	Origin of Data
1. Nagi, S.Z. (1975) (CD-00704)	Reported neglect Neglect, not reported Total	432,000 234,000 666,000	Agency survey, 1972–1973 data Difference between projections from rate of reports in Florida and rate from agency survey, 1972–1973 data
2. Light, R.J. (1973) (CD-00613)	Neglect and other maltreatment incidents excluding abuse	465,000	Reanalysis of Gil's 1965 data
3. American Humane Association (1978) (CD-02538)	Neglect officially reported to state departments of social services[1]	207,227	National study of officially reported cases, 1976 data
4. American Humane Association (1979) (CD-03743)	Neglect officially reported to state departments of social services[1]	95,006[2]	National study of officially reported cases, 1977 data
5. American Humane Association (1980) (*National Analysis of Official Child Neglect Reporting*, 1978, Washington D.C.: National Center on Child Abuse and Neglect, (OHDS-80-30271), September 1980)	Neglect officially reported to state departments of social services[3]	51,148	National study of officially reported cases, 1978 data

94

6.	Burgdorf, K. and Romashko, T. (1981) *Recognition and Reporting of Child Maltreatment: Summary Findings from the National Study of the Incidence and Severity of Child Abuse and Neglect. Draft.* (1981) (Mimeo.)	Neglect reported to and substantiated by CPS agencies, known to some official agency, or identifiable from other official agencies	329,000	National survey of child protective service agencies and front-line professionals, in selected communities, 1979/1980 data
7.	American Humane Association (1981) *National Analysis of Official Child Neglect & Abuse Reporting,* 1979. In conjunction with Denver Research Institute and the National Center on Child Abuse and Neglect. (NCCD: 105-80-067)	Neglect officially reported to state departments of Social Services[4]	154,020	National study of officially reported cases, 1979 data
8.	American Humane Association (1982) *National Analysis of Official Child Neglect & Abuse Reporting,* 1980.	Neglect officially reported to state departments of social services.[5]	248,751	National study of officially reported cases, 1980 data

[1] Includes abuse categories and abuse and neglect categories from all 50 states. Excludes 54,170 reports in the "unspecified" category.

[2] Less than one-third of the total reports were categorized into abuse or neglect categories.

[3] Includes substantiated neglect and substantiated abuse/neglect categories from individual case data of 33 states. 60% of the total cases in the database were unsubstantiated.

[4] Introduction of National Study use of minimal data set. Includes neglect and abuse/neglect categories from individual case data of 33 states.

[5] Includes neglect and abuse/neglect categories from individual case data of 36 states.

Source. Adapted from *REVIEW OF CHILD ABUSE AND NEGLECT RESEARCH,* 1979–81. Prepared for the National Center on Child Abuse and Neglect by the Herner Co., Arlington, VA, 1981.

Table 4-7   Type of Report

Reports	1979	%	1980	%
No. of Individual Case Reports	233,927	***	376,895	***
Reports of Abuse	58,772	25.1	113,068	30
Reports of Neglect	111,162	47.5	180,910	48
Reports of Abuse/Neglect	42,858	18.3	67,841	18
Other	21,135	9.1	15,076	4

Source. National Analysis of Official Child Neglect and Abuse Reporting. American Humane Association, Denver, Colorado. 1979, 1980 (Draft, 1982).

a given year, there is no doubt that AHA findings represent an underestimate of the incidence of abuse and neglect, and may be somewhat misleading because profile data is generalized. However, as is noted in Table 4-8, official reporting since 1976 has increased by 82%. Year to year percentage of change decreases. These findings indicate that laws are becoming more standardized; more agencies are reporting and are improving their record keeping functions; and fewer changes in these laws have occurred in 1980 than occurred in each of the previous 5 year periods. This data may also reflect more and better reporting as awareness of the public increases.

Some discrepancy exists between the 1976 total reported in earlier summaries (1976–1978) and this figure which was used in the 1980 Annual Report. The earlier figure was 416,000.

Table 4-8   Trends in Official Reporting

Year	Total Number of Reports	% of Year to Year Change	Cumulative Change (%)
1976	413,000[a]	. . .	. . .
1977	516,033	+25	+25
1978	614,142	+19	+48
1979	711,142	+16	+71
1980	788,844	+11	+91

[a]Some discrepancy exists between the 1976 total reported in earlier summaries (1976–1978) and the figure which was used in the 1980 Annual Report. The earlier figure was 416,000.
Source. National Analysis of Official Child Neglect and Abuse Reporting. American Humane Association, Denver, Colorado, 1979, 1980, (Draft. 1982).

The National Incidence Study

Although the National Incidence Study does include more than the collection of official reports made to child protective service and police agencies, it does not include interviews with the private sector professionals who serve youth. The definition of child abuse and neglect used in the study is deliberately restrictive. It limits reporting to actual harm, not potential harm. Some of their findings have been affected by these limitations.

The National Incidence Study projected that at least 652,000 children are abused and/or neglected annually in the United States. In terms of incidence, this means 10.5 children for each 1000 children under the age of 18. This figure includes only "in-scope" children, that is, those that meet the study's rather narrow definition of abuse and nelect. They found that only one-fifth of the children reported to the study were also reported to the local Child Protective Service (CPS) agency. Considering the fact that a number of sources (e.g., private schools, day care centers, medical clinics and private individuals) were not included in the study and that they also might report only one-fifth of the children they observe to be abused or neglected to CPS, the actual number of maltreated "in-scope" children is at least 1,000,000. Since American Humane Association data for 1980 shows that nonprofessionals currently make 39% of all reports and the National Incidence Study omits by definition many situations of neglect, even that number is probably low.

Violence in the Family, (Straus et al., 1979)

This study included as abusive a wide range of acts including spanking, slapping, punching, kicking, biting, hitting with an object, beating, or using a knife or gun to threaten, although the Child Abuse Index developed as part of the study did not include spanking or slapping. The results suggest that more than 14 of every 100 American children (age 3–17) are subjected to abusive violence each year (six and one-half million children) and that 3 out of every 100 (3.6%) are at risk of serious injury. Perhaps the most incredible finding is that this actually could be an underestimation of child maltreatment, since the study was limited to physical abuse and excluded children under three. Considering the fact that the information was self reported, the project had to trust the honesty of the parents questioned. It was also possible to physically abuse children in ways other than those noted, for example, burning and scalding. One major category of abuse that was omitted is sexual abuse, a category that is of major significance, especially with teenagers.

The National Survey of Family Violence estimates that between 1.4 and 1.9 million children in the United States were *vulnerable* to *physical injury* from their *parents* during the year of their study. The focus is not on outcome but upon intent and potential for harm. As might be expected, such a figure would be higher than the other two estimates. This estimate still does not include other than physical abuse. It also does not include abuse or neglect by anyone other that the parents of the child. Even this figure, then, may be an underestimate.

Ratio of Neglect to Abuse

Data from the American Humane studies indicates a consistent 2:1 ratio of neglect to abuse. Other studies have suggested an even greater difference. The National Incidence Study found equal amounts of abuse and neglect but comments that the definitions used in the study may have created the result.

Child Mortality Rates

The National Incidence Study estimates that approximately 1000 children die each year because of child abuse or neglect, and notes that evidence from other sources leads the researchers to believe that their estimate is low.

If it is assumed that the 421 fatalities reported by the states which provided individual case data for the 1980 National Analysis represent slightly over 60 percent of all reported cases and that official reporting within states still is not consistent from jurisdiction to jurisdiction, the reported deaths from child abuse and neglect in 1980 are easily estimated at 1000 or more. This figure does not take into account deaths that have not been reported to the agencies providing data for the study, nor deaths that might have been attributed to other causes.

SEARCHING FOR THE QUESTIONS AND THE ANSWERS

Gauging the incidence and prevalence of abuse and neglect is only one part of understanding the problem. The studies already mentioned provide some information regarding the child, the perpetrator, and the various circumstances in which maltreatment takes place. They may also help us to understand official and unofficial responses to reports of abuse. Other studies contribute other information that may be helpful in prevention, intervention, and treatment. Several perspectives on the etiology and characteristics of child abuse and neglect have been suggested by the research. Generally, the work tends to support the observation that child maltreatment is indeed a multifactored condition. Kempe and Helfer suggest that three major variables are present when an incident of abuse or neglect occurs: the parent who has the potential for abuse, perhaps because of his/her own history; the child, who is seen as being "different"; and the situation, generally a crisis. Blair and Rita Justice place these variables in a psychosocial systems model that includes two systems, the family system and the larger system of family, environment, and culture. The variables that they suggest are hosts (parents), agent (child), environment (physical and social), and vector (the cultural "scripting" that governs interactions between the child and parents). (Justice and Justice, pp. 56-57.) Certainly these variables may oversimplify a very complex problem.. They do, however, incorporate the key variables and the ones upon which, in some definition, research has been conducted.

Some observers suggest that research has dealt with the relation of many forces to child maltreatment. These forces include socio-economic and demographic forces, support systems, neighborhoods, networks and isolation, cross-cultural contexts, family dynamics, psychodynamics, specific stressors such as change and life crisis, violence as a means of interaction, and many other areas. Specific findings are cited in many contexts throughout this book. The information that follows summarizes some of the major findings of research and the experience of practitioners into some "intelligent guesses" and more unanswered questions about child abuse and neglect.[2]

Who Is Maltreated?

The maltreated child may be any age, any race, or ethnic group, male or female, and from any socio-economic group, although reports of child maltreatment more often involve children from low income families. In many areas black children are reported at a higher rate than their rate in the total population.

What are the Most Common Forms of Maltreatment?

National Incidence Study (NIS) data indicates that physical assault is the most common form of abuse and that educational neglect is the most

---

[2]Every study has its limitations, some more than others. The design of a study, the way data was collected and analyzed, and the very nature of the topic are all areas that are sensitive to bias. The available findings do not establish clear causal relationships between presenting factors and child maltreatment. The experience of practitioners provides much information about the nature and impact of child maltreatment. However, that experience does not define clear causal relationships. Studies and experience both point to a correlation between certain factors and forms of abuse and/or neglect. Research, where it is available in child abuse and neglect, gives us an intelligent edge to our practical guesses and helps us to set aside some of our myths.

common form of neglect. AHA data (1979 and 1980) indicate that the most common form of neglect is "deprivation of necessities" (over 60%).

Who is Most Likely to Be Injured or Killed?

Children, ages 0–3, are more likely than other age group to be seriously injured or killed through maltreatment. In the NIS, they made up 74% of all fatalities.

Are Males or Females More Likely to Be Maltreated?

Straus et al. found that rates peaked at two ages, the youngest in their study (3–4 years old) and the oldest (15–17 years old). The physical abuse of males, according to NIS data, appears to decrease with age (above 3–5 years old). Straus et al. found that boys are slightly more likely than girls to be abused. (p. 26.)

What Age Group is Most Often Associated with Maltreatment?

The Straus et al. study 1979, which included only physical abuse, indicates some differences relating to age. Eighty-three percent of the children who were 3–4 and 5–9 years old were hit by their parents during the year of the survey. Of the pre-teens and early teens (10–14 years old), 66% were hit. Of the 15–17 year olds, 34% were hit. (p. 23.) The findings of this study also show that child abuse must be assumed to be a chronic condition for many young people. "Extreme forms of parental violence occur periodically and even regularly, in the families where they occur at all." (Gelles and Straus, p. 23.) Martin and Walters found that if one type of abuse had occurred previously, any kind of abuse was equally likely to occur again. (1982, p. 274.)

Is Sexual Abuse Primarily a Problem fo Teenage Girls?

Overall, males and females seem to be equally represented in reports of abuse and neglect, but sexual abuse of females is more frequently reported. Although the study methodology could have skewed the age distribution for the National Incidence Study, the finding relating to sexual abuse is interesting. The study reveals that although the incidence rate for sexual abuse is highest among adolescent females (ages 12–17), half of the female victims of sexual abuse are younger (ages 0–11). AHA data (1979–80) indicates that reports of sexual abuse for girls seem to increase proportionately with chronological age. San Diego data from the Child Victimization Study indicates that reported sexual molestation cases ". . . involved primarily male perpetrators against female victims and were more likely to include middle-class families than either neglect or physical abuse cases." (Smith and Bohnstedt, p. 2.)

What is the Relationship of the Perpetrator to the Child?

AHA data suggest that the physical abuse that occurs when ". . . nonrelatives are perpetrators is significantly higher than in all other instances." Greater than average rates for minor physical abuse exist for step/adoptive/foster parents as a category as well. (This group is associated with the greatest frequency of sexual maltreatment.) Parents are perpetrators in 96% of the reported cases. When they are perpetrators, deprivation of necessities occurs with greatest frequency. Nonrelatives and step/adoptive/foster parents are more often associated with physical abuse. These two groups also are often associated with sexual abuse. Almost half of the children were living with a single, unemployed female caretaker. (AHA 1980.) Peggy Smith and Marvin Bohnstedt found that mothers in single-parent households were most often the caretaker charged with neglect (p. 2.)[3] More abuse seems to occur in homes where there are fewer children, while neglect is more likely to occur where there are more children.

What Characteristics are Associated with Ethnic Group and Income?

NIS data indicate an almost identical rate for nonwhite and white children in middle and upper-income families, but suggest that in lower-income families (less than $15,000) ". . . incidence rates for white children are substantially higher than those for nonwhite." (See also Smith and Bohnstedt.) There appears to be a contrast within each group for higher and lower-income families. The incidence rates for white children in all types of maltreatment is higher in lower-income families. For nonwhite children, although neglect rates were much higher in low income families, abuse rates were ". . . close to constant, at a relatively low level, across income levels." An interesting study might be made contrasting characteristics of white and nonwhite families in lower-income levels. Black children are 14% of the general population, but 21% of reported maltreatment. (AHA, 1980.)

---

[3]Single-parent families have increased in the U.S. to about 20% in 1980, according to the U.S. Bureau of Census. Single-parent families are overrepresented in the distribution of reports across the categories of caretaker composition. [44% of all reported families (AHA,1980.)] Single-parent families are more often headed by a woman than a man.

What Differences and Similarities Are Associated with Geographic Setting?

NIS data indicate that rates are similar across urban, suburban, and rural communities. Types of maltreatment were found to vary, however, the incidence rate for sexual abuse is higher in rural counties, educational neglect is higher in urban counties, and emotional neglect is higher in suburban counties.

What Characteristics Are Associated with Abusive Parents?

Parents of abused children are often characteristically described as being immature, dependent, impulsive, self-centered, rigid, and rejecting. They tend to lack nurturing and coping skills and have a relatively low frustration tolerance. Violence is experienced and viewed as an option. Abusive parents are often socially isolated and distrustful of their neighbors. (Garbarino and Sherman, 1980.) They often live in high-risk neighborhoods, they are under a high level of stress and exhibit a general pattern of "social impoverishment." They have difficulty utilizing resources that are available. They find it difficult to be self-sufficient or to be able to be "counted on" by others in their neighborhood for help. (Garbarino and Sherman, 1980.) Often they have been abused themselves and have a poor relationship with their own parents and spouse. Alcohol abuse on the part of the parent(s) is often a factor in situations of abuse and neglect. Martin and Walters (1982) found an association of abandonment with alcoholism of the mother and an association of sexual abuse with the factor of promiscuous/alcoholic father. Certainly there is no "average" abuser. Many do not fit the descriptors listed here.

Are There Situations That Encourage Maltreatment?

There is no one, given just the right circumstances, who could not abuse a child. No one has a corner on committing violence against children. Parents Anonymous recognizes six forms of abuse. These include physical abuse, physical neglect, sexual abuse, verbal abuse, emotional abuse, and emotional neglect. (Wheat, p. 331–334.) Using the Parents Anonymous forms of abuse and neglect as a guide, most parents at some time have abused or neglected their child or a child who was entrusted in their care.

Most serious injury to children occurs during times of extreme stress in a family. The stress may be in family function, in environmental circumstances, or both. Abuse and neglect always appear to be multifactored conditions. Sometimes the stress is self-imposed. Perhaps the expectations of the parents for the child are inappropriate and unreasonable. Frequent and disruptive change may contribute to the circumstance for abuse as may poverty, extended sickness, loss of a job, and any number of other factors.

Blair and Rita Justice distinguish between two types of crises: situational crisis which involves a rapid series of situational events which may be ". . . compressed together and sometimes accompanied by maturational crises such as marriage, pregnancy, a son or daughter leaving home, or retirement." (Justice and Justice, p. 27.) They see the life crisis as the one which predisposes a person to abuse. It is unpredictable and exhausting. The risk of losing control and not being able to adjust increases as the situations seem to compound one another and efforts to solve the problems fail. From this perspective, the potentially abusive parent, already exhausted by rapid and prolonged change, may see as a crisis what might normally be handled as a minor problem.

THE IMPACT OF ABUSE AND NEGLECT

It is impossible to accurately separate out the impact of abuse and neglect from other factors. We are unable to control for all the rival explanations that might account for our findings. What was the influence of the family, school, friends, system, process of labeling, time, place of intervention, and so on. As we discuss impact, it is also important to focus on the children who have been maltreated but who seem to have somehow taken it in stride. Perhaps a fourth of the children, maybe more, have been able to avoid the many pitfalls described here.

Child maltreatment touches every person and every community. It has an effect on our economic structure and on our mental and physical health as a nation. It spills over into other areas of concern, for example, juvenile crime, violence in society, battered parents and spouses. It is affected by and has impact on our values. The remainder of this chapter is devoted to providing some forms and examples of the possible impact of abuse and neglect on the child, the family, the community, and society as a whole. Other chapters also address impact as a part of the study of the family, human development, etc.

Physical Damage

Physical abuse may result in permanent impairment of limb or body function. Perhaps more tragically, it may result in damage to the central nervous system, leaving the child with seizures, mental retardation, cerebral palsy, hearing or visual damage, or learning disabilities. Neglect, in the form of undernutrition, lack of adequate medical care, etc., may have long-range effects on the normal functioning and the development of the brain.

Poor Physical Health

Maltreated children may be, by virtue of their lack of overall care, more open to distress than other children and generally, in poorer health. A study in Australia of 56 abused children and a control group indicated that the abused children were more than five times likelier to have significant illnesses in infancy. (Dates et al, p. 171.)

Anemia and its resulting consequences of apathy, poor learning ability, listlessness, and exhaustion (which can also be the result of poor nutrition) appear to be common in abused children. (See Ebbin et al., pp. 660–667.) Even among abused and neglected children who are not specifically diagnosed as being failure to thrive children, many pediatricians have observed such problems as poor weight gain, inadequate protein intake, and often below average height for age. Hearing loss, which could easily be the result of absent or inadequate treatment for ear infections or the result of nutritional deficiencies, may also be a major problem for abused and neglected children. Little research on this area is currently available.

Developmental Impact

In addition to physical damage and medical risk issues, the abused and neglected child may be at risk in many other ways, particularly in developmental and psychological areas.

Although there is great variation in the studies as to developmental impact, especially relating to IQ testing, it can be said that there is much consistency in the finding of developmental delays and deviations in abused children. As Harold Martin states, "While an exact risk factor cannot be established, there is no doubt whatsoever that mistreated children have lower IQ's, poorer language, and show less competent academic progress than children who have been well parented." (p. 349.) Even when children with significant handicaps are excluded from IQ studies, ". . . the remaining mistreated children have IQ scores which are significantly below other children from similar socio-economic backgrounds." (p. 350.) Smith and Bohnstedt found that victims of child abuse and neglect had more behavior, discipline, and school attendance problems than comparison subjects. Researchers in Australia found 36% of abused children to be delayed in language compared to 8% out of the control group. (Dates et al., p. 171.)

A summary of federal demonstration projects indicates that over half of the children were significantly below the mean one or more standard deviations in cognitive, language, and motor abilities. (See *Evaluation of Child Abuse and Neglect Demonstration Projects 1974–1977.*)

Psychological Issues

As one abused child stated to one of the authors, "We are all wounded children. And these are wounds that are not easily seen nor healed." The maltreated child often lives in an unpredictable, unhappy, confusing world that may be overtly violent or simply grossly inadequate. Surviving, alone, requires almost all the energy the child can muster. The child may be excessively withdrawn, excessively aggressive, excessively fearful of other people, or indiscriminate in his/her affection (no order of importance to relationships, all adults can be trusted or not trusted equally.)

The issue of self-esteem becomes a major one. A.H. Green studied the self-abusive behavior of maltreated children. He found that 8.3% of abused children with a mean age of 8.5 years had attempted suicide and 20% had self-mutilative behavior. (Green, 1968; Green, 1978.)

T.J. Gaensbauer studied the distorted affective communication patterns of the child and the mother. He found a predeliction for withdrawal, unpredictability, and shallowness of emotional communication. The child demonstrated negative expression of affect and a meager capacity for pleasure compared to the control group. (Gaensbauer and Sands.) There is little question that abused and neglected children are at risk in forming healthy relationships with others.

LONG TERM IMPACT

Longitudinal Issues

Few studies are available that track the abused child into adulthood. This is a particularly difficult area in which to develop valid and reliable findings. True prospective longitudinal studies are expensive and take many years to complete. The complexities of controlling for intervening, elusive variables are great. Retrospective longitudinal studies, although less expensive and more available, have their own design and methodological difficulties. As one "looks back," at data, it may be necessary to operate on some faulty assumptions about the available sample and what factors might have intervened. These studies may also be dependent on someone else's observations and record keeping.[4] Some of the longitudinal questions that we frequently ask are:

[4]An excellent review of some of the problems encountered in longitudinal studies and some possible solutions is found in Cicchetti and Rizley, "Developmental Perspectives on the Etiology, Intergenerational Transmission, and Sequelae of Child Maltreatment." *New Directions for Child Development.* 11, 1981, pp. 31–55. They are presently codirectors of the Development Risk Research Project and the Harvard Child Maltreatment Project.

Do Abused Children Become Abusers?

Thus far, most findings indicate that 20%−25% of persons abused as children may become abusive parents. A recent study found that men who had been abused were more likely to abuse their children and their spouse than women who had been abused.

Is a Life of Failure, Frustration, and Incompetence A Consequence of Maltreatment as a Child?

An Illinois Department of Corrections admission cohort study of youthful offenders found evidence of abuse for 11% and of neglect for 15%. Female commitments had such histories twice as often as males. Referencing recent studies by Wolfgang (1981), Fagan et al., and the Illinois study, Cyriaque states that ". . . violence-dominated lifestyles (in many instances, associated with sexually and physically abusing families), particularly characterize juvenile murderers and sex offenders, regardless of socio-economic background."(Cyriaque, pp. 4−5.) Caution is advised, however, in generalizing such data or of making an assumption of a cause−effect relationship.

Smith and Bohnstedt found arrest rates and convictions slightly higher for victims of abuse than for the comparison group. (p. 4.) Silbert found that 78% of the prostitutes in the Delancey Street Study started prostitution as juveniles. Sixty-eight percent of these were sixteen or younger. Ninety-six percent of the juvenile prostitutes were runaways before they began prostituting. Almost two thirds of the sample were victims of incest and child sexual abuse from the ages of three to sixteen. (Silbert, p. 3.) Preliminary data from runaway centers in several states indicates that a high percentage of the teenage girls who run away from home have been victims of incest and child sexual abuse.

Certainly these are all areas for further study. There are a number of very important unanswered questions here. One of the most important is why do many maltreated children *not* fit this pattern? There are many maltreated children who do not become abusive parents. People who were not abused as children commit violent acts against society. The question may be more appropriately one of risk: the abused child is more at risk in both short and long-term ways than the general population. What is it that decreases the risk?

THE INVULNERABLE CHILD

Julius Segal writes of a child, the invulnerable child, who somehow has managed to not become wounded, even though that child has been subjected to maltreatment and generally has received inadequate parenting. Smith and

Bohnstedt found that 21% of the victims of child abuse and neglect that they studied showed no apparent school adjustment problems, in spite of the abuse reported. (p. 4.) Segal notes that generally this apparent invulnerability is an adaptation that the child has been able to make—a healthy, hopeful view of the world that the child has been able to sustain. He also points out that the invulnerable child has found someone or something outside the home who becomes the "parent" and friend that the child needs. In any case, the child acquires the necessary skills for mastering his environment or at least appearing to live "outside it." We should not be lulled into believing that most children who have been abused will be invulnerable. It is instructive, however, to study the characteristics of this child in order to help the children who are not so invulnerable to achieve some of these characteristics in their own behalf.

Summary

There is nothing controversial about the statement that child maltreatment is a serious and tragic problem. Reaching a common, clear, and concise definition of maltreatment is an important task if we want to determine the nature and scope of the problem. Such a definition will also assist us in effectively preventing child abuse and neglect and in providing effective help to abusing families.

The difficulties encountered in achieving such a definition are many and varied. Child abuse and neglect are defined from many perspectives. Perhaps there are two definitions of child maltreatment: one that defines minimum standards of care and another that defines protection from harm in the positive context of strengthening families rather than the negative context of maltreatment. In either case, clear operational criteria are necessary for each form of maltreatment.

Research in this area is a complex and challenging scientific problem. We are beginning to develop the necessary approaches and controls to assure greater reliability and validity of research findings. At present, our findings must be approached with caution and questions.

We are beginning to develop an understanding of who is at risk of maltreatment. We are learning that once abused, some children appear to be at greater risk than others in their own adjustment as adults and as parents. Child maltreatment is a shared dilemma and a shared responsibility. Its impact is universal and specific.

BIBLIOGRAPHY

Child Abuse and Neglect: The Problem and Its Management. Vols. 1,2, and 3. U.S. Dept. Health, Education, and Welfare Publication No. (OHD) 75-30073, Washington, D.C.

Cicchetti, Dante, and Rizley, Ross, "Development Perspectives on the Etiology, International Transmission, and Sequelae of Child Maltreatment." *New Directions for Child Development,* 11, 1981, pp. 31–55.

Criminal Victimization in the United States: A Description of Trends from 1973 to 1978. Bureau of Justice Statistics, NCJ-66716, December 1980.

Cyriaque, Jeanne. "The Chronic Serious Offender: How Illinois Juveniles Match Up." Illinois Department of Corrections, February, 1982.

Ebbin, A.J., Gollub, M.H., Stein, A.M., and Wilson, M.G. "Battered Child Syndrome at the Los Angeles County General Hospital." *American Journal of Diseases in Children. 118* 1969, 660–67.

Eskin, Marian, and Kravitz, Marjorie (supervising editor) *Child Abuse and Neglect: A Literature Review and Selected Bibliography.* National Institute of Justice, Washington, D.C., February, 1980.

Executive Summary: National Study of the Incidence and Severity of Child Abuse and Neglect. (manuscript.) Westat, Inc. and Development Associates, Inc. for NCCAN. (HEW-105-76-1137), 1981.

Evaluation of Child Abuse and Neglect Demonstration Projects 1974–1977. Vol. 6, Child Client Impact: Final Report. U.S. Dept. of Commerce, PB 278–448, December 1977.

Fagan, Jeffrey, Jones, Sally J., Hartstone, Eliot, Rudman, Larry, and Ermeson, Robert, *The Violent Juvenile Offender Research and Development Program.* The URSA Institute, April, 1978.

Fontana, Vincent J. "Prevent the Abuse of the Future." *Trial. 10,* May–June 1974, 14–16.

Gaensbauer, T.J., and Sands, K. "Distorted Affective Communications in Abused and Infants and Their Potential Impact on Caretakers." *Journal of American Academy of Child Psychiatry. 18,* 1979, 236–50.

Garbarino, James, and Sherman, Deborah. "High-Risk Neighborhoods and High-Risk Families: The Human Ecology of Child Maltreatment." *Child Development. 51,* 1980,188–198.

Geiser, Robert L. *The Illusion of Caring: Children in Foster Care.* Beacon Press, Boston, 1973.

Gelles, R.J. Prepared Statement of Testimony, p. 13.

Gelles, Richard J., and Straus, Murray A. "Violence in the American Family." *Journal of Social Issues. 35,* 2, 1979.

Gil, David G. "Unraveling Child Abuse." *American Journal of Orthopsychiatry. 45,* 3, April 1975, 346–356.

Gil, D. G. *Violence Against Children: Physical Child Abuse in the United States.* Harvard University Press, Cambridge Mass., 1970.

Giovannoni, Jeanne M., and Becerra, Rosina M. *Defining Child Abuse.* The Free Press. A Division of Macmillan Publishing Co., Inc., 1979.

Goldstein, Joseph, Freud, Anna, and Solnit, Albert J. *Before the Best Interests of the Child.* Free Press, New York, 1979.

Goldstein, Joseph, Freud, Anna, and Solnit, Albert J. *Beyond the Best Interests of the Child.* Free Press, New York, 1973.

Green, A.H. "Self-Destruction in Physically Abused Schizophrenic Children: Report of Cases." *Archives of General Psychiatry. 19,* 1968, 171–197.

Green, A.H. "Self-Destructive Behavior in Battered Children." *American Journal of Psychiatry. 135,* 1978, 579–582.

Justice, Blair and Justice, Rita. *The Abusing Family*. Human Sciences Press, New York, 1976.

Kempe, Henry C. *et al.* "The Batthered-Child Syndrome." *Journal of the American Medical Association. 181*, 1962, 105–112.

Light, R.J. "Abused and Neglected Children in America: A Study of Alternative Policies." *Harvard Educational Review. 43*, 1973, 559–588.

Martin, Harold P. "The Consequences of Being Abused and Neglected." In *The Battered Child*. Edited by Kempe, H.C. and Helfer, R.E. 3rd Ed. University of Chicago Press, Chicago, 1980, pp. 347–365.

Martin, Michael J. and Walters, James. "Familial Correlates of Selected Types of Child Abuse and Neglect." *Journal of Marriage and The Family*. May, 1982, pp. 267–276.

National Advisory Committee for Juvenile Justice and Delinquency, Standards For The Administration of Justice. U.S. Dept. of Justice, Washington, D.C., July, 1980.

National Analysis of Official Child Neglect and Abuse Reporting. 1977, 1978, 1979, and 1980 (draft) Annual Reports. American Humane Association, Denver, Colorado.

Oates, R.K., Davis, A.A., Ryan, M.G., and Stewart, L.F. "Risk Factors Associated with Child Abuse." Abstracts: Second International Congress on Child Abuse and Neglect, Pergamon Press, London, 1978, p. 171.

Segal, Julius, and Yahraes, Herbert. *A Child's Journey: Forces That Shape the Lives of Our Young*. McGraw-Hill, New York, 1979, Chapter Twelve, pp. 282–301.

Silbert, Mimi H. "Delancey Street Study: Prostitution and Sexual Assault." Summary of Results, Delancey Street Foundation, Inc., San Francisco, CA., 1982. (NIMH).

Smith, Charles P. *et al.* Reports of the National Juvenile Justice Assessment Center: A Preliminary National Assessment of Child Abuse and Neglect and the Juvenile Justice System; The Shadows of Distress. Office of Juvenile Justice and Delinquency Prevention, Washington, D.C., April 1980.

Smith, Peggy, and Bohnstedt, Marvin. "Child Victimization Study Highlights." (Draft, 1981.) Social Research Center of the American Justice Institute, Sacramento, CA., (NCCAN) 90-C-1870 (2).

Straus, M.A., Gelles, R.J., and Steimetz, S.K. *Behind Closed Doors: Violence in the American Family*. Doubleday/Anchor, Garden City, N.Y., 1979.

The User Manual Series in the Prevention and Treatment of Child Abuse and Neglect. National Center on Child Abuse and Neglect (DHEW), Washington, D.C., August 1979 and July 1980 (HHS).

Viano, Emilio C. *Victimology: An International Journal. 2*, 2, Visage Press, Inc., Summer 1977.

Wheat, Patte and Leiber, Leonard L. *Hope For The Children*. Winston Press, Minneapolis, MN, 1979.

Wolfgang, Marvin E., *Delinquency in a Birth Cohort II: Some Preliminary Results*. Paper prepared for the Attorney General's Task Force on Violent Crime, Chicago, Illinois, June, 1981.

CHAPTER 5

Physical Child Abuse

PREVALENCE OF PHYSICAL CHILD ABUSE

"Statistics indicate that one of every 10 injuries to children is non-accidental and that 15% of all emergency cases involving children under the age of five show some evidence of child battering." Schmitt cites that the incidence of injuries inflicted by caretakers is approximately 510 new cases per million general population per year. (Schmitt, 1980, p. 128.) "The mortality is about 3 percent or 2,000 deaths per year in this country." (Schmitt, 1978, p. 180[1].) AHA (1980) data show that all forms of physical abuse constitute 27% of substantiated reports.

The greatest incidence of physical injury is to infants. Younger children are at greater risk since they are demanding, defenseless, and nonverbal.

DEFINING PHYSICAL CHILD ABUSE

Physical child abuse is defined as an act of commission. A nonaccidental injury inflicted on a child by the child's parent or caretaker is construed as physical child abuse. "Physical abuse or nonaccidental trauma is one of the most common types of child maltreatment seen by physicians." (Schmitt, 1980, p. 128.) Many physically abused children continue to function without

---

[1]This figure is twice the conservative estimate noted in Chapter 4.

110

medical attention but most children who are severely physically abused come to the attention of hospital personnel or physicians. The physician usually has the job of deciding whether the injury is accidental or nonaccidental. An accident is defined as an incident or experience that is unforeseen, unfortunate, and unexpected. An accident implies "no fault" and no intent to inflict injury.

As discussed in Chapter 4, definitions of child abuse vary from state to state. Generally speaking, there is agreement that corporal discipline (shaking or hitting) should not be used on infants. Bruises, cuts, or broken bones should not be the result of any physical discipline administered by the child's parents, caretakers, or others in positions of authority over the child. Instruments that leave bruises, welts, lacerations, or other injuries should not be utilized in disciplining a child.

Ultimately, as in other situations of suspected child maltreatment, the Court makes the decision whether or not physical child abuse exists. Since most cases of abuse and neglect do not go before the Court officially, determination of abuse is made, in a practical sense by other gatekeepers, usually social services. Ultimately, however, social service definitions are shaped, tested, and reshaped in the Courts. Where a dispute exists, the Court ultimately decides.

INDICATORS OF PHYSICAL CHILD ABUSE

Primary indicators of physical child abuse are injuries to the skin, injuries to the face or head, burns, eye injuries, brain injuries, abdominal visceral injuries, or bone injuries. Common injuries to the skin include:

1. Diaper rash and/or uncleanliness.
2. Cigarette burns, bite marks, grab marks, and belt lashes.
3. Abrasions and lacerations unusual for the child's developmental age.
4. Injury of external genitalia.
5. Marks on the neck from strangling by hands or rope.
6. External injuries to ears traumatized by pinching, twisting, or pulling.
7. Unusual skin rashes that deny dermatologic diagnosis.
8. Burns, particularly on the soles of the feet or buttocks.
9. Injuries on two planes of the child's body, often called ping-pong bruises.
10. Lacerated lip.
11. Burns on lips or tongue.

Other indicators of physical child abuse are drawn from interviews with the child's parent or caretaker. Some parents are suspicious, distrustful, and defensive with the interviewer; others are not. Some indicators that may become apparent during the interview of the parents include:

1. A contradictory history given by the parent or caretaker.
2. A history that does not adequately explain the nature and extent of the given injuries.
3. A reluctance on the part of the parent or caretaker to give information or participate in the history-taking process.
4. A history of repeated injuries or accidents to the child.
5. A statement that others caused the injury to the child (brother, sister, or playmate).
6. An undue and unexplained delay in bringing the child in for medical attention.
7. A history of skipping from health-care facility to health-care facility (e.g., going to one doctor in January, another in March, and so forth, all for injuries to the child.)
8. The parent seems detached from the child and from the interviewer.
9. The parent seems to either under or overreact to the situation at hand.
10. The parent cannot be located.
11. The parents or the child present information that indicates chronic family discord or inordinate amounts of stress within the family.
12. The parent seems to have unrealistic expectations of the child.
13. The parent or other members in the family are abusive of drugs or alcohol.
14. The parents refuse to give consent or to participate in further evaluation procedures.

Modified from Helfer, 1980, p. 73.

Behavioral indicators that commonly occur in hospital settings include some or all of the following.

1. The child is wary of physical contact with the parents or others.
2. The child does not look to the parents or other adults for reassurance.
3. The child cries hopelessly under examination and treatment and shows no expectation of being comforted.
4. The child seems less afraid than other children when admitted to the ward and settles in quickly.
5. The child seems constantly alert to possible danger.

6. The child becomes apprehensive when adults approach some other crying child.
7. The child seems to seek safety in sizing up the situation rather than in looking to their parent for comfort.
8. The child continually asks in words or actions what will happen next.
9. The child asks "when am I going home" or announces, "I am not going home," rather than crying, "I want to go home."

Other indicators of possible child physical abuse are in the area of the family dynamics which could include any one or more of the following.

1. Personal and marital problems on the part of the parent or parents.
2. Parents have a history of poor relationships with their own parents.
3. Parents were abused as children.
4. Parents were raised in homes where excessive punishment was the norm.
5. The family is isolated, transient, and lacks external supports.
6. The parents are evasive and contradictory in explaining anything about the family situation.
7. Frequently, little or no interest is shown in the child's treatment.
8. The parents constantly criticize the child and/or blame the child for the injury.
9. The parents have inappropriate expectations of the child.
10. The child is someone who is disliked by the parent or who is accusatory or judgmental.
11. Family members seem to have no approval outlet for their pent-up emotions. (Mayhall, p. 81.)

Although the characteristics noted above are listed as possible indications of abuse, these characteristics may also be present when abuse is not.

DISTINGUISHING FEATURES

Most of us would like to believe about child abuse as we would like to believe about divorce: it happens in other people's families and other families are different from our own. Divorce statistics fast approaching the 50% mark are proof that divorce occurs in a high percentage of families. Child abuse also occurs in a high percentage of families. The image of the family that physically abuses children is one of poverty, lack of education, in high risk neighborhood, and other derogatory conditions. Certainly reported abuse comes disproportionately from families in low level incomes, in many of these conditions. Physical abuse occurs in every type of family and every ethnic, economic, and social background. It can and does occur in our neighborhood, among our friends' families, in our religious congregation, in the families of the people we work with, and in our own homes. The most distinguishing feature of physical child abuse is that there are no boundaries of where it can and does occur.

Other distinguishing features include:

There is no simple cause and effect relationship that will explain why physical abuse occurs in some situations and not in others.

Abusive parents tend to have one or more of the following attitudes about children and the parenting process.

1. Spankings and other more severe forms of physical punishment as discipline are acceptable to these parents.
2. Parents have high expectations of the children that are not consistent with the child's developmental capabilities.
3. The parents have been abused themselves as children.
4. The parents expect the child to be a caretaker to the parent.
5. The parents are more centered on themselves than on the child. These parents have an orientation directed more toward their own satisfaction than the satisfaction of the child.

Physical child abuse is a crime. However, over 90% of abusing parents are neither determined to be insane, nor convicted as criminals (Schmitt, 1978, p. 181.)

Women appear to be involved in physical abuse and may frequently be a passive participant. AHA (1980) data indicate that physical abuse committed by males is 23% and by females 15% of individual case data reports. NIS data indicate that mother/substitutes were involved in 72% of physical abuse cases but were seldom the only involved adult. (NIS, 1981)

Child physical abuse may or may not accompany other forms of abuse and neglect. Most authorities state that physical abuse of children does not occur simultaneously with neglect. Familial correlates with physical abuse appear to be parent–child conflict and biological/nonbiological relationship to the child.[2] (Martin and Walters, 1982.)

ADOLESCENT PHYSICAL ABUSE

Some physical abuse occurs during the adolescent period. One type of adolescent physical abuse is that which has a beginning in childhood and just continues on through adolescence. This form of physical abuse is thought to

[2]AHA (1980) data shows that the ". . . total physical abuse that occurs when nonrelaives are perpetrators is significantly higher than in all other instances."(AHA, 1980, p.23.)

result from inappropriate parental expectations regarding th
mance abilities and/or expectations of the child to nurtu
(Fisher, p. 37.) A second type of adolescent physical ab
actually started in childhood as physical punishment but
changes to physical abuse when the youth reaches adoles
explanation for this change is that the youth is involved in st
become a separate individual from his/her parents and increasi
independence from the family. This struggle results in increasing
between the adolescent and the parent and may escalate the
behavior of physical conflict. (Fisher, p. 38.) Recurring physical abu
third type of physical abuse. In situations of recurring physical abus
parent was abusive to the child in the child's early years, usually up to
three years. Then, following a dormant period, the parent became physica
abusive during the youth's adolecence. This type of physical abuse is a res
of the youth's independence and individuation from the parents. (Fisher, p
39.) The fourth type of physical abuse that characteristically occurs during
adolescence is physical abuse that first occurs during the adolescent period.
The explanation for this abuse is that the youth's emerging sexuality and
separation restimulate the parents' own unresolved adolescent conflicts and
are painful for the parents to deal with, thus creating an atmosphere for
violence. (Fisher, p. 41.)

FORMS OF PHYSICAL CHILD ABUSE

What may appear as physical child abuse may not be. It is difficult for
medical personnel to distinguish between situations of chronic physical
abuse and a mild, one-time situation in which a parent, in a moment of
hopelessness or rage causes an injury to a child. All injuries to small babies
are highly significant and must be investigated in terms of the
psychodynamics of the parent–child relationship and in terms of the parent
expectations in early child raising experiences. (Helfer and Kempe, 1972, p.
69.)

The most common forms of physical child abuse include:

1. Bruises and welts.
2. Abrasions, contusions, lacerations.
3. Burns, scalding.
4. Bone fractures.
5. Wounds, cuts, punctures.
6. Subdural hemorrhage or hematoma.
7. Malnutrition (deliberately inflicted).
8. Skull fractures.
9. Internal injuries.

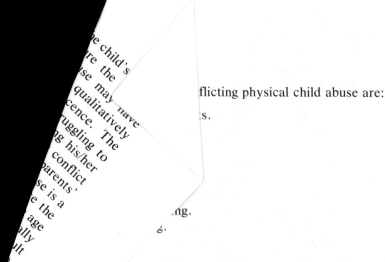

flicting physical child abuse are:

:s.

.ng.

6.

everything is used to inflict injury on a child. Some of the
.nents used in physical abuse include fists, belts, straps, belt
.s, broom handles, baseball bats, coat hangers, cords, hair-
.ghted cigarettes, matches, cigarette lighters, boiling water and
.t liquids, grease, steaming radiators, open gas flames, hot plates,
., shoes and boots, lead or iron pipes, bottles, brick walls, bicycle
.ns, knives, scissors, chemicals, pills, teeth, guns, or any object at hand.

EXPLANATIONS OF PHYSICAL CHILD ABUSE

Aggressive Impulses

Julius Segal has presented a summary of investigations on aggressive
impulses. He notes that abusive parents have been described as immature,
impulsive, rigid, domineering, self-centered, hypersensitive, and more.
However, none of these terms can be operationally defined, much less
agreed upon as characteristics of abusive parents (or potentially abusive
parents). Segal cited that John J. Spinetta and David Rigler came to the
conclusion that abusive parents allow their aggressive impulses to be
expressed too freely. However, these researchers did not come up with a
consensus about the sources of these impulses. (Segal and Yahraes, p. 188.)

Alcohol and Drug Abuse

There is a population of physically abusing parents who are alcohol or drug
abusers or who have been repeatedly involved in serious antisocial violent or

criminal behavior. This group of abusing parents is less than 10% of the total number of offenders. (Steele, p. 2.)

Environmental Issues

David Gil elaborates on what he calls an "environmental model" of physical child abuse. This theory places an emphasis on social and cultural influences of violence that lead to child abuse within the family. Gil asserts that the stress of the inegalitarian society contributes to abuse. If poverty, poor education, and other environmental stresses were eliminated, there would be a major decrease in the incidence of child abuse. People are encouraged to become politically involved in changing laws. This involvement is one way to overcome violence at its roots. (Gil, p. 385.)

Precipitating Problems

Gelles emphasizes another approach to explaining child abuse. The socio-economic position of parents,marital stress, too many children, unemployment, social isolation, an unwanted pregnancy, a problem child, or immediate precipitating situations such as arguments or child misbehavior are focal points. Gelles asserts that parents' socialization patterns contribute to the potential for abuse. (Gelles, p. 613.)

The World of Abnormal Rearing

Helfer coined the concept "World of Abnormal Rearing" (W.A.R.) This concept was devised to explain what occurs when a person's childhood does not provide a favorable environment in which to learn basic interpersonal skills. People who grow up under these circumstances truly miss out on childhood. Helfer states that this cycle has implications for the developing child and the adult who has the task of helping the child during the relearning phase. It is important to remember in considering the W.A.R. cycle that not all children who experience these conditions are beaten. W.A.R. is a never-ending cycle, passing from one generation to another. (see Figure 5-1.) (Helfer, 1980, p. 39.)

According to the W.A.R. cycle model, physical child abuse is explained from the standpoint of circular causality. The situation may actually stem from pregnancy, that is, whether the pregnancy was wanted or unwanted. It is also possible to trace the abuse cycle back to the parent's childhood, to the parent's parent's childhood and so forth. People who have been physically abused are out of touch, out of control, and have learned to mute their own senses. They have not learned how to get their own needs met and are often

Ray E. Helfer

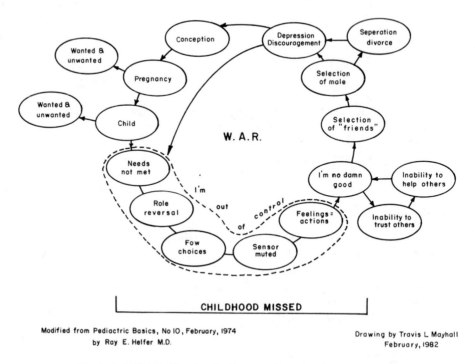

Modified from Pediactric Basics, No l0, February, 1974   Drawing by Travis L Mayhall
            by Ray E. Helfer M.D.   February, 1982

Figure 5-1 W.A.R. (Reprinted with permission of Helfer, 1980, p. 40.)

taught to be responsible for the actions of others. They have little practice in problem-solving and therefore, have few problem-solving skills. They have been convinced that they can not trust others. They often have trouble containing their feelings; they act on their feelings instead of putting limits on their actions and separating actions from feelings. (Helfer, 1980, p. 48.)

A Psychodynamic Explanation

The psychodynamic model for explaining child physical abuse has its roots in Freudian theory where the individual's behavior is based on internal mechanisms of thinking. Combined with an inability to nurture others, physical child abuse is seen as ''. . . an interplay of other dynamics: a lack of trust in others, a tendency toward isolation, a nonsupportive marital relationship, and excessive expectations toward the child.'' (Justice and Justice, p. 39.) This model places less emphasis on environmental stresses and states instead that individuals have a psychological propensity to abuse. A distinguishing feature of this model is that everything is seen as secondary to individual internal psychology. Some people, according to this theory, have a propensity to physically abuse but never abuse. This theory is not an accurate predictor of human behavior. Others have combined this theoretical base with environmental stress in their attempt to understand and relate to issues of physical child abuse. (Justice and Justice, p. 39.)

Common Identifying Characteristics of Parents

Steele asserts that although no two abusive parents are exactly alike, they share common characteristics: (1) immaturity, (2) low self-esteem, (3) difficulty in seeking and finding pleasure and satisfaction in the adult world, (4) social isolation, (5) misperceptions of the child, (6) fear of spoiling the child, (7) strong belief in the value of punishment, and (8) serious lack of ability to be emphatetic in relationship to the child. (Steele and Pollack, p. 15.) These explanations place an emphasis on identifying characteristics rather than in attempting to explain the individual offender as does the psychodynamic model. Other labels or characteristics often used in categorizing abusive parents are chronically aggressive, poor ego functioning, impulse-ridden, etc. Viewing physical child abuse from this standpoint alone is very limiting in that it ignores the context in which child abuse occurs.

Mental Illness As An Explanation

Many mental health practitioners operate from the viewpoint that child abuse suggests mental illness on the part of the offender. (Justice and Justice, p. 48.) However, evidence suggests that less than 2% of abusive parents are psychotic. "The suggestion was that only a mentally ill parent willfully inflicts physical abuse on a child." (Justice and Justice, p. 48.) They further cite research that concludes that abusive parents do not easily fit into the categories included in the psychiatric *Diagnostic and Statistical Manual II*. (Justice and Justice, p. 48.) The same statement might apply for the revised edition, *Diagnostic and Statistical Manual III*.

These parents may have psychiatric disorders in about the same proportion as the general population. Physically abusive parents have about the normal incidence and distribution of neuroses, psychoses, and character disorders which exist rather independently and separately from behavioral patterns expressed in abuse of their offspring. Such difficulties may warrant appropriate treatment in their own right regardless of the coexistence of patterns of abuse.

In the Context of Family

Minuchin and others who approach understanding and working with child abuse from the context of the family say that child physical abuse needs to be defined from this perspective. (Minuchin, p. 4.) Family systems theory does not suggest that people have basic personality structures that remain the same throughout life's traumatic events. Rather, it holds that people are members of social groups and contexts, and act and react within them. The concept of the site of the pathology is much broader than just resting within the individual and so are the possibilities for intervention (Minuchin, p. 4.) There are three major axioms of this model for working with physically abusive families: (1) Everyone lives within a family and is a member of a social system and must adapt to that system; (2) When change occurs in the family structure this change contributes to changing the behavior and functioning of each of the family members; (3) When people work with a family system to help make changes, the helpers become a part of the family system. (Minuchin, p. 9.)

Virginia Satir, a noted teacher and family therapist, has developed a family systems model similar in some respects to that of Minuchin and his followers. Satir states that the family has four primary functions that impact on all the family members and on the group as a whole. The four functions are communication, self-worth, emotional rules, and links to the outside world. "The family is the 'factory' where this kind of person is made. You, the adult, are the peoplemakers." (Satir, p. 3.) Satir shares the ideas of the structured family therapists in stating that the family is the major context that we need to understand in order to understand and explain physical child abuse as well as other problems. The family is seen as the foundation for understanding how people behave and think rather than using psychic, predetermined processes. From this view physical child abuse occurs in a family context when there is low self-esteem, when communication is indirect or vague, when emotional rules for operating within the family are rigid, nonnegotiable, and when the links to society are feared. As with other ideas already discussed, these theories which place child abuse within the context of the family are not predictive specifically of physical child abuse.

A Pyschosocial Systems Model

The Justices build on Minuchin's and Satir's models. They call their model a psychosocial system and shifting symbiosis explanation for physical child abuse. This model takes into account the shifting dynamic forces at work in the family and considers the context (environment and culture) in which the family lives. (Justice and Justice, p. 55.) Physical child abuse is considered to be a family affair and must be understood within this context. "The psychosocial systems model is primarily concerned with two systems: the family system and the larger system of family, environment, and cultures.'' (Justice and Justice, p. 56.) Much like others who view physical child abuse from a family point of view, the Justices suggest that the family system is the arena wherein two basic questions to life must be dealt with: (1) how to be a separate and distinct person and (2) how to belong and have membership in the group. It is the response to these two questions that creates a climate for physical child abuse. If a parent is too involved with a child, the other parent may feel excluded from the attention of the over-involved parent. Stated very simply, this can create a climate for potential child abuse since the parent outside the close relationship believes that it is the child who contributes to the situation. On the other hand, the closeness between the parent and the child may make it very difficult for the child to grow up and become an individual. The child may rebel or ''act out'' in some other ways when the time comes for the child to individuate from the parent. This natural process of individuation may create a climate for the overly close parent to feel or act abusive toward the child. At the other extreme, if the parents are so distant and separate from one another (or their child) that they lack emotional closeness, they may respond to this missing piece by abusing their child out of their own frustration. They may, unknowingly, turn to their child for the emotional nurturing that is missing in the marriage. When the child cannot or does not proovie this emotional nurturing, the parent may physically abuse the child.

A wealth of explanations exist about human behavior, in general, and physical child abuse specifically. It is more productive to draw from this richness rather than be limited by a single explanation. Each has its limitations in explaining physical child abuse, but each also has a special contribution to make to the total picture.

EFFECTS OF PHYSICAL CHILD ABUSE ON THE CHILD AND ON THE FAMILY

How can anyone measure the effects of a tragedy such as physical child abuse? There are innumerable possible short- and long-term consequences to the child, the family, and to the community in general. The nature and extent of the consequences are different for each child.

Immediate Medical Needs

It is important to tend to the immediate medical needs of the physically abused child. Figure 5-2 shows some immediate, physical effects of child abuse. These injuries require immediate attention.

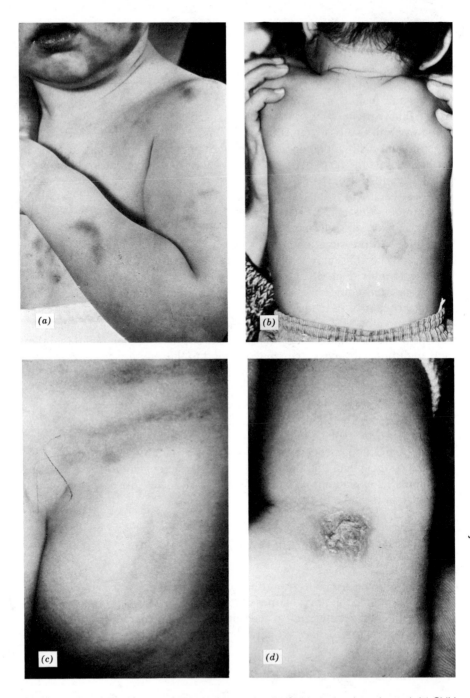

Figure 5-2 Physical Abuse. *(a)* Child with bite marks. *(b)* Child who has been burned. *(c)* Child who has been beaten with a strap. *(d)* Child who has been burned.

"While bruises will fade, burns will heal, and lacerations and welts will rarely lead to permanent impairment, the forms of physical mistreatment for which one must have most concern are those which have the potential to permanently affect the central nervous system. These are injuries which may leave the surviving child with some of the multiple signs of brain damage: seizures, mental retardation, sensory deficits (hearing or visual impairments), cerebral palsy, learning deficits.' (Martin, p. 348.)

Injury-Related Consequences

Anemia, hearing deficits, or poor physical growth may also be the result of the original injury. Researchers have shown that physically mistreated children have poorer developmental prognosis as compared to siblings or matched control groups. (Martin, p. 349.) Children who have been physically abused may later exhibit or develop delay in language development, learning disorders (with either emotional or organic etiology), difficulties in motor abilities, or mental retardation. It is not always possible to predict such problems from the immediate abusive situation and immediate injuries.

Psychological and Emotional Impact

Physical child abuse has psychological and emotional impact on both the perpetrator and the child.[3] The child may lose confidence in his or her ability to effectively cope with life, at least in part as a result of physical assault. Additionally, the child may feel very confused about trusting others, particularly adults, if the child has suffered from physical abuse. The psychological consequences for the child may be dependent upon the interaction of several of the following factors related to the physical abuse.

1. What was the duration of the physical abuse? Was the abuse chronic and of a long and continuing duration or was this an isolated, acute incident?
2. What is the age of the child?
3. What is the developmental task level that the child is dealing with when the physical abuse occurs?
4. What is the nature and extent of the physical injury to the child and what are the long-term medical or physical affects to the child?
5. What is the outcome of the abusive situation? Is the child separated

[3]This topic lacks adequate rigorous study. Intervention and treatment strategies currently in use imply an acceptance of assumptions. Generally, acceptance is based on individual observation, agency policy, and what data is available. If we take a systems position, we can see the possibilities of the material influence of a number of factors. Still, we cannot as yet, predict long term outcomes.

from his or her parents or is the child returned home with assistance from others in alleviating the problems?

6. What are the interactional patterns that the child has developed in situations of long-standing abuse? (Refer back to Chapter 2.)

7. How emotionally stable was the child before the physical abuse? This aspect of the child also considers the stability and functioning level of the family.

8. What is the reaction of the parents, caretakers, and others who are involved in helping the child and the family (doctors, nurses, social workers, child protective services staff, et al.) with the immediate and long-term ramifications of the problem? Do others blame the child or the family or is there acceptance and understanding about the situation with an attitude of expectancy and hope in making changes for both the child and the child's family?

The psychological consequences for the perpetrator also relate to the above conditions. If the physical abuse was an isolated incident and the child is harmed, the parent or caretaker may feel very guilty and may be very motivated to make a change. If, however, the physical abuse has been continued over a long period of time, the parent may feel guilty but may be less willing to seek and accept help in making a change in the interactional patterns within the family and between the parent and the child.

Developmental Issues Revisited

Unlike an infant or very young child who has been sexually abused (but unharmed physically), the infant or young child who has been repeatedly physically abused sustains some sort of pain and physical injury as well as psychological consequences. Infants are completely at the mercy of the world around them. They can do practically nothing for themselves. They rely on their caretakers for food, shelter, warmth, emotional needs, and physical safety. If a child is repeatedly and continuously physically abused during this time, the child may learn that the world cannot be trusted. Since infancy is the developmental period of parent–child bonding, the child may fail to develop a mutually satisfying relationship with his or her parent.

Young toddlers who have been physically abused may feel that they have no control over their lives just at a time in their psychosocial development when they need to achieve some degree of control. Toddlers who are physically abused during toilet training may develop a distorted perception of their own sexuality.

If a young toddler is physically abused and feels that he or she has no control over this fact (and has no coping skills to deal with the physical abuse), the psychological perception of the toddler may well be that "I cannot be in control of my life.'' Some toddlers are physically abused as a part of the process of toilet training which usually occurs during this period. These children may develop distorted perceptions about their sexuality and toilet training.

The preschool-age child who is struggling with the task of initiative and who is physically abused may have difficulty being assertive and asking for and getting what he or she needs and wants from life and from other people. If the physical abuse received by a child during this stage in life is justified by the parent or other caretaker as punishment, the child may easily focus on failures and have difficulty accepting common mistakes. The child at this stage in life is normally able to forget failures quickly and approach what seems desirable with undiminished and accurate direction. ''Initiative adds to autonomy the quality of undertaking, planning and 'attacking' a task for the sake of being active and on the move, where before self-will, more often than not, inspired acts of defiance or, at any rate, protested independence.'' (Erickson, p. 255.)

During the latency period (school-age children), when the child is faced with solving the task of industry, the child learns to find his or her place in the larger world, for examle, school. The child learns to win recognition from others by producing things (schoolwork). The child who experiences physical abuse during this period (beginning at this time or as a continuation from younger childhood) may well give up on the task of industry. Many foster children do poorly in school. It is possible to speculate that these children learned long ago not to venture out and be assertive. This often transfers over into their school performance. Since being a foster child means disruption from a person's home and usually a change in school settings (often several times, even during the foster care experience), this disruption may further add to the difficulties of a child trying to master the experience of school. When a child is worried about events at home (marital discord, violence in the home, or other problems), it is also difficult for the child to concentrate on schoolwork. Success may hinge upon being able to find another significant adult in the school setting who will encourage his/her school efforts.

The period of adolescence is a time for the development of identity, including but not limited to sexual identity. The accomplishment of this task is based on transactions and adaptations along the developmental path. An adolescent who experiences physical abuse in his/her home for the first time during this period, may have better ego strengths (a better self-concept) than the adolescent who has been physically abused for a longer period of time. This teenager may run away or take some assertive action since s/he will probably not feel that s/he is deserving of such behavior on the part of the parent.

In one family, a father and daughter had been living together for years after the death of the girl's mother. The father remarried and the daughter lived with her father and stepmother. The stepmother had three boys who also lived with the family. The stepmother began physically abusing the girl. She immediately told her father, who did not believe his daughter. This man had lived alone for ten years and really wanted this new marriage to work. He told his daughter to try not to provoke her stepmother. When the stepmother heard that the daughter had told her father about the punishment, the stepmother became more incensed and increased her physical assaults on the girl. The stepmother also felt that the teenage girl was spoiled and that she needed some discipline. Finally, out of desperation, the girl ran away from home. In this situation, the girl had a strong, positive self-concept and did not believe that she should have to accept the physical abuse her stepmother was issuing. If the same situation had been one where the mother and daughter had a long-standing physically abusive relationship, the girl might not have been assertive enough to run away from home and seek help.

Help is not always what awaits a youth who runs away from intolerable home situations. Many youths run away from home each year in response to physial and other kinds of abuse. Some youths who try to get away from physically abusive home situations have no place to turn. Returning home may bring more abuse yet the community may have few long term alternatives to offer. During a time of life when the individual is forming an identity, being in an abusive situation and not being able to connect with any help has to be very difficult for the young, developing self-concept.

Physically abusing parents and other caretakers, for the most part, act out of desperation and lack of knowledge about how to better parent their children. The cost of physical abuse is high to them also, particularly in terms of self-respect and self-esteem.

A SITUATION OF PHYSICAL CHILD ABUSE

The case example of Sammy illustrates the difficulty in establishing that harm to a child is nonaccidental. It also illustrates the complexity of the problems and the pain that the family and the child may experience in situations of physical child abuse.

Sammy

Nineteen-year-old Joe was home alone for the afternoon with his son, Sammy, six-weeks-old and his daughter, Malinda, age 3. Joe had been working long hours, many of them overtime at the sawmill. Snow and rain had prevented his working regularly during the winter months, so when an opportunity for overtime came along, Joe jumped at the chance to make extra money for his family.

Joe's nineteen-year-old wife, Molly, was at the market and doing other errands when Sammy began to cry. Joe put Sammy on the couple's bed and began changing his diaper. Molly had not left a supply of diapers in their usual place. Joe went to the other room to get a clean diaper. When Joe returned to the room, little Sammy was on the floor, unconscious. Shocked and frightened, Joe grabbed Sammy and began shaking him. Sammy did not respond. Finally, in desperation, Joe bit Sammy on the forearm. His explanation, later, was that when he was growing up, his mother told him that biting could help a person regain consciousness.

When Molly arrived home, Sammy was lying stiffly in his crib. Molly sensed that something was wrong and rushed Sammy to the doctor. Joe, in the meantime, had begun drinking beer, Joe was known throughout the camp for being a drinker.

After examining Sammy, the doctor assessed that he had brain injuries and would have to be taken to the nearby metropolitan hospital. At the hospital, Sammy was near death. Shunts were placed to drain the fluid from his brain. The doctors notified the police that they suspected this to be a case of child abuse.

The police report noted that Joe was inebriated. The next day, the county attorney's office decided that criminal charges of child abuse would be initiated. Child Protective Services (CPS) was given temporary custody of Sammy by the juvenile court.

No one seemed to believe Joe's story about Sammy falling from the bed. Molly didn't know what to think, but she felt very frightened and alone.

Six weeks later, Sammy was released from the hospital and placed in a foster home. The caseworker chose a foster home that could give Sammy the extra care that he needed to recover. The foster mother was willing to let Molly and Joe visit Sammy in her home. In the beginning, the foster mother asked Joe and Molly little things about Sammy that would help her get to know the baby. Soon the foster mother was telling the couple how to raise Sammy and implying that they were guilty of the charges that were pending. The foster mother had increasing difficulty even seeing the parents since Sammy did not seem to be responding in the ways that would be normal for a ten-week-old infant. The doctor suspected that he would be mentally retarded as a result of the injuries.

Joe's co-workers were openly critical of Joe. Newspaper and radio stories about the incident appeared throughout the state. Molly's parents, who had never approved of the young couple marrying, had called Molly and told her to bring Malinda and come home before Joe hurt her. Molly was confused. She avoided her family. Joe became more and more withdrawn. Although he made many efforts, he had difficulty getting an appointment with his court-appointed public defender. Joe and Molly began fighting over little things and Molly began crying more and more. Malinda, who had always been an easy-going child, became cranky, demanding attention. Joe responded by swatting her. Joe's actions increased Molly's fears and seemed to confirm her suspicions about what really happened with Sammy.

Sammy's story underlines the difficulties encountered in cases of suspected physical abuse. The problems for Joe and Molly have only begun. No one knows for certain how serious or long-term Sammy's injuries are. The outcome of the criminal charges against Joe is unknown. It is possible that Joe will be sent to prison. Should that occur, Molly may have to live with her parents to survive financially. Malinda is still another problem. Her behavior is difficult for her parents to handle especially when complicated by the many other problems they face.

Given the nature and extent of the injuries to Sammy, Joe's story, and the circumstances in which it was told, the hospital staff, police, and CPS had no choice but to suspect child abuse. Even though CPS chose a loving foster home for Sammy when he was discharged from the hospital, the choice to put Sammy into a foster home placement may have created additional problems for both Sammy and his family. Sammy's attachment to his parents could be interrupted by his removal from the home.

It is also possible that Sammy could have had difficulty with the many transitions he experienced during this short period of time. Sammy was only six-weeks-old at the time of his injury and ten-weeks-old when he was placed in the foster home. Over one-third of his life has already been spent in transitions.

Neighbors and friends reported that Molly and Joe had a happy, loving marriage before the incident of the alleged child abuse. Certainly in the weeks following the hospitalization and release of Sammy, the couple experienced turmoil in their lives. Would this turmoil have occurred if the allegations had not been made?

In Sammy's case, the damage is already great. No matter what decision is made in criminal court, the emotional and physical injuries to Sammy are real. It may be difficult for Joe and Molly to ever again have the kind of marriage and family that they might want, particularly, if Sammy were returned home and was severely mentally retarded. Unless this family receives some outside assistance now, their difficulties will probably increase.

Elaine

Five year old Elaine was a "handful" from the moment she was born. Elaine's mother, Laura, was disappointed that Elaine was not a boy. Elaine's father deserted her mother days after Elaine's birth. Elaine had colic and was not an easy baby to care for.

Laura believed that it was important to be firm with children so that the child would not become headstrong. Her parents had raised her by the adage of "spare the rod and spoil the child." Laura believed that this was an important way to guide children.

When Elaine was two years old and Laura was trying to toilet train her, Elaine repeatedly said "no" to her mother when asked whether she had to use the toilet. Each time, Elaine would wet or soil her diapers. Laura was furious. After the third incident, she told Elaine that she was a bad girl and that she would be punished if she ever did that again. The next time that Elaine said "no" and then wet her pants, Laura sat Elaine down on the hot heater grate to teach her a lesson. She did not hold Elaine long on the heater grate, but the lesson apparently was learned, Elaine became toilet trained after that.

By the time Elaine entered kindergarten, she and Laura had a very poor relationship. Elaine was punished frequently by Laura to "keep her in tow." Laura commonly used a belt to discipline Elaine. One day when she was spanking her with the belt, Elaine moved, and the belt slashed across Elaine's arm leaving a welt. The next day in school, Elaine's teacher asked her what had happened to her arm. When Elaine explained, the teacher called the school nurse who subsequently called child protective services.

Laura was disappointed when Elaine was born. Her disappointtment was twofold: First, Elaine was a girl, not a boy; second, Laura's husband left the small family during a difficult time. Elaine grew up in an emotionally and physically abusive home. By the time she reached school age, Elaine did not have a positive self-concept. She not only repeatedly heard her mother tell her she was worthless, but she also received continual physical abuse with the explanation that this was necessary to help Elaine be a better girl.

Elaine was untrusting of other people. She had never learned to trust her mother, her main caretaker. This is an example of physical child abuse that may have escalated or at least continued on into Elaine's adolescence. In this situation, if Elaine and her mother get some counseling, positive changes may occur for both mother and daughter.

Summary

Physical child abuse is a major social problem. It is not exactly like any other form of child maltreatment. Parents have a capacity for physical abuse of their children just as they have a capacity to love their children. Straus found that violence tends to be high in families where people have learned to respond to stress and family problems by using violence. Even in such cases, violence is not an automatic response to stress. "One also has to believe that the problem is amenble to a . . . violent solution." (Straus, p. 100.)

Although there are many proposed explanations for physical child abuse, none seems totally complete without some consideration of the others. A child who has been physically abused may experience both short and long-term effects of the abuse. Consequences may be dependent upon the interaction of a number of factors. Consequences are also experienced by the perpetrator, by all those who interact with the family, and, more generally, by society at large. The nature and extent of the consequences vary with each experience and each child.

BIBLIOGRAPHY

Bolton, F., Kane, Sandra P., and Kruse, Roger F. *Child Abuse: Our Problem, Too.* Arizona Dept. of Education and Arizona Dept. of Economic Security, July, 1979.

Erikson, Erik H. *Childhood and Society.* W.W. Norton, New York, 1963.

Fisher, Bruce, Berdie, Jan, Cook, Jo Ann and Day, Noel. *Adolescent Abuse and Neglect: Intervention Strategies.* U.S. Dept. of Health and Human Service, DHHS No (OHDS) 80-30266, January, 1980.

Floyd, Louise. "A Model For Assisting High-Risk Families in Neonatal Nurturing." CWLA, LX:9, November 1981, 637–643.

Gelles, R.J. "Child Abuse as Psychopathology: A Sociological Critique and Reformulation." *American Journal of Orthopsychiatry. 43,* 1973, 611–621.

Gil, David G. *Child Abuse and Violence.* AMS Press Inc., New York, 1979.

Helfer, Ray E. *Child Abuse and Neglect: The Diagnostic Process and Treatment.* Department of Health, Education and Welfare, U.S. Government Printing Office, Washington, D.C., 1976.

Helfer, Ray E. "Developmental Deficits Which Limit Interpersonal Skills." In Kempe, C. Henry and Helfer, Ray E., Eds. *The Battered Child.* 3rd ed. University of Chicago Press, Chicago, 1980, pp. 36–48.

Helfer, Ray E. and Kempe, C. Henry. "The Child's Need for Early Recognition, Immediate Care and Protection." In Kempe, C. Henry and Helfer, Ray E., Eds. *Helping The Battered Child and His Family.* Lippincott, Philadelphia, 1972.

Justice, Blair and Justice, Rita. The Abusing Family. Human Sciences Press, New York, 1976.

Korsch, B. M., Christian, J. B., Gozzi, E. K., and Carlson, P. V. "Infant Care and Punishment: A Pilot Study." *American Journal of Public Health. 55,* 1965, 1880–1888.

Martin, Harold P. "The Consequences of Being Abused and Neglected: How the Child Fares." In Kempe, C. Henry and Helfer, Ray E., Eds. *The Battered Child.* 3rd Ed. University of Chicago Press, Chicago, 1980.

Mayhall, Pamela and Norgard, Katherine. *Foster Parenting the Abused and Neglected Child.* Pima Community College, Advanced Foster Care Project, Tucson, Arizona, 1980.

McFadden, E.J. (Patricia Ryan, Series Editor) *Fostering the Battered and Abused Child.* Foster Parent Training Project, Eastern Michigan University, 1978.

Minuchin, Salvador. *Families and Family Therapy.* Harvard University Press, Cambridge, MA, 1974.

National Study of the Incidence and Severity of Child Abuse & Neglect, NCCAN, (OHDS) 81-30325.

Rader, Dotson. "Runaways." *Parade*. Feb. 7, 1982, p 6−8.

Satir, Virginia. *Peoplemaking*. Science and Behavior Books, Inc., Palo Alto, CA, 1972.

Schmitt, Barton D. "The Battered Child Syndrome." In Touloukian, Robert J., Ed. *Pediatric Trauma*. John Wiley, New York, 1978.

Schmitt, Barton D. "The Child with Nonaccidental Trauma."In Kempe, C. Henry and Helfer, Ray E., Eds. *The Battered Child*. 3rd ed. University of Chicago Press, Chicago, 1980.

Segal, Julius, and Yahraes, Herbert. *A Child's Journey: Forces That Shape the Lives of Our Young*. McGraw−Hill, New York, 1979.

Shapiro, Deborah. *Parents and Protectors—A Study in Child Abuse and Neglect*. Research Center, Child Welfare League of America, New York, 1979.

Steele, Brandt F. *Working with Abusive Parents from a Psychiatric Point of View*. U.S. Dept. Of Health, Education and Welfare, OHO 76-30076, no date.

Steele, B. F. and Pollock, C. B. "A Psychiatric Study of Parents Who Abuse Infants and Small Children. In R. E. Helfer and C. H. Kempe, Eds. *The Battered Child*. The University of Chicago Press, Chicago, 1968.

Straus, Murray A. "Stress and Child Abuse." *The Battered Child*. 3rd ed. Edited by Kempe, C. Henry and Helfer, Ray E. The University of Chicago Press, Chicago, 1980, pp. 86−103.

CHAPTER 6

Child Neglect

PREVALENCE OF CHILD NEGLECT

In an interview with the authors, Hunter Hurst of the National Center for Juvenile Justice in Pennsylvania stated that discussion of child abuse generates feelings of hysteria, particularly, discussion of sexual or physical abuse. However, as Hurst notes, neglect, which may actually be more deadly to the child, does not generate the same level of concern.

Interviews across the nation with child protection service caseworkers during 1980 indicated that cases of child neglect are given a lower priority than sexual or physical abuse. Not only are these cases difficult to define, but there are a lack of resources available to help the children and the families. Why open a case on a child if there is no way to help? In times of diminishing availability of social services, food, clothing, and shelter options, neglect may become more prevalent.

One difficulty in determining statistical evidence about child neglect is that unlike abuse, neglect is difficult to document. Also, the abused generally receives sympathy for the tragic experience. The child who is neglected may not receive the same support from the community, and may, in fact, be shunned, treated as an outcast, or ignored.

Statistics resulting from nationwide surveys indicate that the numbers of neglect cases are far greater than those of abuse. The American Humane Association indicates that their analysis of the National Reports of Child

Abuse and Neglect (1980 data) showed 30% to be abuse only, 48% to be neglect only, 18% to be a combination of abuse and neglect, and 4% other. Sixty-one percent of substantiated reports involved the deprivation of necessities or in other words, neglect. (AHA, 1980.)

Cantwell reports that deaths resulting from child neglect outnumbered the number of deaths from child abuse in Denver in the last decade. (Cantwell, p. 183.) These deaths were related to situations where the child was unattended in the home. AHA data indicates that 43% of child fatalities were associated with deprivation of necessities.

Certainly all indicators point to an extremely high correlation between reported neglect (and abuse) and family income. This could be in part an artifact of our reporting systems but as more and more evidence indicates such a relationship with unreported cases as well, it is impossible to ignore this factor. Giovannoni (1971) found more neglect families had lower status positions, lower incomes, and lower levels of education than abusive families.

Such a statement, however, should not be read as an inference that neglect only occurs in lower-income families, nor, conversely, that all lower-income families neglect their children. Neglect is found in all income levels. The following situation, for example, was not reported as neglect although it meets the criteria for neglect in many states.

A social worker and a doctor left their home in the fashionable suburbs of a metropolitan area six or seven times a year for weekend trips. They left their two sons, ages 9 and 11, unattended. They felt satisfied in the level of supervision that they left behind; they provided the boys with a telephone number of a close family friend who lived ten miles away. The close family friend felt concern about the lack of supervision of these young boys. However, she made no report to anyone because she felt this would create problems for the boys' parents. Although this situation did not result in serious injury to the boys, the risk to them was great.

DEFINING NEGLECT

Definitions of neglect change with culture and time. States and jurisdictions do not commonly define neglect and often leave its specific definition to protective service practice. Neglect is relatively easy to define in broad terms, but is much more difficult to define in specific criteria that meet the requirements of clear, concise, and common as discussed in Chapter 4.

Essentially, parents or caretakers are expected to adequately provide for a child's basic needs. Failure to provide minimal care to the extent that a hazard exists to the child's health or safety constitutes neglect. How is hazard defined? Possible harm? Demonstrated harm? Harm to what degree?

The complexity of the problem of definition can be demonstrated in the question of adequate supervision. Criteria regarding adequate supervision varies from jurisdiction to jurisdiction and in relation to the child's age, competence, length of time unsupervised, the structure of that time, etc. Is a single mother who leaves her 10-year-old daughter alone at home from midnight until 8 AM because the mother works that shift neglecting her child?

There are literally thousands of children under the age of 13 in the United States, who look after themselves daily without any adult supervision for extended and regular periods of time each day, some in daytime hours and others at night. Latch key children carry a house key around their necks so that they can let themselves in after school or they may be children who get locked in the house while their parents are away.

In the interest of clarity and conciseness, our choice of definition of child neglect from those currently available, is that utilized by the National Incidence Study. A situation of neglect was said to exist if it could be shown that ". . . as a result of extreme parent/caretaker inattention to the child's basic needs for care, protection or control . . ." the child experienced foreseeable injury or impairment of serious or greater severity. NIS required that two questions be answered yes before a case of possible neglect could be included in their study.

(a) Had the caretaker been informed of the child's need or problem by a competent professional, or, under the circumstances of the situation, would the child's need have been apparent to most reasonably caring and attentive adults?

(b) Was the parent/caretaker physically and financially able to obtain or provide the needed care, protection, or supervision?

Although in some cases inherent injury was assumed (as in abandonment or refusal of custody of child), harm generally had to be demonstrated through overt serious injury to the child before neglect was considered substantiated. Neglect in the NIS study included the categories of physical neglect (including abandonment), educational neglect, and emotional neglect.

Minimum standards of care in the NIS definition are categorically similar to those used in many jurisdictions. They differ, however, from most in that they require that the child already be seriously harmed. They omit the area referred to in Chapter 4 as "protection from probable harm." Prevention and protection from possible harm is not considered at all. As discussed in Chapter 4, many jurisdictions are narrowing definitions of neglect, especially restricting when coercive intervention can take place. However, they rarely require that serious harm be demonstrated before formal response occurs.

Although there is some consensus about what constitutes minimally adequate child care, because of the nature of American society there are limitations as to what professionals can do about neglectful parents; laws protect these families from unreasonable intrusion. (Hally et al., p. 2.)

INDICATORS OF CHILD NEGLECT

Indicators suggesting possible child neglect may be physical, emotional, and/or behavioral. In the interest of good citizenship, it is important for each of us to be alert to these cues. It is even more imperative that we be aware of the signs of neglect more than other forms of child abuse because child neglect may be given a lower priority by the child protection services and may therefore require the greatest sense of shared responsibility to help resolve the problem. Possible physical indicators include:

1. Consistent and regular hunger.
2. Unkempt physical appearance, poor hygiene, and inappropriate dress.
3. Consistent lack of supervision: engaging in dangerous activities for long periods of time.
4. Unattended physical problems or unmet medical needs.
5. Abandonment (''Push-outs''—involuntary emancipation). (Adapted, Lauer et al., p. 10.)

Possible behavioral indicators of child neglect include:

1. Begging for and/or stealing food. Withdrawal from the peer group.
2. Extended stay at school, in public places, or at a neighbor's house.
3. Undue fatigue, listlessness, falling asleep at times that inappropriate, or other obvious medical signs.
4. Alcohol or drug abuse, delinquency, child tells you that there is no caretaker. (Adapted, Lauer et al., p. 10.)

Emotional neglect is discussed in relation to emotional abuse in Chapter 7. Some of the possible emotional indicators of child neglect include:

1. Extreme affect (excessive sadness or inappropriate happiness.)
2. Undue anxiety or extreme focus on basic survival needs.

Neglect During Infancy

Children may exhibit different symptoms of neglect at different times in their development. Infants are the least able of any age group to verbalize situations of neglect. If an infant's head is flattened and his/her hair rubbed off from what might be excessive lying in the crib, neglect may be suspected. An infant with poor weight gain, unresponsiveness for his/her age group, a flabby musculature (possibly from lying in the crib too much) may be neglected. These symptoms at least require further investigation. The infant is probably the most vulnerable to harm from child neglect of all age groups since the margin of safety is less for an infant than for any other age group. If the infant does not have adequate stimulation, food, or shelter, the infant is less able to obtain these necessities independently of the caretaker.

Parents or other caretakers may find that infants are easy targets for neglect, since they have a limited repertoire for making their needs known. Physical care, emotional nurturing, and intellectual stimulation are all important elements of growth for infants. Neglectful parents and caretakers disregard the infant's needs in all or part of these areas.

Neglect During the Preschool Period

Preschool children are also vulnerable to child neglect. Since preschool children are often in day care or Headstart programs, symptoms of neglect may be more easily observed by persons outside the family. Caretakers of children must be alert to continuing signs of possible neglect. Neglect tends to be chronic rather than episodic. Where neglect is suspected, the following questions are particularly useful in clarifying symptoms.

1. Do the indicators of possible child neglect occur rarely or frequently?
2. Are they chronic (present most of the time), periodic (noticeable after weekends or absences), or episodic (seen twice during a period when there was illness in the family)?
3. In a given community or subpopulation, do all or only a few of the children display these symptoms?
4. Is this culturally acceptable child rearing, a different life style, or true neglect? (Broadhurst, p. 17.)

Possible indicators or symptoms of child neglect during this period are constant hunger, poor hygiene, or inappropriate clothing, for example, lack of a coat or jacket during the winter. Consistent lack of supervision, constant fatigue or listlessness, and unattended physical or medical needs are other possible indicators.

Neglect During the School-Age Period

Thumb-sucking, nail-biting, bad teeth, difficulty in reading large print on the blackboard, and other symptoms are suggestive of child neglect of the school-age child. The child who appears to be excessively dependent may require the security of an adult's attention because it is absent at home. Children who seem to live excessively in fantasy worlds, are shy, depressed, noncommunicative, or passive may be exhibiting symptoms of neglect.

Neglect During Preadolescence and Adolescence

Preadolescents and adolescents may be misunderstood and mislabeled as delinquents or trouble-makers when in actuality, s/he may be neglected. These children may, in fact, only be struggling to meet their own basic physical needs or the needs of a younger sibling. It is imperative that we not over respond to children who appear to be incorrigible or delinquent until we have first investigated the possibility of neglect. Sometimes, out of wanting to protect their parents or out of sheer embarrassment, the child may be unable to verbally articulate the experience of neglect to authorities.

DISTINGUISHING FEATURES OF CHILD NEGLECT

Even though abuse and neglect are often discussed together in the literature, it is important to note that not only are the definitions of the two different, but the distinguishing features are generally different. Also, the two do not necessarily occur simultaneously within the same family.

Physically abusive families are often cited as engaging in unhealthy, dysfunctional interactional patterns. These familial patterns can ultimately contribute to situations of physical or sexual abuse. (Justice; Kaufman; Norgard.) Parents are the architects or leaders in a family unit and as such, are largely responsible for the creation of the interactional patterns within the family. Since the parents are the family's architects, they share responsibility for neglect that occurs within the family.

Leontine Young's classic study holds that there are some marked differences between abusing and neglecting families. According to Young, only a small number of children who are neglected are also abused. "Whereas abusive parents typically restrict the child's social experiences outside the home, neglectful parents do not actively forbid such attachments. Nor is the neglectful parent so prone to derogatory remarks about his child." (Polansky et al., p. 3.) The fact that neglecting parents do not forbid outside connections and relationships for their child may actually shield the child from some of the emotional side-effects of neglect. (Polansky et al., p. 3.) Segal emphasized in his discussion of the invulnerable child that part of the child's strength appears to be in emotional connections with people outside the family. (This may be a teacher, a boy scout leader, or other person.) (Segal, p. 282; see also Chapter 4.)

Hally, Polansky, and Polansky determined in their work that neglectful parents have certain characteristics that are different from non-neglectful parents. Neglectful parents are seen as less involved with others, less able to plan, less able to control impulses, less confident about their future; less verbally accessible; and less equipped with a sense of workmanship. Further, they are seen as more plagued by psychological and psychosomatic symptoms, socially isolated both formally and informally, and isolated from informal helping networks. Also, neglectful parents are described as scoring lower on intelligence tests and higher on a scale for anomie, the state of being without norms. (Hally et al., p. 10.) Other studies indicate the importance of environmental factors such as inadequate housing and insufficient incomes. (Giovannoni 1971; AHA, 1978.)

Leon Pelton states, "Both evidence and reason lead to the unmistakable conclusion that contrary to the myth of classlessness, child abuse and neglect are strongly related to poverty, in terms of prevalence and severity of consequences." (Pelton, 1981.) A compilation of studies suggests that even though child neglect occurs across socio-economic boundaries, neglecting families are more likely to be the "poorest of the poor." Further, ". . . if parental personality plays a major role in determining how much income is available as well as how it is handled, then programs aimed simply at increasing income will not solve the problem of neglect." (Polansky, 1981.) Polansky observes that although the quality of child care is tied adversely to poverty, child care is also separable from poverty. (p. 80.)

Another important distinguishing feature is the conviction of some researchers that neglectful parents are well aware of values about child rearing common among parents of similar socio-economic status. (Polansky, 1981, p. 25.) Therefore, parents who neglect their children do so for reasons other than divergent values, although they seem not to be practicing the child-rearing values of their particular social group.

Mothers are usually the primary physical and psychological caretakers of infants and children. National data show that biological mothers are almost twice as likely to be the neglecting parent than biological fathers. Biological mothers also have a higher percentage of likelihood of being the neglecting caretaker over any other category of caretaker (stepmother, mother/father substitute, et al.) (NIS, p. 31.) Further, the data indicates that the mother/substitute was the only involved adult for 34% of the children in the sample population, the father/substitute was the only adult involved in 13% of the cases, and both parents/substitutes were directly involved in 41% of the cases. (NIS, p. 32.)

Data from AHA shows that single-parent families are on the rise in the U.S. population and the majority of these families are headed by females. Case data (1980) indicated that almost half of the neglected children reside in single-parent, female-headed families. Single-parent mothers are overrepresented as neglecting parents (AHA, p. 36), but they may also be more vulnerable to the scrutiny of the system, to reporting, and to many of the factors that seem to be correlated with neglect.

Most studies indicate that neglect is more likely to occur in large families than in small families, a characteristic that is not shared with most other types of maltreatment.

ADOLESCENT NEGLECT

Although child neglect can and does occur at every developmental stage, adolescent neglect has some special features. Some neglect begins in infancy or early childhood and prevails into the adolescent years. Neglect may, however, only emerge during adolescence. Family difficulties that arise from conflicts of adolescent and middlescent (midlife) development can result in physical neglect of the youth. (Fisher et al., p. 45.) Fisher et al. suggest two patterns that contribute to adolescent neglect. First, parents literally "give up" their parental responsibilities toward the youth during adolescence, at a time when the adolescent is struggling toward the mastery of internalization of control and identity formation. In some situations, physical abuse may precede the actual neglect. The parents reach a point where they decide that they can no longer effectively discipline the youth. Juvenile court workers are very familiar with this type of child neglect. Children are often turned over to the authority of the court because the parents feel unable to manage their child. These children are often labeled "incorrigible" and the parents often may refuse to participate in the problem-solving process. In these cases, the parents move from a stance of wanting to nurture and control their child to a position of what is described as "self-protection" from further feelings of failure or disappointment.

The second type of adolescent neglect arises from situational factors. The parents may be reacting to their own situational factors (life crisis) which lead them to withdraw emotionally or physically from their child. One problem faced by increasing numbers of adults is divorce. When a parent is in the midst of a divorce, he or she (or both of them) may turn complete attention to "starting a new life." Sometimes starting a new life means returning to dating, finding a new career, learning new skills, returning to school, moving to a new location, or moving to a new neighborhood. Often, people in the midst of an emotional crisis such as a divorce feel very alienated and isolated from former familiar networks of family and friends and they are desperately trying to seek new connections with other people. The adolescent whose parents have divorced may suffer both physical and emotional neglect through improper supervision and inadequate nurturance. (Fisher et al., p. 46.) A crisis is always defined in the eye of the beholder. For some people, a divorce is not a crisis. For others, just the fact of growing older, facing illness, or other changes in life creates a crisis that detracts from the emotional energy necessary to relate to and supervise an adolescent family member.

FORMS OF CHILD NEGLECT

The forms of child neglect that commonly occur within the context of the family include:

Abandonment: This is defined as leaving a young child unattended or inadequately supervised for excessively long periods of time. An example of abandonment is where parents or other caretakers leave children home for long periods of time or where parents totally abandon or desert a child.

Lack of supervision: This is defined as a failure of the caretaker to adequately account for the child's actions and whereabouts. Lack of supervision exists when a very young child wanders into the street or when the child accidentally ingests poisonous substances. The television slogan "It's 10 PM, do you know where your children are?" is a question for parents of teenagers relating to the issue of neglect.

Nutritional Neglect: This is defined as both a failure of the caretaker to provide sufficient quantities of food and failure to provide an acceptable quality of diet, that is, appropriate nutrients. Nutritional neglect might exist when a caretaker provides so little food to a child that the child suffers from malnutrition. (The failure-to-thrive syndrome is a special type of nutritional/psychological neglect that will be discussed in more detail.)

Medical and Dental Neglect: This is defined as a failure of the caretaker to recognize and act to resolve medical and dental problems and other appropriate treatment needs. An example of medical neglect is the child whose caretaker fails to obtain eyeglasses for a badly cross-eyed child after repeatedly having been informed by school or other officials that the child requires glasses.

Educational Neglect: This is defined as a failure to provide for a child's educational development. For example, if a caretaker refuses to permit the child to attend school and makes no alternative provisions for the child's education, educational neglect may be said to exist. The most often identified problem of educational neglect is "permitted chronic truancy." (NIS, p. 24.) To be chronically truant, a student must miss an average of five days a month. If there is evidence that the parents were notified of the problem but did not attempt to alter the child's behavior, the truancy is said to be "permitted."

Inappropriate or Insufficient Clothing: This is defined as a failure by the caretakers to provide minimum quantity and quality of clothing to a child. An example of clothing neglect is a child whose clothes are unwashed, torn, or inadequate to protect the child from the elements of the weather such as rain or cold.

Shelter Neglect: This is defined as a caretaker's failure to provide basic minimum standards of adequate shelter, for example, space, heat, indoor plumbing, electricity, structural adequacy, and sanitation. Shelter neglect might exist when the child has to live in a building that has inadequate heating or is unsafe because electrical wires are exposed.

Hygiene Neglect: This is defined as the caretaker's failure to properly clean the child. The infant or young child may appear smelly or dirty.

Failure-to-thrive (FTT): This is a special category of child neglect. This syndrome of child neglect is more common among infants and young children. Older children who suffer from severe growth retardation without physical disease are often referred to as cases of psychosocial dwarfish. (Kempe et al., p. 178.) The older child in these cases seems to be a child who lives in a multiproblem family that has severe emotional problems that center on the one child. (Also refer to Chapter 3.)

EXPLANATIONS OF CHILD NEGLECT

No Single Explanation

There is no single cause and effect explanation for child neglect. A myriad of explanations and combinations of explanations exist to explain this social problem. The explanations range from individual characteristics and psychopathology to severe incidences of emotional and situational pressures.

Four categories of explanations are used to understand and explain child neglect.

1. *Individual characteristics.* Every individual has unique characteristics such as physical health, mental health, intelligence, personality, and previous life experiences (such as previous maltreatment). These are the most constant influences on our behavior.

2. *Attitudes and values.* Each culture and subculture within the major culture has attitudes and values. Each of us has attitudes and values about children, family roles, violence, punishment, economic and social competition, and religion to name a few. Each family also has a set of family values and attitudes that must be understood in order to be able to understand child neglect within a particular family.

3. *Specific life situations.* Situational forces that may be either chronic or acute affect parents' relationships with their children. Marital relationships, employment situations, extended family members, housing conditions, financial security, and social contact are common stresses that affect parenting.

4. *General community welfare.* Businesses, schools, police, fire departments, and religious institutions are a few social institutions that define the general community welfare. The condition of the general community welfare impacts on the issue of child neglect within a particular family. Society's institutions make up the general community welfare and may be supportive or nonsupportive to the parents and to the children. They may contribute to neglect.

Any of the factors mentioned can have either a positive or a negative effect on the occurrence of child neglect. Child neglect is most likely to occur when there is a combination of negative forces affecting the family. (Lauer, p. 5.)

Lack of Knowledge

Neglectful parenting can also be understood and attributed to the parents' lack of knowledge, lack of understanding, and lack of motivation. Some parents have a lack of knowledge about child development and the basic needs of children at various stages of child development. If a parent lacks knowledge or judgment, the parent may not realize that certain things must be done that the child cannot do for him/herself. (An example of this would be supervision of a young child.) Motivational problems occur when parents refuse to make necessary changes to improve their parenting practices or lifestyles for the benefit of the child. (Kempe, p. 184.)

Kadushin's Formulation

Alfred Kadushin noted three principal factors that seem to be associated with child neglect: (1) Low socio-economic status, (2) One-parent family structure, (3) A large number of children. (Kadushin, pp. 222–228.) Further, Dr. Kadushin noted that a common causative factor shared by both neglecting and abusing parents is "emotional immaturity." The definition of "emotional immaturity" includes a lack of impulse control, inability to love or feel genuine concern about the welfare and needs of another person, an inability to learn from previous experience, and difficulty in making long-range plans. These attributes may result, according to Dr. Kadushin, from poor and instable love relationships during the childhood of the neglecting parent. (Kadushin p. 222.)

Kadushin Questioned

Giovannoni and Billingsley do not agree with Kadushin's ideas about the explanation of child neglect. They claim that Kadushin's studies may have been biased in that they compared neglectful families to the general population which may lead to spurious associations because of the compounding of low-income status, neglectful status, and family patterns. (Giovannoni, p. 171.) Their study, which compared non-neglecting with neglecting parents from low-income backgrounds and similar ethnic backgrounds had five important suggested outcomes: (1) The early family life of neglecting parents was not significantly different from the early family life of non-neglecting parents; (2) high level of stress was a major factor in the neglect of children; (3) neglecting parents seemed to be alienated and disconnected from their extended family network with resulting impoverishment of relationships; (4) neglecting mothers differed from non-neglecting mothers primarily in their acceptance of and in the meeting of the dependency needs of their young children; (5) it was important to understand and evaluate families within the ethnic context. (Giovannoni, p. 176.)

Unwanted-Child – Bonding Issues

Some authors suggest that many neglected children are unwanted children and the parent has dealt with this initial problem. Lack of parent–child bonding is another factor attributed to parental neglect of children. Some obstetricians can detect the likelihood of attachment problems in the last trimester of a mother's pregnancy. A mother may exhibit increasing apprehension, fear of a painful delivery, and perception of her body as distorted and unattractive. In addition, there are signs in the delivery room of possible disturbed maternal attachment that include mothers who see their infants as unattractive, mothers who let the infant's head dangle without proper support, mothers who avoid eye contact with their infants, mothers who do not "coo" or talk to their babies, and mothers who cannot seem to find in their infant any physical or psychological characteristics that they value in themselves.

Failure-To-Thrive Syndrome

The major explanation for the FTT syndrome is a disorder in maternal attachment. (Segal, p. 81.) Potential explanations for this lack of attachment or bonding process include early deprivations in the life of the mother, events during the pregnancy that make it difficult to attach to the new baby, events around the birth of the child that make it difficult to attach (prematurity, acute illness of either mother or infant, congenital defects, or disruptions caused by the doctors or nurses), and current life events such as marital strain, financial stress, or substance abuse of alcohol or drugs. (Segal, p. 83.)

Personality Types

Polansky et al. have classified five prevalent types of personalities that are most frequently observed in mothers in situations of child neglect: (1) apathetic–futile mother; (2) the impulse-ridden mother; (3) the mentally retarded mother; (4) the mother in a reactive depression; and (5) the psychotic mother. (Polansky, p. 21.) In our discussion of these explanations, we would like to expand the discussion to include fathers and other possible caretakers of children.

Apathetic–Futile Personality

A person with an apathetic–futile personality shows very little reaction either to the way that he/she lives or what happens to him/her. This person, according to Polansky's description, gives the appearance that nothing is wrong. There seems to be a lack of emotional bonding between this person and anyone else. There is a pervasive emotional numbness about the person. This person represents what Dreikurs called the person with "assumed disability." (Dreikurs, p. 63.) In other words, when other people are around this person, they begin to believe in the person's emotional disability and expect less of that person. Dreikurs described this person as one who has completely given up and feels that there is no opportunity for success. This person then becomes completely helpless and uses this emotional posture as a way of avoiding any task that may lead to failure. The personality characteristics of this person are explained as having originated in the infant–parent relationship as a result of severe deprivation on the part of the infant. Often a person who has apathetic–futile characteristics is a person who was treated similarly during childhood (in the same way he/she is treating his/her infant or child.)

Children who grow up in homes where one or both of the major caretakers fits the apathetic–futile characteristics will not suffer from the physical absence of a parent or caretaker because the person will be physically present. However, the children in these homes do not have the opportunity to learn how to form meaningful, affectionate relationships with adults and may have trouble learning this skill with children and adults outside the home situation.

Impulse-Ridden Personality

The second explanation for child neglect is parents who have impulse-ridden personalities. These parents are the antithesis of the apathetic–futile parent. They are restless and rebellious. These parents may have periods when they function as mature, adequate parents even though they may have a low threshold for stress and frustration.

The main difficulty experienced by children of these parents is that they may not have the consistent limits and boundaries that are so necessary to growing up and ultimately achieving internal control themselves. "Controls enter the personality by moving from the outside inside." (Polansky, p. 29.) These children may need special protection from the impulsiveness of their parent in addition to needing external controls if their parents are unable to provide these.

Mentally Retarded Parent

A parent who is mentally retarded is not necessarily going to be a parent who will be neglectful of his or her child. However, the extent of the retardation will play a significant role in the abilities of the person to parent. Since the parent who is retarded in the borderline or below category (IQ 63 and below) has limited cognitive abilities, he or she may not be able to adequately care for an infant or a child. If a child is deprived of cognitive stimulation, the child will most likely have difficulties in school, in social situations, and in language development.

Abilities and potentials vary widely among people who are classified as mentally retarded. Some intelligence guidelines place people in the borderline mentally retarded category if their IQ's range between 68–83. (Polansky, p. 33.) Adults who function in this borderline range of intelligence may function at earlier developmental levels than their adult counterparts. However, many mentally retarded people function as loving and adequate parents with support of outside persons and services. Some possible indicators of mental retardation include illiteracy, inability to tell time or count change, and thinking patterns that are characterized by rigidity and concreteness.

Reactive Depression

Most people suffer some form of loss (employment, death, divorce, physical relocation, or other trauma) during the period that they are parenting young children. However, most people are able to give the sadness its due and get on with life after a period of mourning. Some people have a severe, reactive depression as a result of such a loss that may physically and/or emotionally impair their functioning. These persons may have persistent moods of despair and hopelessness. In these cases, parenting may show a dramatic, sharp change from what it was before the person became depressed. "A mother suffering from reactive depression may expose her children to all the hazards of child neglect." (Polansky, p. 44.)

Children who have parents who are depressed for long periods of time may receive a legacy of guilt and constrictedness. The child may also be physically neglected since the parent does not have the energy to fulfill the role of parent.

Psychotic Parent

The psychotic parent may suffer from serious defects in personality. These people may be "out of contact" with reality at certain times. A person who has so much personal difficulty in keeping track of reality will have a difficult time parenting children. The two major groupings of psychosis are thought disorders and mood disorders. Some possible symptoms of psychotic process are social withdrawal, loss of contact, inappropriateness of mood, bizarre behaviors, disturbances in the train of thought, delusional systems, hallucinations, or severe anxiety. (Polansky, p. 49.)

An Interplay of Explanations

After examining hundreds of case histories of child neglect, the authors believe that it is possible that all of the above factors interplay in their relationship to child neglect. There is no single or simple answer to the explanation of child neglect. To date, no study has shown a clear cause and effect relationship between a single factor and child neglect.

Child neglect cannot be predicted even if an assessment of the conditions discussed in this section is made. Unexplainable and unpredictable factors always exist which positively or negatively influence the possibility of child neglect. Sometimes an external condition such as war plays an important role in the possibility of child neglect. The Vietnam conflict created this condition for hundreds of cases of child neglect; children went without shelter, food, or emotional support. It does not necessarily follow that their parents fit in any of the categories discussed in this chapter, rather a horrifying external event created a situation for massive child neglect.

From the previous paragraphs, it is possible to see how child neglect affects the child both in specific and in general ways. Child neglect affects the rest of us as well. If a child does not have adequate shelter, nourishment, or food, the rest of the community needs to respond. Responding in time, before more lasting damage has been done to the child, is critical. When response comes "too late," the cost in human lives as well as dollars can be major. Early response and assistance to the child and the family may prevent the necessity of removing the child from the home. Care of children is financially expensive to the community and psychologically expensive to the child and the family. The long-term consequence of out-of-home care for a child may be the difficulty or impossibility of ever reuniting children and parents.

It is our premise that parents want to be adequate parents. It is also our premise that parents do the best they can at a given point in time. Parents may need help to do their job of parenting.

When a parent is actively psychotic, there may be physical dangers to the child as well as a high potential for child neglect. A child may have difficulty growing up with a positive self-concept when influenced by a psychotic parent. Such a parent can be unpredictable as well as possibly dangerous. The child may learn or genetically be transmitted patterns of living that may be psychotic.

EFFECTS OF CHILD NEGLECT ON THE CHILD AND THE FAMILY

Most forms of physical child neglect have emotional by-products for the child. In Chapter 3, child abuse was discussed within the context of child development. Neglect during infancy may create permanent and irreversible physical affects on the growth and development of the infant, but emotional issues are also present. The baby must establish a sense of trust during infancy. This trust is established by the caretaker meeting the baby's basic physical and emotional needs discussed in Chapter 2. There are generally only two caretakers (the mother and the father) who are available to the infant to meet the infant's basic needs. If the infant is deprived of these basic needs, the infant generalizes this experience to the rest of the world and decides that it is not all right to trust people. The baby's sample of the world is small and he has no way of knowing that just because his parents do not meet his basic needs that there are others in the world who will or can.

The infant and the child are developmentally at risk during each stage of development discussed in Chapter 3. If a child is neglected at any period during his development, the child may fail to acquire a developmental skill as a result.

The consequences of neglect also impacts on the parent. As previously stated, it is the authors' belief that most parents want to do the best job that they can to raise their children. If a parent fails to properly care for the child (through physical neglect) the parent is faced with a sense of personal failure that may be confirmed by the attitudes of others working with or relating to the neglectful parent. Another immeasurable cost to the parents is in the loss of the "connection" with the child. Sometimes these connections are permanently gone because the system intervenes with an out-of-home placement that may temporarily or permanently sever the connections between the parent and the child.

SITUATIONS OF CHILD NEGLECT

Marcia

Mrs. Lofray was asked to come to see the social worker at the local county hospital pediatric department after 8-year-old Marcia Lofray was sent to the clinic by the school nurse. The nurse had noted sores on Marcia's body that did not seem to heal or improve.

Mrs. Lofray did not appear for the first scheduled appointment. When the social worker called to inquire what had happened, Mrs. Lofray had no explanation for missing the first appointment, but did agree to a second appointment. After Mrs. Lofray did not come to the second appointment, the social worker decided to visit Mrs. Lofray at her home.

The outside of the Lofray house was cluttered with opened, empty cans, parts from automobiles, and tall weeds. There were several old cardboard boxes piled near the side door. Three children were playing in the front yard. As the social worker knocked at the front door, she could smell the odor of cooking.

Mrs. Lofray opened the door so that the social worker could come into the living room. Mrs. Lofray told the social worker that she had not noticed that Marcia had sores on her arms and legs. The social worker explained that the sores were impetigo and that they required treatment so that they would not spread. Mrs. Lofray listened but did not seem emotionally involved in the conversation.

When the social worker left the Lofray household, she did not believe that she had developed a relationship with Mrs. Lofray. The social worker did not feel at all certain that if Marcia or one of Mrs. Lofray's other three children contracted impetigo anything would be different until the school nurse or someone else would aid the child. Even though Mr. Lofray did not live with the family, the social worker noted that Mrs. Lofray seemed to be managing on her AFDC payments. During the interview, two of the younger children crawled over Mrs. Lofray and clammered for her attention. Was it patience or indifference in Mrs. Lofray's response to these children as she passively listened to the social worker and literally ignored the children? The children did not seem to be afraid of Mrs. Lofray. If anything, they seemed to crave physical contact. One of the younger children held the social worker's hand as the social worker walked out to his car.

The Lofray case is an example of the ambiguity of defining child neglect. Are these children neglected? The children are fed, clothed, supervised, and housed in an adequate fashion. Even though the Lofrays are a low-income family, the standards are adequate. There does seem to be a lack of medical attention, at least for Marcia. But, is this chronic or just an isolated example? Since the social worker reports in her notes that she has a difficult time relating to Mrs. Lofray who appears to be apathetic and futile in her attitude, Mrs. Lofray might be assessed as an apathetic–futile personality. However, the one incident of untreated impetigo is not sufficient to warrant that the social worker report this case to the child protective services.

What is Mrs. Lofray's level of depression and discouragement? Certainly there does not seem to be any change in sight for this woman as far as how she cares about herself, her household, and her children. Did she have aspirations for herself, her home, and her children at one time that were given up in discouragement or sadness? Who can say what the outcome will be for the children growing up in this environment. Certainly it is not an environment that abounds with stimulation. This is the type of situation where it would probably be helpful if a neighborhood or a religious group or some other concerned person made a connection with Mrs. Lofray to decrease her isolation.

Frank

Louise Alvarez died after an accident as a pedestrian. She was going to meet her son, Frank, who was coming home from school. When the telephone call announcing his wife's death reached Tony, he was out in the field installing telephone equipment. Tony responded with immediate shock.

Tony and Louise had moved to the small midwestern town in an effort to make a fresh start for themselves. Their families lived in the southwestern part of the United States. Both families had been very disappointed in their children for marrying across ethnic lines. Tony was of Mexican descent and Louise was Jewish. Both families were further hurt when the young couple decided to leave the southwest and relocate in the midwest. Neither grandparent had yet met young Frank.

When Tony arrived home on the day of his wife's fatal accident, Frank was at a neighbor's house eating ice cream and waiting for his mother. Tony did not tell Frank about his mother's death immediately. Instead, Tony went about doing the things that needed to be done. He called the local mortuary, notified the relatives, and contacted a lawyer. Tony seemed to do all these things in rote fashion. Later that day when Frank asked where his mother was, Tony, still appearing strong and stoic, related to Frank that his mother had been killed and that tomorrow he should go next door after school.

When the relatives came for the funeral, Tony was not responsive. Tony's mother begged him to return to New Mexico and be closer to her so that she could help with Frank. Tony acted detached and refused all her offers of help.

Three weeks after the accident, Tony still had not returned to his job. Tony's supervisor was sympathetic, called and stopped by Tony's house but did not seem to be able to talk to Tony. When Frank would return from school each day, he would find his father watching the afternoon television programs. One afternoon, Frank, who had been fixing his own meals out of whatever he could find in the cupboard and refrigerator, told his father he was hungry and that there was nothing in the house to eat. Tony replied to his son by saying, "Hush, we don't want anyone to know that we are home." This was only one step in Tony's process of withdrawal from the outside world and from his son, Frank. Tony began to fear that people were after him. He heard strange voices and was not sure they were not real. Tony did not leave the house for anything, even to buy food. Sometimes Tony would sit up late at night waiting for the last television program of the day and then stare at the empty screen until the morning program appeared.

Frank stopped going to school. One day Frank went to the neighbor's house and asked for something to eat. Freida, the neighbor, noticed that Frank was very dirty and unkempt.

After Frank repeatedly begged for food, Freida called the police since Tony would not come to the door or answer his phone. The police had a difficult time getting a response from Tony and their presence only reinforced some of Tony's fear and paranoia. The police finally convinced Tony to admit himself for psychiatric care at an inpatient facility and Frank was placed in the temporary care of Freida, the neighbor. The initial days and weeks after Louise's death had turned to months and Tony had become more and more withdrawn, eventually becoming psychotically depressed. Tony's hallucinations had become so real for him that he was unable to separate them from reality. Psychotherapy and medicine were needed to help Tony pull out of this depression. Tony had had the tendencies for this type of problem before Louise's death, but the lack of supportive network (from which Tony had alienated himself) coupled with Louise's death had been the final straw that separated Tony's hold on reality. Tony was able to return to his home and to his son after his hospitalization.

Evelyn

Eleven-month-old Evelyn lived with her mother and father in a one-room
motel room that they rented by the week. Barbara, the mother, stayed at
home during the daytime, cleaned the one room, and watched television.
Kerry, Evelyn's father, worked as a dishwasher in a nearby restaurant. The
couple paid disproportionately high rent on their motel room, but they never
seemed to save enough to pay the first and last month's deposit on an
apartment of lower monthly rent.

The visiting home nurse had become involved with Evelyn's family
after Evelyn's birth. One of the nurses on the maternity ward noticed that
Barbara was inattentive to Evelyn and often would just prop her next to her
on the bed while feeding her. The nurse had instructed Barbara many times
about how to feed Evelyn but repeatedly she would come into Barbara's
room and find Barbara again feeding Evelyn by propping her bottle. The
maternity ward nurse called a visiting home nurse to work with Barbara after
she left the hospital.

When Kerry came to visit Evelyn and Barbara at the hospital, he was
very happy and attentive to the new baby. He had difficulty handling Evelyn
at first, but learned quickly and soon knew how to care for Evelyn.

For the first month, Barbara, Evelyn, and Kerry seemed happy when
the visiting nurse visited them. One afternoon, Barbara was very talkative
and explained to the nurse that she just could not seem to get both her
housework done and care for Evelyn.

The nurse, who had not visited Barbara for over a week, noted that the
room was dirty and so was Evelyn. The nurse suggested that Barbara let the
nurse take Evelyn to a shelter care facility for young children so that Barbara
could get caught up on her housework and have a rest from caring for
Evelyn. Barbara was delighted with the suggestion and the nurse took
Barbara to the shelter facility.

The next morning, Barbara was on the telephone to the nurse explaining
that she would have to bring Evelyn home because Kerry was very angry
that she was in a shelter care facility. The nurse agreed to help convince
Kerry to let Evelyn stay a little longer at the shelter care facility. Kerry
reluctantly agreed that Evelyn could spend two or three more days at the
shelter home.

Evelyn returned home to a clean motel room. The next time the nurse
visited, Barbara suggested that it would be nice for her to take Evelyn to the
shelter home again. Evelyn was very dirty and unkempt.

The nurse called child protective services (CPS) and suggested that they
talk with Barbara about Evelyn. The social worker was able to form a
relationship with Barbara and soon learned that Barbara had never wanted

Evelyn and that she would really like to have Evelyn adopted. However, Kerry did not agree and sometimes threatened to leave Barbara if she even so much as talked about such a plan. The social worker decided that if some day care services for Evelyn were provided, Barbara might have enough relief during the day so that she would be able to have time to herself and Evelyn could have good care.

Barbara and Kerry's marriage seemed more and more strained when the nurse and the social worker visited. Many times Kerry did not come directly home from work. During these times Barbara felt more pressure and anger about Evelyn. Kerry also did not bring home enough money for the couple to have food. Barbara was not good at budgeting the money. Sometimes when Kerry got paid, they would go to a local coffee shop and eat their evening meal spending all but a few dollars of Kerry's weekly check.

Barbara had frequent medical problems and had to go the county hospital for help with her asthma and seizure problems. Evelyn's stays at the shelter care facility became more and more frequent and for longer periods of time each visit. Finally, against the wishes of both Kerry and Barbara, Evelyn was placed in a foster home. Barbara was very upset because she feared that now Kerry would leave her and she had no way to support herself and besides, she loved Kerry. Kerry felt totally hopeless.

Kerry and Barbara were functioning at a borderline intellectual capacity. Neither of them made long-range plans and their thinking tended to be rather immediate and concrete. The social worker perceived that Barbara did not neglect Evelyn intentionally. Barbara was worried about her marriage and seemed incapable of being concerned about more than one thing at a time. Kerry truly loved Evelyn but did not have the resources to be able to provide economically for her since he, too, had trouble planning and living in more than a day-by-day existence. Another feature of this situation was that Barbara did not want to have a child. She perceived that she and Kerry had a happy marriage before the birth and arrival of Evelyn and she wanted to return to that happy time.

Summary

Child neglect is a problem of major proportions. "Statistics resulting from a nationwide survey indicate that the number of neglect cases are far greater than those of abuse." (Cantwell, p. 183.)

Children of all ages are potential candidates for child neglect. The consequences of unchecked child neglect can be life-threatening. Early child neglect in the form of poor attachment between the parent and child can result in emotional disabilities for the child throughout the child's life. Child neglect at other times in the life of the child can also have devastating outcomes.

Clearly the issue of child neglect is an issue that concerns us all. Child neglect can occur within the context of the family, however, it can also occur within the context of other institutions. There are many programs designed to deal with and monitor situations of child neglect, but these programs are generally overwhelmed, understaffed, and underfunded. There needs to be an approach of shared responsibility throughout different segments of the community to meet the needs of child neglect.

BIBLIOGRAPHY

American Humane Association. 1982 (draft.) *National Analysis of Official Child Neglect and Abuse Reporting.* Denver, Colorado, 1980.

Berkow, Robert, Ed. *The Merck Manual—Thirteenth Edition.* Merk Sharp and Dahme Research Laboratories, Rachway, New Jersey 1977.

Bolton, F.G., Jr., Kane, S.P., Kruse, R.F. *Child Abuse: Our Problem, Too.* Arizona Dept. of Education and Arizona State Board of Ed. and DES, 1979.

Broadhurst, Diane D., Edmunds, Margaret, and MacDicken, Robert A. *Early Childhood Programs and the Prevention and Treatment of Child Abuse and Neglect.* U.S. Dept of H.E.W., DHEW Publication No. (OHDS) 79-30198, 1979.

Cantwell, H.B. Child Neglect. In Kempe, C.H. and Helfer, R.E. Eds. *The Battered Child.* The University of Chicago Press, Chicago, 1980, pp. 183–197.

Dreikurs, R. *Children: The Challenge.* Hawthorn Books, New York, 1964.

Elmer, E., Gregg, G.S., and Ellison, P. Late Results of the 'Failure to Thrive' Syndrome. *Clinical Pediatrics. 8,* 1969, pp. 584–589.

Fisher, B., Berdie, J., Cook, J., and Day, N. *Adolescent Abuse and Neglect: Intervention Strategies.* U.S. Dept. of Health and Human Services, ACYF, January 1980. DHHS 80-30266.

Gil, Eliana. *Prevention of Abuse and Neglect of Children.* San Francisco Department of Social Services Pilot Project and San Francisco Child Abuse Council, 1979.

Giovannoni, J.M., Parental Mistreatment: Perpetrators and Victims. *Journal of Marriage and the Family. 33,* (Nov. 1971), 649–657.

Giovannoni, J.M. and Billingsley, A Child Neglect Among the Poor: A Study of Parental Adequacy in Families of Three Ethnic Groups. *Child Welfare. 49,* April, 1970, 196–204.

Hally, C., Polansky, N.F., and Polansky, N.A. *Child Neglect Mobilizing Services.* U.S. Dept. of Health and Human Services, National Center on Child Abuse and Neglect, DHHS Publication No. 80-30257, May 1980.

Hurst, H., National Center for Juvenile Justice, Pennsylvania, Interviewed by Pamela Mayhall, November 24, 1981.

Justice, Blair and Rita, *The Abusing Family,* Human Science Press, N.Y., 1976.

Kadushin, A. *Child Welfare Services.* The MacMillan Company, New York, 1967.

Kaufman, I. *Psychodynamics of Pratecline Casework, Ego Oriented Casework: Pralilern and Prospectives.* Edited by Howard J. Ponad and Roger R. Miller. Family Service Association of America, New York, 1963, p. 194.

Kempe, R.S., Cutler, Christy, Dean, J. The Infant with Failure-to-Thrive. In Kempe,

C. Henry and Helfer, Ray E. *The Battered Child*. The University of Chicago Press, Chicago, 1980, pp. 163–182.

Lauer, J.W., Lourie, I.S., Salus, M.K., with Broadhurst, Diane D. *The Role of the Mental Health Professional in the Prevention and Treatment of Child Abuse and Neglect*. U.S. Dept. of H.E.W., DHEW Publication No. (OHDS) 79-30-194, August 1979.

Leavitt, Jerome, Ed., *The Battered Child—Selected Readings*. General Learning Corporation, California State University, Fresno, 1974.

Marano, H.E., The Bonding of Mothers and Their Babies. In *Family Therapy News*, September 1981, pp. 9–11.

Minuchin, S., Rosman, B.L., and Baker, L. *Psychosomatic Families*. Harvard University Press, Cambridge 1978.

Norgard, Katherine, Whitman, Stephen T., *Understanding the Family as a System*, Arozina D.E.S., Phoenix, 1980.

Pelton, Leon. Child Abuse and Neglect, The Myth of Classlessness. *The Social Context of Child Abuse and Neglect*. Edited by Leon Pelton. Human Sciences Press, California, 1981.

Polansky, Norman A., Chalmers, Mary Ann, Brittenwieser, Elizabeth, and Williams, David. *Damaged Parents: An Anatomy of Child Neglect*. University of Chicago Press, Chicago, 1981.

Polansky, N.A., DeSoix, C., and Sharlin, S.A. *Child Neglect: Understanding and Reaching the Parent*. Child Welfare League of America, Inc., New York, 1976.

Segal, J. Yahraes, H., *A Child's Journey: Forces That Shape the Lives of Our Young*. McGraw Hill, New York, 1979.

Young, L. *Wednesday's Children: A Study of Child Neglect and Abuse*. McGraw–Hill, New York, 1964.

San Francisco Child Abuse Council, Inc., *Prevention of Child Abuse and Neglect in Out of Home Care*.

Institutional Abuse of Indian Children and The Indian Child Welfare Act. In Linkages for Indian Child Welfare Programs. *1*, 3, October 1981, p. 10.

CHAPTER 7

Emotional Neglect and Abuse of Children

PREVALENCE OF EMOTIONAL NEGLECT AND ABUSE OF CHILDREN

A national study of child abuse indicates that emotional neglect of children is likely to occur about half as often as emotional abuse. Emotional abuse occurs at approximately half the rate of physical abuse. (National Study of the Incidence and Severity of Child Abuse and Neglect, p. 36.) Emotional abuse and neglect of children may be the most elusive of all types of child maltreatment to measure.

Some emotional issues that have emotional impact on the child are circumstances that may occur in the child's home.

- Continuous friction in the home.
- Mentally ill parents.
- Marital discord.
- Immature parents.
- Excessive drinking by the parents or other family members.
- Alcoholism within the family.
- Drug addiction within the family.
- Criminal involvement on the part of one or more family members.
- Illicit sexual relationships within the family.
- Overly severe control and discipline by the parents.
- Encouragement of delinquency.
- Mentally retarded parents.

155

- Harsh and improper language.
- Nonsupport of the child's interests and pursuits.
- Parental values that conflict with society's values.
- Divorce and frequent remarriages.
- Failure to offer motivation and stimulation toward learning.
- Failure to provide wholesome recreation for the family and the children.
- Failure to individualize children and their needs.
- Failure to give the child constructive limit-setting or discipline.
- Promiscuity and prostitution.

All of these issues may contribute to child emotional neglect or abuse. However, none of the situations is guaranteed to result in symptomology within the child; thus, the difficulty in assessing the incidence of emotional abuse and neglect.

Since concrete behavioral standards which detail both parental behavior and the child's response in given situations is missing in the definition of emotional child neglect or abuse, it is difficult to know incidence rates. The inability of protective agencies and others to act given the absence of established criteria is very frustrating to people concerned about children. A child's incomplete relationship with his/her parent is often accompanied by severe feelings of emptiness and depression, a sense of abandonment, deep dependency needs, and a general inability to maintain social relationships. (Bolton, p. 19.)

DEFINING EMOTIONAL NEGLECT AND ABUSE OF CHILDREN

Few would argue with the statement that physical abuse and neglect of children has emotional consequences for both the child and the abuser. Not only are emotional abuse and neglect difficult to measure, they are also the most difficult forms of child maltreatment to adequately and operationally define.

What is the measure for a shattered self-concept? How can you know when someone's self-esteem is harmed? How much emotional abuse or neglect is too much and how are the consequences measured?

These are some of the questions that plague lawmakers and others concerned with the protection of children. Consequently, there is no uniform legal definition of child emotional neglect and abuse. It may be said that emotional neglect is the failure of the parent or caretaker to provide for the appropriate emotional developmental needs of the child. Emotional neglect may occur independently of or along with other forms of abuse and neglect. A child may be adequately and properly fed but never cuddled or provided with physical or intellectual stimulation and emotional nurturance. A child who grows up in a home without feeling loved by his/her parents or other caretakers is emotionally neglected.

Medical and social service professionals tend to see neglect from the point of view of the child. They describe the child with symptoms that imply that emotional neglect has occurred. The social worker, physician, or other person involved with the child may determine that the child has suffered emotional neglect by his/her parents, but others in the legal system or the parents themselves can ask: "How do you know what caused these symptoms?" "How do you know that this is not just the nature of the child?" It is easier to "imply" that emotional neglect has occurred than to prove it and define it.

Infants and young children are rarely exposed to influences other than those in their homes, except where the child is placed in a day care setting. Even in situations where a child is in a day care center, it is the responsibility of the parents to insure that the day care experience provides for the physical and emotional needs and general well-being of the child. Parental action or inaction that leads to what appears to be emotional disturbances by the infant can be described clearly. The infant who is frequently left crying in the crib or with his/her bottle propped instead of being held may possibly be emotionally neglected by his/her parent or caretaker. This infant may demonstrate the emotional neglect by a general lack of affect.

Like child emotional neglect, there is no uniform or commonly accepted definition of child emotional abuse. Emotional neglect implies indifference whereas emotional abuse implies more overt rejection on the part of the parent or caretaker. Emotional abuse is usually deliberate action or inaction resulting in nonaccidental harm to the child. Where emotional neglect occurs at a more unconscious level, emotional abuse occurs at a conscious, knowing level. This is not to say that a parent who emotionally abuses his or her child has the intent to do emotional damage to the child. The parent may not be aware of the long-range outcome of his or her actions toward the child.

INDICATORS OF EMOTIONAL NEGLECT OR ABUSE OF CHILDREN

All children have common emotional needs that include feeling a sense of belonging, having a place and a role within the family, and having a positive self-concept. Other emotional needs of children, which they derive primarily from their parents or other caretakers include affection, approval, consistency, structure (limits and knowledge of consequences of behavior), security, stimulation (growth and exploration of environment encouraged, recognized, and appreciated), and an identity in the form of having a sense and appreciation of oneself.

Just as physical injuries can scar and incapacitate a child, emotional neglect or abuse can handicap a child emotionally for the moment or sometimes for a lifetime. Mental health professionals trace severe psychological disorders in childhood and in later adult life to excessively distorted parental practices. Serious emotional and behavioral problems are common among children whose parents abuse or neglect them emotionally.

It is important for every person to question whether emotional abuse or neglect has occurred or is occurring when any of the following behavior is observed in a child.

The child is withdrawn, depressed, or apathetic.

The child acts out and is considered by teachers and other adults to be a behavior problem in the classroom or in other situations where children need to follow rules or have set standards of behavior.

The child is very concerned about conforming to the instructions of the adult, that is, teacher, doctor or others in authority, and this conformity seems to be disproportionate to other children of the same age group.

The child makes comments about his or her behavior such as "My dad thinks that I am worthless" or "Mother says that I can never do anything right" which might indicate that this child lives with constant criticism in his or her home.

The child displays signs of emotional turmoil such as repetitive rhythmic movements, lack of verbal or physical communication, or an inordinate attention to details.

The child is generally not thriving (unable to perform age-appropriate functions).

The child displays antisocial behavior or obvious delinquent behavior.

The child has inappropriate behavioral expectations from his or her parents.

None of these indicators are proof that emotional neglect or abuse has occurred or is occurring. The indicators are only possible signals to watch for and check further.

DISTINGUISHING FEATURES OF CHILD EMOTIONAL NEGLECT AND ABUSE

Emotional neglect is not easily or readily observable since it usually occurs at an unconscious level and may be received similarly. Emotional neglect is very difficult to assess and to measure. Generally it is possible to question its existence or know about its existence only after the child has experienced chronic exposure to situations of emotional neglect. The consequences of emotional neglect are usually observed only in the child's behavior unless rejection has been overt and blatant enough to be apparent to observers both within and outside the family.

There seem to be four central themes that occur in the emotionally abusive family. First, the infant or child is penalized for positive, normal behavior such as smiling, mobility exploration, vocalization, and manipulation of objects. Second, the parent or caretaker discourages the infant or child from bonding or forming a normal attachment to the parent or caregiver. Third, the infant or child is penalized for showing signs of positive self-esteem. Fourth, the infant or child is penalized for using interpersonal skills that are needed for adequate performance in nonfamilial contexts such as school and in friendship groups.

Emotional neglect and abuse of children must be considered within the context of the family. In some situations a child may appear to be less attractive physically or intellectually than other children in the family. The parents may have difficulty accepting this particular child. Other infants and children have temperaments that make them difficult to rear and live with and less endearing to their parents. In general, however, these explanations are not the distinguishing features of child emotional neglect or abuse.

In many situations of emotional neglect or abuse, the parents bring difficult childhood experiences of their own that almost seem to trigger the patterns of emotional deprivation or abuse. Often these parents recreate the families that they grew up in. These parents, as children, may have been expected to perform in a particular way in order to gratify their parents' needs and then were criticized, punished, or rejected for their failure or inability to do so. (Kempe and Helfer, 1972, p. 4.) These parents had childhoods in which they felt that their own needs were inadequately met by their own parents. Childhood experiences and interpretations about life leave lasting impressions, and are major factors in how we function as adults and make decisions about how to parent our own children.

Growing up in an emotionally abusing or neglecting home environment may deprive a person of basic self-esteem, emotional maturity, and the experiences necessary to cope with the requirements of child-rearing later in life. Children who have poor self-concepts often become adults with poor self-concepts. Children who are emotionally needy may grow to adulthood with the same emotional neediness. As these children become adults and move through the life cycle to become parents, they may look to their children to fill their unmet needs. Role reversal is one distinguishing feature of emotional abuse and neglect.

In role reversal, the child becomes the parent and *vice versa*. The child takes on the emotional role of the adult and "gives" to the adult instead of receiving what the child needs for him or herself emotionally. In these cases, the child may actually become the emotional caretaker of the adult.

Adults who have been extremely criticized as children may continue to be overly sensitive to criticism as adults. These adults are very concerned about performing well. They avoid disapproval from others and seek constant reassurances. Since adults cannot usually get these needs met from other adults in the amount that they may need, they logically turn to their children. These adults, who have grown up unable to meet their basic needs, live in a daily crisis of insecurity. They may repeat the patterns that they learned in childhood with their own children.

Gil's studies of the histories of abusing parents revealed that many of them had experienced living in foster homes, had been hospitalized for mental illness, had experiences with the juvenile court, had criminal records, and had deviant intellectual functioning. (Gil, p. 113.) The Justices' study found, similarly, that 85% of the people included in their sample of abusive parents had experienced deprivation or abuse as children. (Justice and Justice, p. 93.)

It is difficult for an adult entering parenthood with basic feelings of insecurity to provide adequately for the emotional needs of a child, much less of a spouse. Emotional abuse and neglect often appear in generational cycles that are difficult to break unless the basic interactional patterns of the family are changed.

ADOLESCENT EMOTIONAL ABUSE

Fisher et al. have identified two family patterns that usually accompany adolescent emotional abuse. Both of these patterns begin in early childhood and continue into adolescence. The first pattern is associated with chronic and excessive generalized criticism. Parents exhibiting this pattern characteristically have inappropriate expectations of their children and predict that their child will fail. This prediction of failure can become a self-fulfilling prophecy so that the child finally meets the parent's expectations of failure. These parents may start their criticism about a specific issue and generalize into a pervasive statement about the child's general lack of worth. These parents also sometimes prohibit their children from expressing feelings of sadness, fear, anger, or grief. If they do so, they are criticized. Each time the child fails, the parent bears down harder on the child since the child becomes a further threat to the parent's self-esteem. (Fisher, p. 41.)

The second pattern of emotional abuse originating in the child's early years and continuing through adolescence is one of a chronic double-bind. "Double-bind" means that communication has taken place in a contradictory fashion between two people. The double-bind may occur between two different levels of communication. For example, if a parent says "you are wonderful" in a degrading tone, the child may be confused as to which message to receive from the parent. Should the child accept the verbal message at face value or should the child listen to the sarcastic tone of the parent's voice? In these situations constraints are usually placed upon the child that prohibit the child from commenting on the contradictions. Therefore, a child is left in a potentially psychologically damaging situation. Some family therapists suggest a strong connection between young adults ✳ who exhibit schizophrenic symptoms and family interactional patterns that include double-binds. (Haley, p. 287; Winston, p. 33.) The increased internal pressure of adolescent development (both physical and emotional) combined with this type of family functioning may result in the youth's desperate acting out or in a problem such as schizophrenia.

Parents with rigid parenting styles often use physical punishment to enforce their rigid rules. When a youth reaches adolescence it is natural for the youth to begin to experiment with becoming an individual separate from the parents. During adolescence parents are less central to the youth than in earlier childhood. Parents who have parented with rigid standards may no longer be able to physically coerce their youth since the youth may be larger, stronger or faster than the parents. Parents therefore often turn to emotional embarrassment to control the youth. Parents may attempt to use the juvenile court to enforce control over the youth. If parents are not able to enforce obedience to their standards, they may abdicate parenting altogether and "push" the youth out of the home maintaining that the youth can no longer live there since she failed to follow the rules.

A fourth type of adolescent emotional abuse is that which seems to emerge solely during the adolescent period. The developmental stage of adolescence centers on the issue of control. Parents who are in their midlife may feel that they are losing control not only over their children but over life in general. For the parent, this time may be one characterized by questioning. Given these two conditions simultaneously, the parent may react to the youth in an emotionally assaultive manner to "put the youth in his or her place." This can be very discouraging and emotionally destructive to the youth who is trying desperately to test his or her own individual identity and capabilities. "The parental overreaction can compromise the youth's development by damaging self esteem already made vulnerable by adolescence." (Fisher, p. 43.)

Sometimes emotional abuse which emerges in adolescence is associated with previous or concurrent physical abuse. By the time the youth reaches adolescence, the parents are usually not physically able to control the youth. If the parent feels that they have lost their means of control, they may direct their anger at the youth via emotional mechanisms such as criticism, rejection, or unreasonable restrictions. All of these conditions may create the climate for the youth to respond in ways that will ultimately be damaging emotionally to the youth and to the stability of the entire family.

Adults may be facing marital crises at about the same time that their children have reached adolescence. Sometimes, a youth may unconsciously serve as a scapegoat in service of holding the marriage and family together. Even if the marital conflict is open and the youth is not the scapegoat, the self-esteem of the youth may suffer just as a result of the marital strife since the youth's image of himself is closely connected to his parents all during his lifetime. Family instability does not provide a firm foundation from which to grow to independence.

FORMS OF EMOTIONAL NEGLECT AND ABUSE OF CHILDREN

The National Study of the Incidence and Severity of Child Abuse and Neglect (NIS) distinguished three diverse forms of emotional abuse.

Verbal or emotional assault. Habitual patterns of scapegoating, belittling, denigrating, or other overtly hostile rejecting treatment including threats of sexual or physical assault.

Close confinement. Tortuous restrictions of movement such as tying a child's arms or legs together, binding a child to a bed, or confining a child to a closet or similar enclosure for prolonged periods.

Other unspecified abusive treatment. Attempted physical or sexual assault (e.g., throwing something at a child, but missing), "overworking," or economic exploitation, withholding of food, sleep, or shelter as a form of punishment, or similar purposive acts not encompassed elsewhere.

NIS findings indicate that the most common form of emotional abuse was verbal/emotional assault. ("In-scope" children included only those who received substantial injury as a result of the maltreatment.) Study findings relating to close confinement revealed that 73% of the "in-scope" children in this group were inherently traumatically or emotionally injured as a result of the punishment.

The National Incidence Study utilized the following subcategories of emotional neglect.

Inadequate nurturance. Extreme parent/guardian inattention to a child's needs for affection, attention, or emotional support; causing or materially contributing to the occurrence or unreasonable prolongation of a serious physical, mental, or emotional problem including but not limited to nonorganic failure-to-thrive.

Encouragement or permitting of seriously maladaptive behavior. Severe assaultiveness, chronic delinquency, or debilitating drug/alcohol abuse under circumstances where the parent/guardian had cause to be aware of the existence and seriousness of the problem (e.g., the child had been picked up by the police on previous occasions) and had not attempted to correct it.

Other. Includes refusal to permit recommended treatment for a child's diagnosed emotional condition, failure to seek professional assistance for a severely debilitating emotional condition, and extreme overprotectiveness.

Inadequate nurturance was cited as the most common form of emotional neglect. Of all the categories of maltreatment, emotional neglect had the highest (74%) of demonstrably serious injuries/impairments such as attempted suicides, severe failure-to-thrive, and drug overdoses. (NIS, pp. 22; 25.)

EXPLANATIONS FOR EMOTIONAL CHILD ABUSE AND NEGLECT

As in other situations of child maltreatment, there is no single explanation for child emotional neglect and abuse. However, the emotional nurturing of a child is a complex process and several features of parenting are critical to emotional development in children. The following list includes major ingredients necessary to the growth and development of a child from an emotional point of view.

- Love
- Praise
- Acceptance
- Warmth
- Stimulation (mental and physical)
- Individualization (allowing the child to become a separate person)
- Stability and permanence
- Opportunities and rewards for learning and mastery
- Adequate standards of reality and limit setting
- Socialization
- Control of aggression
- Opportunity for extra familial experiences
- Appropriate behavior models
- Sense of security
- Safety

When children do not receive these necessary ingredients in the growing process, they may have difficulty giving emotional support and guidance to their own children when they become adults.

Children who are born prematurely or with low birth weights are at a greater risk for emotional abuse and neglect since there is a greater possibility of maternal illness and the bond of attachment that develops between parents and child may be compromised by the conditions imposed by and associated with the prematurity.

> Deviations in attachment can occur for several reasons: insufficient contact between parent and child; difficulty of the mother in responding to the baby's signals, leading to distortions in development; difficulty of the baby in responding to the mother's signals, leading to a lessening of protective responses; and a baby whose signals are difficult to read, as is frequently the case with premature infants who are delayed in establishing predictable rhythms and who may be ill and irritable. (Newberger, p. 16.)

Certainly, if the attachment between the infant and the parent or caretaker does not form, there is already emotional neglect in that the infant is not getting what he or she needs at that early time in life. For some types of emotional neglect, the lack of a necessary connection between the parent and the child just never occurs and the process of neglect continues.

Emotional neglect and abuse also occurs with adopted children. In the case of adopted infants or older children, the process of parent–child attachment is still necessary for effective parenting. The development of emotional attachment between parent and child requires that there be a reasonable amount of proximity maintained between the child and the parent. What is considered "reasonable" may vary from situation to situation and in the case of an adopted child, stepchild, or foster child it is possible that more consistent proximity may be required than in situations with birth children since the relationship does not have the benefit of time. If the parent is unable to respond to the child's needs or signals for needs, a distortion in the attachment process can occur. However, the child has a part to play, too. The child's well-being and attachment depend on his/her ability to read the parent's signals or cues and respond accordingly.

When people are "attached" to one another, they seem not only to be able to read one another's signals and have a basic understanding of one another, but accept one another as well. If I understand you, I am better able to accept you. The process of acceptance is a basic condition for the emotional well-being of any person, adult or child. The child who lives in a condition where he or she feels that he/she is not accepted or understood by his/her parents or caretakers does not have the necessary emotional stability for growing and development into responsible adulthood.

Families in which emotional abuse and neglect occur often find it difficult to communicate their needs and wants to one another. This communication process coincides closely with the attachment process. If the adults have the skill and ability to communicate clearly with one another, there is an increased chance that they will be able to effectively parent their children and read and understand the needs and wants communicated to them by their children. If communication is stifled between the adults, it is possible that these adults will lack the necessary skills to be able to understand the needs of their children.

It is also important to consider societal explanations for emotional child neglect and abuse. Chapter 2 detailed a focus on societal violence and social conditions such as poverty which create situations for potential emotional abuse and neglect of children. Children live in families, families live in neighborhoods, and neighborhoods are a part of the larger societal structure. Explanations for child emotional abuse and neglect must consider each of these elements and their interaction and interplay with one another rather than any simple linear cause and effect explanation.

One important aspect of emotional abuse is that it may be a by-product of child abuse and neglect. When a child experiences sexual abuse, physical abuse, or physical neglect, a degree of emotional abuse accompanies these other forms of abuse. ". . . children who grow up in abusive and neglectful families can rarely escape psychological wounds of clinical significance." (Martin, p. 351.) On the other hand, it can equally be argued that expecting emotional abuse to accompany these other forms of abuse and neglect may actually create some of the emotional component. The chapter on sexual abuse discusses the fact that when adults overreact to sexual abuse of the child, they may actually make the experience worse for the child than if the adults were able to remain more emotionally calm about the experience. This may be a truism about all forms of abuse and neglect and the accompanying emotional abuse.

EFFECT ON THE CHILD AND THE FAMILY OF EMOTIONAL ABUSE AND NEGLECT

The effects of emotional child abuse and neglect on both the child and the family can be measured, although somewhat arbitrarily, in short or in long-term consequences. If the emotional abuse only occurs over the short run, it may have only short-term consequences. However, if excessive criticism and berating occurs over a major portion of the child's growth and development, the consequences may be more significant. If the child lives in a home environment that is unpredictable, it is usually unpredictable for the adults, too. If the child lives in a home situation that is isolated physically or emotionally from other people, the adults have the same environment. If the home has an inordinate amount of social and psychological stress, it is experienced by both the child and the adults. In other words, all the features in a family (isolation, unpredictability, and stress, etc.) where a child is emotionally neglected or abused effect all the members of the family at one level or another.

Martin holds that the affect on the child may be manifested in one or more of four areas: the child's behavior is typically at one end of the spectrum or the other, the children are usually unhappy, the children generally have poor capabilities with object relations (healthy, gratifying, age-appropriate relationships with adults or peers), and the child generally has impaired peer relationships. (Martin, p. 352.) Although Martin lists these possible consequences in response to physical abuse, the same results are probable as a result of emotional abuse or neglect. The main point to be made about emotional abuse and neglect is that if children do not get their emotional needs met while growing up, it is very likely that they will not be able to respond to the emotional needs of others when they reach adulthood.

SITUATIONS OF CHILD EMOTIONAL ABUSE AND NEGLECT

The following case examples are situations of emotional neglect and abuse of children.

Henry

Twelve-year-old Henry always seemed to be alone on the school ground. Teachers and other school officials had no problems with Henry. He was no problem except that he never seemed to have any interest in his schoolwork. Henry was described as apathetic and lethargic.

In the classroom, Henry would sit for hours in what seemed to be a daydream state. Henry's teacher referred him to the school counselor because she was concerned about Henry's detached attitude. Unable to make any progress on a one-to-one basis with Henry, the counselor decided to visit Henry's family.

The counselor assessed Henry's mother as being depressed. The house was clean and Mrs. Horn was well-dressed. She told the school counselor that she did not know why Henry would not respond to people at school since she had no problems with him at home at all. He always completed his chores on time and never had any problems with his sister. Mrs. Horn told the school counselor that she had spent a great deal of time in the State Hospital over the last ten years. They could not determine what was wrong with her. Mrs. Horn stated that some days she just could not get out of bed. However, Henry was never a problem to her and he just took care of himself. When asked who Henry's friends were, Mrs. Horn did not know. When asked how Henry was doing with his schoolwork, Mrs. Horn did not know that either. As the interview progressed, the school counselor became increasingly aware that Mrs. Horn did not know much about Henry's life and general well-being.

Mr. Horn worked in the Merchant Marines and was away from the family for three months at a time. When Mr. Horn was "on-shore," he would spend a great deal of his time with close friends playing cards and visiting. The Horns had been married for thirteen years and Mrs. Horn said that she thought they had a good marriage. Mrs. Horn did relate to the counselor that Mr. Horn just did not have much time for Henry or his three-year-old sister, Martha.

Child Protective Service staff would have a difficult time intervening on Henry's behalf unless his mother or father exhibited some degree of cooperation in the matter. It would be very difficult to clearly prove that Henry's isolation on the school ground and his lack of attention to his schoolwork was directly correlated with difficulties at home. Henry's mother is physically present and available for Henry, even though it is possible to question her level of availability to him. Henry seems to have the food, clothing, and shelter that he requires. The main missing ingredient to Henry's life is an emotional one. Probably the most that could be offered to Henry and his family would be services aimed at prevention of further emotional neglect. Prevention services are just as difficult, if not more so, than intervention services after neglect has occurred. It also seems that Mrs. Horn would be able to benefit from some services to help her with her detachment and possible depression.

Christie

Eight-year-old Christie would never sit still in the classroom. She was always visiting other children or generally disrupting the class. Finally, the teacher and the principal decided that they would request permission from Christie's mother to get some special psychological testing from the school psychological services.

Mr. and Mrs. Seav were very happy that the school had decided to pursue the psychological testing. Mrs. Seav told the school principal that she had been very concerned about Christie for some time. She never seemed to do anything right. Mrs. Seav went on to explain to the principal that Christie was a bad child at home and had been a problem to the parents almost from the moment she was born. When asked to elaborate, Mrs. Seav noted that Christie was a messy eater, never kept her room clean, fought with her younger brother, did not do her chores correctly, and did not have a good relationship with her parents in general.

During the psychological testing, the astute psychologist heard from Christie that her parents thought she was a bad person. Christie said that she was certain that they were right. They often told her that she was not as good as her older sister, Patricia, or other children that Mr. and Mrs. Seav knew. The psychologist was able to determine that Christie was very afraid of making mistakes and Christie told her that she would go and ask her classmates about her work before turning it into the teacher to try and prevent mistakes. During the psychological testing, Christie would mark one answer, erase it, mark another, erase it and finally ask the psychologist to help her make sure that she found the correct answer.

At the conclusion of the tests, the psychologist recommended that Christie's entire family seek family counseling. The psychologist recommended that the family would need to learn some parenting skills and age-appropriate expectations of Christie.

As in the case of Henry, this case would have little possibility of court intervention. If the family refused family counseling, the case might have been closed. This case of emotional abuse probably would not be considered severe enough to merit intervention by the child protection authorities. However, the time to protect Christie is now. She may well be on her way to developing emotional/behavioral problems if the family does not receive some assistance with their problems.

Ralph

Fifteen-year-old Ralph was the oldest child of Mr. and Mrs. Jones. The other two Jones' children were ages 7 and 5. Mrs. Jones had miscarried three times in between her pregnancy with Ralph and the next youngest child. The Jones' were very disappointed not to have more children since they had hoped to have eight or nine children.

Mr. Jones worked in a local grocery store and Mrs. Jones was a full-time housewife and mother. Mrs. Jones kept a watchful eye on the children and they were prohibited from many activities that the other neighborhood children could do. Ralph was never permitted to stay overnight at anyone's house. The children had a set of chores to do and Mrs. Jones made certain that they did each chore and on time. Ralph did not have contact with many other children his age during his early childhood years.

After the miscarriages and the news that Mrs. Jones was unable to have any more children, Mr. and Mrs. Jones seemed to drift apart. Mrs. Jones put all her efforts into raising her three children. She rarely took part in any activities outside the home. Mrs. Jones was intent on raising these three children with an iron hand so that they would turn out to be good people. By the time Ralph reached high school, he began making friends and wanting to participate in after school sports programs. Mrs. Jones forbade him to stay after school to participate in sports. Until Ralph reached high school, Mrs. Jones had kept Ralph in line with the belt. Whenever Ralph misbehaved even in the slightest rule infraction, Mrs. Jones would take down the belt and use it on Ralph. At fifteen, Ralph had gotten tall and strong. Once when Ralph was in high school, Mrs. Jones tried to use the belt on him and he turned on his mother and grabbed the belt out of her hand. Mrs. Jones and Ralph never talked about this incident but from that point on, Mrs. Jones refrained from putting any limits on Ralph.

Since Mr. Jones had literally withdrawn from the parenting of the children, Ralph found freedom beyond his wildest expectations. All the new found freedom was actually frightening to Ralph. One day when he arrived home from school quite late in the evening, he found himself locked out of the house. When he was unable to get into the house, he went to a friend's house whose mother called the police. It was at that point that the family and Ralph became involved in the juvenile justice system. Mrs. Jones claimed that Ralph was a runaway and furthermore that he would not obey her and that she could not handle him at home.

Ralph's case is an example of adolescent neglect. Ralph had grown up in a very rigid environment as a young child without much physical or emotional guidance and support from his father. The probation officer who did the intake interview suggested that this family seek family counseling to work out the difficulties that they were experiencing.

SHARING THE RESPONSIBILITY

Reporting suspected emotional abuse or neglect may not be the most useful route to alleviating the problems faced by the youth and family unless the local child welfare agency or division is able, through its staff, to offer programs to the families. Observant, involved, caring, and unblaming neighbors and friends may have all the tools necessary to prevent many situations and circumstances of emotional abuse and neglect. At a minimum, they may provide the "caring connection" which can help the child and sometimes the parents to grow positively. The shared responsibility of professionals, paraprofessionals, volunteers, and every member of the community at large to be aware of and to act to prevent child maltreatment is particularly critical in this area. These families will not reach out to make connections and sometimes the ambiguity of definitions of emotional abuse and neglect prevent any formal intervention from taking place until the problem is overt and extremely serious.

The more a shared responsibility is acted upon, the more protection will be made available to children and the greater the possibility that situations and circumstances of emotional neglect and abuse can be prevented and alleviated.

Summary

Emotional neglect is likely to occur about half as often as emotional abuse. For both, however, incidence rates are difficult to determine given the problems encountered in defining and developing operational criteria for emotional neglect and abuse. Indicators of emotional abuse and neglect are open to interpretation. The mere presence of such indicators is not proof that emotional abuse or neglect has occurred.

Two long-standing family patterns that are usually associated with adolescent emotional abuse and neglect are chronic and excessive criticism and chronic double-binding of the youth. Rigid family structures may contribute to adolescent emotional abuse and neglect.

Three major subcategories or forms of emotional abuse are verbal or emotional assault, close confinement, other/unspecified abusive treatment. Major forms of emotional neglect include inadequate nurturance, encouragement or permitting of seriously maladaptive behavior, and other forms (as refusal to permit recommended treatment for a child's diagnosed emotional condition or failure to seek professional assistance for a severely debilitating emotional condition, and extreme overprotectiveness).

Emotional abuse and neglect of children may be, and usually is masked by other problems. Some emotionally neglected or abused children have difficulty relating to others and forming lasting and meaningful relationships with others. Such children may even appear to sabotage a helping relationship. If these children "act out" their emotional needs and frustrations, they may add to the frustration of those around them, creating turmoil which others prefer to avoid.

The responsibility for preventing and alleviating emotional neglect and abuse is shared by professionals, paraprofessionals, system volunteers, and the community at large. The more this responsibility is acted upon, the better the protection that will be available to children and to families.

BIBLIOGRAPHY

Berger, Milton, M. Ed. *Beyond the Double Bind,* Brunner and Mazel, New York, 1978.

Bolton, F.G., Jr., Kane, Sandra P., and Kruse, Roger F., *Child Abuse: Our Problem, Too.* Arizona Department of Education and Arizona State Board of Education, D.E.S., 1979.

Fisher, Bruce, Berdie, Jane, Cook, JoAnn, and Day, Noll. *Adolescent Abuse and Neglect: Intervention Strategies.* U.S. Department of Health and Human Services, OHDS, 80-30266, January 1980.

Gil, D.G. *Violence Against Children.* Harvard University Press, Cambridge, MA, 1970.

Haley, Jay. Family Therapy: A Radical Change. In Haley, Jay, Ed. *Changing Families.* Grune and Stratton, New York, 1971, pp. 272–284.

The Investigation of Child Abuse Incidents, A Field Reference. San Leandro, California Police Department, January, 1980.

Justice, Blair and Justice, Rita. *The Abusing Family.* Human Sciences Press, New York, 1976.

Kempe, C. Henry and Helfer, Ray E. *Helping the Battered Child and His Family.* J. B. Lippincott Co., Philadelphia, 1972.

Kempe, C. Henry and Helfer, Ray E. Eds. *The Battered Child.* The University of Chicago Press, Chicago, 1980, pp. 183–197.

Martin, Harold P. The Consequences of Being Abused and Neglected: How the Child Fares. In Kempe, C. Henry and Helfer, Ray E. *The Battered Child.* University of Chicago Press, Chicago, 1980.

National Study of the Incidence and Severity of Child Abuse and Neglect. OHDS, 81-30325, September 1981.

Newberger, Carolyn Moore, and Newberger, Eli H., The Etiology of Child Abuse. In Ellerstein, Norman S. Ed. *Child Abuse and Neglect: A Medical Reference.* A Wiley Medical Publication, New York, 1981.

Segal, Julius and Yahraes, Herbert. *A Child's Journey.* McGraw–Hill, New York, 1979.

Westat, Inc. and Development Associates, Inc. *Study Findings: National Study of the Incidence and Severity of Child Abuse and Neglect.* NCCAN, (HEW-105-76-1137), DHHS Publication No. (OHDS) 81-30325, September 1981.

Winston, Arnold. Understanding and Treating Schizophrenics: A Review of Some Contributions of Communication and Family System Theories. In Berger, Milton. Ed. *Beyond the Double Bind.* Brunner and Mazel, New York, 1978.

8

Child Sexual Abuse

PREVALENCE OF CHILD SEXUAL ABUSE

Sexual abuse of children, in the broadest sense, encompasses a wide range of behavior including physical and genital fondling, molestation, exhibitionism, forcible and statutory rape, sexual assault, commercial exploitation of children in pornography, pedophilia, incest, and misuse. Children may be sexually maltreated by a parent, a family member, a significant other person trusted by the child, or a stranger. Historical and social taboos are strongest against incest (sexual relations between persons so closely related that they are forbidden by law or custom to marry). The taboo is particularly strong where parent–child incest is concerned. Physical violence is most often associated with sexual abuse by strangers. Persons who are convicted and imprisoned for sexually harming children are often either ostracized or abused by other inmates in the institution.

In 1978, the nation was shocked to learn about the sexual exploitation and murders of young males in Houston, Texas. This and other similarly publicized cases seem to infer that child sexual abuse frequently results in the death of the victim, and that it is committed predominantly by strangers. Actually, most child sexual abusers are respected members of the community and often are family members. (Caplan, p. 46; Finkelor, p. 17.)

Reports of sexual maltreatment increased at a rate of over 100% from 1979–1980. However, in 1980 data, reports of sexual maltreatment represent only 7% of all maltreated children known to CPS. (AHA 1980.) Of that 7%, approximately 2% were incest cases. Increased reporting may reflect increased public awareness and changes in focus and reporting systems rather than an actual increase in sexual maltreatment. As with other forms of child maltreatment, reported sexual maltreatment probably makes up only a part of actual incidence. Some observers suggest that sexual abuse of children, particularly incest, may be grossly underreported. Possible explanations for this underreporting include:

1. Sexual abuse of children is not easily identified or diagnosed since it rarely results in physical injury.

2. Sexual abuse of children is not easily detectable by outward signs other than secondary indicators (pregnancy or venereal disease), unless the child tells someone.

3. Both children and adults may have more difficulty expressing themselves in matters of sexual abuse than in other types of maltreatment because of guilt and other feelings associated with the experience.

4. The sexully abused child is most likely abused by a trusted family member or friend who may tell the child that the experience is a normal part of growing up but that it must be kept secret from others.

5. Young children are taught to respect adult authority figures, especially their parents and family members. Therefore, young children may be more gullible in accepting sexual abuse as "normal" and less likely to tell others.

6. The offender's threat of retaliation or punishment may deter the child from telling others or from reporting the sexual abuse to the authorities.

7. The child may fear rejection, blame, punishment, abandonment, or fear that his/her experience will not be believed, and therefore decide against telling others.

8. Parents often do not report sexual abuse because they want to protect their child from involvement in legal proceedings.

9. Family members may fear censure and blame from neighbors and friends if they report sexual abuse. They therefore rationalize not telling the authorities when physical harm has or has not occurred to the child.

10. Children may not tell others about the sexual abuse because they may feel guilty about any physical pleasure they may have had from the sexual contact.

11. Adults, particularly parents, may respond to a child's story about such incidents, especially incest, with disbelief.

DEFINING CHILD SEXUAL ABUSE

Early Statute Definition

Rape of children, as defined in statutes on child sexual abuse, may or may not involve violence and force. Early statutory rape laws were imported to the United States from England and were designed to protect very young children from sexual abuse "Until the late 1800's most state statutes prohibited 'carnal abuse', 'carnal knowledge', or sexual intercourse with female children age 10 or below." (Kocen, p. 2.) Children above age ten were protected under that law only from nonconsenting sexual intercourse and forcible rape.

Children under ten years of age were considered to be too immature to give consent or to know about sexual behavior. Early laws attempted to protect children both physically and morally. Modern laws are based on these nineteenth century laws but are less concerned with moral issues. They are more likely to treat sexual crimes as matters that threaten physical security rather than as crimes against morality. (Kocen, p. 3.)

Trends in Criminal Definitions

Current major trends in criminal legislation relating to child sexual abuse specifically include definition of the prohibited acts, establishment of a tiered structure of offenses with graduated penalties based on the age of the abused and/or the age of the offender, and penalties for not protecting children from abuse by family members or others in positions of authority. The main purpose of these laws seems to be to protect chidren from harm resulting from sexual abuse. Laws have been expanded in all states to include comprehensive protection of children from sexual abuse.

Most of the laws refrain from punishing sexual activities between adolescents close in age. The focus of the legislation, according to the Kocen report, is not moral standards, that is, preserving an adolescent girl's virginity or chastity or condemning premarital sex. (Kocen, p. 11.)

New Jersey is cited by the Kocen report as one state whose statutes include comprehensive protection of children from sexual abuse.

It has a tiered structure for both sexual contact and intercourse, protecting children in several age categories up to the age of 18. It provides special protection for the teenager from abuse by perpetrators who are older or in several broad positions of authority. The penalties are reasonable and the prohibited acts are specifically delineated. (Kocen, p. 12.)

Sexual Misuse of Children

Sexual misuse is defined as activities that expose the child to sexual stimulation inappropriate to the child's age and role in the family. Examples of sexual misuse range from a child observing sexual activity between adults to child pornography and child prostitution. It is reported that the sexual misuse of children has become a multimillion dollar industry. (Densen–Gerber, p. 77.) Some forms of sexual misuse involve payment in money, drugs, gifts, clothing, food or other items to the child or the child's caretakers. According to some estimates, more than one-half million children in the United States were actively engaged in prostitution in the late 1970s. (Densen–Gerber, p. 77.) Historically, the child has been considered to be an item of property and as such, has been viewed as a marketable commodity in the labor force. Children are often employed for pornographic materials. Child pornography, commonly referred to as "kiddie porn" and "chicken porn," is defined as films, photographs, magazines, books, and motion pictures that depict children under a certain age (usually age 16) involved in both heterosexual or homosexual acts with one another or with adults. "In 1977 there were at least 264 different magazines produced in the United States each month which depicted sexual acts among children or between children and adults." (Densen–Gerber, p. 79.) Further, there is evidence to substantiate that the psychological scarring that occurs as a result of a child's involvement in child pornography is similar to that of children involved in incest. (Densen–Gerber, p. 80.)

> Public outcry against child pornography resulted in a series of congressional hearings in 1977. Testimony presented at the House Hearings on the sexual exploitation of children estimated that approximately 7 percent of the United States pornographic market involved sexual activity between children and adults. (Burgess, p. 1.)

Part of the public outcry arose from information that sex rings exist which involve children. It is believed that these sex rings of children are formed for the purpose of producing pornographic material and delivery of direct sexual services to adults. Such rings are organized to the extent that they actively recruit children and have an extensive network of customers. (Burgess, p. 1.)

Legislation has played an important role in working against what appears to be a rapidly growing problem of child pornography and child prostitution. Since 1977, 48 states have designed legislation to combat the sexual exploitation of children. (Nash, p. 2.) In 1978, the U.S. Congress enacted the Protection of Children Against Sexual Exploitation Act (Public Law 94-224, 18 U.S.C. 2251-53), which prohibits the transportation of children across state lines for sexual exploitation. In addition, federal legislation provides for punishment of persons who use, employ, or persuade minors under the age of 16 years to become involved in the production of visual or printed material which depicts sexually explicit conduct. Punishment is also provided for parents and legal guardians who knowingly permit a minor to participate in such conduct. (Nash, p. 2.)

Pedophilia

Pedophilia is a term used to describe a condition in which the child is the preferred sex object of the adult. Some organized groups argue that sex between adults and children is permissible and desirable both for the adult and for the child. The René Guyon Society states as a slogan, "Sex before eight or else it's too late." The Pedophilic Information Exchange organization located in Wales (Densen–Gerber, p. 78; Caplan, p. 48), and a group in the New England area (Yates) are organized for the purpose of promoting adult–child sexual activity.

SEXUAL ABUSE IN THE CONTEXT OF THE FAMILY

Sexual maltreatment, as we have indicated, includes many categories of sexual activity between an adult and a child and sexual misuse of children. Kempe defines sexual abuse as ". . . the involvement of dependent, developmentally immature children and adolescents in sexual activities that they do not fully comprehend, to which they are unable to give informed consent, or that violate the social taboos of family roles." (Kempe, p. 198.)

This chapter focuses most specifically on child sexual abuse occurring within the context of the family group. Sexual activity between the child and a closely related family member is known as incest. Criteria for "closely related" is often stated as ". . . family members whose marriage would be proscribed by law or custom." (Finkelhor, p. 83.) Legally, incest does not usually include sexual activity between a single-parent's paramour and children in the family. This person may be living in the home, be involved in the family as a family member, and a part of the family environment. Sexual activity between this person and a child in the family may be very similar to incest. The reaction of other family members to it may also be similar.

The sexual contact defined by "incest" is not limited to genital intercourse; it may involve fondling, masturbation, or genital fondling. Another definition of incest, found in some state statutes, refers to marriage between two members of a family who are legally or blood related to one another. This is not the meaning of incest in the context of this chapter.

In sexual abuse, the patterns of adult involvement are different from other forms of maltreatment. The National Study of the Incidence and Severity of Child Abuse and Neglect found that mothers/mother-substitutes and biological fathers were less frequently involved than in other forms of maltreatment. Although mothers and mother-substitutes are often at least passively involved, they are seldom the primary perpetrator of the abuse. Also, biological father−daughter or father−son incest or molestation made up only 28% of sexual abuse cases that the study accepted as "in-scope" cases. In contrast, stepfathers and other adult caretakers (such as the parent's paramour) were more likely to play a major role in sexual abuse than in other types of maltreatment. (NIS, 1981.) This finding is based on cases known to other investigatory agencies and professionals as well as cases known to CPS. It cannot, however, take into account those cases that may exist but are not known to the specific agencies included in the study. Some caution must be taken in the use of this finding. While it is possible that taboos and other relationship restraints may operate to limit the involvement of natural parents, particularly in incest, it is also possible that reporting of stepparents and paramours may be more acceptable than reporting natural parents. This is an area that requires additional study.

Sexual abuse within the family environment, in the opinion of the authors, is contributed to by the entire family environment, not just the person who is the initiator (or offender) of the activity. A nonparticipating parent contributes to incest by directly or indirectly encouraging the activity through silence or failing to provide for the sexual safety of the child. The child may not know how to resist the behavior or may even welcome the activity as a form of attention or caring from a parent or parent figure and in that sense contribute to the situation. "The whole environment of the family is involved in terms of contributing to the conditions under which incest or sexual misuse occurs." (Justice and Justice, p. 32.)

Three characteristics of sexual abuse are: (1) the acts are against children; (2) the acts are considered inappropriate by society; (3) the adults have a substantial advantage in authority, power, and sexual sophistication over their child partners. (Finkelhor, pp. 16−17.) This does not mean that situations of incest are the only times that a child may be victimized or feel overpowered or intimidated by someone else sexually. Children may be involved in incest with other children and feel overpowered, victimized, or intimidated. In cases of sexual contact between the adult and the child, the child is used to satisfy the adult's needs, not the child's. The child lacks the capacity to decide matters of long-range consequence; there is no such thing as a consenting child in matters of incest or sexual abuse. (Caplan, p. 47.)

Most people agree that child sexual abuse interferes with normal, healthy child development. The child is usually unable to cope emotionally, physically, and/or intellectually with sexual stimulation and responsiveness, whether the child finds the experience emotionally satisfying, erotically pleasurable, or negative in some fashion.

Sexuality within a stepfamily unit can be more difficult and ambiguous to deal with than it is within a nuclear family. If two people enter a marriage, each having teenagers who have not previously lived together, sexual attraction between the teenagers may be greater than if they had grown up together. Similarly, stepparents may find stepchildren attracted to them and behaving in seductive ways. These feelings are sometimes shared, particularly when a strain exists in the marital relationship. A new stepfamily is usually a very sexual environment. "Repressed impulses are perhaps less rigidly controlled because of a weakened 'incest taboo' which applies to blood relationships." (Visher, p. 106.) Similar difficulties occur around issues of sexuality within foster homes. Adolescents who are experiencing and experimenting with heightened feelings of sexuality and who may be behaving seductively need the permission and protection to do so within the family unit without becoming involved in sexual relationships with adults in the family.

Taboos Relating to Incest

"Taboo" is a word that is often associated with incest. Most societies have taboos against incest and other forms of sexuality involving children and adults within the family. There are exceptions to rules of incest that generally apply across all cultures. In Teita, East Africa, for instance, it is legally possile to marry your mother or your sibling. However, for most societies such unions are forbidden. These taboos involving marriage and sexual contact are based in kinship and biological rationales.

Five possible explanations for the incest taboo include:

1. The incest taboo may have originated because it was important at different times throughout history for tribes and clans to establish alliances. "By establishing rules requiring marriage and intercourse outside the family, early humans devised a system for expansion and security of the race." (Justice and Justice, p. 26.)

2. Sexual contact within the family can be very disruptive to the family since passion and jealousy are related. It can interfere with a harmonious family life, the well-being of a tribe or community, and the well-being of its individual families.

3. Incest confuses roles within a family. If a daughter has sex with her father or stepfather, what is the wife's role? When does the daughter get to be a daughter?

4. Incest threatens a child's development. "To develop, a child must receive both nurturing and encouragement to become a separate person. The needs both to belong and to separate must be met. Incest keeps these and other needs of the child from being met." (Justice and Justice, p. 28.) If a child becomes sexually involved with a parent, and the emotional and physical attachment is so great that it prohibits the child from separating, the child may not be emotionally or physically able to separate from the birth family and establish his/her own family or complete, separate identity. The overall protection of the family and the individual family members is thought to be the basis for most modern incest prohibitions.

5. Biological rationale for the incest taboo suggests that inbreeding in a population will physically weaken the offspring. Some believe that defective offspring result from incestuous relationships between close family members. Since ancient man probably was not aware of this consideration, it is more likely that early proscriptions had more to do with issues of kinship. Current literature suggests that genetics is not a sound explanation and rationalization for the prohibition of incest between close family members or blood relatives. "Today statistics reveal that the biological risk rationale for incest prohibitions is probably overrated." (Kocen, p. 53.)

INDICATORS OF SEXUAL ABUSE

Indicators of possible sexual abuse occur in three areas: medical, behavioral, and familial. As with other lists of indicators relating to other child maltreatment categories, most of these indicators are not, of themselves, absolute proof of sexual abuse.

Medical Indicators

The common medical indicators are:

1. Bruises in the area of the external genitalia, vagina, or anal regions.
2. Bleeding from external genitalia, vagina, or anal regions.
3. Swollen or red cervix, vulva, or perineum; positive tests for gonococcus or spermatozoa.
4. Pregnancy or venereal diseases. "Gonorrhea infections in children occurring at any body site except the eyes are virtually always a tell-tale indicator that the infected child has been a victim of sexual assault." (Scroi, p. 251.)

Behavioral Indicators

Behavioral indicators of possible sexual abuse include:

1. Regressive behavior. Children who have been sexually abused may withdraw into fantasy worlds. Outwardly, these children may even seem mentally retarded when, in fact, they are not.
2. Delinquent or aggressive behavior. Preteen and teenage children often act out their hurt, resentment, and anger at being sexually abused.
3. Sexual promiscuity.
4. Confiding statements to a friend or an adult that the youth does not want to go home, wants to live in a foster home, etc.
5. Poor or deteriorating peer relationships. This may arise partially out of the child's shame about the sexual abuse or from the emotional disturbance surrounding the experiences. Also, the abuser tends to try to keep the sexually abused child socially isolated from other children to lower the risk of disclosure.
6. Prostitution. Jennifer James reports a strong correlation between child sexual abuse and late teen-age prostitution. A child with a negative self-concept may experiment with prostitution after running away from home and then find that prostitution has become a lifestyle.
7. Unwillingness to participate in physical/recreational activities. This may occur because the child has physical discomfort.
8. Runaway behavior. For some children, running away is a way to escape sexual abuse. Often it is a last resort.
9. Drugs. Teenagers who have been sexually abused may turn to illegal drugs as a way of escaping from their feelings about the experience or as a way of acting out their experiences.
10. Reporting of the offense by the youth.
11. Fear of adults, especially in young children. These children may cling to their parent and generalize their fear of sexual abuse to all individuals of the same sex as the abusive parent.
12. Siblings jealous of child chosen by parent.
13. Excessively seductive child.
14. Hysterical seizures. (Gross, p. 1704.)

Sibling Sexual Abuse Indicators

These may include:

1. A brother and sister who behave like a girlfriend and boyfriend.
2. A child who fears being left alone with a sibling.

3. A brother and sister who appear to be embarrassed when found alone together.
4. A situation in which a child antagonizes the sibling but the sibling does not retaliate (for fear of exposing secret).

It is important to note that not all sex play and/or intercourse between siblings is abusive or harmful. (Yates.)

Familial Sexual Abuse Indicators

The following are possible indicators that sexual abuse is occurring or has occurred within the family:

1. A dysfunctional family system characterized by blurring of generational lines within the family—father and/or mother becomes the child and daughter and/or son take on the role of wife/mother or husband/father.
2. Strained marital relationship.
3. Parent often alone with one child.
4. Favoritism by parent toward one child over other children.
5. Overly protective parent. The parent who is involved in incest may become overly protective and jealous of the youth and try to isolate the youth from other contacts within and outside the family. The parent is not only afraid that the child will tell, but also afraid that the child may find another sexual partner.

Indicators Related to Developmental Stages

Some indicators are specific at various developmental stages of children. Young children may act out their disturbing feelings by fear attacks, night terrors, clinging behavior, or regression. School-age children indicate possible sexual abuse by sudden onset of anxiety, fear, depression, insomnia, conversion hysteria, sudden or massive weight loss or gain, sudden school failure, truancy, or running away. Adolescents may exhibit serious rebellion (especially against the silent parent), venereal disease, pregnancy, drug abuse, antisocial behavior, role reversal with a parent in the household, prostitution, or social isolation.

DISTINGUISHING FEATURES

Child sexual abuse most frequently occurs within the context of family. The perpetrators are usually trusted family members (fathers, mothers, stepfather, stepmother, single parent's paramour, other relatives) or trusted persons close to the family (babysitters, neighbors). The abuse may take many forms. The classic form of incest is father–daughter involvement. However, possibly "... the largest amount of incest occurs between partners of the same generation—brothers, sisters, and cousins." (Finkelhor, p. 87.) The Justices' claim that fathers or father-substitutes are most often the initiators of incest according to statistics and reporting data, but that brother–sister incest may be much more common and less reported since it would more likely be handled within the family than to receive outside help or attention. (Justice and Justice, p. 61.) Some incest is reported between mothers and children. One commonality exists among all these forms of incest. The role of nonsexual needs of the perpetrator, (the need for affection, the need for belongingness, the need to have roots, the need to be dependent and nurtured, and the need to have a haven from stressful outside world), although not overtly stated may be as important or more so than the sexual needs. (Justice and Justice, p. 30.)

Distinguishing Characteristics of Father–Daughter Incest

Roland Summit describes seven distinguishing features of father–daughter incest. ("Father" in this reference can be construed as birth father, stepfather, or other adult male in a parent position within the family.)

1. Incest is surrounded by secrecy since the girl typically is fearful of disapproval, retaliation from the offender, and loss of acceptance and security in her home if she tells her mother or anyone else about the experience.
2. The experience of incest leaves the girl with a helpless feeling since she has been overpowered by someone she has trusted who is in a position of authority over her.
3. The girl usually feels entrapped and accommodates because she feels helpless.
4. Most father–daughter incest is either delayed in its disclosure or is never disclosed at all.
5. If the girl does disclose the incest experience, she may later retract her complaint when faced with the consequences of having to participate in a criminal proceeding. The child may also be affected by the accompanying turmoil in the family and the disbelief in her story that others have expressed.
6. Girls who experience incest usually have a prepubertal initiation. The age of highest risk for girls is about nine years of age.
7. The girl who is molested by her father is usually involved in role confusion since she replaces her mother's sexual function with her father. (Summit, p. 2–12.)

Distinguishing Characteristics of Sibling Incest

Sibling incest may come to the attention of authorities less frequently than father–daughter incest because the taboo against it is not as strong. Sibling incest usually occurs between minors and does not set up as explosive a family conflict. Brother–sister incest is not as likely as father–daughter incest to create an intense rivalry which potentially threatens to upset all the family roles. In addition, brother–sister incest may be less offensive to the partners and the family as a whole.

Distinguishing Characteristics of Mother–Son Incest

Less seems to be known and written about mother–son incest than any other type. It is often held that this type of incest occurs only in the context of psychosis or extreme family disorganization. The few cases of mother–son incest that are publicized usually appear in magazines directed toward male audiences. (Finkelhor, p. 93.)

Adolescent Sexual Abuse

Fisher et al. describe three types of sexual abuse that occur during the adolescent period: that which begins in childhood and continues through adolescence; that which begins in adolescence and is related to emerging marital and personal dysfunction; and that which begins in adolescence and is related to developmental issues.

Adolescent Sexual Abuse Beginning in Childhood

This is the most common form of adolescent sexual abuse. "The adolescents in this category have been sexually abused for at least several years, and often since preschool years." (Fisher et al. p. 47.) In these situations, sexual contact that began in childhood escalates during adolescence. Early sexual contact may have been limited to fondling or masturbation with intercourse first occurring in the adolescent period. Physical coercion in these situations is not as common as psychological coercion. Family disruption and incest usually occur simultaneously whether the incest is confined to childhood or occurs throughout childhood and into the adolescent period. Some observers suggest that the family disruption is a result of the incestuous behavior. Others take the position that the disruption is the cause of the incestuous experiences (Fisher et al., p. 47.) The authors' clinical experience suggests that the incestuous situation is more likely a result of family disruption.

Emerging Dysfunction and Adolescent Abuse

The second type of adolescent sexual abuse begins in adolescence and emerges from long-standing personal and marital dysfunction and role reversal. The sexual abuse appears to be connected to other dysfunctional family and perpetrator–victim interactions (Fisher et al., p. 47.) As in the situation of long-standing sexual abuse, controversy exists as to whether this type of adolescent sexual abuse is the result of the family dysfunction or individual pathology on the part of the perpetrator. From a systems point of view, as discussed in Chapter 2, individual pathology exists in a family context and can be traced to pathology in the individual's family of origin or throughout generations in the family of the individual offender.

Developmental Issues and Adolescent Sexual Abuse

Sexual abuse beginning in adolescence may be strongly connected to developmental issues of adolescence and the developmental issues of parents at midlife or, in other words, to life cycle issues for the youth and for the parent that are occurring simultaneously. It is normal for adolescents to be aware of and to experiment with their emerging sexuality within the family. Functional families can provide a safe, nonincestuous atmosphere in which such experimentation can take place. If the parents in the family are struggling with their own developmental issues of aging at the same time, however, greater vulnerability to sexual abuse may exist. If, for instance, a daughter's adolescent flirtation with her father coincides with a situation in which the father has deep concerns about his own sexual attractiveness, and this concern is reinforced by conflicts with his wife and with doubts about his competency at work, the situation may foster sexual abuse. (Fisher et al., p. 48.)

FORMS OF SEXUAL ABUSE WITHIN THE FAMILY

Father–Daughter Incest

As stated earlier, the most commonly reported type of child sexual abuse is incest that occurs between father and daughter. Cases of stepfather–daughter incest may actually have different dynamics, but the form is similar to that of father–daughter and the potential disruption in the family is the same. Criminal courts prosecute this type of incest more frequently than other types. This type of incest can also be potentially more damaging to the child than incest between siblings or sexual abuse of a child by a stranger. In this situation, both parents may seem unpredictable to the daughter. At one moment Dad may be a loving father and at the next he presents himself as a lover. Mother may alternate between being a loving parent and a suspicious and angry competitor. Mother may also be a silent partner to the incest.

Mother–Son Incest

Mother–son incest is characterized by the father being an absent partner, rather than a silent partner. Freudian theory suggests that this form of incest may be more psychologically damaging to the child than father–daughter incest since mother–son incest represents the fulfillment of the Oedipal desires. Freud theorized that the young male child wants to sleep with his mother and take his father's place in the sexual role, but at the same time the child wants protection against this fantasy. A functional family serves as a safe place for a child to fantasize with protection from fulfillment.

Sibling Incest

Children have a natural tendency to experiment sexually. They may limit their experimentation to masturbation or looking at the bodies of persons of the opposite sex. Some forms of sibling incest may not be traumatic for children, particularly if the children are young and there is no betrayal of trust between them. Some sex play between children is the result of normal curiosity and exploration and is not a major event in the life of the child unless adults interpret it negatively. When incest occurs between an older brother and a younger sister, the older child may feel burdened with the responsibility of having taken advantage of his younger sister. Misuse of power in the relationship so that one sibling is made to feel powerless is a major issue in nonplayful sexual encounters between children. In some situations of older brother–younger sister incest, the older brother seems to be disturbed emotionally before the onset of the incest. Less seems to be known about older sister–younger brother incest. Incest between siblings can be heterosexual or homosexual.

Grandfather–Granddaughter Incest

Grandfather–granddaughter incest seems to parallel father–daughter incest in overall dynamics. One explanation for this form of incest is that the grandfather may be experiencing diminished feelings of self-esteem as a result of the natural physical deterioration of aging. Some grandfathers may also have sexually abused their own daughters.

Mother—Daughter Incest

Current limited data regarding mother—daughter incest indicates that the relationship is characterized by a mother who is severely disturbed, possibly psychotic. (Forward and Buck, p. 117.) It is suggested that this mother does not clearly differentiate herself from her daughter. She stimulates her daughter to satisfy her own needs for pleasure. (Forward and Buck, p. 117.) Sexual abuse by adult women may be reported less frequently than sexual abuse by adult males because social censure surrounding that behavior discourages its disclosure. Feminist authors question the disparity in numbers between father—daughter incest and mother—son incest. "The answer from the feminist perspective, is that within a patriarchial society, mother—son incest is an affront to the father's prerogatives, and this gives rise to the asymmetrical nature of the incest taboo." (Child Sexual Abuse, p. 4.)

Father—Son Incest

Father—son incest violates both the incest taboo and the taboo against homosexuality. Forward states that this type of incest seems to be a result of the father's psychological problems rather than a symptom or the outcome of family dysfunction. Other sources disagree, noting that this form of family sexual abuse can also be explained in terms of family dysfunction. (Yates.)

EXPLANATIONS FOR CHILD SEXUAL ABUSE

The notion of the offenders being "dirty old men," "perverts," or "molesters" is simply not the case. (Elwell, p. 230.) A large proportion of offenders include parents or other people who are familiar to the child. Seventy-six percent of the older persons who had sexual experiences with girls were known to their victims; 43% were actually family members. A similar percentage relates to boys who were abused. (Finkelhor, p. 73.)

> Children abused by persons known to them, including a natural father or stepfather, experienced a high degree of anxiety and ambivalence. If the abuser subsequently was excluded from the family, the child's guilt and ambivalence increased, particularly if court action was involved and testimony from the child was needed. (Shamroy, p. 129.)

The explanations, dynamics, and effects of child sexual abuse vary with whether the offender is a stranger or someone known to the child. If the offender is a stranger, the behavior against the child is more than likely an expression of a sexual preference for children, (pedophilia) or of a need to overpower a victim in order to feel sexually adequate (child rape). In the case of incest, the offender's sexual preference is more than likely for adults but it has been thwarted, disoriented, or inappropriately directed toward a child. "While aggressive sexual offenses, such as rape and sadism, do occur within the family, they are the exception rather than the rule." (Kocen, p. 3.) The majority of cases do not involve penetration or infliction of any serious bodily harm. Often an important danger to the abused child is in how the situation is subsequently handled by the family, CPS, the courts and the community.

Four Theories Regarding Child Sexual Abuse

Finkelhor has outlined four theories that attempt to explain child sexual abuse in relationship to the offender.

1. The abuser is a degenerate. Sexual abusers are seen as moral degenerates and psychopathic personalities. This theory may have been a response to the public outcry and outrage at child sexual abuse. Research does not support this explanation for the offender's participation in child sexual abuse.

2. The abuser had a seductive mother. This theory arose from the early Freudian model of understanding the human personality. According to the Freudian point of view, an offender's sexual interest in children is the result of a disturbance in his relationship with his mother.

3. The adult is fixated on sexuality. This theory explains the adult's behavior in terms of early childhood sexual experiences that encouraged the person to become fixated on sexuality as a child. This fixation carries over into adulthood.

4. Sexual abuse is an expression of the adult's diverse needs. This diversity theory holds that the adult who sexually acts out against children may be influenced by problems with alcohol and fear of adults and adult sexuality. Another part to this theory is that the adult's sexual abuse of children is more an expression of the adult's need for closeness or for aggression than for pure sexual gratification. (Finkelhor, p. 20–22.)

Regression as an Explanation for Child Sexual Abuse

Regression is defined as functioning at a former or more primitive level than the expected level for the age and development of a given person. A temporary or permanent appearance of primitive sexual behavior after more mature forms of expression have been attained (regardless of whether immature behavior was actually manifested earlier in the person's development) may explain child sexual abuse by an adult. (Groth, p. 87.) Groth states that in such situations, the offender has not exhibited any predominant sexual attraction to significantly younger persons during his sexual development. He observes from clinical data that fixated and regressed child sexual abuse offenders occur in equal numbers. (p. 88.) Groth's study has many limitations. He gathered his clinical data from male patients classified as "sexual molesters." His sample of men who engaged in father–daughter incest was smaller than the population of sexual molesters.

Theories That Focus on the Family

Other theories that attempt to explain child sexual abuse place the offense within the context of the family. These theories hold that the family plays a central role in creating the blend of ingredients that permit and possibly encourage child sexual abuse. Social isolation is seen as one key family variable. (Justice and Justice, p. 134.) Isolated families are separated from both the model of functional family behavior by other families and the restraint of public disapproval.

> It has been suggested that some of these isolated families are part of subcultures where incest is not regarded with the same kind of disapproval as in the culture at large. In fairly self-contained communities, the tolerance of incest can be transmitted from generation to generation, relatively unchanged. (Finkelhor, p. 26.)

Another view of sexual abuse within families is related to the sexual culture of the family. Some families allow children in the family to observe sexual experiences between the parents. Other families use explicit sexual language in communicating within the family. Disregard of individual rights to privacy is common in some families. All of these features may provide subtle or not-so-subtle messages within the family about sexuality and may create an atmosphere of permission for incest.

Early studies placed a special emphasis on the physical environment within a family as an explanation for incest and sexual abuse. Lack of space was studied by Weinberg in a sample of 203 incestuous families. Sixty-four percent of these families lived in housing below the minimum standard of one person per room. "However, he found that in only two cases were fathers compelled to sleep with daughters because of congested quarters, and in one of these cases, another sleeping arrangement was possible." (Justice and Justice, p. 137.) These findings suggest that although physical environment may be used as a rationale and overcrowding may contribute to the potential for incest, physical environment may actually be more of an excuse for incest than a viable explanation for it.

Another theory proposes that sexual abuse of children by parents relates to a poor sexual relationship between the husband and the wife, that is, if a husband and a wife have a poor sexual relationship, the parent may turn to the child for sexual satisfaction. Marital conflict can subject the child to contradictory messages about sex. Also, the marital conflict is difficult for the child and leaves the child uncertain about where to turn for protection. "When a child feels unprotected, he or she is more apt to become entangled in a sexual situation with an adult . . ." (Finkelhor, p. 28.)

Minuchin and other family therapists assert that role confusion between the adult and the child is still another explanation for child sexual abuse. (Minuchin, p. 3; Machatoka et al., p. 114.) When adult–child sex occurs in families, the adult has in essence placed the child in an adult role. Sibling sex also may be facilitated by marital discord between the parents and the surrounding lack of protection from the parents who are too busy with their own conflict situations to protect the children and provide a nurturing, yet safe family environment.

The three-level definition of the family, as explained in Chapter 2, will help to clarify explanations of child sexual abuse within the context of the family. In terms of this definition, when sexual abuse occurs, family members are having difficulty finding their places and roles with one another in ways that are acceptable within the larger society and within the family. This confusion within the family system contributes to a lack of developmental (physical and/or emotional) well-being of family members. When sexual abuse occurs, the members of the family are also having difficulty with the inner workings of the family. There may be no clear and equal distribution of power within the family. It may be that the power is vested in the father at the expense of the other family member's self-esteem.

Stern has identified three possible interactional patterns that may occur in incestuous families: (1) the "dependent–domineering" pattern that is characterized by the marriage of an emotionally strong woman and a man who believes himself to be inadequate; (2) the "possessive–passive" pattern wherein there is a patriarchal family configuration; (3) the "incestrogenic" pattern in which both parents have difficulty functioning as adults and the marriage appears to be a union of two children. "Clinging to each other, these emotionally dependent adults cannot meet each other's needs or those of their children and, instead look to their children for parenting and love." (Stern and Meyer, p. 83.)

Communication processes within incestuous families are often unclear and stifled. People are not free to comment on what they feel, hear, see, or believe. The lack of a clear communication flow throughout the family may actually contribute to the keeping of the family secret of incest. People in sexually abusing families pay a high price for these communication dysfunctions. In addition to not receiving and giving clear and meaningful messages (and then perhaps not having the skills to communicate in situations outside the family either), the highest price seems to be to the family's and the individual's self-esteem.

Self-esteem is the gauge by which we measure our self-worth. Self-esteem may also be considered the inner energy that we have to face the daily issues of life inside and outside the family. Self-esteem is intertwined in our feelings of hopefulness, power, choice, and belief about ourselves.

Sometimes the emotional rules within these families do not work to the benefit of the family as a whole. Emotional rules within the family are generally implicit and beyond the awareness of the family members; yet everyone seems to obey them. These rules relate to how people will conduct themselves, what actions can and will be taken, and the general "laws" of the family. (Ford, p. 141.) If, for example, a family's emotional rules included: "don't talk so anyone can hear" and "father knows best," acting upon these rules might actually foster incest. A family's emotional rules, as one part of the inner workings of the family, support the process of communication, the arrangement of power, concepts of self-esteem, and how change will be allowed to take place within the family and work with other elements of a family described in Chapter 2.

EFFECT OF SEXUAL ABUSE ON THE CHILD AND THE FAMILY

"All parents have sensuous feelings toward their children," (Summit and Kryso, p. 52.) These authors go on to state that sexually abusing parents act on these feelings, lack impulse control, and confuse roles.

> Just as there is a shifting and invisible line between constructive discipline and dehumanizing punishment, there is a vague borderline between loving sensuality and abusive sexuality. Just as both discipline and sensuality are vital to the growth of children, the backlash of these qualities by abusing parents can blight a child for life. (p. 52.)

When children are sexually abused by adults, they are robbed of developmentally appropriate sexuality. (Kempe and Helfer, p. 204.) Children are not ready physically or emotionally for the experience of sexuality. Once they have experienced sexual encounters with adults, they may lose a part of their childhood.

Kempe asserts that incest that occurred and stopped before adolescence appears to cause less havoc for the child than incest which occurs into adolescence (Kempe and Helfer, p. 210.) He reasons that younger children are not quite as acculturated to the mores and expectations of society and, as a result, the experience may have less impact on them. Also, they may forget the experience if the adults in their lives handle the experience in a manner that will permit that to happen.

Sexually abused boys seem to have greater adjustment problems than girls. (Kempe and Helfer, p. 211.) Culturally speaking, it may be more acceptable for girls to have these kinds of experiences than boys. More support may be available to girls when the incest is discovered.

The following critical factors may help to determine how a child might react to and assimilate the experience of sexual abuse.

1. The duration of the experience.
2. The child's age.
3. Developmental status of the child.
4. Relationship of the abuser to the child.
5. Amount of force or violence used by the offender.
6. Degree of shame or guilt evoked in the child for participation in the sexual abuse.
7. Reaction of the child's parents and professionals involved in the matter.
8. The extent of coercion versus participation that the child experienced with the sexual abuse.

Sources. Kocen, p. 5; Elwell, p. 23.

Some sources suggest that the psychological trauma is greater for the child when the offender is a family member or close family friend. (Kocen, p. 5.) Finkelhor's study does not substantiate this finding. Most sources agree, however, that (1) the closer the relationship between the child and the offender, the more likely the abuse will be repeated; (2) children seem to have an easier time recovering from stranger-initiated sexual abuse than from abuse that takes place within the family. The major factors apparent in such recovery are:

1. The child is less often blamed as the provoker of the abuse.
2. The child has more family support and protection available.
3. There is less of a personal consequence for the family. (If the offender is prosecuted and sentenced to prison, the child's family membership is not usually disrupted.)
4. The child is living in a family that is not necessarily dysfunctional.
5. The child was emotionally stable prior to the abusive incident. This consideration is closely tied to the emotional stability and the functioning level of the family as a whole.

The Interaction of Developmental Stages and Impact

Infants do not comprehend the nature of sexually abusive incidents as older children do. Of greatest concern is whether or not their needs are being adequately met. Infants who are involved in situations of incest, unless physically injured, may not show signs of having been sexually abused if their basic emotional and physical needs have been met during the experience.

Very young children, like infants, do not have the sophistication of older children. They may not comprehend, either intellectually or emotionally, the significance of sexual abuse. Unless they are told that incest is bad or shameful, they do not necessarily experience shame or guilt about the incident.

"By the time children are approximately three years old, their perceptions of the world have become more sophisticated. They may experience feelings of shame or guilt if these emotions are communicated to them by parents or other adults." (Leaman, p. 21.) When young children find the sexual stimulation pleasurable, they may feel confused and perhaps guilty since they have already assimilated some of their family's and the society's values and expectations by this time in their life. For these children, the separation and distinction between fact and fantasy may be difficult. Children may be more influenced by what they thought or imagined to have occurred than by the actual facts. For instance, ". . . if a child imagines that the offending adult wanted to urinate on him, the incident may be remembered as unpleasant, but it may have no sexual connotations." (Leaman, p. 22.)

Children often act out situations of sexual abuse in their play. Since the play of children is their work, play is the logical outlet for a child's concerns about sexual abuse. Many times children are more aggressive both in play and with peers following incidents of sexual abuse.

By the time children are six-to-ten years of age, they are able to separate fantasy from fact. For these children, situations of sexual abuse are usually more clearly connected with feelings of shame and guilt. The children are particularly influenced by the reactions of family and other meaningful adults.

"Adolescents who become involved in long-term sexual relationships with adults may have particularly severe problems when the relationship is discovered. They often have little self esteem and feel rejected and betrayed." (Leaman, p. 22.) Since adolescents are establishing their identities, particularly their sexual identity, this experience of sexual abuse by an adult may be more traumatic than for other developmental periods. Adolescents are often considered to be sexually provocative (a normal part of growing up), and therefore responsible for the incident. The burden of blame can compound the difficulties of the adolescent, especially if the sexual abuse occurred within the context of the family and resulted in physical and emotional disruption for the entire family.

Long-Term Issues

It is difficult if not impossible to separate the effects of sexual abuse within the context of the family from the effects of the pathological family on the child and his/her membership in such a family. It is impossible to generalize with any accuracy about the effects of sexual abuse on children and adults. Flashbacks, both for adults and children involved in sexual abuse, are common. One foster child who had been sexually abused told the authors, "It is an experience that you never get over. You just sort of have to try and forget it, but some times when you don't even know it is coming, there are all the memories and thoughts again." Another foster child related that the prosecution experience was the worse part of the whole chain of events for her.

A mother who had been the silent partner when sexual abuse occurred in her family of creation told the authors, "I just can't seem to get over the guilt. Sometimes I wake up in the middle of the night and just shake all over when I remember what my daughter went through and how I didn't do anything to take care of her."

In one case of sexual abuse where the child was placed with her grandmother, the grandmother was very protective of the child after the child came to live with her. She rarely let her play with playmates of either sex. The little girl had a difficult time growing up in this overprotected environment.

Increasing evidence suggests that many youths who become prostitutes (both boys and girls) may have been sexually abused as children and that prostitution may be in some way correlated with sexual abuse. No conclusive findings are yet available, but early studies contradict some commonly held views regarding prostitution. A San Francisco study summary states,

> The excessive victimization, physical and sexual abuse, and learned helplessness, coupled with the young ages and disturbed backgrounds of the women, produce a distressing portrait of women trapped in a lifestyle they do not want, and yet feel unable to leave. Almost two-thirds of the subjects in this study were found to be victims of childhood sexual abuse including incest; one-half of the subjects had witnessed violence between their fathers and mothers, and nearly two-thirds of the subjects had been beaten by family members while growing up. (Silbert.)

Impact on the Family as a Family

Child sexual abuse certainly is an offense against the entire family. How does child sexual abuse affect the family? One might ask, "Which family?" Child sexual abuse seems to affect the immediate family within which the abuse takes place, often the extended family, and many times the families that these family members form as future generations.

Compounding the Problem

Two areas that are often very difficult for the child to deal with emotionally are the need to be a part of the prosecution process and questioning by family and others as to whether the child participated voluntarily. One foster child related that people had asked her why she did not use a weapon to fight off her stepfather when he sexually abused her. Another child was accused of voluntary participation in sexual abuse since she told others that some of the encounters with her father had been pleasurable.

Professionals, paraprofessionals, and volunteers working with children who have been sexually abused must take great care not to compound existing problem through their "helpfulness." The legal process needs to be handled in a way that considers the child's circumstances. Medical examinations of children can be very traumatic and must be conducted with sensitivity to the needs and feelings of the child. The press also has some social, if nor moral, responsibilities to the child in situations of child sexual abuse. One girl opened the local newspaper and read the name of her adopted father who had been accused of sexually molesting her in every paragraph of a second-page newspaper article.

Case Examples

Two of these case examples will be accompanied by a diagram of the family of the abused since the authors take the position that sexual abuse is a shared responsibility of the family and its larger context, the neighborhood, community, and society.

Lorraine

Lorraine was born thirteen years ago. She was the third child of a couple about which nothing is known except that they were killed in an automobile accident while traveling in Pennsylvania. Officials were not able to trace any family connections or extended family members for Lorraine. At the time of the accident, Lorraine was three-years-old. She was placed in a temporary shelter care facility until long-term arrangements for her care could be made.

Three weeks later, Lorraine was placed in a foster home with the

Nelson family. The Nelsons had two children of their own. Lorraine stayed with the Nelsons until she was three and a half, at which time she was adopted by the Rubin family. Lorraine was the only child of the Rubins. Lorraine was a very lovable child and the Rubins were very pleased to have her join their family.

The Rubins lived in a small town, about 40 miles from the major metropolitan area where Mr. Rubin worked. The Rubins seldom made social contact with other people in their small town. Their parents lived in distant parts of the country. They had been married for six years and had hoped to have several children. When it was discovered that Mr. Rubin was sterile, Mrs. Rubin was heartbroken. She lost interest in sex and almost lost interest in the marriage. The couple had applied to adopt an infant, but after a three year wait had become discouraged. When the caseworker said that they could adopt a three-year-old child they decided to proceed. Mr. Rubin never told the caseworker that he hoped that the adoption of Lorraine would improve the estranged relationship between himself and his wife. When the social service agency investigated the Rubins for the adoption study, they were found to be financially and emotionally sound. During the waiting period of trying to adopt, Mrs. Rubin had taken a job in the nearby city. She worked long hours and was away from home a great deal. When Lorraine arrived, Mrs. Rubin was ecstatic. She resigned from her job and decided to be a full-time mother and housewife. For several years, the family was happy. The relationship between Mr. and Mrs. Rubin improved, although not to the extent that Mr. Rubin would have liked, particularly in terms of their sexual relationship. The couple did not seek marriage counseling.

By the time Lorraine was in third grade, Mrs. Rubin was diagnosed with kidney failure. The doctors recommended a treatment that meant that she had to be admitted to the hospital every three months for treatment which lasted three days. When these hospitalizations first began, Mr. Rubin was very supportive of his wife. After two years of this process, Mr. Rubin began to feel more and more distant from his wife.

One evening when Mrs. Rubin was away at the hospital, Mr. Rubin persuaded Lorraine to sleep with him in his bed. Lorraine was eight years old when she and Mr. Rubin began sleeping together during Mrs. Rubin's absences. Lorraine welcomed the closeness at first but when Mr. Rubin would touch her genital area she felt strange even though pleasant physical sensations were associated with the touching. By the time Lorraine was in sixth grade, Mr. Rubin had accelerated his fondling of her to penetration by masturbation. Lorraine never asked her adopted father to stop these activities because she was lonely while her mother was away at the hospital and she longed for some attention and physical holding. But she grew increasingly uncomfortable with these encounters with her father. Mr. Rubin said that she should not tell her mother about their experiences together because she would get mad at Lorraine and might not want to keep Lorraine as her daughter.

Lorraine became socially isolated at school. However, her grades did not suffer. If anything, Lorraine buried herself in her school work as an escape.

When Lorraine brought friends to the house to play, Mr. Rubin would ask them to kiss him and hug him. Sometimes, he would touch Lorraine's friends. The only friends that Lorraine had were children much younger than herself who lived in the neighborhood. One weekend, Lorraine had a special friend, Joan, age 11, stay with her. Mrs. Rubin had to be admitted to the hospital that weekend because of kidney problems. While the girls were sleeping, Mr. Rubin came into their room and began fondling Joan. Lorraine, who was 13 years old by this time, was embarrassed when she woke up and heard Joan telling her father to "stop it." When Joan went home the next day, she told her mother about the event. Joan's mother called the police.

The process began. The police visited Lorraine at school and asked her about her father. When Lorraine confirmed Joan's story and added her own account of the last five years with her adopted father, the police decided to place Lorraine in a shelter care facility while the county attorney decided whether to prosecute the case.

When the police took Lorraine to her house to get her clothing, her father was not around, but her mother looked very hurt and angry. She did not speak to Lorraine. Lorraine was frightened. She stayed three nights at the shelter care facility and was not able to attend school during that time. The next week she started attending a new school near the home of the foster family with whom she had been placed pending the settlement of the events surrounding her removal from her home.

Figure 8.1 illustrates what has happened in Lorraine's life in thirteen years. She has had six disruptions in her family life. The first disruption occurred when Lorraine was age three. During this period in her life, she was dealing with the developmental task of autonomy. It is difficult to know how successfully she was able to feel a sense of control over her world at this time, given the dramatic changes that occurred in her family stability. It would seem plausible to hypothesize that she may have had some difficulty accomplishing a sense of mastery over the task of autonomy since her primary caretaker shifted three times during her third year of life.

After Lorraine's adoption, Lorraine again began to feel stable about her family situation. However, by the time she reached third grade, Mrs. Rubin became ill, and there were separations between the two coupled with the feelings in the family about Mrs. Rubin's illness. Lorraine was at the industry stage of development. Lorraine continued to do well in her school

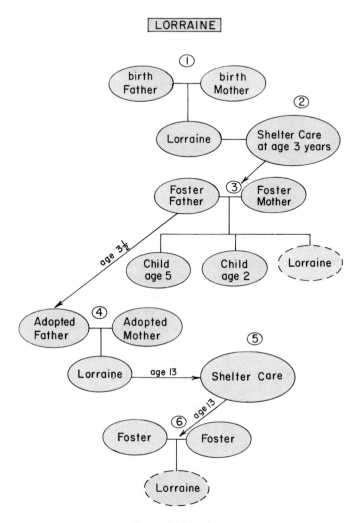

Figure 8-1 Lorraine.

work even when things began to become frightening and confusing at home. She was old enough to have realistic expectations about what was right and wrong between her and her adopted father. Often she would feel very nervous and guilty about what was transpiring between them when Mrs. Rubin was away at the hospital or other times.

When Lorraine was a young teenager, family disruption was again a part of her life. Her mother with whom she had been so close seemed to abandon her after Lorraine talked to the police about her relationship with her father.

Although she never said it out loud, Lorraine's mother seemed to be blaming her adopted daughter for the sexual abuse.

The long-range effects for Lorraine are uncertain but there do seem to be some costly short-range effects. Lorraine feels very frightened and confused. She wants a family badly and believes that if her adopted father is sent to prison for his actions against her, she and her mother can live happily together in their small community. Lorraine's future is uncertain. Fortunately, she is getting professional counseling and is active in a self-help program for sexually abused children. Lorraine is slowly beginning to learn that she is not at fault for what happened. Lorraine still wants to go home. Since the sexual abuse continued through Lorraine's adolescence, the long-term effects for her may be greater than they would have been had the abuse ended when she was younger.

Several factors may have contributed to the sexual abuse. It is apparent that Mr. and Mrs. Rubin had a strained sexual relationship in their marriage and they never seemed to resolve the issue of Mr. Rubin's sterility. Mrs. Rubin's illness placed another strain on the already strained family. The family was isolated from possible support groups. Not only did they live far away from neighbors, but they also had no close friends and no extended family support. When Mrs. Rubin was hospitalized for her treatments, there seemed to be some role confusion on the part of both Mr. Rubin and Lorraine. Further, Lorraine felt so lonely and longed so for affection when her mother was gone, that the attention that Mr. Rubin gave to her seemed good. Mr. Rubin may have been an individual who confused sexuality with getting his emotional needs met. He seemed estranged from his wife and had no other close bonds with people in his life.

Margaret

Fourteen-month-old Margaret was taken to the emergency room of the local community hospital by her grandmother because of vaginal bleeding and bruises. The examining doctor discovered vaginal irritation and was suspicious of sexual abuse. The grandmother, Mrs. Sinkle, reported that the child lived with her mother, Janice, the grandmother's daughter, and the mother's boyfriend, Ralph. Margaret's mother was divorced from Margaret's father who was currently serving time in prison.

The doctor decided to admit Margaret to the hospital for further examination. After the hospital social worker obtained a social history from Margaret's mother, the staff learned that she was divorced from Margaret's father and had been living with Ralph, a 35-year-old unemployed man from another state. Janice, Margaret's mother, was 20 years old and worked nights as a barmaid in a local tavern. Ralph had agreed to babysit for

Margaret while Janice worked since he was unemployed. Many times when Janice came home at 2:00 in the morning, Ralph would be at her apartment playing cards and drinking alcohol. Janice's usual pattern was to say hello to Ralph and then go in to check on Margaret.

One night, Janice came home from work and Ralph was asleep on the couch with the television still playing. Beer cans were piled all around the living room and the smell of alcohol permeated Ralph's clothing and the room. When Janice went in to check on Margaret, she noticed that Margaret was very wet and was moaning in her sleep. Janice thought that she must have been uncomfortable from the wet diapers. When she changed her, she noticed what seemed to be bleeding from her vaginal area and what looked like a bruise at the tip of her tailbone. She also noted that Margaret seemed to have diarrhea. The following morning she took Margaret to her family doctor to have the diarrhea checked. The pediatrician gave her some medication for the diarrhea and sent her home with Janice. Although Janice had been concerned about the bleeding, she did not mention it to the doctor when he examined little Margaret. Janice felt relieved when the doctor gave her the medicine and sent her home. Margaret had hollered and screamed while being examined by the doctor. Margaret had never been such a bad patient before when Janice had taken her for visits to the doctor.

Later that afternoon, Ralph said that he would be out that evening and would not be able to watch Margaret while Janice worked. Janice took the baby to her mother's house. When Janice's mother, Mrs. Sinkle, changed Margaret's diaper, she became very alarmed at the bruise near her anus and the discharge. Janice had given her mother the medicine for the diarrhea and told her mother that she had taken Margaret to the doctor that day. Mr. and Mrs. Sinkle did not like Ralph and they did not approve of his babysitting Margaret while Janice worked. In fact, they felt that they should be caring for Margaret full-time as they had one of their other daughter's baby.

Mrs. Sinkle took Margaret to the emergency room soon after Janice left Margaret in her care. Lori, Janice's older sister who still lived at home with her parents, accompanied Mrs. Sinkle to the emergency room. Lori, like her parents, had no good feelings about Ralph and had often told her sister to have him move out since he did not contribute to the household expenses and Janice financially supported him.

While Margaret was hospitalized, the child protective service staff became involved. The evaluation of the child protective services social worker and the evaluation of the hospital psychiatrist concluded that Margaret had been sexually abused and the case would be given to the county attorney to prosecute Ralph. Since Ralph was still living at the apartment, it was decided that Margaret would be placed in a shelter care facility. Mrs. Sinkle did not feel confident that she would be able to keep

Margaret at her house if Janice wanted to take her home. The decision to put Margaret in the shelter care facility was to protect Margaret from possible further harm.

Figure 8.2 is an illustration of the family systems that are pertinent to Margaret's life. Margaret's father left her mother when Margaret was six-months-old. Janice reports that she had been very sad during that time and had to live with her parents while she found a job that would support her and her baby.

She met Ralph at about the same time that she moved into her own apartment. It is difficult to speculate what effect these influences had on Margaret, but she may have perceived some basic insecurity in her life during these times. She reportedly received good care and loving affection both from her mother and from her mother's family. She may have been able to establish trust which was the developmental task that she needed to master during her first year of life.

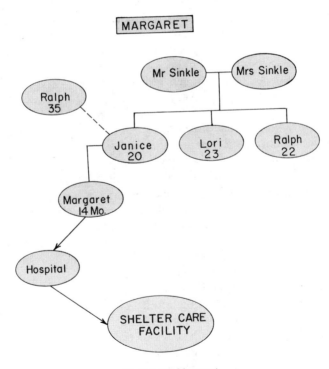

Figure 8-2 Margaret.

BIBLIOGRAPHY

Bolton, F.G., Kane, Sandra P., and Kruse, Roger F., *Child Abuse: Our Problem, Too.* Arizona Dept. of Education; Arizona Dept. of Economic Security, Phoenix, AZ, July 1979.

Brady, Katherine. *Father's Day.* Seaview Books, New York, 1979.

Burgess, Ann Wolbert. The Use of Children in Pornography and Sex Rings. In *Legal Response: Child Advocacy and Protection.* American Bar Association, *2,* 4, (Summer 1981), pp. 1, 10.

Burgess, Ann Wolbert, Holmstrom, Lynda Lytle, and McCausland, Maureen P. Child Sexual Assault by a Family Member: Decisions Following Disclosure. *Victimology. II,* 2, (Summer 1977) pp. 236–250.

Caplan, Gerald M. Sexual Exploitation of Children: The Conspiracy of Silence. *Police Magazine.* Vol. 5, No. 1 January 1982. pp. 46–51.

DeMause, Lloyd. Our Forebears Made Childhood a Nightmare. *Psychology Today.* April 1975, Vol. 8; 98, pp. 85–88.

Densen–Gerber, Judianne. Child Prostitution and Child Pornography: Medical, Legal, and Societal Aspects of the Commercial Exploitation of Children. *Sexual Abuse of Children: Selected Readings.* National Center on Child Abuse and Neglect, Children's Bureau, DHHS Publication OHDS 78-30161, November 1980.

DeVine, Rayline A. Sexual Abuse of Children: An Overview of the Problem. *Sexual Abuse of Children: Selected Readings,* National Center on Child Abuse and Neglect. Children's Bureau, DHHS Publication OHDS 78-30161, November 1980.

Elwell, Mary Ellen. Sexually Assaulted Children and Their Families. *Social Casework.* April, Vol. 60, 1979, pp. 227–235.

Executive Summary: National Incidence Study. Westat, Inc. and Development Associates Inc., 1981.

Finkelhor, David. *Sexually Victimized Children.* Free Press, New York, 1979.

Fisher, Bruce, Berdie, Jane, Cook, JoAnn, and Day, Noel. *Adolescent Abuse and Neglect: Intervention Strategies.* U.S. Department of Health and Human Services, Office of Human Development Services, 80-30266, Issued July 1980.

Ford, Frederick R. and Henrich, Joan. Family Rules: Family Life Styles. *Treatment of Family–Sexual Abuse.* University of Minnesota, Department of Family Practice and Community Health (no date).

Forward, Susan and Buck, Craig. *Betrayal of Innocence, Incest and its Devastation.* J. P. Tacher, Publisher, Los Angeles, 1978.

Giovannoni, Jeanne M. and Becerra, Rosina M. *Defining Child Abuse.* The Free Press, New York, 1979.

Gross, Meir. Incestuous Rape: A Cause for Hysterical Seizures in Four Adolescent Girls. *American Journal of Orthopsychiatry. 49,* 4, (October 1979) pp. 704–708.

Groth, A. Nicholas and Birnbaum, H. Jean. Adult Sexual Orientation and Attraction to Underage Persons. In *Sexual Abuse of Children.* National Center on Child Abuse and Neglect, DHHS 78-30161, November 1980, pp. 87–90.

James, Jennifer and Vitaliano, Peter Paul. Factors in the Drift Towards Female Sex

Role Deviance. Study supported by National Institute of Mental Health Center Grant, undated, unpublished paper.

Justice, Blair and Justice, Rita. *The Broken Taboo*. Human Sciences Press, New York, 1979.

Kempe, C. Henry and Helfer, Ray E. Eds., Incest and Other Forms of Sexual Abuse. In *The Battered Child*. 3rd Ed. University of Chicago Press, Chicago, 1980.

Kiersh, Edward. Can Families Survive Incest? *Corrections Magazine*. April 1980, Vol. 6, pp. 31–38.

Kocen, Lynne and Bulkley, Josephine. Analysis of Criminal Child Sex Offense Statutes. In *Child Sexual Abuse and the Law*. Edited by Josephine Bulkley. A report of the American Bar Association National Legal Resource Center for Child Advocacy and Protection. July 1981, pp. 1–51.

Leaman, Karen M. Sexual Abuse: The Reactions of Child and Family. *Sexual Abuse of Children*. National Center on Child Abuse and Neglect, DHHS 78-30161, November 1980, pp. 21–24.

Machotka, Pavel, Pittman, Frank S., and Flomenhaft, Kalman. Incest as A Family Affair. *Family Process*. 67, 6(1), 1967, pp. 98–116.

Markham, Margaret. MD's Urged to Be Alert To Sex Abuse of Infants. *Psychiatric News*. February 1, 1980, p. 1B.

Minuchin, S. *Families and Family Therapy*. Cambridge, MA, Harvard University Press, 1974.

Nash, Daniel. Legal Issues Related to Child Pornography. In *Legal Response: Child Advocacy and Protection*. 2, 4, (Summer 1981), p. 2.

Rosenzweig, Herschel D. Indications and Management of Sexually Abused Children. An unpublished, undated paper. Dr. Rosenzweig, former Director of Sexual Abuse Treatment Team, Children's Hospital Medical Center, Boston, MA 1981.

Sarles, Richard M. Incest. *Pediatric Clinics of North America*. 22, 3, (August 1975) pp. 633–642.

Scroi, Suzanne, M. 'Kids with Clap!', Gonorrhea as an Indicator of Child Sexual Assault. *Victimology*. II, 2, (Summer 1977) pp. 251–267.

Sexually Abused Children and Teenage Prostitution. Center for Women Policy Studies. 2000 P Street NW, Washington, DC 20036, May 2, 1980.

Sexual Exploitations of Juveniles: Chickenhawking. A Peace Officer Information Handbook, produced by the San Leandro Police Department, Training Division 1981.

Shamroy, Jerilyn A. A Perspective on Childhood Sexual Abuse. *Social Work*. 1980, pp. 128–131.

Silbert, Mimi H. *Prostitution and Sexual Assault (Delancey Street Study)*. (Unpublished summary.) February 1982.

Stern, Maddi-Jane and Meyer, Linda C. Family and Couple Interactional Patterns in Cases of Father/Daughter Incest. *Sexual Abuse of Children*. National Center on Child Abuse and Neglect. DHHS 78-30161, November 1980, pp. 83–86.

Summit, Roland and Kryso, JoAnn. Sexual Abuse of Children: A Clinical Spectrum. *Sexual Abuse of Children: Selected Readings*. Washington, D.C., NCCD, DHHS 78-30161, November 1980, pp. 51–58.

Summit, Roland. Typical Characteristics of Father–Daughter Incest. An unpublished paper. Roland Summit, M.D., Head Physician, Community Consultation Service, Assistant Professor of Psychiatry, Harbor–UCLA Medical Center, 1000 W. Carson, Torrance, CA.

U.S. Dept. of Health and Human Services. *Child Sexual Abuse: Incest Assault and Sexual Exploitation.* DHHS No (OHDS) 81-30166, April 1981.

Visher, Emily B. and Visher, John S. *Stepfamilies: A Guide to Working with Stepparents and Stepchildren.* Brunner/Mazel, New York, 1979.

Yates, Alayne. Chief, Child Psychiatry Division, University of Arizona, Health Science Center, Comments on manuscript, February 22, 1982.

9

Making the System Work

Child maltreatment is a community problem. It belongs to everyone. People involved in protecting children are part of a larger response network, whether or not they identify formally with such a network or are even aware that one exists. A single agency such as a department of public welfare provides only a small portion of the total formal and informal response to child abuse and neglect in any given community.

This chapter is about people and their motivations. It is also about the parameters and nature of the roles within which services are provided to children and families. Often a discussion of this sort focuses only on the functions and not on the people who provide them. People are helped by people. Agencies may facilitate or hinder the helping process. The law and administrative policy may help to define (and sometimes confuse) the parameters and nature of the help. Only people humanize and individualize the process.

Both the people and the roles are important. People who respond need to have clear personal goals and realistic expectations of others in order to secure positive change. Working with others requires self-awareness, energy, commitment, genuine caring, and respect for people.

On the other hand, the roles within which people function must be clearly defined in terms of what is offered, how it is offered, and how each role and its functions interface with others in the network. Clearly defined roles assume that the efforts of professionals, paraprofessionals, lay volunteers, and clients compliment rather than compete with or duplicate each other.

Better understanding of the roles of those who respond to child abuse and neglect brings better understanding of how to be most effective and how to interface individual roles with those of other people who might be touching the lives of members of a family.

WHO RESPONDS TO THE PROBLEM?

Child maltreatment is a legal, medical, social, and psychological problem. The need for response occurs across many disciplines and at many levels. Ideally, response can provide a wide range of service options and a network of many people available to help the abuser and abused. In reality, what is often provided is a fragmented, confusing array of services or no services at all, with much duplication of effort and many different and competing approaches to the problem. Communication and coordination are difficult to achieve in any context. In child abuse and neglect that difficulty is compounded by the complexities inherent both in the problem and in the variety and range of the responses. Sometimes personal jealousies, battles over turf, and even hostility intrude on objective decision-making within and among agencies. Other times, the issues experienced in communication and coordination are the result of differences in the philosophical foundations of the many disciplines involved.

Assume, for example, that you are a caseworker in child protective services, employed in a state welfare agency. You are working with a child named Paula whom you feel needs to be placed in a special program for sexually abused children. Approval from your supervisor, Mr. Travis, which has not been forthcoming, is important if you are to accomplish this placement. However, your commitment is firm. You truly believe that Paula will benefit from the program. Your agency has contracted with an independent review team composed of a psychiatrist, a psychologist, and a social worker who as a part of their contract, review all changes in case plans. You have the option of taking the case to them. Mr. Travis, who has worked closely with these people in the past, documents his disapproval of your plan. When the independent consultants review the case, they align themselves with Mr. Travis. You know that your agency also hires other consultants on selected abuse and neglect cases. One such consultant, a psychiatrist named Dr. Joseph, is someone with whom you have worked before and you know that he shares your philosophy. You arrange to have Paula evaluated by Dr. Joseph. He, who does not like the three people who have previously reviewed the case, sees the child, and, as you have predicted, recommends the program you support. Mr. Travis, furious at what he perceives to be your insubordination and challenge to his authority, orders you not to place this child, even though you now have the support of Dr. Joseph. Dr. Joseph, upon hearing the latest development in this drama, consults with a friend of his, Janice Light, who is a leader in the community and a well-known child advocate. She is a volunteer with several child care agencies and also privately assists a number of local children financially. Mrs. Light immediately calls the Director of Services (a minimum of two levels above your boss, Mr. Travis) and complains that the child is being deprived of an appropriate placement. The Director, Ms. Smith, works her way down the heirarchy. She orders an investigation of the situation immediately and a summary of that investigation brought to her. That order finally rests on the desk of the supervisor of Mr. Travis. In the meantime, the date for court review of this case has come due. The officer assigned by the Family Court to coordinate this matter calls you, reminding you that your report has not been sent to him for presentation to the judge. You explain to this officer the pending plan for Paula. He agrees. He has worked with some of the counselors in the program on other cases and thinks that their approach is one that would be helpful to Paula. Ms. Smith, upon review of the facts in the summary she has received, decides, given the psychiatrist's report and your recommendation, that she will support your position. You quickly write the report for court review including Dr. Joseph's and Ms. Smith's comments. You prepare to attend the court hearing with some relief. At last, it seems this matter will be concluded, not without a residue of hard feelings but, at least, you believe, in Paula's best interest. The judge reads your report and the report from his own officer. He has very strong feelings about this program. He does not believe that any child should be placed in a specialized sexual abuse program. At the hearing, he refuses to order such a placement.

This vignette includes only a few of the many agencies and individuals who share responsibility for Paula's welfare. It also deals only with a single decision-making issue rather than the many that might have to be faced in such a problem. But even in this narrow perspective, it illustrates some of the issues that are experienced by persons responding to child abuse and neglect.

Most areas now have a multidisciplinary child protection team that is supposed to focus, generally, on utilizing the expertise of each member. This team's major function may include the investigation, assessment, and treatment of cases of child abuse. Some teams achieve a high level of coordination and cooperation with others who are a part of the response network but not necessarily a part of the team. Other teams are teams in name only. No two are organized and implemented in precisely the same way. A discussion of the multidisciplinary team concept and its implementation is the subject of a later section of this chapter.

The child protection team is only a part of the broader child protection network that responds to problems of abuse and neglect. This group includes both private and public organizations and agencies. It includes people at various levels of training and expertise whose services are used in specific roles. Among these are professionals, paraprofessionals, and volunteers.

Professionals are usually considered to be people who are engaged in occupations that require a high level of training and proficiency. They are characterized by the standards of a particular profession or occupation. Professionals might be called on to function as expert witnesses in a hearing or trial. They would be asked to provide factual information and professional opinions based on their field of expertise. Professionals might include people working in criminal justice, juvenile justice, social work, education, medical, and ancillary service areas such as police officers, pediatricians, therapists, child protective service workers, teachers, judges, probation officers, psychiatrists, et al.

Paraprofessionals are generally considered to be people who have been trained in specific service areas, who are paid for their services, and who function in the systems mentioned above. The training and function of paraprofessionals is often formalized but not as intensive nor as extensive as that required for professionals. Paraprofessionals provide supportive services to the family and to the agency they serve. They work with professionals but their range of responsibility is not the same. They may or may not be employed full-time. Lay therapists, parent aides, social service aides, and teacher aides are all examples of paraprofessional positions.

Volunteers are people from the community who offer their time in some specific service-related area. They come to a public or private agency from all walks of life and with many different levels of education and experience. Their services expand the response that agencies can make to problems of abuse and neglect. Generally, they are offered specific orientation and training in their specific service areas. Volunteers are not paid for their services and they usually do not work full-time. They may function in all the systems mentioned above and more. They generally provide supportive services to the family and to the agency, sharing their own life skills with troubled families. In some cases, their service is identical to that provided by paraprofessionals. Volunteers respond as caring community members providing service to other community members. They often become advocates for children and families in the system of formal response (Figure 9-1).

A System of Response

The professionals, paraprofessionals, and volunteers who respond to child abuse and neglect situations usually do so through some part of the more formalized system of response. This system includes:

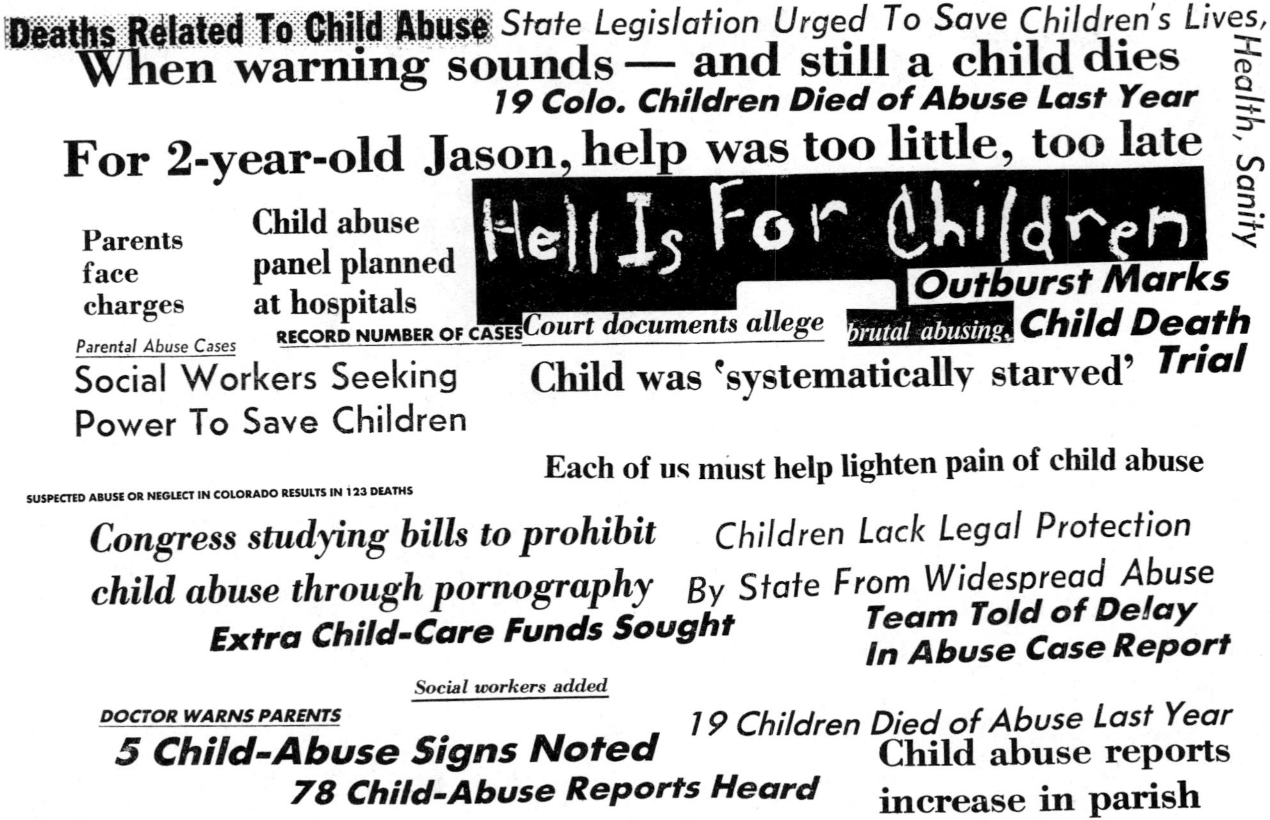
Deaths Related To Child Abuse
State Legislation Urged To Save Children's Lives, Health, Sanity
When warning sounds — and still a child dies
19 Colo. Children Died of Abuse Last Year
For 2-year-old Jason, help was too little, too late
Hell Is For Children
Parents face charges
Child abuse panel planned at hospitals
Outburst Marks
RECORD NUMBER OF CASES
Court documents allege
brutal abusing.
Child Death Trial
Parental Abuse Cases
Social Workers Seeking Power To Save Children
Child was 'systematically starved'
Each of us must help lighten pain of child abuse
SUSPECTED ABUSE OR NEGLECT IN COLORADO RESULTS IN 123 DEATHS
Congress studying bills to prohibit child abuse through pornography
Children Lack Legal Protection By State From Widespread Abuse
Extra Child-Care Funds Sought
Team Told of Delay In Abuse Case Report
Social workers added
DOCTOR WARNS PARENTS
5 Child-Abuse Signs Noted
19 Children Died of Abuse Last Year
Child abuse reports increase in parish
78 Child-Abuse Reports Heard

Figure 9-1

- Child Protective Services
- Law Enforcement
- Medical Services
- Legal Services
- Juvenile or Family Court
- Adult Justice Process
- Community Child Care Programs
- Schools
- Public and Private Social Services
- Church-related Groups

Many key services are provided to children and families through this network of response. Roles and responsibilities associated with each are discussed below. Some are formal and legally mandated roles; others are informal and not mandated. Still others combine some type of legal mandate and informal response.

CHILD PROTECTIVE SERVICES (CPS)

CPS is the agency that is primarily responsible for decisions relating to prevention, intervention, and treatment of child abuse and neglect in all states. Usually CPS is a part of the state or county welfare or human services system. Specialties within this unit may include, for example, a child sexual abuse unit. CPS has primary access to people supervising specialized shelter care and short-term foster and group care of abused and neglected children who have been removed from their homes. Services are provided by professional, paraprofessional, and volunteer staff.

CPS provides direct services to families and monitors child abuse and neglect cases. CPS is the agency that, in most states, is mandated by law to evaluate reported child abuse and neglect cases and to ensure that ". . . preventive, evaluative, and treatment programs are responsive first to the needs of abused and/or neglected children and then to the needs of their families." (Jenkins et al., p. 7.)

In some states, the parameters and minimum criteria for the treatment to be provided or coordinated by CPS is mandated by law. In other states, the implication of the legislation is that once a situation of abuse or neglect is reported, all services will simply fall into place. (Smith, et al., p. 19.) The effectiveness of the CPS delivery system has a major impact on the nature and effectiveness of intervention and treatment in child abuse and neglect situations. CPS is unique in that it provides, as Jenkins suggests, an "involuntary" social service. The worker may be a manager of resources, a provider of services, and/or a purchaser of services.

CPS responsibility includes a broad range of response areas.

Identification and reporting of child abuse and neglect situations.

Intake and investigation of reported cases.

Assessment and planning for children and families in substantiated cases of abuse and neglect.

Treatment and referral.

Termination and follow up.

Coordination and implementation of required procedures in every reported case. (Jenkins et al.)

A CPS Perspective

CPS workers trained in social work concepts are more likely to approach problems of child abuse from within the context of the family than from the context of criminal justice. Where possible, CPS seeks the cooperation of the family in an intervention and treatment plan. If cooperation is present, police intervention and criminal justice proceedings may be avoided. In some cases, however, working with the police may add protection to the child and provide additional services to the family. Police, as authority figures, can also bring power to the child who has felt powerless in the situation.

Offenders and passive parents (parents who did not actively abuse the child but who permitted the abuse) may appear cooperative at first, but may not follow through on treatment plans. In these circumstances, the criminal justice system involvement can add more assurance of the parents' continued compliance with treatment and child supervision agreements. Monitoring of the offender's behavior by the system is increased.

Removal from the home is not considered by most CPS workers to be necessarily the best way to protect every child. If the child can remain at home, and the family remain intact while supportive services are being provided, the chance for positive change is enhanced. If anyone has to be removed, the better choice might be the offender. Some children do need to be removed in order to protect them from further abuse. Of these children, some may later return home once the home situation has stabilized and the parents are better able to offer protection. Others never return home.

Response Issues

Typically, CPS units are understaffed, have limited in-service training options, and are provided with inadequate funds to achieve outreach work.

Consequently, the conscientious worker is generally overworked and underpaid. The worker spends much time writing reports, justifying time spent, and having plans reviewed by supervisors, review boards, and protection teams. It is sometimes difficult for CPS to gain the cooperation of other agencies. Workers often have difficulty finding placements that match the needs of the child.

Fluctuation in public opinion on such issues as the cost of foster care and other care of children placed out of their homes, the rights of parents, and the definition of appropriate child discipline affect the policies and procedures within which the CPS staff operates and the resources available to workers. Other systems issues have impact on CPS function. According to Ann Nichols, D.S.W., Professor, Arizona State University School of Social Work, one such issue is the concern of many professional social workers about an apparent deprofessionalization of social work practice in the field. States where graduate level licensure exists appear to have less difficulty than others in maintaining high educational qualification for employment in CPS units. Walter Friedlander and Robert Apte comment more broadly, "A growing proportion of [professionally trained social workers] are persons without graduate degrees. Since 1970 persons holding a baccalaureate degree in social work have been entitled to membership in the NASW [National Association of Social Workers]." (pp. 486–487.)

CPS workers are easy targets to blame. They get the wrath of the family, the awesome mandated responsibility for protection of the child, pressure and criticism from the community and the courts, and advice, generally in hindsight, from other agencies and individuals. Often they even lack support within their own agency and have to contend with a negative stereotype of the "welfare worker." Emotional exhaustion combined with a lack of personal and agency resources to replenish their depleted energy supply leads to "burn out." Discouraged workers create new problems through decreased sensitivity to the needs of their clients and a cynicism toward the work in general.

A Positive Note

Considering the odds, CPS workers provide a significant service. Where they are provided with a support system, outlets to vent their own frustrations, and resources, they are able to offer protection and support to children and families. Changes in the reporting laws and increased community awareness of child abuse and neglect have resulted in a greater volume of cases. These changes have brought accompanying pressures on CPS, since personnel increases have seldom kept pace with the demand for services. The same changes, however, have also helped to clarify the CPS service role. CPS is increasingly seen as serving an important function. Available federal funding within the last ten years has provided many such units with the opportunity to test new programs of intervention and treatment and to enhance the ability of CPS to respond.

LAW ENFORCEMENT

In matters of neglect and abuse, law enforcement agencies are mandated to receive and investigate reports, to report, and to intervene where the child's immediate safety is in question. They share some of these responsibilities with CPS.

Law enforcement officers represent a key resource in child abuse and neglect. They are available 24 hours a day, 7 days a week in every community. They are known as a resource to most people, easy to reach and recognize, and quick to respond when force is an issue. Police are called, even by CPS and other network members who might have made the initial response.

Some police agencies have specially trained child abuse units. Generally, officers who are a part of these units are also a part of an identified multidisciplinary community team. In addition to intervention services, these units also participate in community prevention programs, making presentations, participating in developing and implementing media events and seminars. Even in communities where such units exist, the officer who is the first to respond to emergency calls regarding child abuse is most often the line officer on patrol. He or she also is the law enforcement representative who is most likely to be in a position, routinely, to report suspected incidences of child abuse and neglect.

The Police Perspective

The police image is one of authority. Many police officers tend to see themselves as crime fighters, even though most research since the 1950s has indicated that police agencies devote less than 20% of their time and energy to crime-related problems. Most of it is spent in public service activities. (Mayhall and Geary, pp. 99–117.) Some police agencies, as a matter of policy, automatically refer cases to CPS for processing without investigation by their own agency. Such matters are seen as "social work" issues rather than police issues.

Such a view is not universal in police work, however. Many large agencies have trained officers in the specialty of handling family crises. This change has come about not only because of the need to respond to child abuse and neglect situations, but also because family disturbances are particularly dangerous situations for police officers. The Uniform Crime

Reports indicate that from 1970–1979, 181 officers were killed responding to disturbance calls. *(Uniform Crime Reports for the U.S.*, p. 311.)

One situation requiring the specific services of law enforcement is the death of a child through maltreatment. This situation is treated as murder and is investigated and processed though the criminal justice system. Hopefully, an important part of this investigation is also in relation to other children in the home. Are these children safe? What are the living circumstances of the home? The investigating officer is a person who can offer protection to the other children in the home.

Police officers are more likely to see maltreatment at its extreme, usually as physical or sexual abuse. They are less likely to be involved in emotional abuse, neglect, and less serious situations of all types of abuse. (Child abuse and neglect are, at least, an emotional experience for all who respond.) Police officers rarely see the resolution of the problem, so their emotional residue is from the scene of the crisis and the sometimes incomprehensible harm to the child. The police officer's experience contributes to his/her overall view of what abuse and neglect are and what should happen to offenders.

Response Issues

Generally speaking, police officers on the street who are the first to respond to emergency situations are very possibly the least prepared to deal with them. Through no fault of their own they usually lack the specific training and diagnostic skills to evaluate the seriousness of abuse and neglect situations. Law enforcement agencies are generally understaffed. Priorities for action are set in response to community pressures and an administrative police perspective of the police role in the community. Child abuse investigations are not high on the priority list in many agencies.

Police officers, by the very nature of their training and their work, are somewhat isolated and alienated from the community as a whole. The threat of danger brings with it a certain distrust. Working closely and sharing information with child protection services may appear to be in conflict with agency policy and police function. Some police officers disagree in principle with treatment programs for abusive parents. From their vantage point, offenders, at minimum, should be arrested, brought to court, convicted, and sent to prison. It is easy to feel impatient with a social service approach that seems soft and unjust.

On A Positive Note

The establishment of a child abuse unit as part of a police agency is, in itself, a very positive move on the part of an agency toward cooperation and coordination of response efforts. As Cathy Schmitz of the Sexual Assault Unit, Harborview Medical Center in Seattle, Washington points out, the power and authority vested by law in police agencies can be used to empower the child and can encourage the cooperation of family members in treatment efforts sometimes by the simple fact of its existence. Arrest as an available option and institutionalization as an alternative to failure to seek treatment, if used in a therapeutic context, can be positive motivators toward necessary change.

MEDICAL SERVICES

The health-care system includes many disciplines, many facilities, and a wide variety of private and public agencies under its broad umbrella. This is a rather fragmented system at best. Yet members of this system are very likely to come in contact with and have the opportunity to diagnose and document situations of abuse and neglect. This discussion centers on a few of the key members of this system who are most frequently placed in this position—the physician, nurse, emergency room staff, and mental health professionals.

The Physician: A Perspective

Dr. George Commerci, a pediatrician who works with many abused children, states that,

> . . . the prime responsibility of the health professional who confronts a case of suspected abuse is to care for the child. Once the immediate medical needs have been met, the appropriate authorities will enter the case. They, and not the doctor, will conduct the investigation. The doctor can contribute by determining whether the child's caretakers have supplied an adequate explanation for the trauma.

He cautions that the fact-finding focus of the health professional is on *how* the injury occurred rather than *who* caused it. (Letson, p. 7.) The chief role of the physician is centered on the welfare of the patient. The physician needs to be an accurate diagnostician who can prescribe and provide medical treatment where appropriate. The law in many states requires that a diagnosis of damage to the child through nonaccidental means be made by the physician, psychiatrist, or, in some cases, a psychologist, in order for CPS to coercively intervene to protect the child. The physician is also mandated by law to report suspicions of abuse and neglect to CPS or law enforcement. The physician may also be required to testify in court. Many states eliminate the privilege that usually exists under law that protects the communications between doctor and patient from being used in court.

Responding Issues

Physicians may find diagnosis of abuse difficult. Even radiologists, orthopedists, surgeons, ophthalmologists, and persons in other medical specialties sometimes do not recognize cases of abuse and neglect. Their focus is not on child-rearing and family function. Although they might question exceptional cases, they might never ask and a parent or child might not volunteer information about the true nature of the circumstances of the injury to the child. Many times, when they do ask, abuse is denied and no follow up is made. Although pediatricians might be more likely than other physicians to query these areas, even they would not be as likely as social service professionals to observe for interactional data between the child and caretaker that might provide information regarding abuse. Many are simply unwilling or unable to confront the issue.

Other issues that act as barriers to the reporting of abuse by physicians include: (1) their own concerns regarding confidentiality, privacy of the family, and what they see as professional ethics; (2) the possibility of liability; (3) damage to their practice; (4) the ordeal of testifying in court, both in terms of the time lost from their practice and the experience of being a witness in court; (5) the possible wrath of parents. (Eskin and Kravitz, pp. 38–39.)

On A Positive Note

Many physicians, particularly pediatricians and emergency room physicians, have become members of child protection teams and actively participate in prevention, intervention, and treatment efforts. Many hospitals have established internal child abuse teams so that if abuse is suspected by any diagnostician, the report can be made to the team. Team members will examine the patient and follow up on the case. They will be called to testify in juvenile (family) or adult court as to their firsthand information. They are particularly well prepared for court hearings with complete data and with an understanding of court protocol and adversary proceedings. (See Chapter 11 for more information on testifying in court.)

Obstetricians and gynecologists may be in an excellent position to prevent abuse by listening to parents and by establishing a positive doctor–patient relationship. Early referrals made by a concerned physician to other community resources can give parents an opportunity to gain parenting skills and realistic expectations of themselves and their children.

Physicians also can be helpful after abuse has occurred in the healing process for the child. In addition to healing the body, the physician can help the child to know that he or she is physically whole—a complete and adequate person. This is a very important concern for children who have been sexually abused. (Schmitz.)

Nurses: A Perspective

The nurse's role in response to abuse and neglect is actually much broader than the physician's. Although the nurse may be less likely to testify in court, he may be a part of the identification, the treatment, and the prevention aspects of child maltreatment. Nurses can be a nonthreatening and available resource to children and families. Parents and children are sometimes more willing to confide in nurses than in other adults. Nurses may be employed in schools, doctor's offices, hospitals, and public health agencies. The very nature of their profession is caretaking and concern. They are in a position to act as an advocate for the child. Nurses and other health service professionals are mandated by law to report child abuse and neglect. They may face charges of negligence and malpractice if they do not.

Response Issues

Often, the barrier to reporting and active participation of nurses is lack of information as to what to report, where to report, and what services they can provide. Reporting abuse in rural communities, established neighborhoods, military installations, and Indian reservations is difficult for nurses as well as other possible reporters because of the personalized nature of the community and the fact that confidentiality becomes very difficult to maintain when people are related, close friends, or working and living in close proximity. Customs and culture must also be considered not only in determining whether or not to report but also how to report and how best to be an advocate for the child. Nurses may also find themselves in conflict with people for whom they work who may have objection to reporting, or who establish reporting procedures that may actually complicate and dilute the reporting function.

On A Positive Note

In states where an aggressive educational program in matters of abuse and neglect has been instituted for school nurses, the nurses have, in turn, become a central resource in the education of their respective agencies and institutions and in the establishment of policies and procedures for reporting. School nurses receive reports from other school personnel; public health nurses, working in the neighborhood and the home, have the opportunity to prevent, identify, and treat maltreatment in the home; nurses in all settings including hospitals and doctor's offices may act as a resource for children and parents, and through that function, prevent abuse and neglect. They also have opportunities to observe inadequate bonding in delivery rooms and maternity wards. They are also in position to identify high–risk cases and to provide appropriate links between parents and public health services and parenting programs.

Emergency Room Staff: A Perspective

This staff works with others in a hospital or clinic setting. Often they are the first to see the abuse. They deal with the family in crisis. If they act quickly (taking appropriate x-rays, a thorough history, and if directed by proper authority, photographs), they may be able to document abuse that will be more difficult to document at a later time.

Response Issues

Response issues are similar to those mentioned regarding other health professionals. The chief problem with emergency room response is the fact that documentation may not be very clear, nor complete. Unless a system of response is established so that a physician regularly takes the responsibility of working with CPS and the court, testimony presented may be weak and inadequate for a finding of dependency.

Dependency is a legal status given to children who are determined through juvenile or family court process to be abused, neglected, or without the proper protection of parent or caretaker, either because that person was unable or unwilling to provide proper care. In contrast, delinquency is a legal status given to children who are determined through juvenile or family court process to have committed an act against the law. In a delinquency petition, the offense(s) of the child are alleged and the petitioner requests that the child be adjudicated (or officially labeled, judged) a delinquent. In a dependency petition the conditions that prove that the child is in jeopardy are alleged and the petitioner requests a finding of dependency in order to protect the child. Documentation in the emergency room may provide the proof necessary to legally protect the child. Lack of proof could leave the court with insufficient evidence of dependency, which may result in dismissal of the petition.

On A Positive Note

Clear policies and procedures can be developed that will assure such information will be gathered. If the staff suspects abuse, they can admit the child to the hospital for further x-rays and tests. Frequently, evidence of old injuries will show up on x-rays. Hospitals that have established clear policies and procedures and that operate a medical protection team provide more immediate protection for the child and are better able to document that protection for CPS.

JUVENILE OR FAMILY COURT

A Perspective

The juvenile or family court is, in effect, a parent of last resort. Generally, by the time the court responds officially to a situation of child abuse and neglect, several other agencies and individuals are already involved. Apparently, there is a need for the legal structure and authority of the court in decision-making regarding the child and family. Although less than 20% of all reported cases of abuse and neglect are formally petitioned through the court process, the court's role is a particularly important one. It is given the power and jurisdiction by law to monitor and maintain authority over matters relating to the protection of children. Central to its function is jurisdiction over issues of delinquency, dependency, and children in need of supervision (CHINS) for reasons such as incorrigibility or unruliness.

The court's authority is broad. It may include temporary removal of children from their home, severance of parental rights, decisions relating to the welfare of children (e.g., whether or not medical treatment should be given to a child even though the parents refuse consent), permission for children under legal age to marry. Essentially, the court's concern is to act in the child's best interest. In recent years, the changes in interpretations of the authority of the court, the definition of due process in juvenile court, and the appropriate balance of the rights of children and parents have changed the nature of the procedures and the hearings in the court. Chapter 11 deals with many of these issues in depth. At this point it is only important to state that the court has a particularly powerful overseer role over such matters.

Response Issues

Depending upon one's position in relation to the daily workings of the justice system in relation to child abuse and neglect (e.g., administrators, legislative planners, social workers, police, prosecutors, medical workers, parents, and children), the legal process of intervention may be seen as fragmented, feeble, or futile. (Smith, et al., p. 18.)

There are few easy decisions in dependency matters. Goldstein, Solnit, and Freud reflect on the difficulty of the placement decisions that the court is required to make: "While the law may claim to establish relationships, it can in fact do little more than give them recognition and provide an opportunity for them to develop. It may be able to destroy human relationships; but it does not have the power to compel them to develop." (1973.) There is doubt that decision-making under such circumstances is at best difficult. Judges and referees who hear dependency cases need to be aware of the concerns and issues surrounding dependency situations. Often they are not. People who come before the court, whatever their roles, need to understand the court's function and how it can best be used to protect the child. Often they do not. People working within the court on dependency matters need to be particularly careful to pursue cooperation, communication, and coordination among the various members of the response network. This task belongs to all people who perform the functions of the court process, from those who first come in contact with the child to those responsible for carrying out the orders of the court including those responsible for temporary care of children outside their homes and volunteer services. (Chapter 11 discusses the court process in greater detail.)

One such service, the volunteer *Guardian Ad Litem* Program, which is available in a few courts across the country, trains volunteers to function as officers of the court and as advocates for children. There is some similarity in this volunteer function to that of an attorney appointed guardian *ad litem*. An attorney appointed as advocate for the child legally represents the child's interests in court and attempts to keep in focus the question of "What will be best for the child?" The volunteer guardian approaches the same question but not from the same perspective as an attorney. The volunteer becomes a very practical resource for the court. He or she is the one person who contacts everyone involved in the case in an effort to determine what is the child's best interests. On the surface, this role seems to duplicate functions of many other agencies involved in the case. In reality, rarely has any other person communicated with all other parties from the perspective of the best interest of the child. In all too many cases no one has even spoken with the child for more than a month prior to the hearing.

Courts of all types and in all jurisdictions, including tribal courts, face many difficulties. Some are jurisdictional issues, but most are the same as those experienced by other agencies. They are understaffed, have long dockets, and a large backlog of cases. In matters of child abuse and neglect, delay in itself can be harmful to the child. Education of judges and their staff in dependency matters is often lacking. The majority of cases in juvenile courts are delinquency matters. These are more familiar to most staff members. Attention to children and families in neglect and abuse is important in preventing delinquency. Recent studies indicate that a CPS and the juvenile or family court for dependency matters were later referred for delinquent acts. (See Smith et al.)

There seems to be almost a tradition of competition and hostility between CPS and juvenile courts. The power struggle for control is apparent, particularly in adjudication and dispositional matters. (CPS does the major portion of the intake activity.) Adjudication is the finding of the court that the allegations of the petition are true. This judgment occurs after sufficient evidence has been presented to support the allegations or the allegations have been admitted. Following adjudication, the court must make a decision as to what placement and what treatment plan will be in the child's best interest. This decision is based on input from all interested parties and court staff. CPS workers accuse the court of making decisions to confirm its authority rather than as a response to the needs of the child. They suggest that the court has no concept of the problems they face and do not cooperate with protective services, thus making their job even more difficult. The court accuses CPS of being inept, of providing the court with inadequate and incomplete reports, and of not making effective plans for children and families. Yet these two systems are required by law and by the nature of their functions to work together and to share in the protection and supervision of children. As Giovannini and Becerria state, "... the potential for conflict between courts and social workers is clear. Perspectives on child rearing may exist along a continuum, but interventive action does not." (p. 97.) Judge Robert Mallard talks of the role of a judge, "The legal issues that face a judge, the role that we really play as judges in this child protection or abuse prevention field, is that we have to make these decisions that affect a family's life."(Mallard, p. 71.) Later, in the same article, he adds, "... we don't operate our courts on the theory of punishment. We operate our courts on the theory that we will look at this case. We will determine the facts. We will make a decision which will be ... in the best interests of this child and his or her family." (Mallard, p. 74.)

A Positive Note

Many judges are very conscientious and deeply concerned about the many issues related to dependency. Support for training and the sharing of ideas among juvenile court judges are important. New technologies promise some continuing opportunities for such sharing. A judicial college for juvenile and family court judges has not only been offered at the University of Nevada campus, but with the support of local judges and the National Council of Juvenile Court and Family Judges has also been presented in workshop formats around the country. (Wittman.)

Volunteers in the court process are also a vital part of the present day court. They involve the community in the functions of the court and provide some very powerful and meaningful advocates for kids.

THE LEGAL PROFESSION

Less than twenty years ago, an attorney was a rarity in any case in juvenile court. Today there can be as many as seven or more attorneys in the courtroom, each representing various interests in a single dependency case. Imagine being the judge in a case that includes an attorney for the state, an attorney for the child, (sometimes in addition to a guardian *ad litem),* an attorney for each parent, an attorney for the foster parents, another for the grandparents, and yet another for some other relative. Although this situatiion is unusual, the very fact that it does occur points to the dramatic change in the nature of juvenile and family "informal" matters. It also opens a new area of specialty for attorneys, one which is so new that many attorneys are still struggling to understand the juvenile justice system.

When Giovannini and Beccera surveyed attorneys, pediatricians, social workers, and police officers, for a definition of child abuse, they found that the attorneys were the most conservative in their definitions. They were also far more concerned with the rights of parents than any other group. (Giovannini and Beccera, 1981.) Attorneys have insisted upon more structure in the juvenile justice process and more clarity and preciseness in the evidence presented. They are concerned with legal precedence. They tend to support their arguments with reference to law while social workers support theirs with references to psychiatric, psychological evaluations, family history, or the child's needs. Both are concerned with both areas, but the attorney seeks an element of regularity in procedures; she may in fact find him/herself attempting to prevent "well-intentioned efforts to help that proceed via legal shortcuts." (Fox, p. 159.)

In addition to representation in juvenile court, the caretaker's attorney also may represent him or her in adult court, where the caretaker may be facing criminal charges. Although in many states the privileged communications between physician and patient, therapist and client, and husband and wife are specifically disallowed in child abuse matters, the privilege between attorney and client continues to be protected.

Response Issues

Accustomed to and trained in an adversary process, attorneys have brought many elements of the adult adjudicatory system into juvenile courts including some of its delays. More motion are made and points of law argued routinely in juvenile and family courts than ever before. The arguments themselves serve to slow down the court process. While assuring that the rights of all persons involved are protected, they sometimes interfere with the best interests of the child. The balance between these interests is a difficult one to achieve. To have a child returned to the parents because of a legal loophole might make the child vulnerable to continued abuse. The attorney is in a new ethical dilemma in such matters.

Mutual misunderstandings between attorneys and medical experts interfere with the presentation of evidence and therefore with the protection of children. Medical experts often have little understanding of court procedure and presentation of evidence. Attorneys often do not know the best questions to ask their medical witnesses in order to provide complete and concise medical data. Communication and mutual education between these two disciplines is imperative if the interests of children are to be served. (See also Chapter 11.)

On A Positive Note

The attorney with the most facilitating role in the dependency matter is the child's attorney. This person, whose function is to assure that all evidence is heard that will be in the child's best interest, will have an opportunity to cross-examine other witnesses and ask questions that others might have avoided or not been permitted to ask. All parties seek this attorney's cooperation and understanding, if not his/her alliance.

Attorneys are taking their new role in juvenile and family courts seriously. They are developing local and state councils of attorneys for children. They are sharing information through the American Bar Association and through its National Legal Resource Center for Child Advocacy and Protection that will guide attorneys and others who need answers to legal questions related to children. They are joining with professionals from many other disciplines to sponsor and deliver seminars and to develop training materials that are multidisciplinary in nature. The American Bar Association is currently involved in an NCCAN supported project to develop a compendium of case law bearing on issues of child abuse and neglect.

Attorneys are actively seeking a better understanding of the children they represent. Many are increasing their knowledge of child development and their skills in interviewing children, centering on the child's feelings and being respectful of children. They are seeking ways to encourage the participation of children in decision-making regarding their own lives wherever possible. As is true for many other people who respond to child abuse and neglect, their most difficult task is in learning how to avoid pitting child and parent against each other, and how to understand the child's loyalty to the parent who has been abusive to the child.

The legal profession is now involved in dependency hearings, severance of parental rights, reviews, and criminal court trials. Attorneys involved are from both private and public sectors: the state or county attorney, the public defender's officer, and many private attorneys engaged by the parents or appointed by the court. Individually and as a group, they help to bring checks and balances to the juvenile justice process elements.

THE ADULT JUSTICE PROCESS

A Perspective

The adult justice process responds to matter of child abuse and neglect when the abuser is prosecuted. This court focuses on the illegality of the offense, the finding of guilt or innocence, and the punishment appropriate under law. This system was designed to focus on the offender and the offense, not upon the victim and his/her needs. The nature of the trial, the disposition, and its implementation do have an impact on the child and the family. In some cases, where positive change in the family is highly unlikely and protection of the child or other children requires it, a prison sentence may be in order. This may be particularly true for the repeat offender. More often, it is possible for the court and probation officer to work with CPS and other intervening agencies in order to provide a structure within which treatment can take place.

Response Issues

As with other systems, this one moves particularly slowly. In the process of fact-finding, the child and other family members may be required to testify against the caretaker who actively abused the child. This may be a very emotional and disturbing experience for the child. It may also create additional pressure on an already crisis-laden family, especially if the cultural rules of the family forbid speaking out against a family member. Since abuse occurs behind closed doors and in intimate circumstances, many circumstances of abuse may be very difficult to prove in court. The child may see the person who abused him/her acquitted.

Intra- and interagency cooperation and coordination may be difficult to achieve. Control over the program and/or its goals may be an issue. It is possible to fight over the most inconsequential of issues. Who is to be included in staffings? To whom should copies of progress reports be sent? Should the inmate be required to pay some money toward his "board and room" at the jail while he participates in a work/treatment program?

On A Positive Note

Cooperation requires an informed judge and staff, coordination between the adult probation office, CPS, and community agencies offering treatment. Support staff in all of these areas must be involved. If the offender is convicted and sentenced to time in an institution, yet will be returning home, the state correctional system needs to begin working with the offender and the family from the outset to protect the child.

This sort of cooperation does occur. An example exists in the Harborview Sexual Abuse Program. There, the police, medical staff, juvenile and adult courts, supervisory probation staff, treatment programs, child protective services, and the child abuse unit work together, each providing a specific function. Others may also be involved in a specific case. Members of the "team" have joint meetings. They have training sessions that are commonly attended as well as some sessions that are designed as in-service for a specific agency. Every member of the group has a clear role that contributes to the long-range protection and health of the child. This means the strengthening of the family, strengthening the child, and stability for the child. The probation officer, in this situation, supervises the offender who has been convicted and is placed in a community treatment program. Supervision adds to the security of the child and the likelihood that the offender will continue with treatment.

SCHOOLS

A Perspective

The National Incidence Study found that ". . . public schools are the source of 65% of the children reported by non-CPS agencies and accepted as part of the study, or 'in-scope' group as meeting project criteria. Indeed the schools were the source of more than half of all reports on 'in-scope' children made to the study from all sources." They actually ". . . reported to CPS only 13% of the 'in-scope' children which they recognize and reported to the study." At that, public schools still reported more than twice as many children (in-scope) to CPS than any other type of agency. (Executive Summary, pp. 22–25.)

School personnel are a major reporting resource but they only report a very small percentage of the total abuse and neglect that they are aware of. Educators have many roles in response to the problem of abuse and neglect. They assist in identification, treatment, and prevention of abused and neglected children. They are major resources in that they see children for long periods of time on a regular basis. They have the opportunity to observe the child in learning situations and in interactions with others. They also may be able to gain first-hand insights into the child's home situation as well.

Educators are in an excellent position to prevent abuse and neglect through parenting programs for parents and youth in the school, in-service programs for staff, and the use of the school as an information and service resource for families. Teachers and administrators can participate in the development of educational policies and procedures through the school board that will encourage local schools to be involved in response efforts.

Response Issues

Many teachers do not report abuse and neglect, either because they overlook it, perhaps believing that harsh punishment of children is appropriate, or because they do not wish to get involved. Reporting is particularly difficult for teachers in small communities. Reporting can be seen as an intrusion into a family's private life.

Charges can be and are brought against schol personnel who have not reported abuse. If convicted, such personnel can be fined or, in some jurisdictions, face a possible jail term.

School involvement in prevention programs can be seen as increasing the already heavy burden of responsibility for children already assigned to the district and the individual teacher. In some cases, reporting may have been a negative experience. The teacher may have reported cases to authorities and either nothing was done or the solution was unsatisfactory in the teacher's eyes.

Some educators argue that the confidentiality of records laws that were passed in the Federal Family Education Rights and Privacy Act of 1974 prevent reporting child abuse without the parents' consent. Most situations require observation of the child, not school records. Even if reports from records were necessary, recent interpretations of that Act make it clear that it does not bar reporting of suspected abuse. If a health or safety emergency exists, if release of information to state or local authorities is required, or if a judicial order, or subpoena has been issued commanding release of information, that information may be released so long as some attempt is made to notify the parents in advance. (Broadhurst.)

On A Positive Note

Schools include a variety of personnel who all interact with children. In addition to classroom teachers, most schools have a principal, vice-principal, office staff, counselors, school nurse, special-education teachers, teacher aides, and parent volunteers. For a school to effectively respond to problems of abuse and neglect, all of these people need to be educated to recognize symptoms of maltreatment. They also need to know what procedures should be followed in the event that such situations are observed. The procedure could be spelled out in a memo to all staff, describing what is to be done if a person observes what might be abuse or neglect, what documentation is to be required, and who specifically should be notified. Many districts have developed and distributed such information.

Schools have several roles in relation to child maltreatment. If the school is concerned with the "total child," then an abused child is the school's problem. It is their legally mandated responsibility to report the problem. It is also their opportunity to act as a resource for children and families and to confirm the interrelatedness of emotional, academic and physical growth, and development of the child. (Jones, p. 19.) Next to the time they spend at home, children spend more time at school than in any other social institution in our society. If the school does not act as a part of the solution, it becomes a part of the problem. Garbarino suggests that there are many things the schools can do: model nonviolent interpersonal relations, act as a support system for children and families, work cooperatively with other resources, and act as advocates for children. (Garbarino, p.206.)

Many suggest that the teacher's role for many of these children is that of a psychological parent. This parent, as defined by Goldstein, Solnit, and Freud, is ". . . one who, on a continuing, day-to-day basis, through interaction, companionship, interplay, and mutuality, fulfills the child's psychological needs for a parent, as well as the child's physical needs." (1973.)

Reports from the Education Commission of the States suggest that there has been an increase in services provided by schools to abused and neglected children. These reports also indicate that school systems are increasingly becoming involved with other network members in response efforts, often through representation on interdisciplinary child protection teams. (pp.6−7, Report # 109.)

center, and create additional financial problems for the program, too. In some agencies, no reporting procedure has been established and therefore staff may be uncertain as to what, where, and how to report.

On A Positive Note

Much improvement in reporting has occurred in child care programs. Public awareness has sharpened general sensitivity to the problem. Caretakers in such facilities are receiving training in recognizing and intervening on behalf of the abused and neglected child. Programs for parents and children are being sponsored by such agencies. Parenting classes are offered.

The possibilities for response by child care programs are endless. They could offer services such as family day care as a treatment resources. Parents could attend the center with children in order to learn improved parenting skills. The fact that staff has an opportunity regularly to interact with the parents may also allow them to observe the parents and offer nurturing and support.

SELF-HELP GROUPS

A Perspective

Self-help groups are very much like the social agencies and programs already discussed. They may be privately sponsored or sponsored by one of the agencies working with families. They may be informally or formally structured. Self-help groups have a goal that is clearer and more singular than many of the other agencies and programs that have been discussed in this section. These groups are specifically geared to be supportive of the client and to encourage the client to be supportive of others within the group(s). Such groups include Parents Anonymous, Parents United, Alcoholics Anonymous, Drug Abuse self-help programs, etc. Such groups usually focus on sharing pain, but also on modeling approaches for change. The assumption made is that a person who "has been there" and has been able to change positively is not only a model for others but also a sign of hope. In the very act of reaching out to help others, the person who has gained control over his/her life, strengthens that control.

Response Issues

Sometimes abusers who do not seek treatment in addition to the self-help group, do not make the necessary changes to provide protection for the child. The support group may or may not be willing to report one of their own. It is difficult to do. It is also difficult to assess the point at which coercive intervention is the best choice.

On A Positive Note

Self-help group members have experienced the dynamics of family violence and the process of change. They often include in their support group professional therapists and others who can assist in some decision-making. Peer influence, the commonality of experience, and an opportunity provided by the group to normalize experience and relationships all help to make the self-help programs successful.

Other People Who Respond

There are several other individuals and groups that might be mentioned separately as part of this broad response network. Certainly, foster parents serving through human services departments, through the juvenile court, or some private agencies respond to abuse and neglect. Group homes and other long and short-term residential care facilities can be considered a separate category of response. The response of people working in these areas must, of necessity, be in offering support supervision and treatment, often after the fact. Their greatest opportunity for help may be in nurturing the child and family and in assisting both or either to gain life skills and self-esteem.

Secretaries, dieticians, and groundskeepers in the schools and in private and public agencies, ministers and priests, people who are responsible for driving children and/or parents to appointments are all an important part of this network. The very fact that they are not one of the "professionals" with whom the child and parent are required to interact makes them more appealing. Since they do not seem to be directly associated with the "department" they may be easier to talk with or at least easier to talk freely with. These people do not attempt to replace others in the program. In fact, they have to be very aware of their own behavior in order to be nurturing and helpful, even though the parents and child may not always present them- selves positively to them. Self-awareness and situation awareness is impor- tant to anyone who responds. Without these, interactions with the child and family may undermine the work that has already been accomplished.

A Positive Note

Food represents nurturing as well as nutrition for most people. Food will sometimes break down communication barriers that seem to be permanently concreted in place. For some children and parents it may be a beginning, however small it may seem.

Jo was a failure-to-thrive child, who was nurtured back to health in a foster home and adopted at the age of two years by a childless couple in their late forties. Jo's adoptive father died when she was five. She and her adoptive mother had many problems. Jo was a very active child and her mother seemed confused by Jo's energy. Although she appeared to care about Jo, she rarely touched her and never told her that she cared. There were few meals cooked in the home. The two either snacked, ate sandwiches, or went out for hamburgers. When Jo became a teenager, she wanted out of her home. It took Jo very little time to convince her mother that separation was the best of all possible options. By this time, Jo had been seen by a series of psychiatrists, as the mother and Jo had moved from city to city and state to state. Jo also had attended many schools. She had few friends. Eventually, Jo was placed in a foster home, then a rapid succession of foster homes, and finally, a group home. She got along nowhere. After two days at the group home, the other girls went to the house mother as a committee and asked that she be made to leave.

The house mother in this group home suggested that the other girls needed to give Jo a little more time. This house mother was a very good cook. She also took great care to learn what foods the girls in the house enjoyed. Every week, each girl could count on having her favorite foods being the center of a very nutritional meal, fixed especially because she was special. It was a tradition of the house. The girls were invited but not required to help to fix the meals.

At first, Jo had difficulty thinking of anything that she liked to eat. Soon she not only had ideas but was helping with the meals. As she and the housemother worked, Jo began to talk. One evening the housemother asked her if she would like to invite her mother to dinner. It would soon be her mother's birthday. Jo could fix the meal herself. Jo first said no, but by morning had changed her mind. It was the first thing that she had been able to give to her mother that seemed to connect the two of them in a positive way. Both benefited from the nurturing provided through the food itself and the context in which it was offered.

The Child and Parent As Part of the Response Network

The child and the family also need to be considered in the context of response. They have very clear roles to perform if positive change is to occur in such situations.

At first, the child and parents may sometimes seem to be only takers. They may question whether or not they have anything to give. Since they may be caught up in their own needs of the moment, they may need to selfishly cling to every bit of nurturing they can, just in case tomorrow they will be faced with "starvation" again. Even if they wish to reach out, they may not know how to do it. Eventually, a part of their success will be the fact that they too can give. Therefore, even from the beginning, they must be considered a part of the response network.

Coordinating Child Protection

Perhaps the most impressive thing about such a list as this is its sheer volume of people who respond to situations of child abuse and neglect. Surely every possible need that a family or individual has can be met. The variety and level of skill available to respond is amazing. Yet, somehow we are not always able to use it effectively for the benefit of our shared client. In fact, even with all this help available, the child may continue to be abused, either at home or in the system.

Generally speaking, there are two broad views on how the problem of child maltreatment should be approached so that endangered children can be protected.

> *Punish the Abuser.* This approaches child abuse and neglect as crimes which someone is guilty of committing and for which they should be punished. The punishment will deter this person and others from abusing children.

> *Treat and rehabilitate the abuser and the family.* This approaches abuse and neglect as a family problem which should be solved in the context of the family if possible. The treatment and rehabilitation will strengthen the family unit, and, in the long run, perhaps even prevent the child from abusing his/her own children.

Both approaches exist today. The social service and medical components of the response network take a dominantly therapeutic approach to the problem. The criminal justice system, in both its juvenile and adult processes, has become increasingly legalistic. The law enforcement and the school approaches are less clearly defined. Philosophical arguments are frequent. Agencies and individuls are often at odds because of unresolved differences relating to the question of approach.

Since the responsibility for immediate intervention and investigation is generally given to two community agents who have traditionally approached the responsibility from opposite positions, namely, child protective services and the police, the stage is set for problems in cooperation and coordination from the outset. Given the fact that the difficulties between the two, as has been demonstrated in this chapter, are only a few of many, even the idea seems monumental, much less the realization of it.

A Summary of Issues

1. A lack of understanding or misunderstanding among the many disciplines of the philosophy, roles, and functions of each other.
2. A lack of mutual respect from discipline to discipline and agency to agency.
3. Ineffective communication from one agency to another, one discipline to another, and sometimes one division or level of one agency to another.
4. Lack of clear policies and procedures that could define the appropriate interface of the various agency representatives in a given situation.
5. Lack of professionalism, in the sense of misplaced agency loyalty at the expense of other agencies, and often at the expense of clients which exhibits itself in turfism, territorialism, and critical asides made to other co-workers about other agency representatives.
6. The system and individual worker overburden. Too much to do in too little time with too few resources and no improvement in sight.
7. Lack of basic trust between individuals and agencies.
8. Differences among agencies in priorities.
9. Legitimate differences in professional judgment as to what is in the best interest of the child.
10. The problem itself, in its complexities and the variety of reactions it evokes on the part of all those who respond.
11. Lack of placement options.
12. Frequent changes in agency policy and administrative and service staff.
13. Frequent turnover in many states of juvenile court judiciary.
14. In large metropolitan areas, lack of information systems to trace cases effectively.

A Multidisciplinary Model

Where have we heard this before? Everyone talks of "teams," "cooperation," and "coordination" and certainly "multidisciplinary" continues to be an important buzz word in conjunction with all of these. Teams may even be an excuse for inaction. They may keep the hounds from the door and look good to management, but they may serve no useful function for children and families. It is also possible to coordinate and cooperate to the point of sterility. Teams may defer difficult decisions to someone willing to take responsibility for their judgment and assign complex tasks to whoever will do them instead of whoever would be most effective in the tasks.

Even when the committee or team is established and goals and objectives are assigned to the committee as a unit and to individual members as well, the task has scarcely begun. Once the activities of the group begin to take place on a regular basis, and the temptation is to call the team successful, some of the most difficult tasks of the group remain to be completed. The group itself requires monitoring. How is it functioning? Do the procedures need to change? How effective are the decisions made? Is a workshop necessary so that respective roles of members are clarified? Do interpersonal difficulties need to be resolved?

It is fine for different agencies to have different goals. The differences, if understood and used positively, can strengthen the services of both. For example, joint initial investigations by CPS and the police are an effective use of services because they capitalize on the strengths of both agencies. After that investigation and a comparison of findings, each agency will have a different function to fulfill.

No two committees or teams will be exactly alike. In order to be effective, each team needs to operate locally, responding to the strengths and problems of the local community. Generally, the decision as to who will be on the team or committee is in part determined by the proposed group function(s) and the local child maltreatment response network. A number of references and a review of existing teams suggests that there are some major elements that a community team should provide in matters of abuse and neglect.

1. Identification of abused and neglected children.
2. Verification and diagnosis of situations. (This step includes investigation, intervention, assessment and disposition phases of the process.)
3. Treatment of child and family.
4. Education and training of all people who respond and of the community as a whole.

Many different agencies and individuals might be involved in each of these elements. Interdisciplinary models can be used to develop teams around any of these elements or in a larger coordinating sense encompassing all four elements.

Effectiveness of any team or committee is defined in terms of its ability to deal with the barriers to success and in terms of its identity as a functioning system. Each person and each agency must understand his/her contribution to the group.

Some examples of multidisciplinary models include:

Alliance: A program in Syracuse, N.Y., which, as a division of Catholic Charities, acts as a coordinator for services in all the elements mentioned above. The program educated the service community to a guiding philosophy and approach to the problem, and then has developed a long-term treatment approach which uses teams of agencies in the community working together. The program, by all reports has been phenomenally successful.

Harborview Medical Center, Sexual Assault Unit: mentioned earlier, this center places major focus on all of these elements, specifically in relationship to sexual assault. Other units, through the Harborview model, have been able to achieve similar goals in other areas of abuse and neglect. Another hospital based program is that of the guidance of Dr. Eli H. Newberger.

The National Center for the Prevention and Treatment of Child Abuse and Neglect: this center offers several programs and several teams under one encompassing philosohy of involvement. Spearheaded by Dr. Henry Kempe, the project now includes family group care, parent aides, foster grandparents, and a number of other projects. This center also sponsors a community review team which meets to staff all reports of child abuse and neglect and make recommendations as to what should happen in each case.

A study of each of these programs and other successful ones across the United States indicates attention to the characteristics discussed. All continue an aggressive education and training program. All have developed a level of trust and mutual respect among the members of the group.

Summary

Problems of child abuse and neglect belong to all of us. Both the people and the roles they play are critical to making the system work. A network of response is only a functional network when the people in their roles find ways to enhance resources and complement one another's efforts. People, no matter their position or agency, requires nurturing, and teams, no matter their original design, will only function well as long as their goals are respected and shared.

BIBLIOGRAPHY
Arthur D. Little, Inc. *Volunteer Services.* Washington, D.C., U.S. Dept of Justice. Office of Juvenile Justice and Delinquency Prevention. (#J-LEAA-013-77).
Broadhurst, Diane D. *The Educator's Role in the Prevention and Treatment of Child Abuse and Neglect.* N.C.C.A.N., U.S. DHEW (OHDS) 79-30172, August 1979.
Child Abuse and Neglect: The Problem and Its Management. Vol. 3. The Community Team: An Approach to Case Management. Washington, D.C., HEW (OHD) 75-30075.

Education Commission of the States. Education Policies and Practices Regarding Child Abuse and Neglect: 1978. Report # 109, ECS Child Abuse Project, Colorado, October 1978.

Eskin, Marian and Kravitz, Marjorie, (Eds.) *Child Abuse and Neglect: A Literature Review and Selected Bibliography*. Washington, D.C., U.S. Dept of Justice, February 1980.

Executive Summary: National Incidence Study. Westat, Inc. and Development Associates, Inc., 1981.

Fisher, Nancy. *Reaching Out: The Volunteer in Child Abuse and Neglect Programs*. Washington, D.C., NCCAN, DHEW Publication (OHDS) 79-30174.

Fox, Sanford, J. *Juvenile Courts: In a Nutshell*. West Publishing Co., Minn., 1971.

Friedlander, Walter A. and Apte, Robert Z. *Introduction to Social Welfare*. 5th Ed. Prentice–Hall, New Jersey, 1980.

Garbarino, James. The Role of the School in the Human Ecology of Child Maltreatment. *School Review*. Chicago, Ill., February 1979, pp. 190–213.

Giovannoni, Jeanne M. and Becerra, Rosina M., *Defining Child Abuse*. Free Press, New York, 1979.

Goldstein, Joseph, Solnit, A., and Freud, Anna, *Beyond the Best Interest of the Child*. The Free Press, New York, 1973.

Jenkins, James L., Salus, Marsha K., and Schultze, Gretchen L. *Child Protective Services: A Guide for Workers*. Washington, D.C., (NCCD) DHEW Publication (OHDS) 79-30203, August 1979.

Jones, C.D., Jr. Project Director, Child Abuse and Neglect Curriculum in Schools of Education. Education Commission of the States, Colorado, August 1980.

Letson, Mike. Child Abuse: First Priority: Protection of the Child. *InforMed*. Dodie Gust, Editor, Information Services, University of Arizona Health Sciences Center, Tucson, Hal Marshall, Director, March, 1981.

Mallard, Hon. Robert. Judge Family Court, Charleston, South Carolina, Due Process—Guidelines for Fair Play and Protection of Rights. *Fourth National Symposium on Child Abuse*. American Humane Association, Colorado, 1975.

Materials from the states of Louisiana, Colorado, Arizona, Tennessee, West Virginia, New Mexico, Kansas, Nebraska, and California.

Mayhall, Pamela D. and Geary, David. P. *Community Relations and the Administration of Justice*. 2nd Ed. John Wiley and Sons, New York, 1979.

Newberger, Eli H., M.D. Interdisciplinary Management of Child Abuse: Problems and Progress. *Fourth National Symposium on Child Abuse*. American Humane Association, Colorado, 1975, pp. 16–26.

Schetky, Diane H. and Benedek, Elissa P. *Child Psychiatry and the Law*. Brunner and Mazel, New York, 1980.

Schmitz, Cathy, M.S.W., Sexual Assult Center, Harborview Medical Center, Seattle, Washington. Interview: 10/81;1/82.

Smith, Charles P., Berkman, David J., and Fraser, Warren M. *A Preliminary National Assessment of Child Abuse and Neglect and the Juvenile Justice System; The Shadows of Distress. Reports of the National Juvenile Justice*

Assessment Centers. Washington, D.C., U.S. Dept. of Justice, National Institute for Juvenile Justice and Delinquency Prevention. April, 1980. (© 1979 American Justice Institute.)

Uniform Crime Reports for the U.S., U.S. Dept. of Justice, Federal Bureau of Investigation, 1979 (Washington, D.C., U.S. Government Printing Office.)

Wittman, Gerald, Training Coordinator, University of Nevada, National Council of Juvenile Court and Family Judges. Interview: 11/81.

CHAPTER 10

Formal Response: From Identification to Assessment and Planning

The process of formal response to child abuse and neglect can be divided into several broad stages: initial identification and reporting, intake and investigation, assessment and planning, court adjudication and disposition, treatment, termination, and follow up. In a given case, the process does not necessarily include all of these stages of response. In one situation, formal intrusion into the family might end at the intake and investigation stage, with the decision that either no situation of neglect or abuse exists or that, although reports of abuse or neglect may be founded, no further intervention is recommended by the investigative staff. In another, noncoercive, voluntary intervention might take place, and treatment, termination, and follow up be provided without court adjudication and disposition. In still another situation, involuntary coercive intervention might be required to protect the child. In this instance, court adjudication and disposition is not only a part of formal response, but central to it.

Prevention, although an integral part of every step in the process, is discussed as a separate topic in Chapter 14, in the primary sense of reaching out, personally, to families that might have potential for abuse or neglect. The goal of such efforts is to expand the options and resources of families *before* a problem occurs. The spirit in which such positive reaching out takes place is the spirit of support, nurturing, and friendship, not of labeling, criticism or judgment. The authors take the position that it is only when this sort of prevention is not actively provided or when the potential for abuse and neglect has already resulted in probable abuse or neglect that the formal response process becomes a necessary, but not always effective, protective network for the child and the family. Figure 10-1 describes the various steps in the formal response process.

STAGE ONE: IDENTIFICATION AND REPORTING

The first step in any problem-solving process is to identify the problem. Recognition that a possible problem exists is necessary if action is going to be taken to solve it. Recognition must then be translated into a report of suspected abuse and neglect situations if the formal protective process is to begin. Responsibility for identifying and reporting such situations belongs to everyone. How willing the people of a community are to accept such responsibility may depend on a number of factors, among them:

1. Community awareness of symptoms of abuse and neglect.
2. The belief that these symptoms constitute child maltreatment.
3. The belief that the community as a whole, rather than a designated few, is responsible for the welfare of its children.
4. The availability of a simple, clear procedure for reporting suspected situations of abuse and neglect.
5. The faith of community members in the formal intervention system available to them.

REPORTING AS A PROCEDURE

Who Must Report

In most communities, the mandated responsibility for identification and reporting belongs to the people most likely to be in direct contact and have children as a part of their job or profession. Reporting statutes in individual states vary in their specific requirements. Most name physicians, nurses, and social workers, and require that reports be made to some specified agency. Although 39% of all reports of suspected abuse and neglect are made by nonprofessionals (AHA, 1980), this group of reporters is not specifically mentioned in the reporting laws of most states, and fewer of the cases they report are substantiated by the investigating agency. Generally, these reports are also given lower priority for investigation than those received from professional sources.

People who report are generally given immunity from liability, and in many cases, anonymity, as long as the report is made in good faith. A report of suspected child abuse or neglect is an expression of concern and a request

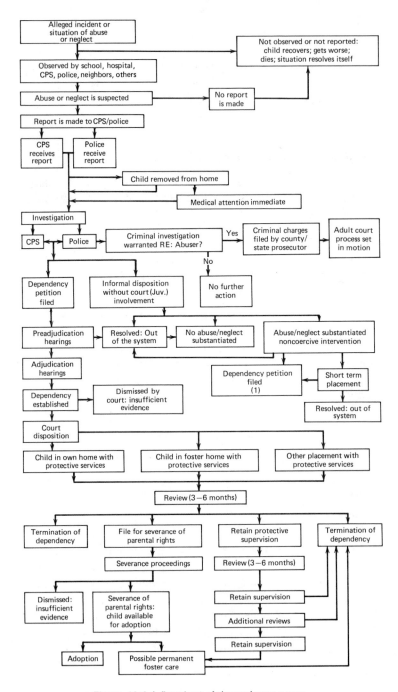

Figure 10-1 A flowchart of dependency cases.

for an investigation. It should not be viewed as an accusation. Reports are made, presumably, to protect a child, not to punish his/her caretakers. Good faith would be questioned, for example, if an investigation showed that the neighbor who reported the abuse had been reported by the ''abuser'' the day before for not keeping his dogs in his own yard. Feuding neighbors, fighting parents, and angry children may all report child abuse or neglect with questionable motivations and a lack of good faith. Even these reports should be investigated, however, since the fact of inappropriate motivation for reporting does not eliminate the possibility of abuse or neglect. Police agencies, child protective service agencies, and, in some states, juvenile courts may be designated as reporters of abuse, receivers of reports, and investigators of reports received from others.

Privileged communications between husband and wife, physician and patient, and clergy and confessioners that are normally protected from admission as evidence in court are generally not protected in cases of abuse and neglect. In such cases the protection of the child is considered the paramount concern. Therefore, in most states, communications, except for those between attorney and client, are not deemed privileged.

Where Should Reports Be Made

Some statutes do not specify a single agency to receive reports. When responsibility is specified, it is most frequently placed with a state department of human services and implemented through a division of Child Protective Services (CPS). Some states place responsibility with law enforcement, a central register, or more than one agency. One state requires that reports be made to the juvenile court.

What Should Be Reported

Any condition that constitutes suspected physical or sexual abuse must be reported in every state. At least 48 states and jurisdictions also include neglect and emotional abuses as reportable conditions. Color photos and x-rays may be taken without parental consent in most states.

Reporting needs to be immediate. Some states require oral and written reports, others specify only oral or written. No state requires that the reporter have absolute proof in order to report.

The minimum information usually required includes:

The child's name, age, and address.

Location of the child.

The parents' names and address(es).

The nature of the injury or condition that has been observed.

The extent of the injury or condition.

Other pertinent information that might assist the investigator.

STAGE TWO: INTAKE AND INVESTIGATION

The Intake Process: Receiving Reports

Child Protective Services (CPS) is the agency or unit most frequently mandated to receive reports of suspected abuse and neglect. Experience dictates that where other agencies are also mandated to receive reports, one agency (again, usually CPS) is or should be designated as the agency to maintain a central recording function and have primary responsibility for intake and investigation of all reports. That agency needs to provide:

1. Round-the-clock availability to receive reports.
2. Advertisement of availability to receive reports.
3. Immediate response to emergency situations.
4. A central register of reports.
5. A system of effective communication and consultation with others in the interdisciplinary response network. (Child Abuse and Neglect, Vol.3.)

If CPS is the agency designated primary responsibility to receive reports, even though mandated responsibility is shared with law enforcement, an agreement can be made that all reports received by law enforcement will be referred for investigation to CPS. Such an agreement does not preclude a preliminary investigation by law enforcement before referral. Cooperation in the investigation between the two agencies can be helpful in some cases, especially in situations of serious physical injury or sexual abuse or where the parents are extremely hostile and refuse to voluntarily work with CPS.

Concern for the Reporter

Reporters need the support of the agency. Confidentiality may be very important to the reporter. Assurances that the report is appropriate may also be necessary. Reporters want to believe that their action will be helpful to the child and family and not add to the already existing hurt. To the extent that state law allows, feedback is very important. At minimum, a call back is helpful to inform the reporter that an investigation is underway.

The Reporter As An Investigative Source

Without being asked very specific questions, the reporter may provide very sketchy information regarding the suspected situation of abuse or neglect. Often this person can be the source of much more detailed information. It is important to take the time initially to learn whatever is possible from this person.

The reporter might provide:

- The name, age, sex, and permanent address of the child.
- Present location of the child and the location where incidents occurred if different from permanent address.
- Name of the person or institution responsible for the child's welfare (and address, if different from the permanent address of the child).
- Name and address of the person alleged to be responsible for the abuse and/or neglect.
- The family composition, that is, names, sex, ages of siblings, and other adults normally present.
- The nature and extent of the suspected abuse or neglect including any available information on prior injury to the child or siblings.
- The action taken by the reporting source or others including whether or not the child has been placed in protective custody.
- The reporter's name, telephone number, and address, if he/she is willing to provide this information.
- The type of reporting source: (1) mandatory, required to report by law; (2) permissive, voluntarily reporting and willing to claim personal responsibility for the report; and (3) anonymous, willing to report, but unwilling to be identified.
- The relationship of the reporter to the child and family.
- The willingness of the reporter to share with the family his/her role in initiating the report and his/her willingness to participate in the assessment process if appropriate.
- The motives of the reporter, if it is possible to evaluate them.
- Possible witnesses to the incident that caused the child's condition.
- The date and time the oral report is received.

Source. Broadhurst and Knoeller, pp. 35–36.

This reference also noted ethnic background as an information item to be provided by the reporter. The authors have omitted it from the list. A request for such information at this point may infer that an agency has a dual standard for handling reports based on ethnicity and race. This information is more appropriately recorded at the time of actual investigation.

Procedures for Logging In and Screening Reports

The agency receiving information must establish procedures for handling reports. Most agencies include (1) procedures for logging in and screening reports, (2) referral of reports to other agencies, and (3) case assignment. This may include registering the report in a state or local central register.

The Function of the Central Register

Some states require the creation and maintenance of a central register. Others have developed a central registration of cases either on a local or state basis, but do not require such registration by law. Central registers are somewhat controversial—existing ones do not collect the same information, nor do they collect information for the same purposes. Generally, centralized information is used for diagnostic or statistical purposes. If the collection of data is complete enough, it may be used for both. If data is collected haphazardly with no clearly established purposes, it may be very limited in its usefulness.

The major issue with registers is one of confidentiality. In a computerized, centralized system that collects information from many areas, (and depends upon people in those areas to provide follow up information on each case after investigation), available data may reflect the original report, but not the investigation results. Although a system for deleting information may exist, it may be seldom utilized. Accuracy and currency may be questioned in these instances. Also, since the information must be accessible to professionals from many disciplines in many areas of a state, access is difficult to control and confidentiality is threatened.

Another issue with the use of central registers is in the danger of false assumptions. It cannot be assumed, for example, that abuse or neglect does not exist, just because no prior reports regarding a given family have been made. Neither does the presence of a prior report prove that abuse or neglect currently exists. At best, the register is one source of information among many.

Central registers can provide useful data. On a local or state basis, they can help to coordinate a system of protection for children, particularly those from highly mobile abuse families. Registers can be a source of information for immediate or long-term planning for a child or family. If complete information is available, registers may assist in documenting the services already provided. In a broader sense, registers may provide important evaluative data regarding the system and its effectiveness in working with families. They may pinpoint procedural problem areas early. Finally, they can be useful in collecting and sorting statistical data that may be helpful in the study of abuse and neglect.

The Status of The Case: The Question of Emergency

When a report is received, the first question which must be answered is whether or not the child is in possible imminent danger. Verification of the report and determination of needs of the family and child must also be addressed promptly. The answer to the question of imminent danger, however, helps to determine whether or not the case is to be assigned for immediate action or for nonemergency investigation. Theoretically, all reports must be investigated at some level and investigation must be prompt. Some cases will be closed after preliminary investigation indicates that the report is unfounded. Others may be closed even though the potential for abuse or neglect exists and the child may be considered at risk. In most states, if the investigation reveals no evidence of actual abuse or neglect and the family is unwilling to participate in noncoercive, voluntary programs, formal intervention may not be legally possible. According to AHA (1980) data, nearly 40% of cases reported to CPS were closed after investigation even though investigation substantiated the abuse or neglect.

If the report alleges serious physical abuse, bizarre punishment (e.g., locking the child in a closet), or sexual abuse, an emergency situation is assumed. In addition to these categories, most agencies also treat as emergencies:

1. Reports of young children (usually under age 8) being left alone.
2. Reports of children and families in need of food and shelter.
3. Reports of bizarre behavior by parents of young children, where severe psychiatric disorder or the influence of drugs or alcohol might be suspected.
4. Reports that a child or youth is possibly suicidal.
5. Reports of an abandoned child.
6. Self-referrals from parents.
7. Referrals from hospital emergency rooms regarding children presently in their care.
8. Cases in which protective custody is authorized by the court.

A source of information immediately available to the agency receiving reports is a records check. A routine check of central register, court, police, and local CPS records can reveal in moments any prior reports (and sometimes their outcomes), services presently being provided to a family, and information on the reporter's reliability (e.g., has this person made prior reports re: this family and under what circumstances?) Such information can assist in determining imminent danger as well as preliminary verification of reports.

In cases of sexual abuse and in most serious physical injury cases, law enforcement will want to be advised so that they can investigate the possibility of criminal charges against the perpetrator of the abuse. Delay may not only endanger the child immediately but may also eliminate evidence that will be necessary to assure protection over a long period of time. It is important that the two investigators interact positively in the best interest of the child. Emergencies, because they may require taking a child into custody, require more paperwork under very tight time constraints than is usually required for emergencies.

Nonemergencies

If the situation is not considered to be an emergency, but preliminary review of other sources indicates further investigation is appropriate, a field caseworker should make a home visit. Promptness of investigation is important, even in nonemergency situations.

The difficulty, in practice, of prioritizing responses to received reports is that some cases may never be investigated properly. It must be observed, however, that the number of cases reported in a given jurisdiction is often far greater than what the existing CPS staff can adequately and promptly investigate. Prioritizing may be, to some extent, the agency's response to its responsibility and its own limitations of an overburdened and sometimes poorly trained staff. Perhaps it is wishful thinking to hope that we might someday offer children something more than the better of two marginal options.

The Investigation Process: Sources of Information

The investigator has several primary and secondary sources of information, some of which have already been discussed.

The primary sources are:

- Interview with the child.
- Interview with the parents.
- Observable physical data regarding the child, parents, and home environment.
- Observable behavioral data regarding the child and parents.

The secondary sources include:

- Medical evaluation and previous medical records.
- Psychological/psychiatric evaluation.
- School records.
- Police records.
- Photographs.
- Records of other agencies.

All of these sources provide data that will assist the investigator and child protection council or team (if such a group is participating) in the assessment process. The underlying need at all times is to ensure the safety of the child.

Standardizing Information Generated by the Investigation

Interagency cooperation is required to develop questions and categories of information which might be used by several agencies and which could be gathered during a single part of the investigation. This will prevent duplication of effort and the necessity of several agencies asking the same client the same questions. If the information can be made available to all pertinent agencies and is acceptable to those agencies, much time and effort will be saved, to say nothing of the savings in wear and tear on the clients. Formulating and standardizing procedures is important to ensure the protection of confidentiality rights of the family and to allow access to the information *only* to those who have a need to know.

The Medical Evaluation

If the case is considered an emergency, immediate medical intervention may be needed. In nonemergency situations, medical examination may be a part of the total investigation but may not be considered critical nor immediate. If the parent refuses permission for treatment or is unavailable to give consent, authorization for medical treatment may be given by a judge.

In some situations, hospitalization is indicated. It is sometimes used as a means of offering protection to a child and of providing an opportunity for a more thorough evaluation. If a child is hospitalized under such circumstances, special policies are in order. Special care may be needed, both in terms of attention to the child and his/her needs and in controlling access to the child by others. Concern by the hospital staff for the feelings of the child and parents is very important at this critical time. Support from medical personnel can provide a relatively neutral environment that is neither blaming nor condoning and yet is secure. A pediatric examination and a mental health evaluation may be an integral part of the total medical evaluation, or may be arranged as necessary by the investigator independently from this evaluation.

Photographs and X-rays

Determinations of who may take photographs of alleged circumstances of abuse or neglect and under what circumstances they may be taken are made in local jurisdictions. In most areas, photographs may be taken without parental consent where abuse or neglect is suspected. Sometimes state law designates authority to photograph or to supervise photographing to CPS or law enforcement. In almost all areas photographs taken by the investigator or by medical professionals and/or law enforcement are encouraged. Time and location of photographs is important documentation of abuse and neglect. In most cases, photographs, taken immediately, are critical documentation of injury. (Follow up pictures are also very useful where contusions exist.) The quality of the photographs is important. Color photos are generally preferred to black and white. Pictures are most valuable when they incorporate body "landmarks" which may serve as focal points for comparison.

X-rays of injuries may be taken during the medical evaluation and usually include x-rays beyond those indicated when the child was first brought in for evaluation. X-rays can document injuries that are not otherwise visible, for example, broken bones in various stages of healing, injured internal organs, deformations possibly caused by abuse etc.

CONTACT WITH THE CHILD AND FAMILY

Contact with the family and child is usually initiated by the agency receiving the report. (Since the agency in this position is usually CPS, we will use CPS as the example agency.) This first contact is extremely important. Not only is it important for gathering information about the family and child, it is also important in gaining the family's cooperation and encouraging a commitment to change. The attitude of the investigator is critical. The importance of the investigator's ability to set his/her own feelings aside and approach both the child and the family from a position of concern can not be overemphasized.

Some parents may seriously doubt that help exists, others may believe that they need no help, and still others may doubt the competency of those offering help. In some cases, they may be correct. Even if they are not, the investigator must begin where the family is. Many agencies assume that they are more effective in protecting the child and working with the family if investigative and therapeutic functions are separated. The investigator may have to take the brunt of the family's anger, denial, and confusion. After this initial process is complete, the family may be able to respond to a different person in the role of therapist. Other agencies assign both functions to one worker, which reduces the number of people with whom the family has to interact.

Few families can tolerate the bombardment of many agencies asking many questions and all providing their own version of "help" at once. If too many agencies and too many people approach at once, especially asking the same questions, and sometimes offering the same advice or "help," the result may be increased anger, frustration, confusion, and resistance on the part of the family. It is also disrespectful to a child or a family to intrude more than necessary or to require that the family repeat information again and again. Being respectful will model and encourage mutual respect.

The Rights of the Family

Unless the rights of natural parents have been relinquished (given up voluntarily) or severed by the court, parents have the right to be involved in the decision-making regarding their own lives and the lives of their children.

They have the right to consent or refuse consent to:

Medical services and/or surgery.

Adoption of the child.

A driver's license for a minor.

Marriage of a child for whom permission to marry is required.

Military service for a child for whom permission to enter the service is required.

In some cases the court may override parental decision and coercively intervene if it determines that the child's health and welfare is threatened. However, such an override is not made automatically, nor lightly by the court.

Parents have the right to:

Determine the religion of the child.

Have access to their child.

Know the allegations of the report, although not the identity of the reporter, and the findings of the investigator.

Plan with the worker for the child and share in decisions that are made.

Know what conditions will be necessary to assure the agency that protection by the agency of the child will no longer be necessary.

Receive services that will increase their ability to protect the child.

The Search for Answers

In addition to seeking answers to questions relating to the existence of abuse and neglect and how best to protect the child, investigation must also ask questions such as: What does this person and this family need for themselves? What do they want for themselves? How do they perceive the problem? The investigator and possibly the therapist must be constantly aware that the family and the child are participants in the solution. If they are not, the proposed solution may not be implemented.

Experience has indicated that different abuse situations may require slightly different interventions. In adolescent sexual abuse, for example, it may be necessary for the abuser to move from the home or that charges be brought in order to ensure safety. In some cases of preadolescent sexual abuse, when parents are willing to admit their behavior and accept family counseling, danger may be lessened. In situations where parents refuse to accept responsibility for their actions, the danger appears to be greatest. (*Child Abuse and Neglect: The Problem and Its Management*, Vol. 2, pp. 24–25.) In the opinion of the authors, however, if we are to err, it should be on the side of protecting the child. Caution is certainly indicated when available research shows that other forms of maltreatment recur during treatment at a rate of 30%. (Berkeley, 1977.)

In situations of neglect, a nonaccusatory approach, awareness of the family's cultural rules, and assistance to parents in the prioritizing and solving of their problems, are most helpful. Assistance in coordinating needs with resources may be of the greatest help. In more serious cases, however, voluntary placement or court placement of children may be necessary in order for changes to begin to take place.

Interviewing the Child

Sometimes the investigator interviews the child in the home setting, but the interview could just as well take place at school, in a doctor's office, in a child care facility, or in any number of other places. Whether or not the child should be interviewed is determined by a variety of factors. Basically, a child should not be interviewed if it will increase the danger or trauma to the child. The child's age, emotional and physical condition, the attitude of the parents toward the child, and the possibility of placing the child in the position of being "the only one who tells" and therefore guilty of violating the rules of the home and harming his/her family, are all issues that must be questioned in making such a decision.

If the only source of necessary information is the child, then an interview may be required, even when other dangers are present. The child who has reported his/her own abuse or neglect must be interviewed as a primary source of information.

If a child is interviewed, care must be taken to assure that the child will not have to tell the story again and again. Many agencies (in addition to CPS) may need information that the child can provide, for example, investigating law-enforcement officers, the prosecuting attorney, other attorneys, and juvenile court personnel. This can be achieved by recording the information and making it available to other agencies that might require it or by having someone from another key agency present to assist with the interview.

Effective Listening

Being an effective listener is critical to interviewing. An effective listener listens to the words that are said, but that is only a small part of listening effectively. Communication is verbal, nonverbal, and symbolic.

Verbal communication is what is said. What people say is important. They describe facts and insights as they view them. Words are also meaningful because they are an encoding system for our feelings and our experiences. The language that people choose is important. The person speaking and the person listening must share some common language symbols, in order for mutual understanding to take place. Language that an interviewer uses that a child does not understand will limit an effective response from the child. If a child does not understand English and the questions are in English, the child will not be able to respond to those questions adequately.

Nonverbal communication is multidimensional. There are at least three types of nonverbal communication: proxemics, kinesics, and paralanguage.

Proxemics is the use of physical and social space. People "talk" about themselves in how they sit in a chair, how close or how distant they sit from the interviewer, and when and if they move during the interview. When interviewing a child, if approaching seems to make the child uncomfortable, it is best to respect the distance. The space itself may have different meanings to the child and the interviewer. A desk between the child and the interviewer may make the interview more formal. If the child sits and the interviewer stands, the child may feel overwhelmed, overpowered, and threatened by the interviewer's use of the space.

Kinesics is the use of gestures, that is, body language. A person's body talks constantly. The messages are sometimes the same as the words that are said, sometimes supportive of, and other times contradictory to those words. Astute observation of changes in the pupils of the eye, the tightness of a jaw, quivering of lips, movement, and change in the position of hands, feet, etc., may add meaning in the context of the interview. Sadness, weariness, excitement, fear, concern, etc. are all expressed in body movement.

Paralanguage is the pitch, tone, and speed of what is said. It is also the way that silence is used. Paralanguage provides the message between the line and between the words. These are very important messages. They show changes in emotion. They also may indicate skills, abstraction ability, sensitive and comfortable subjects, etc.

The interviewer's sensitivity to these areas will help him or her decide whether to continue a topic or drop the subject, and whether to respond to the feeling behind the person's answer rather than the words that were said, and to be able to guess about that feeling. Sometimes, the only feedback the person needs to continue talking is a nod or an ''uh huh'' to indicate that the interviewer is listening.

It is important for the interviewer to keep the interview centered on the person or persons being interviewed. If it is the child, the child's perspective is important; if it is the parent, then the parent's perspective is important. It is particularly critical that the interviewer not be judgmental about the person(s) who is not there in order to appear supportive to the person being interviewed. Honest concern for the persons being interviewed, for their feelings, their problems, their concerns is necessary if any level of trust is to be established.

Symbolic communication occurs through the passive symbols the interviewer and the client carry with them. These symbols help to determine the meaning of what the other says. All of us own these symbol out of our own experience. They are prompted by the present, but are anchored in our past prejudices and biases. All of us use symbolic communication to some extent. We are not always aware that our symbols are helping us determine meaning. Yet they have much impact in how we feel about the other person and how we hear what they have to say. The following are a few stereotyped statements.

''All people who wear mustaches are crooks.''

''People who are on welfare don't want to work.''

''People who drive cadillacs are rich.''

There are many ways to finish:

''Social workers are . . .''

''Children who tell family secrets . . .''

''Anyone who wears a uniform is . . .''

In this context, it is important that the interviewer be aware of his or her own symbols and the possible symbols of the person being interviewed. The interviewer may be having great difficulty with his own feelings of anger and shock, but he must not condemn the parent. It is necessary that he be supportive and nonjudgmental in his approach to all parties.

The uniform of a police officer, the fact that the interviewer has a beard, a particular color of hair, or works in a particular agency (particularly the "welfare" department or the "police") may be symbols that will contribute to or interfere with the establishment of a trusting relationship. Yet feelings about these factors may never be stated. Sometimes it is helpful for the interviewer to make the symbols explicit in conversation. "I realize that some people see the police as the bad guys. Don't let the uniform fool you. I am here because I want to help you and your family."

The interviewer needs to listen for attitudes and prejudices. What do these parents think about children in general? How do they view other adults in their life? How do they see themselves?

Observable Data

Observation is integral to an interview, but it is much more subjective. Observation of physical surroundings is the least subjective; observation of interactional patterns among family members and attitudes and emotional health of the family members is the most subjective. Some of the data will be "educated guesses." The interviewer's skill in gathering data from many sources and many avenues increases the accuracy of those educated guesses.

Observable physical data might include: What is the physical nature of the home? How much space does the family and each person have? How is the space used? Is the home clean? Is there adequate food available? Is the environment safe for children at the age(s) of those who live in the home? What was the injury or situation of abuse/neglect? Did the physical circumstances of the home contribute to the abuse or neglect? Does the situation continue to exist? Are weapons of abuse evident?

Behavioral data includes emotional factors. How do family members respond to each other? How does each parent perceive the other and the children? What is the relationship of the other children in the home to the child who is abused? Do parents appear to understand child development. Do they understand the basic skills in caring for a child? What are the child-rearing rules in this home? Is there eye contact among family members? What is the nature of the interaction among family members? Are they supportive and positive of each other? Do they indicate respect for one another, a willingness to listen, express feelings, be helpful, etc. How were the parents raised?

Cultural and Generational Differences

What are the cultural issues here? Have the parents been transplanted into a culture that they are unfamiliar with? Are they bringing cultural rules that conflict with rules of the culture in which they now live? Have they misunderstood the rules of their culture?

What is the family lifestyle? How is it different from the lifestyle of their parents? Are these parents attempting to apply rules from one setting into another without adapting the idea to the change in time and culture.

Sometimes the religion of the parents specifies that medical treatment not be provided. The abuse or neglect may simply be in terms of not providing such treatment even though the life of the child is threatened. In such cases, intervention of the court may be required to secure treatment for the child. Follow up counseling may be necessary to help the family adjust to the fact of intervention. The issue here is one of adequate care.

Interviewing Other Family Members

Interviews may be important with the boyfriend, stepfather, and other adult males in the family. These interviews may shed additional light on the observations made based on primary data.

ASSESSMENT AND PLANNING

Once the investigation is complete and all supportive data is in, an assessment must be made in at least four areas.

1. Does child abuse or neglect exist?
2. If so, what is the degree of risk to the child in this home?
3. What are the strengths and weaknesses of the parents? What is the level of functioning of the family?
4. What action will be necessary to ensure safety for the child and long term protection for the child and family?

From this assessment, a plan may be made through which services may be provided to the family.

Finally, six types of decision are possible. (Jenkins et al.)

1. Abuse and/or neglect exists and the family will cooperate voluntarily with services.
2. Abuse and/or neglect exists but a court order will be required to gain the cooperation of the family.
3. Abuse and/or neglect exists. There is imminent danger to the child. The child must be removed with consent or court order.
4. No abuse and/or neglect. Case closed.
5. No abuse and/or neglect, but other services offered.
6. No abuse and/or neglect proved, but suspected problems. Further investigation is necessary.

In any assessment, a diagnosis and prognosis are necessary. These may be defined (*Child Abuse and Neglect: Its Problems and Its Management* Bibliography, p. 44) as

Diagnosis: "An evaluation of the facts to determine whether or not the child's injuries or the parent's behavior can be classified as child abuse under State Law."

Prognosis: "An evaluation of the facts to determine the possibility of effective treatment for the abuser and the child."

Removal of the child, with or without the parents' voluntary agreement, is a last resort. Many references (including Helfer) suggest that children should be hospitalized instead of being placed in shelter or foster care. This is less traumatic for the child and the family. At least, the "state" did not remove the child. Indeed, more recently, coercive or noncoercive removal of the parent has been encouraged as an alternative. Most states do provide, however, for the removal of the child in an emergency, often without the voluntary consent of the parents and even without a court order if the police or CPS believe the child to be in imminent danger. Some states require a court order for such removal. Most states require that a petition be filed within a specified period of time (usually 24 hours) and that the matter be scheduled for court review promptly if the child has been removed without the parental consent.

RELIEVING STRESS AND ENHANCING RESOURCES

Crisis: An Opportunity for Change

The crisis of a situation of child abuse or neglect, or the crisis of confrontation with the situation, can be an opportunity for change. Openness to confront the need for change may be more likely in crisis than at any other time. The role of the investigator or intruder into the family at this time becomes even more important. This person is not only involved in ensuring safety for the child, but also in helping people to confront the crisis as an opportunity for positive change and, in a long-term sense, to develop the ability to better deal with crises out of this experience.

Characteristics of Crisis

Borgman (pp. 2–5) states that the characteristics of a crisis are:

1. An unanticipated or unusual event.
2. Unfamiliar feelings of vulnerability and helplessness.

3. Involvement of several persons in the situation.
4. Involvement of a series or chain of events.
5. Linkages to previous problems.

A crisis is difficult to cope with because it is in unfamiliar, uncharted territory. A conflict exists between wishes and reality. Sometimes major conflict exists even in the perspectives of all the people involved in the crisis as to what the problem is and how it might be solved. It is more of a crisis if, when the person or persons involved look into their experience to find possible ways of handling it, and find instead that it brings with it many other problems and the shadows of other crises that were not resolved well. The realization that other crises have not been solved is frightening. It generates crisis on top of crisis. The result is overwhelming. For some people, the feeling of being overwhelmed is temporary, for others it is continual. Generally a crisis is an event that includes the elements of timing (in another time and place this would not have been a crisis), a special situation (the situation is unique because of the combination of factors that have come together), and the personal characteristics of the people involved (their coping skills, their attitudes, their emotional and physical well-being).

The Effects of Crisis

Crisis affects functioning. To cope with it some people become more impulsive, doing "something" even if it is inappropriate. Others become immobilized, unable to take action at all. Crisis may disorganize a person's thinking, making it difficult for the person to problem-solve and to order priorities. Some people become hostile and violent in a crisis, as if external furor will help them regain internal balance. Some react in just the opposite way, detaching themselves from external interaction and input and becoming increasingly isolated, again with the hope of achieving internal balance and control. As effective functioning decreases in a crisis, the need to be dependent on someone else for support, sustenance, and decision-making increases.

Crisis Intervention Techniques

Ostbloom and Crase suggest that family dysfunction that leads to abuse and neglect is a stress–resource imbalance. They imply that the abusive family considers violence a resource. Stress issues, they believe, can be dealt with through stress relieving services, of which crisis intervention is a major option. They point out that often it is ". . . not the technique, however, but the strength of the worker or his or her ability to transmit to the client a successful manner of functioning that can produce lasting change." (p. 170.) Building positive resources, both within the family and external to the family, is a long-term process and much more difficult to achieve than stress reduction but equally important and also dependent upon ". . . strength and motivation from a helping person." (p. 171.)

Effective crisis intervention techniques include those suggested earlier in this chapter as positive interviewing techniques. Borgman lists the following as effective crisis intervention techniques:

1. Maintain a neutral, matter-of-fact attitude about the alleged mal-treatment.
2. Be supportive whenever possible.
3. Provide validating statements and recognize positive intentions.
4. Keep the focus upon the welfare of the children and the parental caretakers.
5. Keep attention upon what the parent caretakers themselves reveal and what is directly observable.
6. Be reassuring.
7. Be acutely aware of nonverbal communication and look for signs of hostility, fear, and affection among family members.
8. If possible, talk to family members separately at first.
9. Use open-ended questions.
10. Recognize and label feelings. Restate the parents' answers to make sure they are understood and to give the parent a chance to provide more information.
11. Avoid agreeing with or seeming to condone everything, but make it clear that facts and feelings are understood.
12. Do not take verbal abuse personally.
13. Convey a desire to alleviate the stress and help change the situation. (Borgman, pp. 13–15.)

POSSIBILITIES FOR HELPING

The person who intervenes can help the child and family to sort, prioritize, and manage the problems facing the family. He/she can explore various coping strategies with the family and suggest new resources which the family has not tapped. He/she can provide emotional support for the parents and for the child. If the child is to be removed from the home, the person working with the family can help to reduce the shock of that separation. Many options and resources may be available: alteration in family activities; trips to clinics; counseling, ongoing protective services; removal of child combined with some of these other services; public financial assistance; homemaker services; day care; community youth programs, etc.

THE CHILD PROTECTION TEAM

The possibilities for helping may increase when an effective child protection team participates in the assessment and/or disposition of severe or difficult cases. Eleven states have child protection teams that are given decision-making authority. Many others have consultant or advisory councils, boards, or teams that assist in the assessment process. The shared assessment may include a medical diagnosis, psychological and/or psychiatric evaluation of the parents, an evaluation of the dynamics of the home, and a realistic understanding of community resources. Each team member may evaluate a different component, but the team as a whole can share in making the recommendations for intervention, referral, and treatment for the family. The team may include professionals from major resource agencies that can facilitate and offer services to the family. As discussed in the last chapter, teams may be organized for many different functions. Even if a formal team does not exist, the CPS worker who is faced with the problem of assessment and planning may develop an informal team in an individual case to assist in this process. Hopefully, in cases of serious physical abuse and sexual abuse, the police investigator will participate in this part of the process.

FAMILY PARTICIPATION

In order for assessment and ultimately a treatment or referral plan to work effectively, the family, including the child, must participate in the assessment and planning process. Their involvement in the process helps to eliminate some of the key problems for famlies in working with the system.

1. The label of abuser.
2. The issue of the authority of the court and the dependency of the family.
3. The difficulty the family has in reaching out, or asking for help.
4. The importance of feeling in control of their lives, a great issue in the midst of crisis.

One of the most critical themes of this book and of successful intervention is that the "helper" needs to reframe the problems observed and the strengths and needs of the family, in a way that will assist the family to believe that they can help themselves and assist in the decision-making. Assessment must be with the family, not for the family. Some families may feel so impotent that their contribution to the assessment process is limited. Even in this instance, and perhaps especially in this instance, it is important that they participate. For the child, depending on age, maturity, and circumstance, participation at some level in the decision-making process increases his control and responsibility for his own life. Participation of the child can increase his self-esteem. The child should not be placed in the position of deciding whether or not he should be removed from home. Such a decision has implications of "deciding against one's parents," "labeling parents as bad," etc. Instead, allowing the child to have input in decisions relating to treatment, use of resources, suggestions of what might be helpful to her family will be much more productive for the child and the family.

In some cases where the family is unwilling to participate and there is no family unit upon which to build, permanent placement of the child may be the only legitimate option available. In this situation, assessment and planning should include the people who will be the child's caretakers, insofar as possible.

The Report

The results of the investigation and the assessment and plan will need to be documented in written form. The categories of the report should include all those in which information was gathered. The report should include data gathered from all primary and secondary sources. It should include factual information and impressions of the investigator. It is important that the impressions be clearly labeled as such and be supported by observational data.

The Decision

Recommendations may come from the child care team, the family, agencies that have worked with the family in the past, the worker assigned to investigate, assess, and develop a plan of protection for the child, and others involved in the intake and investigation stage of the process. If CPS is working with the family on a voluntary, noncoercive basis, the ultimate decision will be made by the CPS caseworker and her supervisor. If coercive intervention is required and the matter has been petitioned in juvenile or family court, then adjudication and disposition will become the responsibility of the court. The decision will be based on the recommendations of those involved, the options available, and the circumstances of the case. Any service plan that is recommended and implemented has as its goal the establishing of a safe environment for the child, and, if it is at all possible, the maintaining and strengthening of the family as a unit.

Goldstein, Freud, and Solnit warn that ". . . safeguarding the well-being of every child has to be frustrated by the limits of our knowledge, by the limitations of all those who seek to help, and consequently by society's need to restrict coercive intervention to 'objectively' definable grounds."

They suggest a standard of intervention that asks for the least intrusive disposition and demands a test of "less detrimental alternative" for the child in jeopardy. (Goldstein, et al., 136–137.) Their arguments are particularly potent in the framework of our dilemmas, that we often intervene too early or too late, offering too much or too little. If we are unable to offer something that is less detrimental than what the child in jeopardy now has, intervention should not take place.

TAKING CARE OF BUSINESS

It is not easy to stand on the firing line, keep emotions and discouragement in check, deal with the everyday hassles associated with large agencies and with interagency cooperation and communication, and make decisions regarding the less detrimental alternative for a child when all the evidence is less than clear and convincing on any count. Just as the caring process can increase the self-esteem of children and families, it can replenish depleted energy supplies for those who respond to situations of abuse and neglect, especially in crisis. A part of taking care of business, then, is taking care of oneself and others who respond.

Agencies can assist in taking care of business by providing mental health days, workshops, positive feedback, and a support system for the staff. Often, however, this sort of support from an agency is, at best, erratic and, at worst, nonexistent.

One of the most successful approaches to reenergizing has been the self-help support group concept. These groups are usually established by the staff themselves. Sometimes meetings are held after work. Other times during compensation time on the job set aside by the agency for these meetings. These groups provide the opportunity for "dumping" the feelings of anger, injustice, impotence, and discouragement, while at the same time gaining recognition and strokes for efforts made, and regaining goals and perspective. Permission can exist in such a group to laugh and cry. The danger in such efforts is that the group could become a "bitch" session. In doing so, it would be an additional drain on energy rather than an opportunity to recharge. Safeguards can be built into the structure of the group to assure a balance, however. Self-help strategies for all those who respond are discussed in more detail in Chapter 14.

Summary

The formal response process begins when primary preventon has failed to provide support and assistance to families whose potential for abusing and neglecting children is high. The first stage of the formal response is identification of probable situations of abuse and neglect and the reporting of such situations to the agency designated by law to receive such reports. This stage is the responsibility of everyone.

The second stage of response is intake and investigation. Primary responsibility for this stage is usually assigned by law to CPS or law enforcement. This responsibility is shared with many primary and secondary sources of information. Investigation tasks may be shared with other professionals including physicians and law enforcement.

The third stage of response is assessment and planning. This stage, although the primary responsibility of the investigating agency, may be shared with a child protection consulting team, and hopefully will be shared with the family including the child. Cooperation of the family will help to determine whether or not intervention, if it is indicated, will be coercive or noncoercive. Intervention, at its most effective, occurs only when it is the less detrimental alternative.

Investigation, assessment, and planning include the element of short-term crisis intervention. The effectiveness of crisis intervention efforts has a direct relationship to the ability of the family to enhance their resources and face future crises positively.

Those who intervene at these early stages of formal response are particularly vulnerable to raw hostility and pain and to criticism and blame no matter what their decision. They are less likely to receive recognition for a job well done. Support systems for those who respond are critical.

BIBLIOGRAPHY

Aguilera, Donna C. and Messick, Janice M. *Crisis Intervention, Theory and Methodology.* 3rd Ed. C.V. Mosby Co., St. Louis, 1978.

Benjamin, Alfred, *The Helping Interview.* 2nd ed. Houghton Mifflin Co., Boston, 1974.

Berkeley Planning Associates. *Evaluation of Eleven Demonstration Projects.* NCCAN, (DHEW/OHD), Washington, D.C., 1977.

Bolton, F.G., Jr. Arizona Community Development for Abuse and Neglect, Law Enforcement Manual, DES-5039 (3-78) Grant No. 90-C-600.

Borgman, Robert, Edmunds, Margaret, and MacDicken, Robert A. *Crisis Intervention: A Manual for Child Protective Workers.* NCCD, DHEW Publication No (OHDS) 79-30196, Washington, D.C., August 1979.

Broadhurst, Diane D. and Knoeller, James S. *The Role of Law Enforcement in the Prevention and Treatment of Child Abuse and Neglect.* NCCD, DHEW Public. No. (OHDS) 79-30193, Washington, D.C., August, 1979.

Burch, Genevieve and Mohr, Vicki. Evaluating a Child Abuse Intervention Program. *Social Casework: The Journal of Contemporary Social Work.* Feb. 1980, pp. 90–99.

Child Abuse and Neglect: The Problem of its Management. Vols. 1,2,3. DHEW (OHD) 75-30075, Washington, D.C., 1975.

Education Commission of the States. *Trends in Child Protection Laws—1979.* ECS, Colorado, 1979.

Eskin, Marian and Kravitz, Marjorie. (Eds.) *Child Abuse and Neglect: A Literature Review and Selected Bibliography*. U.S. Dept. of Justice, Washington, D.C., February 1980.

Garrett, Annette, *Interviewing: Its Principles and Methods*. 2nd Ed. Family Service Association of America, New York, 1972.

Goldstein, Joseph, Freud, Anna, and Solnit, Albert J. *Before the Best Interests of the Child*. Free Press, New York, 1979.

Helfer, Ray M. The Etiology of Child Abuse. *Pediatrics. 51*,4, Part II, April 1973.

The Home Visit: How to Recognize the Forms and Indicators of Abuse and Neglect. Paper, distributed by the National Indian Child Abuse and Neglect Resource Center. Fall, 1980, (NCCD: 90-C-1744(02).

Jenkins, James L., Salus, Marsha K., and Schultze, Gretchen L. *Child Protective Services: A Guide for Workers*. (NCCD), DHEW Public. (OHDS), 79-30203, Washington, D.C., August 1979.

McGovern. James I. Delicate Inquiry: The Investigator's Role. *Victimology: An International Journal. II, 2*, Summer 1977, pp.277–284.

National Advisory Committee for Juvenile Justice and Delinquency. *Standards for the Administration of Justice*. U.S. Dept. of Justice, Washington, D.C., July, 1980.

Ostbloom, Normal, and Crase, Sedahlia Jasper. A Model for Conceptualizing Child Abuse Causation and Intervention. *Social Casework: The Journal of Contemporary Social Work. 61*, 3, March 1980, pp. 164–172.

Sexual Assault Center, Harborview Medical Center. Interviewing Child Victims: Guidelines for Criminal Justice System Personnel. 10/1/79.

CHAPTER 11

Child Abuse and Neglect and the Courts

The legal aspects of child abuse and neglect have become of much concern and interest in recent years as the rights of children and of families have become issues. Reporting laws regarding abuse and neglect have become more specific. Child protection laws have a much greater scope than they have had in the past and they address intervention as well as investigation issues. Community awareness regarding indicators of abuse and neglect has increased. As a result, more cases come to the attention of a formal response system, bringing with them a variety of legal questions about everything from when should a state intrude into the family to when and whether a child should be returned to his home.

There seems to be no issue relating to the legal aspects of child abuse and neglect that is totally resolved. Precedence in law can be cited with some authority in a few issues. Law and its application, however, continue to be relative to time and culture.

What people wish and need to know about the legal aspects of child abuse and neglect varies widely. Some are interested in the philosophical foundations of decision-making and the evolution of law; others are much more concerned with the practical implications of law, e.g., how they should behave in court, what are the steps in the legal process, etc. This chapter begins with an overview of some of the major issues, and then presents a discussion of the differences between criminal and juvenile justice procedures. The role of the witness in juvenile court and the child's role as witness in any court, as both philosophical and practical concerns, are included as special topics of this chapter.

ISSUES: FAMILY INTEGRITY VERSUS THE BEST INTEREST OF THE CHILD

The growth of a child into a socially acceptable, functioning adult is the concern of a nurturing family and the law. As a dependent member in a family group, the child's safety and experience of human and legal rights depends upon others. A nurturing family is able to help the child develop trust, affection, and a sense of belonging. It provides the modeling of values and the encouragement of the child to grow and learn. The law, through the Fourteenth amendment to the U.S. Constitution, protects the rights of parents to rear their children as they see fit without undue interference of the state. There are some exceptions: immunization, a common school education, and situations of abuse or neglect.

Family integrity, a concept which recognizes the wholeness, completeness, autonomy, and privacy of the family unit, must exist if essential guidance and nurturing are to be possible. Goldstein et al. in *Before the Best Interest of the Child* take the position that family integrity encompasses three liberties which have direct impact on children: parents' rights to autonomy, the right to have parents who are autonomous, and privacy. These, when recognized in law, protect the family from state intrusion and give parents the opportunity and permission to establish bonds within the family which can meet the physical and emotional needs of their child. The role of law is to safeguard the psychological parent–child relationship that has been developed or in other words, to safeguard the maintenance of family ties. (Goldstein et al., pp. 4–12.)

From this perspective, the first priority of the state is to safeguard family integrity from intrusion. If intrusion should be required (and the criteria for when and how it might occur should be clear, although it rarely is), the state's priority is to strengthen the family and to keep intervention to a minimum. The assumption in these two statements is that the child's interests are best served by making the family whole and not on treating the child as if s/he were a person with interests separate from that context.

If the state overcomes the assumption that parents should determine what is "best" for their children, and terminates the child's relationship with the parents, then the right of the child to a permanent "place of his own" and to a psychological parent–child relationship in other than a biological family becomes the state's priority and responsibility. In this context, the child's interests conflict with family integrity.

Many U.S. Supreme Court decisions from the mid-sixties and the early seventies seem to focus on the rights of children. Beginning in the seventies others began to seek a definition of parent's rights. Some of these decisions suggest an attempt by the Supreme Court to regain some balancing of rights and to reconfirm the concept of family integrity. For example, *Stanley v. Illinois*, 405 U.S. 645 (1972) provides that a natural father has rights to his out of wedlock child. *Yoder v. Wisconsin*, 406 U.S. 205 (1972) confirmed the right of parents to limit, to some extent, their child's education or for religious reasons, to secure an alternative form of education. More recently, a major decision, *Parham v. J.R.*, 442 U.S. 584 (1979), upheld the right of a family to institutionalize a child in a mental facility as long as support for the placement was provided by an independent physician. The *Parham* decision has effectively limited court intervention in decisions regarding medical or psychiatric treatment of children as long as professional support is present. Among the difficult questions that must be decided are those regarding the right of parents and mature adolescents to choose or refuse medical treatment, even if the result is death. Thus far, the principles upon which such cases are decided are certainly not commonly agreed upon. (Wald, p. 17.) Goldstein suggests that the choice should be with the parent or child unless the ". . . result of the operation or procedure will be a substantial chance at a reasonably normal life." (Goldstein, p. 645.)

The question of the parent's right to counsel in termination of parental rights matters has recently been addressed in the U.S. Supreme Court. In *Lassiter v. Department of Social Services of Durham Co., N.C.*, the mother was found not to have a right to counsel. The court argued that only when ". . . the parent's interests were at their strongest, the State's interests were at their weakest, and the risks of error were at their peak . . ." would due process require appointment of counsel. (See also *Mathews v. Eldridge*, 424 U.S. 319, 335.)

Study of the juvenile justice system and the recommendation of standards for that system have been the task of a number of presidentially appointed commissions, the American Bar Association, the Institute of Judicial Administration and others. From the perspective of model legislation and standards regarding intrusion and intervention of the State into family integrity several other organizations have suggested model legislation, among them the American Humane Association, the Child Welfare League of America, the National Center for Child Abuse and Neglect, the Office of Juvenile Justice and Delinquency Prevention and its many programs, The National Association of Indian Juvenile Court Judges, and many other sources. Generally, the current theme seems to be minimum intervention, with noncoercive voluntary cooperation of the family if at all possible. Coercive intervention is urged only when ". . . harm or risk of harm to the juvenile is cognizable under the jurisdication of the family court . . . and there is no other measure which will provide adequate protection.''

The question that never seems to be addressed is how to support and encourage family "wholeness," not simply to allow it. How can the presence of a nurturing family be assured and facilitated without intrusion and without labeling the family as "bad." If the real hope for children is in family integrity, in the broader sense of that concept, we need to establish some means of reaching out to families, without finding that the family is doing something wrong or has a potential for abuse. Since the legal system must find cause or fault in order to have jurisdiction (Evans), it is prevention, before the possibility of legal intrusion, that offers positive hope. All families have a potential for "wholeness" and all of us have the responsibility as a community to support and develop that potential. The question then becomes: what do we all agree is a nurturing, sound family? The Arizona Supreme Court in *Hernandez v. State ex rel. Arizona Department of Economic Security* stated,

> We are not only concerned with the rights of the natural parents but also the rights of the minor child, which include the right to good physical care, adequate food, shelter and clothing, the right to emotional security, the right to be free from injury and neglect and the right to be with his natural parents and siblings. (See also *In the Matter of the Appeal in Gila County Juvenile Action.)*

The definition of these elements, however, is not commonly agreed upon from state to state.

ISSUES: THE RIGHT OF THE CHILD TO THE LEAST DETRIMENTAL ALTERNATIVE

Goldstein et al. define the least detrimental alternative as

> . . . that specific placement and procedure for placement which maximizes, in accord with the child's sense of time and on the basis of short-term predictions given the limitations of knowledge, his or her opportunity for being wanted and for maintaining on a continuous basis a relationship with at least one adult who is or will become his psychological parent. (p.6.)

There is no issue about the need to find such an alternative for the child. The difficulty is in finding the placement. Certainly, the courts and CPS wish to attain this goal. Appropriate placement options are frequently not available and funding for placements is limited. The luxury of matching child to placement is rarely present.

Part of the planning by CPS needs to be long term. The child who is not expected to return home should, if possible, be freed for adoption. If severance or relinquishment is not a possibility, the child should be placed in permanent foster care with an identified family and with the assurance that he will be able to grow up with that family. Reviews of the plan and its implementation by Foster Care Review Boards, Child Protection Councils, Juvenile Court, and staffings are available, sometimes all of them in a given case. Children may be placed in 16 foster homes in 3 or 4 years, even though recent legislation in some states has severely limited these movements by requiring that they be sanctioned in court and that good cause be shown for the requested placements. Often these placements seem unavoidable due to the extraordinary problems of the child and the limited resources of the state. Many times the review boards, councils, and hearings provide a *pro forma* function rather than their professed function of vigorously protecting the child from system pitfalls.

ISSUES: CONFIDENTIALITY

Confidentiality has already been discussed in regard to privileged relationships and as an issue in the establishment of a central register. Confidentiality is also an issue in not publicizing the name of the reporter. Most states assume such confidentiality unless release is ordered by the court. Many confidentiality issues, however, are also privacy issues. If the Supreme Court can hold that laws that ". . . require parental approval of abortion for minor females are an unconstitutional invasion of privacy interests," the privacy of one's body seems guaranteed. (See *Planned Parenthood v. Danforth.*) Privacy is also the issue in sharing information regarding a case with other professionals and nonprofessionals. Receiving such information is usually on a need-to-know basis. Information shared, theoretically, is only the minimum that will satisfy that need.

Another issue for parents and children is the right to see records written about themselves. This right is now granted in some states within limits of "harm to the reporter," or "harm to the person about whom the record is made". There are still many grey areas in law regarding this issue. The U.S. Supreme Court did not clarify the issue in its review of the *Moore v. Sims* case, a case focusing on the right of parents to have access to abuse and neglect reports and the appropriate scope and operating practice of the Texas Child Abuse and Neglect Report and Inquiry System (CANRIS). A federal district court found several sections of the Texas Family Code unconstitutional, particularly, CANRIS and the statute pertaining to confidentiality of abuse and neglect investigation reports and records. The Supreme Court held that the lower federal court should have abstained from hearing the case and instructed the lower court to dismiss. The issue remains an open question and is resolved differently in different states. (*Moore v. Sims*, ___ U.S. ___, 99 S.Ct. 2371 (1979). (National Legal Resource Center.)

THE CRIMINAL JUSTICE SYSTEM

The Concept of Criminal Justice

Crime is a public offense; it is assumed that a person who commits a crime commits an offense against society and therefore, against the State. Criminal law defines what act is criminal and what punishment is required if the offender is found guilty. The law generally reflects public opinion about what is acceptable and not acceptable behavior in that society. The criminal justice system, then, is basically a legal system that has as its foundation, the criminal law. Its purpose is social control. It regulates the behavior of citizens in society and therefore helps to maintain order in that society. The system assumes that a person who breaks the law does so intentionally. Punishment, or negative sanction, includes fines, probation, imprisonment, the death penalty, or some combination of options. Procedural laws in each state's penal code define the rules for "processing" the offender from the point of arrest through arraignment, trial, sentencing, carrying out of the sentence, and release.

Characteristics of Criminal Procedure

Generally, criminal charges against abusers are drawn from a State's criminal code for such crimes as murder, assault, rape, mayhem, and child molesting. Sometimes a state also has a specific criminal statute defining specific types of abuse (usually physical abuse resulting in serious physical injury or sexual abuse or exploitation) as crimes. There is sufficient substantive law upon which to bring charges against perpetrators in most states. If the accused is found guilty she/he will be sentenced by the court. The court has jurisdiction over the adult, but not over the child victim.

Procedure includes a criminal trial, appointment of experts, the right to have a jury, the highest standard of proof beyond a reasonable doubt, right to counsel, cross-examination of witnesses, and a public and speedy trial. In a criminal trial, rules of evidence are strictly adhered to.

The Threat of Prosecution

It is the threat of criminal prosecution that permeates the entire chain of child abuse responses: self-incrimination, privacy, and due process issues are raised at the threshold of response—at the reporting stage—and continue through each stage until the threat is removed, actualized, or, in the alternative, traded for cooperation. The threat of prosecution affects the attitudes and behavior of all of the actors: they include the reporters, the parents, the child, and the intervening social workers (whether they be intake workers or therapists), not to mention the prosecutors and judges. The threat can be seen to have both beneficial and detrimental effects. (Smith, pp. 107.)

The problems surrounding the prosecution of abusers are many.

1. In many cases, the punishment through incarceration of the offender is not only of no positive value, but actually may break up a family or at least add to its dysfunction.
2. Collection of evidence is difficult in such cases. The crime is generally perpetrated in the privacy of the home. Many times there is only circumstantial evidence available or the testimony of a child so young that s/he is not deemed competent to testify.
3. The child will often be the only witness against the offender. Providing testimony in court against one's parent is very difficult and adds to the burden that the child already carries.
4. If the prosecution is unsuccessful, the child may be in additional danger from the abuser.
5. The abuser herself is often a victim of abuse, so the impact of criminal prosecution and imprisonment may be to further victimize rather than to help.
6. The criminal justice system is not programmed to cope with or to adequately protect the young victim in his/her interaction with that system. It is designed for a victim who can defend herself on the witness stand and who understands abstractly the issues before the court. (Lennon.)

Positive Use of the Criminal Justice System

There are occasions where prosecution is useful. Where the negative impact can be minimized and the sentencing structure used positively for the child's protection, it can be a powerful tool in the child's best interest. Harborview Hospital Sexual Assault Center in Seattle, Washington provides support to the victims and assists them through the process of testifying. At the same time, the criminal justice professionals work as a part of the child protection team. An offender who is convicted and sentenced into a treatment program, is closely supervised and encouraged toward positive change. The family receives help at the same time. Thus far, the project and others like it have demonstrated positive results.

Even if prosecution never occurs, *The threat of it may assist the worker(s) in gaining cooperation and agreement* from parents for treatment or alternative custody that they might otherwise refuse. This threat may *also protect the child,* since further abuse will be prosecuted without question, and, should that occur, charges will be brought on the first instance as well.

The decision to prosecute or not belongs to the prosecutor. The prosecutor does not have to consider the best interest of the child. Some do, but it is not required. More important might be the weight of the evidence, the severity of the offense, the public outcry, and other factors.

THE JUVENILE JUSTICE SYSTEM

Juvenile justice, as a separate concept from criminal justice, began officially in the late nineteenth and early twentieth centuries. It was based on the doctrine of *parents patriae,* in which the judge is the ultimate protector or parent of the child. The state stands *in loco parentis,* in place of the parent, and has ultimate responsibility for the child. The juvenile court was not created to be a criminal court. It was given exclusive (only) and original (first) jurisdiction over matters of delinquency, dependency, incorrigibility, and/or unruliness. It was created to provide services to children (predominantly poor children) who needed protection, reform, or rehabilitation. The process of juvenile justice includes many components and often a broad spectrum of resources available in a total community. The court itself is a fulcrum of the process but much of the work is the responsibility of other formal and informal components of the system.

Conceived as a civil process rather than a criminal process, the juvenile justice system was designed to be informal, protective, and provide individualized treatment. It was to provide ''wise direction'' to children without labeling them criminal and without processing children through an adversary criminal procedure.

It is not the formal role of juvenile justice that has changed, but the interpretation of that role in practice. One of the interpretation issues that has changed the behavior and influence of juvenile justice is the question of the rights of children. Children were not deemed to have rights in juvenile court. After all, why would they need them? Due process for children was to be more substantial than for adults. The court would act in the child's best interest and in a sense of fair play. The whole process of juvenile justice through the intake, screening, formal petitioning, adjudication, disposition and treatment/supervision would be framed in this definition of due process. The emphasis was on acting *for* the child, rather than *to* the child. Children were too young to have rights anyway. Rights and decision-making were for adults. It follows that there was little distinction among the situations of and the services provided for the delinquent, the destitute, and the neglected. All were provided protection and often were placed in the same institutions.

Children were not viewed as "parties" before the court and, for the most part, the interest of the child and the interests of the parents were not seen as being contradictory. The child's interest was considered to be the same as that of the State. After all, the state was bound to be the child's parent.

Juvenile justice has always had to strike a balance between legal aspects and social service function. In its early development, the emphasis was largely on social service function, although, even in its most idealistic days, what was promised and what was delivered were very different matters.

As the juvenile justice system grew and changed, the balance between legal and social service functions has been more difficult to achieve. A large proportion of the juvenile population is referred for delinquency, rather than for dependency matters. Many people today are not aware that juvenile justice jurisdiction includes that of dependency. In some places, the juvenile justice role is a part of the jurisdiction of the family court. This court has jurisdiction over matters that directly affect the family, including child custody in divorce matters, family support, and some adult offenses against children.

Major court decisions have brought rights to children involved with delinquency in juvenile court processes. The balance between legal and social service functions has slipped heavily to the side of legal, especially with regard to delinquency cases. Yet, no one knows just what to do with the juvenile justice concept, how to reconcile its original philosophy with the U.S. Supreme Court decisions of 1966 (Kent), 1967 (Gault), and 1970 (Winship), which all served to change the nature of the juvenile justice process. If it is difficult for the court to assess its appropriate role in delinquency matters, it is even more difficult to do so in child abuse and neglect cases.

It is through the juvenile court or the family court that we coercively respond to child abuse and neglect. We ask that court to make findings of fact regarding evidence presented and then to determine, legally, what will be best for the child. The options of the court are essentially the same as they would have been had the family worked voluntarily with CPS, and sometimes less; however, the court has greater punitive sanctions.

Legal answers to the very hard questions that have been asked in earlier chapters about protection of children are no easier to find. Even those "experts" who come to recommend dispositions to the court disagree, sometimes dramatically, among themselves, as to what is best for the child.

The court and CPS share the tasks related to the case. They must share in providing intake, investigation, referral, assessment, recommendation, suggested treatment, and supervisory options. The increasingly adversary nature of juvenile court procedures has been cited as a major problem in working with neglect and abuse cases because it in turn increases the difficulty of maintaining a balance between the legal and social functions of the court. (Wald, p.15.) Smith comments, however, that

> The adversary character of the juvenile court proceedings can be held in bounds in two ways. A showing of the beneficial effects of certain types of intervention, coupled with resources that diminish the threat of separation of the child from the parents, would enable the court to dispense with many of the more disturbing features of adversary hearings."(p. 114.)

Legislatures have not been consistently clear as to the role of the juvenile or family courts in neglect and abuse. Recent legislative tendency seems to be toward limiting and restricting the court's ability to intervene in child abuse cases and to commit juveniles to mental health centers. (Ferlanto.) The court is assigned the function to protect the child from further injury, to work closely with social service professionals to provide supervision and treatment of the child and the family, and to ensure that the legal rights of both the parents and the child are protected. Perhaps more than anything else, the juvenile court becomes a place to test the appropriateness of solutions that have been offered and to review the implementation of solutions.

PRIMARY CONSIDERATIONS

Taking Into Custody: Emergencies

The first juvenile court involvement in abuse and neglect situations in some states is the removal of a child from his/her home in an emergency. Some states require a court order before removal is possible; many, however, allow removal without a court order but specify that if the child is removed under such circumstances, the court must be notified and a petition of dependency filed. Although most states allow removal only in circumstances of imminent danger, some provide much broader discretion. (See Trends in Child Protection, Chapter Four.) There is increasing objection to initial temporary custody orders that are obtained in certain jurisdictions without requiring initial notice to the parties affected. *(Ex Parte.)*Lack of procedural due process is the principal argument in these cases. Some states, for example, Arizona, require that a child be seen by a physician or psychologist to confirm abuse. If that is not confirmed, the child is to be returned home within 12 hours.

ARIZONA DEPARTMENT OF ECONOMIC SECURITY

TEMPORARY CUSTODY NOTICE

On *(date)* _____ at *(address)* _____

(time) _____ am pm, *(child(ren))* _____

was placed in the temporary custody of the Arizona Department of Economic Security. Temporary custody was necessary because:

_____

_____

_____

Your rights under Arizona State Law *(A.R.S. 8-223)*

1. Your child(ren) must be returned within 48 hours *(excluding Saturdays, Sundays, and holidays)* unless a Dependency petition is filed. If your child was removed for the purpose of an examination to determine whether he or she had been abused, your child must be returned within twelve hours unless a medical doctor or psychologist determines that he or she is suffering serious physical or emotional abuse.

2. If a Dependency petition is filed, and your child is made a temporary ward of the court:

   a. And you want the Juvenile Court to hold a hearing to review temporary custody, you must file a written request with the court within 72 hours of receiving this notice *(excluding Saturdays, Sundays and holidays)*.

   b. The Court will notify you of the date, time and place of the Hearing to review temporary custody.

   c. If your child is returned to you within 48 hours, a Hearing to review temporary custody will not be held.

   d. The Court shall hold the Hearing to review temporary custody within five days of receiving your written request, and shall determine whether it is clearly necessary for the Department of Economic Security to keep your child in temporary custody, pending the Dependency Hearing.

3. The initial hearing on the Dependency petition shall be set not later than twenty one days from the filing of the petition.

4. You may request appointment of an attorney through the court. Qualification is based on financial need.

5. _____ County Juvenile Court is located at *(address)* _____

_____ , *(phone)* _____ .

CHILD PROTECTIVE SERVICES   TELEPHONE

ARIZONA DEPARTMENT OF ECONOMIC SECURITY ADDRESS *(Street, City, ZIP Code)*

_____

METHOD OF NOTICE

On *(date)* _____ , *(time)* _____ I served notice to *(parent, guardian or custodian)* _____ .

Method used:

☐ hand carried   *(signature of parent, guardian or custodian)* _____

☐ mailed to parent   ☐ left at residence   ☐ other *(specify)* _____

CHILD PROTECTIVE SERVICES

Figure 11-1 Sample custody notice.

275

Once a child has been removed without a court order, most states specify what steps are required. Generally, they include the following categories of information. Since every state is different in what is specifically required, the reader may wish to study the statutes in his/her own state.

1. *Notification.* Notification is usually required to the juvenile/family court, the parents, guardians or custodians, and CPS, if that agency has not been involved in the removal. Some states also require notification of a district or county attorney and others.

2. *Promptness of Notification.* Most states prescribe notification within a specified number of hours. Some within 12 hours, others within 24 or more.

3. *Filing of a Report.* A report is generally required in writing as a follow up to verbal notification. It may be directed to the court, the central registry, CPS, or others. The report is usually written by the person who removed the child from the home. Although promptness of filing the report is urged in most states, usually more time is allowed than is allowed for verbal reporting. Despite the requirement of prompt notification, calendar limitations often make it difficult to schedule contested custody hearings in a timely fashion.

4. *Temporary Placement of the Child.* Every state deals with questions relating to placement. Some require that the child be placed in designated shelter care agencies, some allow placement with a relative. Some states do not permit placement of abused or neglected children in a detention center for delinquent children.

If a court order is necessary for a child to be removed, the court may also state who is to pick up the child. Although in some states almost anyone could be appointed by the court to remove the child, in others the statutes are vey specific and require that a sheriff or a peace officer pick up the child.

Generally, the procedure to get the order is similar. First a petition alleging the child's circumstances is filed, along with a summons for the parent to appear at a hearing regarding the matter. The court determines whether or not an emergency situation exists. If so, authorization is given for the child to be removed from the home. The child is then picked up and the parent(s) served with the summons.

WHEN IS PETITIONING APPROPRIATE?

A petition is mostly likely to be filed when one or more of the following circumstances is present:

1. When the child's home is considered unsafe for the child.
2. When abuse has been found to exist and the child is believed to be

IN THE SUPERIOR COURT OF THE STATE OF ARIZONA
IN AND FOR THE COUNTY OF PIMA

JUVENILE COURT

PETITION

IN THE MATTER OF:

PETITION
JUVENILE NUMBER _____

A Person(s) Under The Age
of Eighteen Years

Personally appeared before me this _____ day of _____ 19 ___,
_____ who being duly sworn upon information and belief,
complain and say:
　　1. That _____
_____, residing at _____
_____ years, is/are within the jurisdiction of this court:
　　2. That the father of said child _____ is _____
_____ residing at
　　3. That the mother of said child _____ is _____ ;
residing at _____ :
　　4. That the person(s) having guardianship, custody or control of said child _____ is/are _____
_____
residing at _____ :
　　5. That the said child _____ (is/are) (is not/are not) presently detained _____
_____ having been taken
into custody by the _____ on the _____
day of _____ 19 _____ at _____ hours;
　　6. That the child _____ is/are _____
child _____ within the purview and provisions of Arizona Revised Statutes, Sec. 8-201, as amended, in that said child _____ :

_____

SUBSCRIBED AND SWORN to before me this _____ day of _____ 19 ___.

My Commission Expires:
　　　　　　　　　　　　　　　　　　　　　　　_____
　　　　　　　　　　　　　　　　　　　　　　　　　　　　　Notary Public

ORIGINAL

Figure 11-2 Petition sample.

in need of protection, but the parents refuse to work voluntarily with the social service agency.

3. When voluntary efforts have been attempted and have failed and the child's adequate care is still in question.

4. If the child has suffered institutional abuse or neglect by a school, residential facility, foster home, social service agency, etc.

THE JUVENILE JUSTICE PROCESS: AN OVERVIEW

Intake

The juvenile court does not go out and search for cases. If the case is referred to the court, it is usually referred by either CPS or other professionals who are concerned for the welfare of the child. Sometimes situations that have been referred to the court for delinquent or incorrigible behavior, appear upon investigation, to be dependency matters. Some courts refer such cases to CPS for processing; others might petition the case, process it, and even supervise the case under protective supervision.

If dependency matters are handled from the outset through the juvenile court, a process similar to that used for delinquency matters is followed. Screening occurs during intake at some juvenile courts; others separate the two functions. Often the screening is done by a probation officer assigned to the intake function. Only limited investigations are performed by such personnel. These are usually for the purpose of developing a court social history and dispositional plan for the child and/or family. If further fact-finding investigation is deemed necessary the responsibility will usually rest with the county attorney's office. Generally speaking, many cases are adjusted and/or referred to other agencies at the intake screening level. This function is one of preadjudicative diversion. If the juvenile court is a primary agency to receive reports the adjustment and informal resolution function might be one that will be used in many neglect cases. The possibility of formal processing is always a threat in the juvenile court. The nature of a court, even if one of its functions is social service, is coercive. The authority of the court exists, whether or not it is invoked.

Often the intake and screening of neglected and abused children has been completed, for the most part by CPS. The function of the intake officer at the court is to coordinate the juvenile court and CPS and to prepare for court.

Advisory and Preliminary Hearings

If the child is removed from the home, a protective custody hearing is required soon after the placement in order for the court to review the appropriateness of that decision. Usually, a petition is filed within 24 hours after a child is removed and the hearing held within 48 hours. Evidence supporting the decision to remove the child from the home is presented by the worker and other sources such as the examining physician. The hearing concludes with the decision of the judge regarding temporary custody of the child. This is not a hearing on the allegations of the petition of dependency. It simply determines where the child will stay until an adjudication hearing can take place.

Preadjudication Matters

Some legal and procedural matters are resolved before an adjudication hearing takes place. If more time is needed by one of the parties to prepare the case, a continuance might be requested. If the parents contested the petition but later changed their mind and decided to admit to its allegations, this change can be entered into the record at this time. Questions of admissibility of evidence and various court procedures might be heard as preadjudication matters. Sometimes a pretrial conference can be instituted. This may hone down issues or dispose of collateral matters which will save court time: Some cases are adjudicated or dismissed at this level. (Ferlanto.)

The Adjudicatory Hearing

The adjudication hearing is formal. It is the juvenile court's version of an evidentiary trial. Evidence is heard regarding the allegations of the petition, relative to the injury sustained by the child. It is up to the state to prove by a preponderance of the evidence, or in some jurisdictions, clear and convincing evidence that the child has been abused or neglected. If the parent(s) admit to abuse or neglect, no evidence has to be presented; if they "contest" the petition, however, witnesses will be called and evidence presented to substantiate the allegations. Although the standard of proof required in criminal cases is *beyond a reasonable doubt,* this is not a standard usually required in abuse and neglect situations. Some states now use the intermediate standard of *clear and convincing evidence* in dependency cases. Since the U.S. Supreme Court decision (1982) in 80 U.S. 5889 regarding *John and Annie Santosky v. Bernhardt S. Kramer, Commissioner, Ulster Co. Department of Social Services, New York,* all jurisdictions are required to use this standarrd in cases concerning what have been termed "fundamental rights," i.e., termination or severance of parental rights. This standard was earlier required by the Indian Child Welfare Act of 1978 which provides that ". . . clear and convincing evidence that continued custody of the child will result in serious emotional or physical damage to the child" must be presented before a child can be placed in foster care. (NICAN,

Implementing.) Until the U.S. Supreme Court decision, however, most states required a preponderance of the evidence in these matters, or in other words, the least precise burden of proof.

Beyond a reasonable doubt is the highest standard of proof required in American courts. Using this standard, if any reasonable doubt remains that the facts alleged took place, the decision of the court should be that they did not. Since 1970, with the U.S. Supreme Court decision in *Winship* this has been the burden of proof required in delinquency matters.

People who support preponderance of the evidence as an appropriate standard in dependency matters argue that matters of abuse and neglect are sometimes difficult to prove in precise evidentiary terms, even though abuse does exist. The higher the standard of proof, the greater the danger that a child may not be protected adequately. On the other hand, the higher the standard of proof, the more the autonomy of the parents will be protected.

Both parents, if their parental rights have not been relinquished (given up voluntarily) or severed by the court, have a right to notice and a right to be heard, even if they are not and have not been married. Most states provide right to counsel in juvenile proceedings, although some states only make counsel mandatory if the outcome of a delinquency hearing may be confinement of the juvenile. (Caulfield, p.33.) The U.S. Constitution requires that counsel be provided in delinquency adjudication, but that requirement has not been interpreted to extend to dependency matters. Unless a state statute requires it, the court does not have to appoint counsel for indigent parents. Many states provide for the appointment of a *guardian ad litem* to protect the interests of the child. (Caulfield, p. 34.) *McKeiver v. Pennsylvania* has determined that a jury trial is not necessary in juvenile matters.

Once all parties in the matter have called witnesses and presented evidence on their behalf, the judge makes a finding of fact. (A jury trial is not generally required in juvenile matters. Some states do require them, however, or provide them at the request of a party to the hearing.) If the judge finds that no abuse or neglect has occurred, the case is finished. If the judge finds that abuse or neglect has occurred, the court assumes jurisdiction over the child, adjudicating the child a ward of the court. A second step, either a second hearing or a separate part of this hearing, is necessary to determine what will be done to assist the family and protect the child.

The Dispositional Hearing

Will treatment be required for the family and/or child? Will the child remain at home or be placed in another setting? A predisposition report is written by the intake officer and possibly by the CPS worker, summarizing available information and making a recommendation to the court regarding the ability of the family to care for the child. The child is a ward of the court at the time of this hearing. The judge has the option of accepting or rejecting recommendations presented. If the professionals involved and the family agree on one recommendation, the judge will usually order the treatment suggested. Cooperation among community agencies and the court, especially, CPS and its resources, is critical at this point. Resources used by the court for the child are accountable to the court.

Reviews are generally scheduled on a regular basis to monitor progress and to determine if the decision of the court has been followed. The decision of the court is not final until this dispositional phase is completed. The state has a continuing obligation to show that a status of dependency continues to exist at each review. If parents can demonstrate improvement to the court, they sometimes can regain custody of a child, even over the supervisory agency's objection.

Monitoring

1. Protective Supervision. Protective supervision in abuse and neglect cases is usually placed with the department of human services or the department of welfare. Some states specify that protective supervision can be provided by court officers. Protective supervision is different from probation, predominantly in the options available to the supervisor and the consequences to the child. If a child violates the terms of her probation, that child's probation may be revoked and the child may be committed to a correctional facility for delinquent children. No child under protective supervision could, by their behavior, violate probation, since that is not the nature of the supervision. Protective supervision infers that the child requires the protection of the court through no fault of the child. Probation infers that the child has committed an offense and his behavior is being monitored. Most states now explicitly specify that a child under protective supervision cannot be committed to state institutions for delinquent youth. Usually, children under protective supervision are not detained in centers where delinquent children are detained, although children may be and frequently are placed in treatment programs with delinquent children.

2. Reviews. Are the orders of the court being carried out? Have circumstances changed enough to warrant a change in plans? Are the resources being utilized the appropriate choices for this child? Should dependency status continue?

Generally, reviews are made every three to six months in dependency matters, and sometimes more frequently. The final review of the case ends with termination of the court's jurisdiction.

3. Severance of Parental Rights Hearing. Severance of parental rights may occur if (1) parents have abandoned their child (usually 6 months without contact) or (2) if it appears that the home from which the child has been removed will not be an appropriate home for the child to return to, either because the parents will not or are unable to provide safety and nurturing to the child. The court hears evidence as to whether or not parental rights should be terminated and the child be placed for adoption at a severance or termination hearing. Since the U.S. Supreme Court decision in *Santosky,* clear and convincing evidence has become the common burden of proof in severance matters.

Severance often requires months or even years to achieve. A child may be in "limbo" for that time and longer, moving from placement to placement. As the child grows older, opportunities for adoption decreases. Where the likelihood of the child's returning home is extremely low, yet the probability of severance and/or adoption is also low, some agencies opt for permanent placement of a child in a designated foster home rather than initiating severance proceedings. Permanent placement has its disadvantages as well. (See Chapter 12 and 13 for more discussion of this topic.)

4. The Foster Care Review Board. The foster care review board is a monitoring system used by several states for all children in foster care. In Arizona, boards are appointed and trained in the various districts and a chairperson appointed for each one. Each board is assigned supervision of a set number of cases which are reviewed every six months. At the time of review, input from the worker, other professionals, the foster parents, the parents, and other interested parties are invited.

The advantage of the FCRB is that it provides a community group of citizens who participate in the care and planning for children. A regular review is required. Caseworkers, aware of the review, may be more precise in their recordkeeping and more likely to maintain up-to-date plans. One disadvantage is that it adds one more layer to an already overburdened system. Sometimes board members are unable to offer anything more positive than the better of the two worst choices that the worker was already struggling with. If review boards are not effective, they may become a time-consuming exercise.

5. Appeals. Cases appealed from the juvenile court are appealed to Courts of Appeals and to State Supreme Courts. Some states provide that the appeal first goes to the trial court, where it may be heard *de novo* or as a new case. Generally, however, findings of juvenile court judges are final, and appeals are usually made on some specific issue, as would be true in adult matters. Appeals generally are restricted to questions of law—not matters of facts.

THE COURT ENVIRONMENT

The Expert Witness

Two major types of witnesses testify in court: lay witnesses and expert witnesses. The difference between the two are based in whether or not their opinions can be stated as testimony on the witness stand.

Lay witnesses are assumed to have no specialized knowledge or skill in a subject and generally can testify only to what they have seen or heard first-hand. They are generally not allowed opinions. Many times, however, it is possible to describe facts in enough detail to assist the judge in drawing his own conclusion. Occasionally, a witness is called on to testify to the character or reputation in the community of one of the parties to the hearing. How is the person viewed by his/her own community? Although the line between admissible and nonadmissible testimony in this area is not always clear, generally, neither rumors nor personal opinion can be stated. The character witness must show the nature of her association with that person, that she is reliable, and does know the person's reputation in the community.

Expert witnesses are called because of their specialized knowledge and skill. They can draw conclusions from facts. They can make professional judgments (sometimes intelligent guesses) in their area of expertise. Expert witnesses are very important in child abuse cases. A pediatrician, for example, can explain why a child is failure-to-thrive, or can describe the healing stages of various injuries several times over a period of time. Often, the worker who has first-hand knowledge of the case, especially the investigating worker, may testify as an expert witness.

The expert witness must qualify in order to testify. This may be done through providing information as to how his/her expert status was achieved. It may be through formal education, training, practical experience, etc. Membership in professional associations may be cited; years of experience in the specialized area noted may be helpful. Essentially, the hope of the court is that this person's informed professional opinions will assist the court in making the best decision in this case. The expert is considered an expert only in the specialty field. In any other area, the expert is a lay witness. An expert may be subpoenaed to testify, but cannot be forced to give an expert opinion. (Caulfield, p. 42.)

Example

Lay witness: The child had bruises on his left arm and left cheek. When I took his shirt off, I also saw a mark across his back.

Expert Witness: There were multiple bruises on the child's left forearm and left cheek. Some of the bruises appeared to be fresh. Others were in various stages of healing. The wounds appear to have been inflicted on at least three different occasions. A mark across the child's lower back appears to have been caused by a belt with a large belt buckle.

Understanding the Roles of the Primary Participants

The Juvenile Court Judge. The judge is in charge of the proceedings and is the decision maker. This is the person who assures that everyone who should be heard is heard. Finally, this is the person charged with acting in a way which will protect the child.

The Referee. This person sits in the place of the judge at some court hearings. His/her decisions are in the form of recommendations to the judge who will make the final decision.

The Child's Attorney. This attorney represents the interests of the child. Sometimes, this may be a *guardian ad litem*. In other situations, this attorney is appointed to legally represent the child, while another person is appointed to act as child advocate (and may be a witness in the proceeding). Streib suggests that children's lawyers could be a new specialty in law, not limited to representing children in juvenile court matters. (Streib, p. 53–59; Ray–Bettineski, pp. 65–70.)

Parent's Attorney. This attorney is engaged by the parent(s) or appointed for them to represent their position and asure that their rights are protected in court.

The State/County Attorney. This person acts as the attorney for the people, files petitions, and represents the state in seeking the finding of fact.

Caseworker/Probation Officers. These are agency representatives responsible for analyzing and diagnosing the problems relating to the child and family and recommending and monitoring/implementing a plan of treatment.

Parents/Guardians. The parents or guardians have family and individual rights in dependency matters. Documented attempts must be made to notify them of the hearing in the child's behalf. They are usually represented by counsel, although they may elect to waive that right. Lobbying exists in several states to permit grandparents limited standing in dependency cases.

Foster Parent. If a child is placed in a foster home prior to the hearing, the foster parent may be the person who has had closest contact with the child recently. This person can testify to the child's behavior and any changes which might have occurred in that behavior.

Witnesses. Expert witnesses, e.g., a psychologist, psychiatrist, pediatrician, social worker, or other professional person, may be subpoenaed to testify. Lay witnesses might include members of the family, neighbors, community members who will testify to what they saw, heard, smelled, touched, and the reputation of the parent(s) in the community.

Guardian Ad Litem. If appointed separately from the child's attorney, might be a volunteer advocate for the child and an officer of the court who may submit a report of his/her findings and testify to them in court. (See Ray–Bettineski, pp.65–70.)

Other Persons. The bailiff, court clerk, and court reporter may also be present in court.

Protocol

Several resources are listed at the end of the chapter that depict various aspects of dependency hearings and help the potential witness to understand the form of such hearings.

Some elements of proper behavior in court are:

1. In most courts, all persons stand when the judge is announced and enters the courtroom.
2. The State's evidence will be the first to be presented, followed by the parent(s), and/or the child's.
3. Every witness will be directly questioned by the attorney who called him/her and then may be cross-examined by other attorneys. A second opportunity at questioning by the first attorney (generally called rebuttal or redirect questioning) is permitted on issues that emerged during questioning by the other attorneys, and then recross-examination is permitted by the other attorneys.
4. Leading questions, those which appear to encourage the witness toward a particular response, are generally allowed, except in direct questioning. They may be allowed in all stages when the witness is a young child, who may need help in forming a response.
5. Attorneys may object to questions or approaches taken by other attorneys during the hearing that they feel are improper. If so, they will interrupt and say "I object" or "Objection." Often they will be asked to explain their objection. The judge then makes a determination or ruling on the matter, either sustaining, (supporting) the objection or overruling (not supporting) the objection.
6. Sometimes questions will be asked of witnesses deliberately to discredit their testimony. Usually such questions attempt to con-

fuse the witness or get the witness to contradict some answer already given.[1]

THE CHILD WITNESS

A child may be a witness in criminal or juvenile court cases, although in many situations, the child is not even present in dependency hearings in juvenile and family courts. Generally, the child's competence to testify is determined by the judge and is based on the child's ability to understand "the difference between truth and falsehood, as well as of his duty to tell the former." (Wheeler v. U.S.; see also U.S. v. Spoonhunter.) Generally the child's capacity to testify includes his/her ability to receive an accurate impression of the event, ability to recall the event accurately, and the ability to relate the event accurately in court. (*People v. Delaney; State v. Segerberg; Bradburn v. Peacock;* Caulfield, p. 47.)

Interviews with defense attorneys and being a witness in criminal court are two very traumatic events for the child. Since the adult court is not geared to children, the following discussion centers around what supports can be offered a child who must testify, especially in adult court, and how the experience can be softened for her/him.

Familiarization of the Child with the Court Room and Court Process. A physical walk-through of the entry into the courtroom, sitting in the witness chair, a general orientation to where everyone will be sitting, and the role of those who will be present will help the child to see the courtroom as a less threatening place. Discussion of the stages of the procedure, a review of the possible types of questions that might be asked on the witness stand, and a review of court protocol may be helpful to the child.

Personal Support For the Child. Caring people who understand the process and understand the child's fears, ambivalence, and mixed feelings of guilt and anger at having to testify against a parent or caretaker, need to walk the child emotionally and physically through the entire process. They need to be physically present both before, during, and after the court hearing. Sometimes a peer support group of children who have been in similar circumstances may be helpful. In Pima County, Arizona, the Victim–Witness organization provides this support to children who are witnesses in adult court. In Seattle, Washington, the Sexual Assault Center assumes this supportive role.

The Question of Conviction. Whether or not the accused is convicted of the abuse, the child needs to believe that it was appropriate to have testified.

---

[1]A general reference for much of the preceeding material in this chapter is Norgard, Katherine and Mayhall, Pamela. *Legal Aspects of Fostering.* Pima College/Arizona Department of Economic Security, Tucson, AZ., 1980.

The child needs to know that the lack of enough evidence for a conviction for abuse does not mean that anyone believes that the child is lying or that the abuse did not occur. If the accused is not convicted, the child's safety needs to be assured.

Summary

The child is the concern of the family and the state. The child has a right to a safe, nurturing family and the court has the responsibility to allow the family to function with autonomy and privacy toward this end. The state's first priority is to protect the integrity of the family. If the family does not act in the child's best interest, however, the state is required to act on the child's behalf.

Legal intervention into a family is coercive. It is based on the right and responsibility of the court to intervene when a crime is committed or when a child is in need of protection. The court is a legal mediator of disputes in both civil and criminal matters. The court hears the proof, based on whatever standard of proof is required, and makes findings of fact. If the finding is that an offender should be found guilty of an offense (in criminal cases) or that a child should be made a ward of the court (in juvenile matters), a disposition is made by the court to determine what should happen next. Persons and agencies carrying out the disposition then become responsible to the court for complying with the decision.

Witnesses are generally of two types, lay and expert. Both perform important but different roles in the court process. Only qualified expert witnesses are allowed to state opinions and conclusions. People who understand court procedure and the facts that they need to present in a case will be more effective as witnesses. A child who is required to be a witness needs to be oriented to the courtroom and court process and given a great deal of personal support before, during, and after testifying in court. Generally a child is held to be competent to testify if s/he can receive accurate impressions of an event and to relate them, accurately, at a later time.

BIBLIOGRAPHY

Bradburn v. Peacock, 135 C.A. 2d. 161, 286 p. 2d. 972 (1955).

Berkeley Planning Associates, *Planning and Implementing Child Abuse and Neglect Service Programs: The Experience of Eleven Demonstration Projects.* Children's Bureau, NCCAN, 1977.

Caulfield, Barbara A. The Legal Aspects of Protective Services for Abused and Neglected Children. A Manual. USDHEW, (OHDS), Washington, D.C., 1978.

Danforth v. Planned Parenthood of Missouri, 428 U.S. 52 (1976).

Evans, John R., Esq. Tucson, Arizona, Comments on Manuscript. February 1982.

Ferlanto, Joseph, Chief Referee. Pima County Juvenile Court, Tucson, AZ, Comments on manuscript. February 1982.

Fraser, Brian G. Independent Representation for the Abused and Neglected Child: The Guardian *Ad Litem.* *California Western Law Review, 13,* (1976–77), pp. 16–45.

Gault, In Re, 387 U.S. 1, 70 (1967).

Goldstein, J. Medical Care for the Child at Risk. *86, Yale L.J.,* 645 (1977).

Goldstein, Joseph, Freud, A., and Solnit, A. *Before the Best Interests of the Child.* The Free Press, New York, 1979.

Helfer, Ray. *A Self Instructional Program on Child Abuse and Neglect.* Units 1 and 2. 1974, Helfer, Professor of Human Development, College of Human Medicine, Michigan State University, Lansing, Michigan, 48824.

Hernandez v. State ex rel. Arizona Department of Economic Security 23 AZ App/ 32, 530 p. 2nd 389 (1975).

Implementing the Indian Child Welfare Act of 1978. Spring 1980. Paper developed and distributed by National Indian Child Abuse and Neglect Resource Center, Tulsa, Oklahoma.

In Re C.G. Okla. Sup Ct. 11/10/81.

In Re Gila Co. Juvenile Action, SCt.AZ. 11.42.81.

Jenkins, James L., Salus, Marsha K., and Schultze, Gretchen L. *Child Protective Services: A Guide for Workers.* DHEW Publication No. (OHDS) 79-30203, Washington, D.C.

Kent v. U.S. 383 U.S. 541 (1966).

Lassiter v. Dept. of Social Services of Durham Co., N.C., ____ U.S. ____, 101 S.Ct. 2153, (1981).

Lennon, Beth. County of San Diego, Human Services Liaison, Assigned to San Diego Police Dept. Special Abuse Unit, interview 2/82.

Mathews v. Eldridge, 424 U.S. 319, 335.

National Legal Resource Center for Child Advocacy and Protection. *Access to Child Protective Records*—A Basic Guide to the Law and Policy. A Monography American Bar Association, Young Lawyers Division, Washington, D.C., April, 1979.

McKeiver v. Pennsylvania 403 U.S. at 547, 91 S.Ct. at 1987, 29 L.Ed.2d at 662 (1971).

Norgard, Katherine and Mayhall, Pamela. *Legal Aspects of Fostering.* Pima College/Arizona Department of Economic, Security, Tucson, Arizona, 1980.

Parham v. J.R., 442 U.S. 584 (1979).

People v. Delaney, 199 p. 896 (Cal. App. 3d. 1921).

Ray–Bettineski, Carmen. Court Appointed Special Advocate: The Guardian *Ad Litem* for Abused and Neglected Child. *Juvenile and Family Court Journal.* August 1978, Vol. 29, no. 3, 65–70.

Santosky v. Kramer, 80 U.S. 4889, (1981).

Smith, Charles et al. *Reports of the National Juvenile Justice Assessment Centers.* National Institute for Juvenile Justice and Delinquency Prevention, Washington, D.C., April, 1980.

Stanley v. Illinois, 405 U.S. 645 (1972).

State v. Segerberg, 131 Conn. 546, 41 A. 2d. 101 (1945).

Streib, Victor L. The Juvenile Justice System and Children's Law: Should Juvenile Defense Lawyers be Replaced with Children's Lawyers? *Juvenile and Family Court Journal.* Nov. 1980, Vol. 31, No. 4, pp. 53–59.

United States v. Spoonhunter, 476 F 2d 1050 (10th Cir. 1973).

Wald, Patricia M., LL.B. Introduction to the Juvenile Justice Process: The Rights of

Children and The Rites of Passage. In Schetky, Diane H. and Benedek, Elissa P. *Child Psychiatry and the Law*. Brunner and Mazel, New York, 1980, pp. 9–20.
Wheeler v. United States, 159 U.S. 523 (1895).
Winship, In Re, 397 U.S. 358 (1970).
Yoder v. Wisconsin, 406 U.S. 205 (1972).

Resources

Norgard, Katherine, Burke, Terry, Levey, Stephen, and Cornett, Joan. The Dependent Legal Process: Roles and Perspectives in a Review Hearing. Biomedical Communications, University of Arizona Health Sciences Center, Tucson, AZ, 1980. A color videotape presentation with instructional guide. (24:30 min.).
Duncan, Alex, J.D., Evans, John R., J.D., Fisher, Hon. Lillian S., Johnson, Helen, M.D., Mayhall, Pamela, M.Ed., Norgard, Katherine, M.S.W., Rubin, Stephen M., J.D., The Medical Witness and Juvenile Court. Biomedical Communciations, University of Arizona Health Sciences Center, Tucson, AZ. 1981. An award winning color videotape production with instructional guide. (35:28 min).
Highlights of the 1st National Conference on Juvenile Justice. Presented by the National Council of Juvenile Court Judges and the National District Attorneys Association. Tapes 3 and 4, The Role of the Judge, District Attorney and Public Defender in the Court.

12

Toward a Safe and Nurturing Place to Live

INTRODUCTION

The immediate crisis is over. The imminent danger is past. It is time to begin to assure that the child will have a safe and nurturing place in which to ". . . live and grow up with a sound mind and a sound body." *(In the matter of Sampson.)* A wide range of intervention services can be made available to the child and the family in most communities. They include those that can be provided to families while the child remains in the home, those that can be provided whether or not the child is at home, and alternative care and treatment options for the child outside the home on a short-term or permanent basis. Some of these services can be provided by volunteers and lay therapists coordinated by a case manager. Others are professional services provided by many different individuals and agencies, both public and private. The cost of these services varies. But none costs as much as additional harm to the child.

In this chapter, the authors describe a few of the options that might be utilized by a protective service staff, either directly or indirectly, as part of the therapeutic plan for strengthening the family and/or protecting and nurturing the child. Although some communities have more resources than others, the possibilities are phenomenal.

In a sense, such a descriptive list is always theoretical since even when these options exist in a given community, many barriers stand in the way of getting the appropriate resources to the people who need them most. This topic is also addressed in this chapter.

SUPERVISION IN THE HOME

The most frightening decision of all for the person who intervenes is: Should an abused child be allowed to remain with or be returned to the family who abused him/her? Many children are abused again. Some are killed. Some parents, once the child has been returned, move out of the state and no one knows for sure what has happened to the child. The situation for the neglected child may be just as questionable and even more dangerous because the damage that may occur can be more subtle and more private. Change in the neglecting family may take a very long time. Yet most authorities seem to agree that if safety and adequate care can be assured, supervision in the home is the best choice for the child. If help can be offered to a family to increase its integrity, society gains a nurturing, productive family in addition to a protected child. Many supportive and very concrete services can be offered to families and children, among them medical, educational, employment, financial assistance, community outreach, and recreational services.

MEDICAL OPTIONS

Community Public Health Nurses

Community public health nurses visit a home as often as once or twice per week. They work with parents and child in solving normal childhood problems and understanding child development. These nurses can suggest specific techniques to parents for physically, nutritionally, and emotionally caring for the child, for the environment, and for themselves. Parents may find the nurse to be less threatening than the protective services worker and may be more open to his or her suggestions. Nurses, who are able to visit the home frequently over a period of time, are able to add a valuable dimension of protection to the child by their presence and their awareness of the home environment. Their assessment of family functioning at different points in the intervention process is valuable input into the development and implementation of a treatment plan.

Public health nurses could also function as a primary prevention resource. Their services could be provided to all families with newborn infants. If such services were commonly provided and accepted, the presence of a public health nurse would not appear to be negative evidence that someone had identified this family to be at risk and that, somehow, the family was not "up to par." This universal approach is not currently an accepted function of public health nurses in this country. However, other community public health nurse services are available in most communities.

Referral to Comprehensive Health-Care Services

Health-care services include health care screening, dental care, prenatal, postpartum and well baby care, specialized information and treatment services, and mental health services. Public health departments are a source of information and service that may be tapped regarding many health-related problems.

> *Health-Care Screening.* Private or public health-care clinics may be resources for regaining family health. In some situations, all family members participate in a health-care screening program, which may be the family's first experience at medical evaluation. It is important not only because it will help to correct and/or rule out physical problems of the parents as a reason for continued abuse, but because it may be the first effort of this family to do or accomplish something positive as a family.
>
> The clinic helps to provide health information to the family and treatment where it is required. The clinic also assists in the supervision of the child, helping to assure his/her protection and nurturing.
>
> *Dental Care.* Dental care has been almost totally neglected in many children referred to child protective services or the juvenile court. Neglect in dental care increases susceptibility to disease, increased possibility of headaches, and a poor self-image. A dental examination is a legitimate part of the total health-care evaluation for the entire family. Often, however, federal or state funding prohibits this level of care, even though funds are available for the treatment of specific dental problems.
>
> *Child Care Clinics.* Prenatal, postnatal, and well-child care clinics are offered to families in most communities. The focus of these clinics is preventive and supportive. Risk can be assessed and services offered. A young 16-year-old mother who takes her child to a well-baby clinic has an opportunity in a protected environment to learn to care for her child and herself. Another mother, referred to child protective services for physically abusing her two children, ages 3 and 18 months, is also pregnant with her third child. She may be able to receive services throughout her pregnancy during the post-partum period and as her baby grows. The experience may give her the first positive parenting

information she has ever received, as well as support through the early months of the baby's life. Handling of infants can be modeled for her and proper nutrition can be taught and enjoyed. Even more importantly, all three children may be able to benefit from her experience.

Birth Control Information. Information can be made available to parents on birth control through some health clinics and such centers as Planned Parenthood. Many states now provide through statute that children also have the right to receive birth control information if they wish it, with or without the consent or knowledge of their parents.

Venereal Disease. Diagnosis and treatment of venereal disease is provided through public health clinics in most communities. Many states have given youth the legal right to seek treatment without the permission or knowledge of their parents.

Immunizations. Free immunization against whooping cough, diptheria, polio, measles, rubella, small pox, and several other diseases is provided through public health departments, often at public school sites. All 50 states now require immunization against the first five diseases for children who are attending public schools. Immunizations are provided, however, only with parental consent.

Mental Health Services

A comprehensive variety of mental health services exists in most communities. These include public, private, and church-supported mental health clinics and associations. Psychiatrists, psychologists, and social workers are available in most communities to provide individual psychotherapy, group therapy, family therapy, play therapy or, in some cases, these therapies in a residential setting. Specialized counseling for drug and alcohol-related problems may also be available. The supervising agency may make a referral to a clinic or individual or the client may seek treatment at his own expense. Often, payment for treatment is set on a sliding scale. Insurance, where it is available, for instance, through a job group plan, may also cover such expense.

Although adequate mental health services are available, adequate service to the family is much more difficult to assure. Most abusing and neglecting families will not seek out help. Even those who are referred by child protective services or ordered into treatment by the court may pursue treatment with active or passive resistance. Missing or arriving late for appointments is the most common form of resistance. Families may also leave the community or the state before treatment is completed. The few studies that have addressed success of treatment with abusive and neglecting families have agreed on the importance of "staying with" such families for "a substantial period of time." (Shapiro, p. 112.)

EDUCATIONAL OPTIONS

Early Childhood Education Programs

These programs can be a safety valve to a family in crisis. They offer protection to the child and relief for the parents, giving them time to deal with crisis. Most Human Service Departments contract with a variety of such programs in the local community. The supervisors of such programs have the opportunity to get to know the child and the parent(s) on a rather intimate basis because of the number of hours that the child spends in the program. Many have program components designed for parents as well as for children. Among these programs are:

> *Therapeutic Play School.* Many communities, through private or public early childhood education programs or a mental health center, provide a therapeutic play school environment for children who have difficulty in developing positive relationships with others, expressing themselves, resolving their anger, fear, or other issues. Through therapeutic play, they are able to learn skills, solve problems, and "play out" their problems.

> *Day Care.* Day care is available in almost every community. It provides for care of children between specified ages, usually age two to six, sometimes two to ten, on an hourly, weekly, or monthly basis. Many day care centers have day and evening hours. Activities include arts and crafts, music, and playground activity. Often, day care facilities will not accept infants. If infants are accepted, the hourly fee is higher, since most states have more stringent standards which centers must meet for infant care including a narrower staff to child ratio. Day care may be offered by a wide variety of providers, most of them private organizations, some of which contract with the department of Human Services for placement of children in their program. Day care supported by the Department may be provided free or at minimum cost to parents supervised under departmental programs. Day care might be arranged for the child in order to help the parents structure their own day and to give them some relief from the constant responsibility of the child. It can provide regular supervision of the child while parents work or attend school. A day care center can be a refuge for the child and can provide support to the parents. Children are a part of the total day care program and their behavior can be observed over an extended period of

time. Usually, the monitoring of day care providers is a regular function of the agency that contracts for services.

The quality of services provided in day care varies widely and usually with the level of skill and caring of the staff, number of staff, management approach, and level of professional and financial support from the welfare agency.

Family Day Care. Family day care providers are people who offer child care services in their homes. They may be part of a family day care organization that coordinates such care, one of several components of a day care facility, or individuals who are operating a service independently for people with whom they contract individually and privately. Most such providers see their role as more than babysitting. They are able to establish personal relationships with the parents and the child. They can even be used as 24 hour or on-call child care services in family crisis situations.

Family day care is a very important form of day care. It has some advantages that other forms lack. It offers infant and toddler care facilities, flexible hours, neighborhood convenience, an ability to accommodate different age groups (therefore, brothers and sisters) in one setting, and the security of a smaller group with one adult. (Az Day Care Manual, Trainer Notes.)

Again, quality of care varies from provider to provider. Brochures listing hints in selecting day or family day care are available in many state and federal government pamphlets.

Preschool. A preschool is similar to a day care center except that the program is centered around preschool and kindergarten activities, with a focus on mastery of beginning reading and math skills, and possibly, beginning science. Often the child who remains at a preschool for a full day will participate in the preschool program in the morning and day care recreational activities in the afternoon or *vice versa.* Preschool staff generally have specialized training and meet certification or other requirements specified by state law. Preschool options may be more expensive than day care since more extensive educational requirements may exist for the staff.

Special Education Programs. These may be provided through community agencies, private clinics, or universities and colleges. They have traditionally been provided through specialized residential or day care settings such as treatment and education of the deaf and blind or schools for the severely mentally retarded. With the passage of P.L. 94-142 in 1975, special education programs are a mandated part of the public school system. Some of the funding for these programs is provided by the federal government; however, funding commitments change frequently. As federal sources become more limited, other funding sources will have to be tapped. Loss of funds may mean loss of programs.

Special education programs vary in focus and in quality from school to school, district to district, and state to state. All feature specialized, individualized assistance for the child, especially in basic skills areas. Some children are inappropriately placed in special education programs, either because adequate screening is not available or the goals of the program are unclear. In some areas these programs are seen as alternative education for a child who is difficult to manage in the classroom, even though the child may not exhibit a need for special education. Abused and neglected childen are prime candidates for placement in such programs, and often legitimately so. The trauma of abuse and neglect appears to retard intellectual achievement and emotional growth and development. In many cases, however, encouragement and individualized attention has provided an almost "miraculous" change for a youngster. Follow up testing has demonstrated that intelligence appeared to be temporarily "blocked" rather than permanently retarded. Care must be taken to provide services only when and for as long as they are necessary. Special education needs to be framed positively in the total educational setting and in the special education classroom, so that someone who is participating in such a program does not further damage his/her already bruised and damaged self-esteem. Special education programs are usually provided, at least through the public schools, at no individual cost to the child.

Parent Education Classes

Parent education is offered in most communities. It may be offered as a community service course, a college level course, a weekend workshop or seminar, an on-going program through a church, school, or family-centered public or private health or social service agency. The classes may focus on general parenting skills and child development information or they may target parenting of particular ages of children, types of behavior, or specialized groups of parents such as foster parents or prospective adoptive parents. Scheduling of the classes varies. A popular schedule is an 8 to 10 week course of 2 to 4 hours per week.

Many abusive and neglectful parents are hesitant to join such classes, especially if they are labeled as "education." They also are hesitant to join groups. Once involved, however, the experience is usually a positive one. They have an opportunity to expand their social skills and decrease their isolation. They are able to offer something to the group as well as take something for themselves. They can also become aware that no one has a corner on perfect parenting and that difficult situations have been or will be faced by most parents. They are able to try on new parenting skills and to learn alternative techniques to those they have been using.

In practice, the parents who are motivated to go to parenting classes and are motivated to change may not be the most "at risk" parents. If "at risk" parents can be coaxed to join parent education groups, their lack of group skills and their level of discouragement may undermine success. This is particularly true if the group leader is not skilled in group dynamics and is not aware of the needs of these parents. Although parent education is important and parent education classes appear to be effective for some parents, the structure of parent education for others may need to be individualized and focus more on parenting the parent and the modeling and practice of positive parenting skills.

Parent education, at its most effective, may actually be "family" education offered to children and youth throughout their elementary, junior high, and high school educational experience. (See Chapter 14 for further discussion of this topic.)

EMPLOYMENT OPTIONS

Many times one of the major stressors in the family in child abuse and neglect situations is economic. High unemployment in a community or a nation increases the possibility of child abuse and neglect in families.

Helping a parent to find an adequate job has a direct impact on the family situation. The difficulty in a tight job market is to match job skills and available positions. Many abusing parents do not compete well in the market. Sometimes the necessary place to start is in assessing and improving a parent's skill in seeking and holding employment, and in helping the parent increase her level and variety of employable skills. These may be accomplished through several different resources. Vocational counseling, which may be offered through a federal or state agency or a private organization, may be helpful. Many times the family has not explored counseling options, nor seems to be aware of available job banks that could be tapped. Training in work skills and job development and placement are services that may be available in the community, either through public or private agencies or both. Community colleges and skill centers may contract with the Department of Human Services to provide training for persons whom they sponsor. For many people, the difficulty in getting and holding a job is in learning how to apply for it and how to deport themselves on the job. Simple behaviors, such as being on time and appropriate dress, may have never been modeled for these applicants.

Youth in the Job Market

Teenagers in the home may also be seeking a job. Their own safety or the safety of others in the home may depend upon their being able to spend constructive, structured time away from home. A part-time job or if that is not possible, a volunteer job, may provide such a structure and increase the youth's job skills and self-esteem. Youth may also benefit from vocational counseling, training in work skills and work habits, job development and placement, and help in dealing with problems they have with authority.

Today's employment marketplace still does not provide equal employment opportunities to people of all groups. In many jobs, women continue to receive less pay than men for equal work. Black youth continue to have a much higher rate of unemployment than other groups. The impact of such problems are felt most intensely by applicants who are also poorly educated and poorly skilled. Change in this area may be a major factor in protecting children and preventing child abuse and neglect.

FINANCIAL ASSISTANCE OPTIONS

Unemployment Benefits

Unemployment benefits may be a temporary resource for the family. These are generally provided through a governmental agency of the state.

Grants/Loans/Work Study

Educational grants and loans may be available through a community college or university. These may be federally funded, community funded, or college or private organization sponsored options. Veterans benefits, although more limited in recent years, may also be a source of income for those veterans interested in an approved educational or training program and who qualify under the current requirements.

State Social Service Programs

These programs include public assistance and food stamp programs. They may also include specialized assistance programs designed to assist a parent through an educational or training program. Such programs include an educational grant, stipend payment, day care supplements, and other assistance.

COMMUNITY OUTREACH

Homemaker Services

Homemakers, also known as home health aides, provide a variety of services depending upon the needs of the individual family and the goals of the overall treatment plan. Generally, homemakers assist with functions such as shopping, cleaning, cooking, and caring for children. A homemaker is with the family for extended periods of time and offers direct and specific sorts of help. Homemaker services are more likely to be beneficial in situations of neglect rather than abuse. Homemakers provide modeling, emotional support, and an opportunity for a family to, sometimes literally, get their house in order. By sharing some of the tasks that seem overwhelming to the family, homemakers help parents gain the strength to cope with problems. Homemaker services are usually provided through the state welfare agency. Occasionally, a private organization will provide some of these functions, either as volunteer or contracted services.

If homemaker services can be provided by caring, sensitive individuals over an extended period of time, they have much to offer. They are rarely tested at their best because:

1. Many parents are vigorously opposed to having someone come into their home telling them ''what to do and how to do it.''
2. Many agencies have far greater demand for homemaker services than they are able to provide. Service may not be provided in a timely manner, nor over a long enough period of time to be effective.
3. Homemakers require in-service training and support to gain the cooperation of the parents and adequately meet their needs. Often these are not available.

Lay Therapy—Parent Aides

Lay therapists, also sometimes called parent aides, work closely with families over an extended period of time to provide reparenting and nurturing to the parents. Their service is directed toward the parents rather than the child. Lay therapists are usually trained by the agency and the unit through which their service is provided, and receive professional supervision and support. Some are based in hospital programs. Most are assigned responsibility for only two or three families at a time. Although some lay therapists are paid for their work, many volunteer for these positions. Lay therapists are considered by many professionals to be an important part of the child care team. Their efforts are designed to support the overall plan for the family. Vincent Fontana, Henry Kempe, Ray Helfer, and a number of others have argued for some time that parents can and do benefit significantly from the intense relationship between the lay therapist and the parents. Some of the better known lay therapy programs exist in Denver, San Diego, Lansing, Michigan, and through SCAN (Suspected Child Abuse and Neglect) programs in several other states.

Street Workers

Also known as detached workers, street workers generally work with youth and families in a specific neighborhood or defined area. They provide mediation of disputes, referral services, counseling, recreational program planning and implementation. They may act as community organizers, for example, helping to develop a community youth center or other needed facilities or services. They seek to understand the families and the character of the neighborhood and to strengthen both positively.

Parent Self-Help Groups

Parent self-help groups provide an opportunity for their members to receive and give support and acceptance on a long-term basis. Self-help groups decrease the isolation of families and help parents to believe that change is possible by modeling it. Parents Anonymous and Parents United are two self-help groups that focus on child abusers. Parents Anonymous was organized in 1973 by Jolly K., an abuser. Today it exists nationwide. Every chapter is led by a chairperson (a parent) and a sponsor (a professional social worker, psychologist, or psychiatrist). Members operate a "crisis intervention" service that includes supportive phone conversations, visits to a parent's home, or temporary care of the child until the crisis has passed. Members usually meet weekly to discuss their own experiences (positive and negative) and share feelings with the group. There are no dues or fees.

Parents United was first organized in Santa Clara County, California. It was incorporated in 1975 and is specifically designed to provide assistance to families that have been involved in sexual abuse. Parents United provides professionally guided group therapy sessions and is closely allied with the Child Sexual Abuse response systems and treatment programs.

Alcoholics Anonymous and various drug abuse self-help programs are also available in most communities and provide support for family members in those respective problem areas. There is no charge for self-help services, although there may be a charge for medical and professional counseling services if these are also provided. Many self-help groups sponsor recreational activities and evening and weekend events that encourage social interaction and communication.

Self-Help Groups for Youth and Spouses

Many of the adult groups have started groups for children or, at least, for teenagers who have abusive parents and/or parents who are alcoholics or drug abusers, for example, Parents United offers Daughters and Sons United, and Alcoholics Anonymous offers Alateens and Alanon. In addition to an educational component that is designed to help the child and spouse understand the parent and the problem, steps are suggested for helping the parent and strengthening the family. Perhaps even more important is the focus of these groups on self-awareness and dealing with one's own feelings about the family situation and the parent or spouse.

Criticisms of self-help programs generally center around the alleged refusal of members to report other members to CPS, even in situations where no positive change occurs or parents drop out of the group and the safety of the child is questioned. Some argue that the child is better protected if, as in the Parents United Group, child protective staff or other agency representatives are actively involved in the group and have made some of the original referrals to the group. Maltreating parents, who have never been reported, may have greater difficulty, however, admitting problems in this situation.

Other criticisms include:

1. Such groups lose track of people who drop out of the group or who move out of the area. (Certainly self-help groups are not alone in having this particular difficulty.)
2. Such groups can actually support the negative and not act as an impetus for positive change. (The presence of professional sponsors in the organization is designed to help prevent this possibility.)

Legal Services

Legal services may be provided at no charge or at minimal charge for the child and/or parents for representation in court or other services that the family might need.

In many areas, public legal services are very overtaxed. Case preparation time may be short and, in some instances, almost nonexistent. Private attorneys may supplement this public service by offering a percentage of their services on a sliding scale.

Advocacy for Children

Advocacy may be provided in a local community through community foundations for children and legal advocacy groups. It may also be offered through organizations such as Big Brothers and Big Sisters which provides an adult friend for the child (and sometimes a long waiting list for the service). Juvenile courts and child protection agencies may have an advocacy component through a volunteer program that provides a variety of services to children such as guardian *ad litem,* one-to-one supervision, lobbying, etc.

RECREATION OPTIONS

Since families in which abuse and neglect takes place are usually isolated from the community, they may not even be aware of the recreational options available to them at no or minimal charge or have the energy to seek them out. Adult and youth activities are provided through local parks and recreation programs, schools, churches, sports leagues, and many public and private individuals and organizations. Recreation, in addition to structuring time, can be a healthy means of relieving stress, meeting people, developing skills, and having fun as a family. Families in which abuse and/or neglect is common are not likely to seek out these possibilities on their own. Help in taking the first step and in developing enough connections with other people to get involved in the activities may be necessary.

CRISIS-ORIENTED SERVICES

These services have been mentioned in other contexts. Since crisis, either situational or chronic, seems to be a frequent factor accompanying or precipitating abuse or neglect, knowledge of available crisis hotlines, crisis nurseries, self-help group members, or a worker who is willing to be called in a crisis, gives parents immediate relief and an opportunity to deal with crisis with less danger of abuse to the child. Many of these services can be utilized by the parents and/or child whether or not the child is living at home. Some day care programs offer a form of part-time alternative care. The child spends a regular part of the day outside of the home in a preschool or day care environment. Such a plan may in itself increase the child's safety because parents have an opportunity to separate from the intensity of the moment to moment, hour to hour care of the child. These options do not decrease the parent's access to the child, only the continual contact.

UTILIZING THE FAMILY'S RESOURCES

If the child remains in the home with supervision or if it is likely that the child will be returning home, the family's assistance in determining what services to utilize and when to utilize them is imperative. Helping the family to strengthen and use their own resources is the only way for them to be eventually self-sufficient and to have self-esteem and family integrity. If the parents do not learn how to problem-solve, there will be difficulties again, as soon as the problem-solver leaves and a new problem emerges. If the family does not develop its own internal and external resources before the providers of services withdraw, the family's resources will shrink to the same level as before intervention. If family members do not have an opportunity to give as well as to take help and nurturing, they will continue to see themselves in an impotent position.

ALTERNATIVE CARE

If parents are unwilling or unable to provide a safe and nurturing environment for the child, 24 hour care outside the home, either for short or long-term placement must be considered.

THE LEAST DETRIMENTAL ALTERNATIVE

When children are removed from their homes and into alternative placements, the interest of the child should be paramount, but a "best" alternative is rarely among the available choices. Intervention carries a major burden of responsibility for the safety and nurturing of the child but governmental systems are notoriously poor at nurturing. Intervention brings about some type of change, and, in situations of abuse and neglect, change is highly desirable. Every change that is made, however, also brings a new risk to the child.

Over a period of years, it is not uncommon for a child to have been placed in a variety of alternative care settings, possibly several foster homes, group homes, and a therapeutic residential placement. No one wants this to happen. The difficulty often lies in such factors as the limited number of options available, especially for teenagers; the turnover in foster homes; the sometimes inappropriate placement of a child in a foster home because it was the only available choice rather than because it could meet the needs of the child: and the skill of some children in sabotaging placements, making it more and more difficult to find a place for them. In spite of the difficulties, some placements are very successful and wisely used. Many more could be. It is not impossible to meet the needs of children in alternative care.

ALTERNATIVE CARE OPTIONS

Foster Care

Foster care is probably the most common choice of the alternative care options. It is less expensive than most of the other choices. Foster homes are substitute family settings. A family home is licensed by the appropriate state licensing agency and must meet physical standards set by law. Foster parents are screened and trained, usually by the state department of human services. Homes are licensed for a specific number of children, ranging in some states from one to six. Foster parents may or may not be compensated. Usually some compensation is available, and at minimum, foster parents are reimbursed for actual expenses. Compensation is generally highest for those who care for teenagers and severely physically, mentally, or emotionally handicapped children. Training both in quality and quantity, varies from state to state and locality to locality. Generally training for foster parents has increased nationally in recent years. Whether or not that training has resulted in more effective foster parenting has not been reliably answered. Many areas report that preservice training serves as a useful departmental screening and self-screening tool for foster parents. That in itself is one legitimate and important preservice training goal.

The authors were involved in two major training projects in Arizona (1978–1980): a districtwide project to deliver preservice training and a statewide project to develop and test advanced foster parent educational materials and options throughout Arizona. Project studies, which were made in cooperation with the Arizona Department of Economic Security and the Arizona Consortium for Education in the Social Services (ACESS), indicated a significant increase in knowledge on training topics (based on pretest-post-test scores). A second project study was conducted by Dr. Billie Underwood in an effort to determine the effects of a specific six hour workshop (Conscience Development), which was a part of the advanced foster parent education project, on foster parents' attitudes toward children's moral development. Nine questions were abstracted from that workshop and were sent as a series of attitudinal questionnaires to a number of foster parents in their homes. No attempt was made to select parents who were to be in workshops. Thus, the questionnaire was administered to two groups—those who participated in the workshop and those with no such exposure. Answers to the questions were not considered to be right or wrong. Instead, the study was made solely upon change in scale position (0–5) from one test administration to another. The initial responses of the two groups (before exposure) were very similar. Responses were analyzed to determine the amount of change from one questionnaire to the next. Changes in responses were found to occur in both groups. More occurred, however, in the group that took part in the workshop(s). As Underwood points out,

> The impetus for these changes cannot be identified but one possibility may be that the discussions and subsequent reflections may have precipitated more reflection on these issues of children's morality. Such reflection can in itself be

an educational goal when the educational experience is focused upon a theme as ambiguous as moral development in a diverse society. It is surprising that this degree of reflection may have been accomplished after a six-hour discussion, and suggests that this experience did have impact on the attitudes of foster parents. (Underwood, p. 34.)

There are several types of foster homes. The following definitions, although typical, are certainly not precise. The numbers of children specified in the definition vary slightly from jurisdiction to jurisdiction.

A *foster home* is usually defined as a home maintained by any individual or individuals to care for or control minor children other than those related by blood or marriage to the foster parent or who are legal wards of such individuals. In some states the home of a relative can be licensed as a foster home for a specific child.

A *receiving foster home* is a licensed foster home for immediate placement of children taken into custody or pending medical examination and court disposition. Receiving homes may also be called shelter care, crisis, or "time out" homes.

A *regular foster home* is a licensed foster home for the placement of not more than five minor children.

A *special foster home* is a licensed foster home capable of handling not more than five minor children who require special care for physical, mental, or emotional reasons or have been adjudicated a delinquent. The definition of a special foster home may also include those homes handling foster children ages twelve through seventeen.

A *group foster home* is a licensed regular or special foster home for placement of more than five minor but not more than ten minor children.

Another specialized category, not necessarily defined separately by statute, is the *professional foster home*. Criteria includes that two parents are available in the home and one of the parents is not employed. Educational and training requirements are higher, a professional child-care skill level is expected, and monetary compensation is generally better than in the other categories. The professional foster home can accept up to five children who are hard to place. Often they are teenagers. Special and professional foster homes are sometimes referred to as therapeutic or treatment foster homes.

Use of Foster Homes as Placement Options

Foster homes are often misused as placement options for children. Such a placement is unacceptable when intended to provide a substitute home for very young children for a long period of time and/or when the foster care plan is not reviewed at least every six months. (Martin, p. 23.)

Martin suggests that the appropriate uses of foster care are:

1. As a short-term living arrangement for children in emergency situations, while investigation, assessment, and planning are in progress.

2. As a diagnostic placement, to assess inadequate physical growth (which requires about two weeks) or developmental progress needs (which might take six months). Will the child's physical growth or developmental progress accelerate in foster care?

3. As a therapeutic milieu for an extended period of time. An assumption is made that foster parents are trained and supported in being therapeutic agents for the child. In this instance, the foster parents might, at some point in the future, work with the family as well.

As Martin points out, "Foster care is only appropriate if it is part of permanent planning for the child." (Martin, pp. 22–23.) Many times such planning is fragmented at best. Foster care, as it is frequently used, does not achieve its goals. The following are some of the reasons generally offered for this failure:

1. Lack of adequate, consistent, on-going agency support for foster parents while children are in their homes.

2. Inadequate training.

3. Inadequate initial screening of prospective foster parents.

4. Poor matching of child to placement, for many reasons, including not enough foster homes to meet the needs.

5. Inadequate resources for foster parents or lack of information regarding these resources.

6. Long-term placement of young children who will eventually return home.

7. Placement of children in a series of foster homes because of adjustment problems, choice of foster parents to leave foster care (moving, burn-out, change in personal circumstances, and other reasons).

8. Lack of foster parent support groups.

Group Care

According to the National Advisory Committee Standards,

a group home is "an open community-based residential facility which provides care for juveniles who can reasonably be expected to succeed in a nonrestrictive environment in which a substantial part of their time will ordinarily be spent in the surrounding community attending school or working, pursuing leisure time actives, and participating in community service programs recommended by the family court or the treatment staff. (Standards, p. 436.)

Group homes for children generally include from 6 to 12 children housed in a renovated community residential structure. Group homes are usually supervised by a staff that includes a director, who has a minimum of a bachelor's degree in a casework/counseling area and some counseling experience, house parents and substitute house parents, or a child care staff that works a three-shift, 24 hour schedule. In some states group homes are licensed as group foster homes. Some program counseling services may be provided by the director and staff, but more frequently psychotherapy services are contracted. Group homes also make use of various community services such as employment, vocational, and academic training, recreation, and medical care.

A group home might be an appropriate placement for a child who has difficulty coping with the intimate relationships of a foster home and who is unable to return home. The level of supervision is usually greater in a group home than in a foster home. Group homes are also used as "halfway houses" for delinquent youth when they are released from institutions. Children labeled delinquent and dependent are often both placed in the same facility. Many observers feel that this places the dependent child at risk of learning delinquent behavior. Others suggest that although the legal label of the two may be different, many times their experience and level of sophistication is similar. Both statements may be true. Certainly this risk factor should be considered, both at the time of the initial placement decision and once any placement is made.

Family Residential Care

In this type of care, the entire family moves into a group therapeutic environment. Several communities are now establishing various versions of this type of treatment. Some programs refer to this care as family shelter care. The advantage of such an alternative is that safety and nurturing are assured for the child while emotional bonds and attachments between the parent and child are strengthened. The oldest program of this type is through the National Center for Prevention and Treatment of Child Abuse and Neglect in Denver. Other well-known similar programs exist in the Family Stress Center in Pittsburgh and the New York Foundling Hospital. Available space may be a determining factor in whether and how long such care is available to a family. Many communities still do not provide this care option.

Residential Care for the Child

A child who is seriously disturbed or severely retarded may require placement in a residential treatment facility. A residential facility, as we use it here, is defined as a facility housing more than 10 children in cottage or dormitory style (or both) and providing many services in residence, for example, schooling, recreational facilities, and various counseling services. Often the program is specialized for a specific target population, such as severely emotionally, mentally, or physically handicapped, or violent youth. Such placements are typically much more expensive than foster care or group home placements and are usually reserved for children who have difficulty adjusting in other settings. Placement is usually for a minimum of one year. Many of these settings are listed in psychiatric journals.

Supervision of a residential placement is usually continued by the placement authority. Individualized treatment plans for each child should be made and reviewed regularly. Residential care is not a preferred treatment option. Residential care, by its very nature, has an institutional component which, particularly over a long period of time, may be damaging in itself to a child. It is also more difficult to monitor residential care and therefore more difficult to protect the child from possible institutional abuse. This is not to say, however, that such placement is not appropriate in some cases, nor that residential care cannot be safe, nurturing, and therapeutic.

The Menninger Foundation in Topeka, Kansas is a well-known residential treatment program that offers children therapeutic experiences in group living. This facility can accommodate up to 70 boys and girls, ages 6–16. The youth live in cottages, receive schooling, and individual and group psychotherapies. The Brown School in Texas and the Devereaux programs are similar.

HOSPITALIZATION

If the child has been seriously injured, has a severe psychiatric disorder, or is malnourished or physically ill, hospitalization may be advisable for the child for a brief period of time. Although hospitalization of the child can act as a stabilizer for the family and provide a relatively neutral environment for the parents, it should be used only when the child needs the specialized services of such a facility. The hospital environment is not geared to be, nor was it ever intended to be, a nurturing home for a child. Hospitalization, if coordinated well, can be positive for the child. Interaction with the health care staff can be assurance to the child that he or she is safe and physically and emotionally sound.

Hospitalization may also be advisable for a parent, particularly where the parent's behavior has suggested the possibility of psychosis. Physicians who are members of the child protection team in a community can assist in determining when hospitalization might be indicated and in setting up a coordinated health care service for the family.

Comprehensive Residential Treatment Programs

Some residential treatment programs offer a wide range of placement and treatment components to hard to place, difficult to manage children, especially teenagers. Such a program might include residential care, treatment group homes, therapeutic foster homes, and in-home treatment. Some include some form of day treatment or a "street" component, in which the child lives at home but spends his days participating in program activities. Such programs may be privately incorporated or operated as nonprofit corporations. They may accept children who have been processed through the normal system as delinquents, dependents, and/or children in need of supervision. They may also accept private placements. Some such programs are listed in nationally published psychiatric journals; usually, however, they are state or region centered.

Some programs may be both conservative and traditional yet attempt to provide a wide range of services for children. Often centers that take severely emotionally disturbed children may include residential, group home, foster home, specialized education, and other components.

Traditional and Nontraditional Approaches

Alternative care programs may be traditional or nontraditional. Traditional programs are usually defined as those that fit one of several current, standard models. Nontraditional programs are usually defined as those that are, at least in part, exceptions to the current standard. They may be greeted with some reservations. Obviously, definitions of traditional and nontraditional are relative to time and place. A "new" program may seem very innovative and nontraditional when it is introduced. In time it may become the standard. The "new" program, in fact, may not be new at all. We have, for instance, rediscovered many times, the concept of placing children who are institutionalized in cottages rather than dormitories. Each time the concept is rediscovered, it is innovative, new, and somehow nontraditional. A program that has received recent media attention is one that includes flying an airplane as part of the child's optional program experience.

Nontraditional programs are more likely to receive the public eye, positively and negatively. VisionQuest, Inc., for example, has been a center of media attention in England, France, and the United States. It maintains group homes and schools in several states. It also utilizes as a key part of its

program design, "high impact" components such as Wilderness Quests and
the VisionQuest Wagon Train. It is an action-centered treatment program
designed to work with youngsters who are "raging" and who have failed in
many other settings. VisionQuest attempts to confront the rage and the
reasons behind it. Because the program is nontraditional, controversial, and
expensive, licensing agents have difficulty evaluating the program with
traditional criteria. (Not every program includes a Wagon Train as part of its
therapeutic approach.) The evaluator's legitimate concerns always include
no harm to the child and opportunities and encouragement for growth and
development. The challenge for a program like VisionQuest is to increase
their control over risk of harm, while continuing to provide an important
"high impact"' opportunity for growth for difficult to place youth.

Many subtle treatment gains may be made in developing such relationships. A bridge may be built to new and positive interpersonal attachments.
Issues relating to commitment, responsibility, mutual respect, and caring
can be addressed. VisionQuest has found encouraging such relationships
to be positive. A New Mexico foster mother has used this concept for years
in working with children in her home. The film, "Wild Horses, Broken
Wings," describes her approach and philosophy. Each child is given a pony
to care for and each has responsibilities on the challenging summer caravan
to and from the family's summer camp.

No program is designed for all children. Some children may respond
better in one program than in another. All require monitoring by supervisors
within the program and by the placing agency to assure the safety and
nurturing of the child.

PERMANENT PLACEMENT

Adoption

It is generally assumed that if returning the child to the home is clearly
unwise or impossible, voluntary relinquishment of the child by the parents or
failing that, severance of parental rights should be sought at the earliest
possible time. In this way the child will have an opportunity to have a
permanent adoptive home. This, however, is only the first step. Most agency
records show that many children who are adoptable are never adopted. The
child in this position over a period of years has, literally, no place to belong.
Much of his growth will have occurred in turmoil. The older the child, the
more unlikely the prospects of adoption and the less likely the child will be
emotionally adoptable. Finding adoptive homes for black children at any
age seems to be more difficult than finding homes for other children at the
same age. If adoptive homes for the child are not sought immediately, the

system itself may be contributing to the fact that the child will not have a place. Several steps may be taken to protect against this possibility.

1. Frequent reviews of treatment plans and placement options should occur throughout placement.
2. Where adoption seems appropriate, efforts to find an adoptive home must be vigorous and timely, perhaps including some of the news media, "Wednesday's Child" or "Tuesday's Child" features, especially for older, harder to adopt children, certainly reaching out to the community to increase possible resources for these children.
3. Support for adoptive homes can be provided on many levels. Support by the worker during adjustment periods, consultation over a period of years with social and psychological services, adoptive parent group support, for example, the Open Door Society, which can help parents through some of the difficult times. Subsidized adoption should be provided for children with special needs. Often a family is willing to adopt and could provide a safe and nurturing environment but cannot financially provide the treatment support that the child will need.

Permanent Foster Home Care

Permanent foster home care is appropriate if it is determined that it is unwise or impossible for a child to return home, relinquishment or severance is not a possibility, or the child has been free for adoption for over a year and the likelihood of adoption is low.

Some states now provide that foster parents who have already provided a home for the child described above over a period of time and who have established a close relationship with the child may contract with the state to provide a permanent home for the child if the child agrees to the placement. Other foster parents may elect to be permanent foster parents in their original contract with the agency. Compensation to the foster parents and medical or treatment support for the child will continue. Such an option provides a safe and nurturing place for the child and eliminates the temporary nature of foster care. The permanent foster family is given more integrity as a family group with less intrusion from the state, even though the state continues to monitor the placement and is ultimately responsible for the child.

Independent Living Options

Sometimes older youth, for whom going home is inappropriate and placement in foster homes or group home settings untenable, have more success in independent living centers. This type of program provides an opportunity to learn independent living skills through modeling and practice (for example, budgeting, cooking, buying and cooking food, cleaning, managing an apartment, saving money, getting and keeping a job, adult decision making, improving interpersonal relationships, etc.). Youth are supervised in apartmentlike complexes which may be shared with another youth and are provided support and assistance. All youth in the program are expected to work and save half of what they earn during the time they are in the program, and take care of their own apartments. They are given as much freedom as they can handle responsibly and are given opportunities to take risks and to problem-solve. Such a setting is ideal for youth who will be an adult in approximately a year and who will need to be living on his own.

The Issue of Coordination and Cooperation

A community may be rich in resources and all of them may be made available to the child and family. If, as often occurs, coordination of the resources and cooperation among the providers does not exist, the investment in money, energy, time, and skill is wasted. Services that trip over each other are not services at all. Services that exist but are not accessible to those who need them most serve the community poorly.

If the child is at home and the family is receiving services, every service provider is a team member and needs to understand the treatment plan and his/her role in relation to the other team members. One member, usually the caseworker, needs to be a case manager, guiding the ''helping'' so that it is centered on the child and family, is timely, and is appropriate. A very real danger exists. Providers of services who do not observe the safety of the child and who do not work to provide their particular services within the framework of the treatment plan in a way that complements other services being provided, may actually cause damage to the child.

Need for coordination increases if the child is temporarily or permanently removed from the home. If the child will be returning home, coordination of visits and strengthening of bonds between the parents and the child help to assure a healthy family. If the child is not returning home, coordination and cooperation can assure that the child gets the best that the system can offer and that that child, as a person, does not get lost in the process.

Coordination and cooperation are not accidents. They exist only where the providers commit a continuing effort toward their existence. That is not an easy task. Given competition for funding, frequent changes of personnel, heavy caseloads, procedural and legal constraints, personal turf, and philosophical issues, this effort is uneven at best.

The Concept of Therapeutic Milieu

Stated simply, a therapeutic milieu is a helpful and healing setting. This does not mean that the setting provides the therapy itself. It does mean that the setting and every aspect of it, if utilized well, can work together toward meeting therapeutic goals.

Obviously, the most helpful setting for a child is one that meets the child's needs and allows and challenges the child to grow and develop. Physical structure of a home or residential setting, arrangement of the rooms, lighting, decoration, color scheme, staffing (including the cook, plumber, gardener, etc.), characteristics and number of children in the placement, rules, activities, and all aspects of programming are a part of the therapeutic milieu, whether or not they are deliberately so designed. The impact of such a statement is that some of the elements in the setting may be operating at cross purposes. Understanding the nature of a therapeutic milieu may help to correct such problems. (See Trieschman et al.; Klein.)

It is possible to apply the concept of therapeutic milieu to the total service ''package'' provided to a family and the context or environment in which it is provided. The interaction of all of the services, the personalities of the persons providing them, the setting(s) in which they are provided, the timeliness of service and the attitudes of all concerned are part of this therapeutic milieu. Coordination, to be most effective, must deliberately consider all the elements of this setting.

Psychological Parenting and The Residential Setting

Most of the research cited throughout this book has suggested that in order to reduce the impact of abuse and neglect on a child and on future generations, the child needs to be cared for and to care for someone (or several someones) in a parenting role. This person(s) does not have to be the natural parent, but does have to be a psychological parent(s). A caring, nurturing connection needs to be present in the relationship. (Goldstein et al.; Segal and Yahraes.)

This connection is most difficult to form, in a long-term, large, residential setting. The nature of the environment, the turnover in staff, the necessity of planning for and working with an increased number of children, the monetary limitations, the nature of the problems exhibited by the child population all contribute to this difficulty. Awareness of the need and of the elements which are barriers to meeting it are part of the solution.

Disruptive Behavior: The Issue of Restraint

Disruptive behavior creates a need for action in any alternative care setting. The danger in overreacting is institutional abuse. The danger in underreacting is that the child may harm himself or someone else.

There are many possible approaches to disruptive behavior. However, as the intensity of the disruptive behavior increases, options for control often decrease, with those remaining being more restrictive and sometimes more punitive. At the request of the authors, several agency administrators and staff members developed a brainstorm list of methods of coping with disruptive behavior. This list is similar to one developed by Russo and Shyne from their survey of agencies. The brainstorm list included:

Talking with the child individually or as part of a group.

Consequences, usually in the form of loss of privileges or assigning added tasks.

Time out, or removal of the child from the group to a quiet, safe place.

Physical restraint, or the physical control of the child by two or more staff members, possibly wrestling the child to the ground and literally sitting on him/her until the child regains self-control.

Use of medication, temporarily, to control "out of control" behavior.

Mechanical restraint such as handcuffs or straitjackets.

External restraint such as police arrest or security control.

Removal from the program.

Secure detention (not always an available option).

Shadowing, one on one, or assigning a staff member to stay with the child constantly.

The standards developed by the National Advisory Committee for Juvenile Justice address the issue of discipline and restraint. The focus of the standards is on the least restraint possible and only as much as required to prevent the child from harming himself or others. Three restraints were mentioned most cautiously and with many stipulations for the child's protection. These were medical restraints, mechanical restraints, and room confinement. (Standards, pp. 493–510.)

Many youth care facilities have discovered that if staff is observant, many disruptive problems can be dealt with before they get out of control. If a sufficient number of staff are available, fewer situations seem out of control. One agency administrator suggested to the authors that out of control incidences at that facility had almost disappeared after the rule was imposed that any incident had to be reported in writing and discussed at staffing in order to find ways to help the child deal with problems before the child became out of control.

Trieschman's concept of the stages of a temper tantrum may be used to identify and intervene in accelerating disruptive problems. He suggested that a temper tantrum occurs as a "developing series of events," each of which has its own characteristics. (Trieschman et al., p. 173.) He suggests different therapeutic management possibilities at each stage. The six stages he identifies are (1) Rumbling and Grumbling, (2) Help−Help, (3) Either−Or, (4) No−No, (5) Leave Me Alone, and (6) Hangover. The intensity of the tantrum increases from an irritable, grumbling beginning to a noisy engagement of adults through some breaking of rules to threats and demands and the setting of impossible alternatives to a full blown refusal to do anything that an adult might want the child to do followed by a sort of hollow avoidance of adults and finally, sadness, a headache, or no apparent concern about the storm that has just passed. Trieschman suggests that the early stages of the tantrum are also early calls for help. An early awareness on the part of a worker of the child's issues and the stages in the temper tantrum process could diminish and possibly eliminate the eventual need for restraint. (Treischman et al., pp. 170−197.)

INSTITUTIONAL ABUSE AND/OR NEGLECT OF CHILDREN

Most reported abuse and neglect occurs at home. According to 1980 AHA data, 96% of the perpetrators are the child's parents. It should not be assumed that parents are the only perpetrators of abuse and neglect. Private and public agencies can and sometimes do abuse and neglect children. Institutional maltreatment can be defined as

> . . . any system or program policy or procedure, and any individual interaction with a child in placement which abuses, neglects, or is detrimental to a child's health, safety, or emotional and physical well-being or in any way exploits or violates the child's basic rights. (Institutional Abuse of Indian Children, and the Indian Child Welfare Act, p. 10.)

Institutional maltreatment of children occurs at three levels: system, program, and individual. Except for individual abuse, institutional maltreatment is often subtle. Although condemned by child advocates, institutional abuse may be on-going and is seldom part of abuse and neglect reporting.

System Maltreatment

System maltreatment is imposed on children by a system that allows them to drift through many placement settings, that fails to take positive action in their behalf, and does not make definitive plans by either terminating parental rights or freeing the child for adoption or reunification with the family of origin. Many factors combine to create situations of system maltreatment. Suitable placement options are lacking, the system for placing children is disorganized, the monitoring systems are inadequate, licensing regulations are sporadically enforced, childrens' and parents' rights are ignored, a confusing mix of contradictory policies seem to create inertia followed by crisis management, and a paucity of programs and funding limit options from which to choose. These have all been discussed elsewhere in this book.

Program Maltreatment

Simply placing a child in a foster home or other alternative care placement does not insure that the child's needs will be met. Although no accurate count is available, it has been estimated that 500,000 children were in out-of-home placement in the United States in 1980. (San Francisco Child Abuse Council, Inc., p. 4.)

These children may be in double jeopardy since they are faced with the tremendous emotional upset of family separation and the need to adjust to a new home setting, sometimes without emotional support. Foster care is just one example of a program within a larger institutional system in which program abuse and neglect can occur for children. Program maltreatment occurs within programs because of policies, regulations, or practices that tacitly encourage or allow attitudes and behaviors toward children that disregard their basic rights. Some examples of program abuse and neglect include:

1. Lack of adequate supervision.
2. Lack of stimulation, attention, or meeting of basic needs.
3. Lack of a provision for obtaining medical, dental, or psychological services when needed.
4. Punitive, harsh, or extreme disciplinary practices.
5. Lack of minimally standard nutritional programs.
6. Infringement of the child's sense of personal safety.
7. Infringement of the child's basic rights to shelter and physical comfort.
8. Withdrawal of food as punishment.
9. Emotional chastisement, constant criticism, or public humiliation.
10. Impeding the child's right to contact with his natural family as a form of punishment.
11. Sexual harrassment and/or imposition of judgments and values on the child's sexual preference.
12. Lack of culturally relevant activities or insensitivity to the child's right to continue to practice his or her own culture. (Adapted from San Francisco Child Abuse Council, Inc., p. 6.)

Perhaps the most frightening aspect of this list is that these examples are very familiar to those who work with dependent and delinquent children in alternative care placements.

Individual Maltreatment

Individual foster families, child care workers, and others engaged in providing services to children become frustrated just as parents do. Even though these individuals are often trained in many aspects of youth care and have special skills for working with children, they come to their work with certain expectations, hopes, and predispositions. Well-meaning caretakers without adequate support can become completely overwhelmed by the job and the limitations of the system. They may encounter great difficulty in developing relationships and facilitating positive change with children who resist relationships and have already established behavioral patterns that are difficult to change. Children who have learned interactional patterns of provoking and scapegoating may be very difficult to manage. The time available to work with an individual child may be very limited, both in a short and long-term sense. Individuals involved in child care may pressure themselves with unrealistic expectations and then feel as if they have failed if these expectations are not met. Some, for example, may see themselves as rescuers, or they may expect gratitude and love from the children whom they serve. Failed expectations, unrealistic or not, can lead to anger toward or withdrawal from children. Some individuals may be poorly trained and not prepared to deal with developmental issues compounded by separation issues or the pseudomaturity of the sexually sensitized child. (See Chapter 8.)

Children may be physically, sexually, and emotionally abused and neglected while in the alternative care system. The maltreatment may be subtle or overt and may or may not be reported. What is the impact of the abuse and neglect imposed on children by the response system? Is it possible that many of the problems experienced by abused and neglected children as adults are as much the responsibility of the "helping" system as of the original situation? Would many children be better served by not being served at all, or at least not being removed from their homes for extended periods of time? Specific answers to these questions are ambiguous. As we have discussed previously, longitudinal studies, particularly the preferred prospective rather than retrospective designs, are expensive and time-consuming. Reliability and validity issues are by necessity compounded. It is not necessary to wait for such results. Common sense alone dictates that abuse and neglect underwritten by the system itself over a period of time greatly increases damage to children. The very fact that these children are seen as being "different from" other children and are treated differently than other children may contribute in subtle ways to their view of themselves and their place in society. The least that we owe our children is not to add harm. However we explain system, program, and individual abuse and neglect, however clearly we understand it and even sympathize with the difficulties that provoke it, institutional abuse and neglect of children is unexcusable.

Supervision of Placement Issues

Institutional abuse and neglect occurs when adequate supervision of placement does not. In a recent case, the Gannett News Service investigation of institutional abuse in Oklahoma state institutions for dependent and delinquent children revealed a level and variety of abuse against children that, according to the report and by the state welfare director's own estimate, amounted to about 8000 claims of abuse in that state's juvenile facilities in the last three years. Reports of maltreatment actually included all categories of institutional abuse and neglect. (Hanchette and Sherwood.)

In addition to protecting the child from institutional maltreatment, supervision of placement can also help to achieve positive goals set for and with the child. Frequent visits to the facility, visits with the child outside the grounds, routine inspections by health, fire, and welfare authorities all have their role in supervision of placements. In some agencies, alternative care settings are monitored by specialized staff who are responsible for supervising all out of home placements of children. Every person who works with the child in any capacity is in part responsible for the supervision of the placement. Regular and frequent formal reviews of the plan for the child and progress on achieving specific objectives in that plan add still another check and balance to supervision. More importantly, all of these efforts help to assure a safe and nurturing place for the child.

The volunteer guardian *ad litem* program and the foster care review board (described in Chapter 11), which have recently been established in many areas of the United States, are responses to institutional maltreatment of children. These programs attempt to assess the individual needs of children and determine whether these needs are being met by the system, the programs, and the individuals working within the social institutions serving children.

The Family Protection Act of 1977 was passed by the California state legislature in response to increased concern about the large numbers of children in the "limbo" of indefinite foster care. Its goal was to test the effectiveness of innovative legal and social approaches to the problem of foster care. Its premise is that the natural family is the best setting for a child and should be supported whenever possible. San Mateo and Shasta counties in California have designed pilot projects based on this Act that facilitate keeping children in their homes safely with the provision of services and financial allocations.

Removing a child from home may appear to be the most expedient route to providing a safe and nurturing environment for the child. This may seem especially true in times of diminishing in-home services to families and when mobility of families discourages the forming of supportive networks that could help them develop healthier relationships. Unfortunately, 50% of all children removed from their birth homes stay in alternative care until they reach 18 years of age. (Gil, p. 11.) The risk is great that these children may be more neglected by an inadequate system than they ever were in their home situation. As one girl said after being removed from her neglecting birth home at the age of 8 years and waiting in foster care for three and a half years for an adoptive home, "Sometimes I just wish I'd of stayed with my mom. Then at least I wouldn't have had to live in all these homes and maybe never get adopted."

Alternative care is the best choice for some children. It can be a better choice than it currently seems to be for many children now in out of home care. The same may be said for in-home services. Strengthening families, both the child's family and the alternative care family, while also helping the individual child to gain some invulnerability, may require a fresh look at available resources and the ways in which they might be most useful.

Summary

A wide range of intervention services can be made available to the child and family in most communities. Some of these may be provided while the child remains at home. Others are offered in short or long-term alternative care for the child outside the home.

Supervision in the home, where it is a viable option, offers the best choice for the child. If children must be removed from their homes and into alternative placements, the interest of the child should be paramount. The option that provides the safest, most nurturing environment, most healing setting, and the least detrimental alternative to the child is the option of choice. The child needs to be able to form a mutually caring connection with a person in a "psychological parent" role. Care in resolving issues of restraint and close supervision and monitoring of residential placement helps to ensure positive placements for children.

Many issues continue to stand in the way of providing a safe and nurturing place for children. Among these are:

1.   Many communities have very few resources from which to choose.
2.   Often resources that are available have waiting lists for services.
3.   Mismatching of resources to people needing services often occurs.
4.   Families needing services may refuse help or may not have the energy required to know about or to use the resources available to them.

5. Abusing and neglecting families are very mobile and may leave the state or jurisdiction before treatment is completed.
6. Social service agencies often compete for funding that may affect quality of screening and types and quality of programs available.
7. Many agencies pay very low wages for long hours and emotionally demanding work; high turnover of staff seems almost inevitable in such situations.
8. Basic skills training and improved work habits may be necessary for people needing help before many of these persons will be prepared to compete in an already constricted job market.
9. Many resources do not provide the long term support and follow up services necessary to assist abusing and neglecting families.
10. The special needs of hard to place children are often stated, but not realistically considered, when solutions are sought.
11. The foster care system continues to lack adequate screening, training, and treatment supervisory support.
12. Coordination and cooperation among agencies and individuals who share the same client are difficult to achieve in an on-going way.
13. System policies, programming, and inadequate supervision of placement may foster institutional abuse and neglect.
14. Long-term realistic planning and implementation in abuse and neglect cases is frequently inadequate or nonexistent.

There are many parts to the puzzle of achieving a safe and nurturing environment for a child. Resources must be developed and used in ways that will protect the child, strengthen the family, strengthen the alternative family, and strengthen the child.

BIBLIOGRAPHY

A Parent's Guide to Day Care. Prepared by the Center For Systems and Program Development, Inc., DHHS Publication No. (OHDS) 80-30254.

Arizona Department of Economic Security Day Care Manual. Tucson, Arizona. Trainers Notes. University of Arizona, 1980.

A.R.S., Title 8, Children 8-501 Definitions, 8-515 Local Foster Care Review Boards.

Broadhurst, Diane D., Edmunds, Margaret, and MacDicken, Robert A. *Early Childhood Programs and the Prevention and Treatment of Child Abuse and Neglect*. (NCCAN), DHEW Publication No. (OHDS) 79-30198.

Child Abuse and Neglect: The Problem and its Management. Vol. 3. The Community Team, An Approach to Case Management and Prevention. (NCCD), DHEW Publication No. (OHD) 75-30075.

Community Planning For Addressing Child Abuse and Neglect Issues. (NCCD) National Indian Child Abuse and Neglect Resource Center, (OHDS) Grant No. 90-C-1744 (02).

Gil, Eliana. *Prevention of Abuse and Neglect of Children*. San Francisco Department of Social Services Pilot Project and San Francisco Child Abuse Council, California, 1979.

Goldstein, Joseph, Freud, Anna and Solnit, Albert J., *Before the Best Interests of the Child*. The Free Press, New York, 1979.

Group Home Management. Prepared for the Office of Juvenile Justice and Delinquency Prevention by Arthur D. Little, Inc., March, 1979.

Hanchette, John and Sherwood, Carlton. In Oklahoma child care, stories of abuse abound. *Tucson Citizen*. Gannett News Service. Tucson, Arizona, February 17, 1982, p. 4A.

Heindl, Cathy, Krall, Carol A., Salus, Marsha K., and Broadhurst, Diane D. *The Nurse's Role in the Prevention and Treatment of Child Abuse and Neglect*. (NCCAN) DHEW Publication No. (OHDS) 79-30202.

In The Matter of Sampson. New York Family Court, Ulster Co., 1970. 65 Misc. 2d 658, 317 N.Y.S. 2d. 641.

Jenkins, James L., Salus, Marsha K., Schultze, Gretchen L. *Child Protective Services: A Guide for Workers*. (NCCD), DHEW Publication No. (OHDS) 79-30203.

Klein, Alan F. *The Professional Child Care Worker*. Association Press, New York, 1975.

Martin, Harold P. *Treatment for Abused and Neglected Children*. (NCCD) DHEW Publication No. (OHDS) 79-30199.

National Analysis of Official Child Neglect and Abuse Reporting Annual Report, 1980. American Humane Association, Denver, Colorado.

Russo, Eva M. and Shyne, Ann W. *Coping with Disruptive Behavior in Group Care*. Child Welfare League of America, Inc. Research Center, New York, 1980.

San Francisco Child Abuse Council, Inc. *Prevention of Child Abuse and Neglect in Out of Home Care*. San Francisco, California, 1980.

Segal, Julius, and Yahraes, Herbert. *A Child's Journey*. McGraw–Hill, New York, 1978.

Shapiro, Deborah. *Parents and Protectors: A Study in Child Abuse and Neglect*. Research Center of the Child Welfare League of America, New York, 1979.

Standards for the Administration of Juvenile Justice: Report of the National Advisory Committee for Juvenile Justice and Delinquency Prevention. (OJJDP). Washington, D.C., U.S. Department of Justice, July 1980.

Treischman, Albert E., Whittaker, James K., and Brendtro, Larry K. *The Other 23 Hours*. Aldine Publishing Co., Chicago, 1969.

Underwood Billie. Effects of a Workshop on Foster Parents' Attitudes Toward Children's Moral Development. In Mayhall, Pamela and Norgard, Katherine. *Project Report: Advanced Foster Parent Education*. Pima College, Tucson, Arizona, 1980.

Zitner, Rosalind and Miller, Shelby Hayden. *Our Youngest Parents: A Study of the Use of Support Services by Adolescent Mothers*. Child Welfare League of America, Inc., New York, 1980.

CHAPTER 13

Treatment: Making a Difference

DEFINING TREATMENT

Treatment is defined as any measure designed to ameliorate or cure abnormal or undesirable conditions. (Hinsie and Campbell, p. 784). Since over 50% of abused and neglected children suffer serious developmental, medical, or psychological problems, a high percentage of these children require treatment for these conditions. (Martin, p. 2.) Treatment of these children must first deal with the physical and/or emotional safety of the child.

Treatment is more than just protecting the child from further emotional and/or physical injury. Treatment can be many things. Treatment may be dealing with the child's medical problems, ensuring that the child has a safe and nurturing place to live, providing for the developmental needs of the child or offering the psychological therapy or services described in Chapter 12 to the child and the child's family. Since treatment can be so many different things and can be provided by so many different people in so many different capacities, it is imperative that there is case management.

Case management is an approach to treatment that emphasizes decision-making, coordination, and service. Case management may include a needs assessment on behalf of the individual child and the child's family, coordinating interagency services both to the child and to the family, coordinating intra-agency decision-making, standardizing information systems, or any combination of these. If the case management approach is not utilized, delivery of services becomes fragmented.

The first step in the case management approach is to assess what abnormal or undesirable conditions exist and what measures can be designed to ameliorate them. The first condition that has to be assessed is the safety of the child. The child's physical and emotional safety is always the first priority of the treatment process and must be continually evaluated during the treatment process. The child must have a safe place to live. If the child is not safe, all other attempts at treatment of either the child or the family may be wasted effort.

Medical, developmental, and psychological conditions must also be assessed. Each of these may be singularly problematic or problematic in conjunction with another. Measures must be defined that will help to change any condition found to be undesirable to the child while offering the child the necessary protection and safety. The cast of characters that offer help to the child and family come from various disciplines. The authors believe that one of the most important tools in the treatment process is the person who offers the help.

THE HELPER

Helpers are professionals and paraprofessionals, volunteer and paid. Whether the helper is a social worker, nurse, psychiatrist, pediatrician, counselor, speech therapist, teacher, occupational therapist, or volunteer, there are some important questions and issues to consider before the helping process can begin. Knowing the personal strengths and weaknesses, the prejudices, and the hopes that are brought by the helper to the situation, (i.e., self-knowledge) will assist people who respond to abuse and neglect to better focus their efforts and to avoid compounding the problems that already exist in the situation.

Self-Knowledge

Abused and neglected children and the caretakers who abused or neglected them are usually resistant to help. In the caretakers' views, "help" threatens their lives, takes away what little power they have, requires energy when they feel depleted, and, in a sense, underscores their failure. The caretakers may have agreed to participate in the helping process only because they want to avoid coercive or additional coercive intervention. The challenge and frustration in working with people who are resistant to the help is great. Those who plan to work with abusing families, in addition to having specific knowledge and skills, must honestly answer the following or similar questions for themselves.

1. Can I work with resistant clients and comfortably use authority to the benefit of the client's treatment? In other words, can I capitalize on the fact that this person is mandated to participate in treatment and does not want help on the basis of his own choice?

2. Do I have long-term relationships in my life and do I enjoy them? How involved can I become with a person or a family over a long period of time, particularly when they may need me and not be able to respond to my needs?

3. Am I optimistic? Can I find something positive in almost every situation?

4. Am I realistic? Can I recognize and tolerate negative factors while at the same time try to reinforce new and positive attitudes and behaviors in my clients?

5. Can I depend upon myself to follow through in times of crisis or am I easily frustrated and overwhelmed by crisis?

6. Do I enjoy people and can I remain confident in unfamiliar situations?

7. Am I tolerant of other people's attitudes, values, and beliefs?

8. Do I usually stick to the goals that I set for myself?

9. Can I see past, unpleasant, immediate situations and anticipate results, even though they may be delayed?

10. What kind of a person am I? Am I basically happy and content? Is my personal life and family situation stable, rewarding, and happy so that I do not have to turn to the abusive parent or abused child to satisfy my own needs? What are my motives for doing this work?

If the answer to any of these questions is no, working intensively with child maltreatment situations may not be in the proposed helper's best interest, nor in the best interest of the children and families with whom that person might work. Certainly the question needs further attention before a decision is made. The decision whether or not to be involved in the treatment process in a direct helping capacity is an important one. Self-assessment allows for self-screening in another sense. It is possible to be involved in the helping process but not have direct contact with the family. For some helpers, an indirect helping role is more meaningful and productive. Working directly and indirectly with child abuse and neglect requires a major commitment of time and emotional energy. It is important for helpers to be aware of their willingness to invest such energy and time and their ability to work in crisis and stressful situations. All of these factors contribute to the nature and quality of the relationship that the helpers wish to form with the child or the family who have already experienced much tragedy, disappointment, and discouragement in other relationships. Every failure contributes to the next, just as every success offers new possibilities for another. These family members need success, however small, in establishing positive relationships with helpers. The better helpers understand that positive long-term change in behavior and attitude may occur only in slow and sometimes seemingly inconsequential steps, the better they will be able to set achievement goals that encourage change and build hope on the part of the family members that change is desirable and possible. For some people, participating in a meaningful and positive relationship with another person, even at a marginal level, is a new and frightening experience.

Making Contact

"Contact" is the very first step in working with a child or parent. Making contact means being able to hear what the other person is saying, understanding what the other person is feeling, and finding qualities in the other person that both people can appreciate. Satir has the following to say about making contact.

I want to love you without clutching,
appreciate you without judging,
join you without invading,
invite you without demanding,
leave you without guilt,
criticize you without blaming,
and help you without insulting,
If I can have the same from you then we
can truly meet and enrich each other.

Satir's words capture the essence of a relationship shared by two people. The helping relationship may not involve all of these elements. The purpose of a helping relationship is to meet the needs and deal with the problems of the person being helped, not the person giving the help. A helping relationship usually involves a great deal of giving and very little taking. "Forming a relationship depends on a worker who has strong convictions about the needs of children, and no great need to be popular with everyone she meets." (Polansky, p. 56)

Once contact has taken place, the undesirable conditions and issues of both the child and the family must be confronted. The child's safety is, as always, the first priority.

THE SAFETY OF THE CHILD

Many times it is necessary for children to be removed from their parents and placed in living situations outside their homes in order to ensure their safety. The decision to remove a child from home is not an easy one. This decision must take into consideration the child's developmental needs and circumstances as well as the long-range goals for the family as a whole. The decision where the child lives is crucial to the overall treatment of both the child and family.

When and to the degree possible, parents and other family members need to be involved throughout the decision-making process regarding the child. "If parents are unable to meet their child rearing responsibilities, they deserve professional help in acknowledging their incapacities and in developing a plan of substitute parental care for their child." (Hally, p. 29.) Parents have a right to know what is being planned for both them and their child, to understand the reasons for the plan, and to receive sensitive emotional support throughout the decision-making process.

Chapter 12 discusses the range of options for alternative child care and living arrangements as well as in-home support for families. Each of these options is an integral part of the overall treatment process.

Providing a Safe, Nurturing Place

Following safety, stability is the second treatment goal for the child. Children who have experienced abuse or neglect should not be placed in living situations where the caretaker or parent-surrogate will be changing frequently. A stable home or living situation can be helpful in the healing process.

Becky is a teenager who is still in foster care. Her case illustrates the importance of stability. Figure 13.1 is a flowchart of Becky's life experiences from the time of her birth to age eight years old.

Becky

Becky's original family was composed of her birth mother and father, two older brothers, and an older sister. The family lived together until Becky was four. At that time, Becky's father abandoned the family and was never heard from again. Becky's mother had a difficult time providing for the family of five by herself, even with the help of welfare assistance and a part-time job.

Becky's second family experience is depicted by the circle around Becky, her mother, and her three siblings. After six months in this difficult family situation where there never seemed to be enough to go around, Becky's mother remarried a man whom she had known for two months.

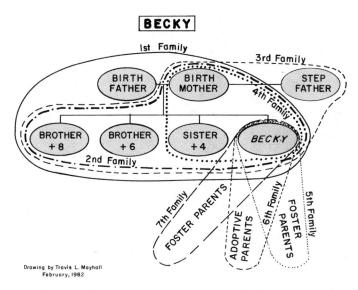

Figure 13-1 Becky's life experiences.

Becky moved to her third family unit at age four and a half. Becky remembers that her mother and stepfather fought continually. The fights were verbal and physical. Becky's mother seemed very unhappy. Becky's stepfather sexually molested Becky and her older sister several times before anyone discovered the abuse. The authorities intervened and the family was again in turmoil. Becky and her sister had to testify in court. The stepfather was sent to prison.

Becky, her mother, and her sister moved into a small apartment. The welfare department sent the two older boys to a foster home after the court determined that they could not be managed and controlled by their mother. Becky remembers how sad her mother was after the boys left. Becky's mother remained sad and was unable to take care of the girls. After a neighbor reported the family to the child protection services, Becky and her sister were placed in foster care and their mother was given psychiatric help.

At age seven, Becky was placed in an adoptive home (her sixth family unit). Her new parents were nice people, but Becky never quite felt that she belonged. She had no contact with her original family and did not even know where any of them lived. Becky developed a severe bed-wetting problem which neither the doctors nor her adoptive parents were able to correct. Becky began playing with matches and one day started a grass fire in a vacant lot. Becky developed more behavioral problems. Finally, in desperation, the adoptive parents decided that they could not manage Becky and asked that she be returned to the care of the state.

At age eight years, Becky was again living in foster care. Becky continued to long to see or talk to her mother and the rest of her family. Nothing seemed to be able to touch Becky's inner pain. Becky's tragic case is illustrative of the need for children to have emotional and physical stability in their home settings after being removed from their family.

No provisions were made for Becky to see her mother. No information was provided to Becky as to the whereabouts of her family. Becky felt cutoff from the family bonds that she longed for and was too young and too inexperienced to know how to maintain them. "Whenever possible, attempts should be made to avoid the weakening of existent bonds and attachments between children and their natural parents, siblings, and other relatives." (Martin, p. 26.) Children need to be able to maintain some sense of their identity in relation to their birth families. Mother and father are the first connections that we make. It is through the ideas that we have about our parents that we begin to form ideas about ourselves as people. When children do not have actual connections with their parents, they may fantasize about what their parents are like (good or bad etc.) and apply these meanings to themselves.

Years later when Becky was asked by her therapist what she had learned, she replied, "I am a bad person. No one wants to keep me." Becky still longed for that vital connection with her family and had not found a viable substitute. Her fantasy was that one day someone would love her enough to adopt her and give her the home and family that she so desperately wanted. Becky developed many problems in her short years. Through the course of her therapy, she will need to come to understand and believe that she has many good parts to herself, that she is lovable as a person, and that she does have a place with other people.

Since removing children from their natural home is such a major decision and such disruption not to be taken lightly with the scant hope that life will be better for the child out of the home, there are those who argue that out-of-home placement should be used only as a very last resort. Levine and McDaid state that a family-based approach to treatment of child abuse problems (working with children and their parents in their home) is far superior to any options that exist outside the home. These authors maintain that removing a child is analogous to major surgery and should only be done when every effort has been made to restore the family. Children should only be removed after efforts at providing psychological and other concrete services to the family do not succeed, or the probability of their success is minimal. (Levine and McDaid, p. 270.)

Electing to place Becky out of her home did not seem to improve her life. In fact, Becky's story is a case in point that out of home placement can be not only disruptive but potentially damaging to a child. Another option available to the case manager in Becky's case would have been to work with Becky and her family in the family environment.

Unfortunately, keeping Becky in her home has no guarantees of a successful outcome either. The case manager often has to make a decision from two or more poor choices with no guarantees about outcome and little or no guidance from research. Had the case manager elected to keep Becky with her family, supportive services would have been required, perhaps family therapy and the services of a homemaker.

For the sake of discussion, let's return to that decision point and assume that this is the choice made in Becky's case. The case manager and the therapist will have to define goals and objectives of this treatment and develop some means of measuring outcomes. The goals are easy enough. They will center around Becky's needs to be continuously physically safe from sexual abuse by her stepfather; her need to be provided adequate basic food, shelter, and emotional care by her parents; Becky's mother's need to resolve her feelings of inadequacy and depression; and the family will need to become self-sufficient. Objectives might be designed around services that can be provided, for example, a job training program and child care. Measurement of outcome could be in whether or not the training was completed, child care was utilized, and possibly in whether or not the family financial resources improved. Keeping Becky physically safe involves more risk and is difficult to assess. Her safety requires the cooperation of the family group. Strengthening the mother is also complex and because of the subtleties involved, is difficult to measure. There are no easy choices.

MEDICAL PROBLEMS AND ISSUES OF DEVELOPMENTAL DELAY

After establishing that the child has a safe and stable living environment, the child's medical, developmental, and psychological needs must be assessed and met. "Children who are abused or neglected frequently have had inadequate medical care in the past; the family may have neglected the child's hygiene, well-child care, nutrition, and illnesses." (Martin, p.11.) The immediate medical needs of the child receive first attention. If the child has medical problems that will require attention over a long period of time, one primary care physician should be identified to oversee and coordinate the medical care. Pediatricians, neurologists, orthopedic specialists, and others may be called upon to provide services to the child. Case management of medical care may be just as important as case management of social services. Designating one primary physician for the child should simplify this process.

Some common medical problems of abused or neglected children are inadequate immunization, hearing deficits, anemia, poor nutrition, infection, vision, dental health, congenital anomalies, and general hygiene. Good health is central to psychological well-being. It interacts with the child's overall development.

Fifty percent of abused and neglected children suffer significant problems in development delay (the range is from 30% to 90%, depending upon who is reporting), yet developmental issues are often ignored. One researcher noted that 88% of a group of abused children had developmental problems such as mental retardation, emotional disorder, speech problems, or marked physical defects. (Martin, p. 27.) Developmental problems are identified under the category of mental ability, speech and language, motor skills, and learning ability. These problems must be assessed and plans made for the short and long-range needs of the child.

Screening for developmental problems should occur as early as possible. Realistically, assessment of these needs is rarely a top priority. The assessment and screening for developmental problems needs to include a complete history of the child and his/her family and observation of the child, particularly when the child is not under undue stress or participating in formal screening tests. The evaluator must have a clear understanding of normal development. Test results must allow for individual differences within the range of developmental milestones. Table 13.2 is a chart of developmental milestones that was developed by Harold P. Martin.

Developmental problems can be assessed by a pediatrician trained in developmental issues, a child psychologist who knows how to evaluate infants and young children, a multidisciplinary team that specializes in such evaluations, public school personnel, some social workers or child psychiatrists who have special training and experience in conducting such evaluations, or a child neurologist. Many times this evaluation and ultimate treatment planning for the developmental needs becomes the responsibility of the CPS worker. The following questions should be addressed by the evaluator.

What is the status of the child's development?

If the child has delayed functioning, what are the likely reasons for the delay?

What can be done to help accelerate the child's development?

Charles

Charles was reported to CPS at age four after neighbors became aware that he was being physically abused by his stepmother. When Charles was examined by the pediatrician at the local hospital emergency room, severe and multiple injuries to his skeletal system as well as bruises and lacerations

Table 13.1 Developmental Milestone*

Age	Motor	Mental	Language	Special
3–6 months	Will bear weight on legs Can roll over stomach to back Engages hands in midline When pulled to sit, head is steady, does not fall back When on abdomen, can lift shoulders off mat When on abdomen, can lift hand and look about Will begin to reach for and grasp objects Sits with support	Looks at objects in hand Locks after a toy which is dropped Uses a 2-hand approach to grasp toys Looks at objects as small as a raisin Turns head to voice, follows with eyes	Coos Gurgles Chuckles Laughs aloud Squeals Has expressive noises	Has a social smile Will pat a bottle with both hands Anticipates food on sight
6–9 months	Rolls from back to stomach Gets feet to mouth Sits alone, unsupported, for extended period (over 1 minute) Stands with hands held On back, can lift head up Beginning attempts to crawl or creep When sitting, reaches forward to grasp without falling	Bangs toys in play Transfers objects from hand to hand Reaches for a toy with one hand Picks up a toy he/she drops Is persistent in obtaining toys Would pull a toy to self by attached string	Responds to name Vocalizes to social stimulus Has single consonants, i.e., ba, ka, ma Combines syllables, i.e., da-da, ba-ba Likes to make sounds with toys Imitates sounds	Expects repetition of stimulus Likes frolicky play Discriminates strangers Smiles to mirror image Takes some solid food to mouth Bites and chews toys Beginning to enjoy peek aboo

331

Table 13.1 Cont.

Age	Motor	Mental	Language	Special
9–12 months	Crawls well Can sit steadily for more than 10 minutes Stands holding on to furniture Can pull to sitting position Walks, holding on to a hand or to furniture	Will uncover a toy he/she sees covered up Can grasp object small as raisin with thumb and one finger Beginning to put things in and out of containers Goes for an object with index finger outstretched Likes to drop objects deliberately Shows interest in pictures	Understands no, or inflection of "no" Uses mama, or dada, first inappropriately, then with meaning By 12 months has at least one other word Knows meaning of 1 to 3 words	Cooperates in games Will try to roll ball to another person Plays patacake and peekaboo Waves goodbye Will offer toy without releasing it Likes to interact in play with adult
12–18 months	By 18 months, walks well alone Creeps up stairs Can get to standing position alone Can stoop and recover an object Walking, pulls a pull-toy Seats self on chair	Looks at pictures in a book Will scribble spontaneously with pencil or crayon Uses spoon Drinks from cup Will follow one or two directions, i.e., take a ball to	Has 3–5 words Will point to one body part Will point to at least one picture Uses jargon, i.e., unintelligible "foreign" language with inflection Imitates some words	Cooperates in dressing Holds own bottle or cup Finger feeds Points or vocalizes to make desires known Shows or offers a toy

332

Age	Gross Motor	Fine Motor	Language	Personal-Social
18–24 months	Can run, albeit stiffly Walks up and down stairs with one hand held Hurls a ball Can kick a ball or object Jumps with both feet Stands on one foot with one hand held	Can tower 2 or more 1 inch blocks Turns pages of a book, even if 2 to 5 at a time Will try to imitate what an adult draws with pencil Can point 2 to 3 body parts	By two years, has at least 20 words By two years, is combining two words in a phrase Jargon, which was elaborate by 18 months, is gone by 24 months Verbalizes desires with words	Uses spoon, spilling very little Removes one piece of clothing Imitates housework more and more Handles a cup quite well
2–3 years	Can walk up stairs without hand held Can balance on one foot for one second Can jump in place Can walk on tiptoe Can jump from the bottom step Kicks ball forward Can throw a ball	Can tower 6 one inch blocks Can dump a raisin from a bottle to attain without hints Can imitate a vertical line, possibly a horizontal line, with pencil Can anticipate the need to urinate or defecate If worked with, can toilet self	Uses 2–4 word phrases Uses plurals Names at least one picture Talks incessantly Vocabulary 100 to 300 words by 3 years Uses some personal pronouns, i.e., I, me, mine Points to several parts of a doll on request Identifies over 5 parts of own body	Puts on some clothing Washes and dries hands Has parallel play with peers Can pour from a pitcher

Table 13.1 Cont.

Age	Motor	Mental	Language	Special
3–4 years	Rides a tricycle Alternates feet when going up stairs Can stand on one foot for 2 to 5 seconds Can broad jump Uses scissors Swings and climbs	Can tower 8 to 10 one-inch blocks Says full name Can match colors Has sense of round, square, and triangular shaped figures and can match them Copies a circle, line, cross with pencil Can repeat 3 digits	Can answer some questions Knows rhymes and songs Asks questions Has understanding of on, under, and behind	Knows own sex Beginning to play *with* other children Unbuttons Dresses with supervision
4–5 years	Runs well and turns Can hop on one foot 1 to 2 times Beginning to skip Stands on one leg for 10 seconds Throws ball well overhand Walks down stairs one foot to each step	Can copy a cross with a pencil Can pick the longer of two lines Can copy a square with pencil	Vocabulary over 1000 words Can match colors, and by 5 years, name 3–4 colors Counts 3 objects with pointing 90% of speech intelligible Can define words in terms of use Can answer questions like, what do you do when you are cold . . . ; hungry . . . tired. . . .?	Can separate from mother easily Dresses with little supervision Buttons Likes to play "dramatic" play, make-believe Imaginative play with a doll

| 5–6 years | Skips on both feet alternatively
Can catch a bounced ball
Can walk heel to toe on a line
Can hop on one foot for 10 feet | Can copy a square or triangle from looking at a copy
Gives age
Knows morning from afternoon
Draws a person with a body, with 3 to 6 parts
Prints simple words | Can repeat 4 digits
Asks questions about meaning of words
Counts 10 objects
Names coins
Can tell what some things are made of
Can define some words | No supervision necessary for dressing
Plays "dress-up"
Elaborate dramatic play
Does simple chores unattended at home |

*If child is not accomplishing two or three of these milestones, consider developmental consultation.

Source. Martin, Harold P., *Treatment for Abused and Neglected Children.* U.S. Department of Health, Education and Welfare, OHDS 79-30 199, August, 1979, p. 32–33.

335

on his body were discovered. The pediatric social worker visited Charles daily while he was hospitalized and spent time with his father and step-mother. A thorough history of the family noted that Charles probably had been physically and emotionally abused by both his birth mother and by his stepmother. Charles' stepmother was very remorseful. She reported to the social worker that often after hitting Charles she would hold him, rock him, and try to comfort Charles.

The social worker noted that Charles' speech seemed delayed. His motor and social skills and his mental abilities seemed within a normal range. Charles stuttered and was unable to answer simple questions. In consulta-tion with a speech therapist, treatment was planned for Charles. He was to have speech therapy on a regular basis while in the hospital in conjunction with other supportive therapy offered by the social worker and the play therapist.

His speech improved considerably during his one month stay in the hospital. By the time of discharge, his speech was more spontaneous and he seldom stuttered. Family therapy and speech therapy facilitated Charles' successful return home.

There are many treatment options to help children deal with develop-mental delays. One option is a special or therapeutic preschool that specializes in the education of children with developmental delays. A second option is to employ the services of an occupational or physical therapist who can work individually with the child and/or offer supportive services to the parents, foster parents, or other caretakers of the child. Creative options must be developed to meet the needs of each child. Physicians, speech therapists, occupational and recreational therapists, and others are identified as helpers in dealing with children's medical and developmental delay problems.

TREATING PSYCHOLOGICAL ISSUES OF CHILD ABUSE

The remainder of this chapter will focus on the treatment of psychological issues related to child abuse. Children may be involved in many forms of treatment at the same time due to the multifaceted nature of their problems.

A thorough assessment of the psychological issues is important before beginning the treatment process with either the child or the family. Family and individual strengths and deficits must be assessed in order to establish treatment objectives.

A Search for Competency

In what ways is this family and each family member competent? What strengths does the family bring as a unit and as individuals to solving their own problems? It is easy to overlook strengths when a child has been emotionally and/or physically harmed in a family. At first glance, it may seem that no competency exists here. Such an observation may be more a product of the observer's reaction to the situation than objective assessment. Sometimes it becomes necessary to actually ''search for'' the areas of individual and group competence.

''In spite of our optimism, we may be skeptical when we see a parent reacting tenderly to the child we know he or she has abused.'' (Ryan, p. 13.) Tender feelings are important strengths for the helper to know about. These tender feelings may be the basis for repairing broken or damaged relationships between a child and an adult. Given time, certain strengths of the abusive individual and of the family will surface. Helpers need to be ready to discover them and must not be blinded by their own prejudices and emotions.

The primary basis for helping people rebuild their self-esteem and shattered relationships is to build on their strengths. People need to be encouraged to become aware of and to build on their strengths in order to begin to feel in control of their lives and to be able to behave in positively powerful ways. The helper who is closed to discovery of a client's strengths is doing that client a disservice. Treatment goals need to be based on the assessment of the strengths of the individuals and the family as well as on a thorough evaluation of the difficulties within the family.

Setting Goals

Treatment is aimed at helping people move out of their isolated, trapped, hopeless patterns of living into a greater sense of self-esteem. Ideally, treatment can enhance the ability of a person to find gratification in the world. The helper acts as a catalyst to this process and encourages and allows the child or the adult to try out new ways of relating to other people and to the world. A primary aim of child abuse treatment is to break the all too familiar generational cycle of abuse. This goal deals with not only the immediate problem, but is aimed at making a better future for the family and other people affected by the family. A primary aim of child neglect treatment is to help the family to better understand and attend to the child's needs and to the needs of the total family.

The following general objectives form a foundation for setting specific treatment objectives for each child and each family.

1. Increase the individuals' belief in their ability to be helped and changed from their dysfunctional patterns to more productive ways of behaving and interacting with one another and with others outside the family.

2. Balance the needs of the child with the needs of the family.
3. Help the parents deal with and meet their unmet dependency needs.
4. Encourage the parents and the child to develop an ability to use people or activities as lifeline supports. The parents must learn how to turn to others for help when they feel overwhelmed or in need of specific help or support.
5. Assist the parents and the child to improve upon their interactional patterns both within and outside the family.
6. Help the parents and the child improve their self-esteem and enhance their self-concept.
7. Encourage the parents and the child to decrease their isolation from other people outside the family and increase their interest in pursuing friendships, extended family, or activities outside the home.
8. Assist parents in learning how to sense their child's needs and wants as well as teaching them how to deal with these needs and wants and to be able to set limits.
9. Teach children how to be more direct in stating their needs.
10. Facilitate the parents' and child's ability to improve their communication process and skills so that they will be more in touch with their feelings and be better able to communicate in a more open and direct fashion with one another.
11. Assist the family in making their emotional rules (see Chapter 2) more explicit so that they can become more flexible and responsive to the needs and protection of the family members.
12. Teach parents how to set age-appropriate limits on the behavior of their children.
13. Work with the marital pair to improve their relationship in order to lessen their fear of rejection, desertion, or loss of one another.
14. Continually reevaluate and assess the progress of the individuals and the family in this process.

Situations of incest have unique dynamics that require specific objectives.

1. The offender must take full responsibility for the behavior and be able to verbalize this responsibility to the abused and to the other family members.
2. The spouse of the offender must take full responsibility for being an ineffective parent and be able to refrain from projecting responsibility and blame onto the abused or onto other people.
3. The abused needs to be informed about who to contact should

molestation occur again. The abused also needs to have the skills to seek help should help be required in the future.

4. Family members need to learn to respect privacy and individuality within the family.
5. Power within the family needs to be redistributed so that one member is not all-powerful over the rest of the family.
6. Distinctions need to be made between generations. Adults need to act as adults. Children need to be seen and act as children.
7. Family roles need to be clarified.
8. Spouses need to find mutual emotional/sexual satisfaction together so one or both spouses are no longer needy, lonely, depressed, or isolated.
9. Family members need to learn to distinguish fantasy from reality.
10. The parents need to provide sexual protection for the child.
11. Parents need to be able to discuss openly their own upbringing and learn how they gave themselves permission for sexual molestation to occur within their family.

Specific objectives for physical abuse treatment include:

1. Help the parents accept responsibility for their role in the physical abuse.
2. Help the parents learn how to control their lives to lessen the number of stressful events.
3. Help the spouses find emotional satisfaction with one another, rather than frustration which might lead to physical abuse of the children in the family.
4. Encourage parents to learn age-appropriate expectations of their children.

Objectives that are generally part of the treatment plans in situations of neglect include:

1. Discover the factors that have encouraged the parents to move away from their children emotionally and/or physically.
2. Discover the parents' needs that interfere with their ability to nurture the child.
3. Separate environmental and psycho–social factors involved in neglectful situations so as to better determine the parents' role.
4. Help the parents improve upon their chaotic home situation if the home life is chaotic.
5. Help the parents meet basic human needs: food, shelter, or unsafe conditions.

6. Help to motivate the parents to improve their lives and develop skills to effect changes.
7. Help these parents learn how to delay gratification so that they can better plan for long-term needs within their family.

Most forms of child maltreatment are accompanied by emotional abuse. Parents often truly do not understand or accept that they are emotionally abusing their child. Rather than denying the emotional abuse out of self-protection or defense mechanisms, parents honestly do not believe that they are causing harm. It may be difficult to convince emotionally abusing parents that any harm even exists. Because emotional abuse is so elusive to identify, it is also difficult to know whether or not it has stopped.

The foregoing objectives apply to parents. The most common objectives for dealing with children who have been abused or neglected are: (1) to help them improve their self-image; (2) to help them learn how to discuss and deal with their feelings surrounding the abusive situations; (3) to help them learn how to be children with all the rights and responsibilities of people their age; (4) in situations of child sexual abuse, to help the children learn age-appropriate sex education; (5) to help learn interactional patterns that will not incite continued or further abuse; (6) to help the child be safe from physical and emotional harm (this objective bears repeating since it is paramount).

Treatment Modalities

The stress of deprivation, neglect, sexual abuse, or battering requires the child to psychologically adapt to the situation. "The younger the child, the smaller repertoire of adaptive behaviors he/she has. What are the options to the child: withdrawal, fearfulness, obeisance, fighting back?" (Martin, p. 44.) Whenever children select an adaptive response to the abusive situation, there is a good possibility that psychological difficulties will follow. The child's adaptations to the abuse may be adaptive in the sense of survival value, but maladaptive in that they impede learning, social ability, and may affect the child's happiness and maturation.

> Often the emotional scars of abuse and neglect are much more far-reaching and severe than the physical scars. If intervention is impossible at this point, and if it is not possible to alter these children's psychological development, there is little hope of preventing future abuse and neglect, or of substantially decreasing the incidence of violence towards future children. (Martin, p. 45.)

Before deciding on a particular treatment modality or a combination of modalities, the case manager should request a thorough assessment and screening which takes into account psychological and social milestones and developmental stages. The symptoms that the child may exhibit inside or outside the context of the family are important and affect his or her mood (for example, an expression of sadness, excessive seriousness) etc., and must also be assessed. After this assessment has been completed, the answer to the question of whether the child and/or the family needs and can benefit from psychological treatment can be answered.

The treatment modalities delineated in this section are conducted by professionals from various training backgrounds. Selections are usually based on their skill level and interest. Social workers, psychologists, counselors, and psychiatrists are among the professionals who generally provide mental health services. It is important to reiterate at this point that even though mental health professionals are designated as the people to "do therapy," all people involved in the planning and care of the child and the child's family can be therapeutic.

Treatment approaches need to deal with the problems of abuse and neglect from the standpoint of what has occurred within the context of the family. The content of the therapy may be multigenerational if the parents explore their own backgrounds and rediscover old processes. The treatment modalities discussed in this section are limited to types of therapy from a psychological framework. Chapter 12 discussed community outreach options (homemaker services, self-help groups, etc.) which can be powerful therapeutic tools and often are part of the overall treatment plan. Sometimes, these community outreach services are used exclusively; psychological treatment is not used if it is decided that the other services are sufficient to meet the child's best interests.

The first consideration in selecting a treatment modality is the question of match. "The matching up of parent, worker, and treatment modality is difficult and is usually managed on a less than ideal scientific basis." (Steele, p. 21.) Abusive parents are usually reticent to become involved in any type of therapy. Therefore the type of treatment selected may be what the parents will accept rather than what the case manager might chose. Realistically, services can only be selected from available resources. Therefore the supply of available resources dramatically affects treatment options. "There is at present no data derived from thorough comparative studies which indicate how or why any one modality of treatment is more effective than another for particular kinds of parents." (Steele, p. 21.) However, it also is known that treatment can fail or be successful in accomplishing treatment of objectives from all the various approaches and points of view.

Although psychoanalytical oriented dynamic psychotherapy in the hands of skilled practitioners has been successful in some situations, it is not the treatment of choice for abusive parents. Practically speaking, the general character structure and life style of most abusive parents makes this procedure quite impractical and probably unsuccessful. (Steele, p. 21.) The more commonly used therapy modalities for abusive parents are individual psychotherapy based on an eclectic model, family therapy, marital therapy, and group therapy.

Individual Therapy

"The design of individual therapy can be beneficial to abusive and neglectful parents because it provides the parent with individual attention and recognition." (Lauer et al., p. 58.) It is important that the treatment goals be specific and focus on immediate problems. The parent needs to be a participant in designing treatment goals, but the therapist must consider the parent's present situation, ability to verbalize feeling, to make changes, and to draw on external supports. After immediate treatment goals have been met (for example, helping the parent have other types of interactions with the children rather than just in times when discipline is needed) and a good relationship has been established between the therapist and the parents, the parents will be more likely to deal with deep-seated, emotional problems since they now have a successful experience and can believe that the therapist will allow their therapy to be self-directed. Dealing with deep-seated problems such as the parent's own unmet dependency needs or the anger that they feel toward their own parents, takes time and patience. Many parents do not reach the point of being willing or able to deal with or resolve these issues. The therapist therefore must be willing to set realistic goals for the therapy and evaluate the accomplishment of these goals.

The therapist may help the parent learn specific skills such as assertiveness and problem solving. The therapist may purposefully serve as a role model for the parent. However, most therapy focuses on family issues. Even though individual therapy is not technically "family therapy," child abuse and neglect occur within the context of the family and family issues are a major part of individual therapy content.

Individual therapy is sometimes offered to all children in the family. Younger children usually profit best from play therapy (discussed in the next section), but children who are too old or too sophisticated for play therapy often profit from individual therapy. Individual therapy may focus on the child's feelings about the abusive or neglectful situation or the child's feeling about his/her parents.

Adolescents who are involved in group or family therapy may also benefit from concurrent individual therapy. Sometimes individual therapy is all that can be offered to either a child or an adolescent when the parent(s) are unavailable or unwilling to participate in the treatment.

Family Therapy

Family therapy is a mode of therapy for the family as a group. Family therapy can mean working with the whole family in the same room at the same time or working with family members in small groups, each group meeting at a separate time. Working with families requires a clear understanding of the four mainstays and the three-level definition of the family, as discussed in Chapter 2. Some family therapists intimate that a person only becomes a family therapist after having worked with several hundred families.

During the process of the family therapy, the family therapist must become aware of the family's emotional rules. When these rules are ones that allow or encourage abusive situations, the therapist must find ways to help the family improve and expand these operational rules. Therapists may work at helping the family with their rules through the process of communication or by helping family members enhance their self-esteem. The family therapist deals with all the first and second-level definitions of the family by helping the parents restructure the family so that it will function without violence.

In working with neglectful families, the focus may be on helping the family deal with the third-level definition of the family—the external influences. The therapist may encourage the parents to become better connected not only to one another but with people outside the family.

The ultimate aim of family therapy is to help the parents become positive leaders in the family in order to facilitate meeting the basic needs of all of the family members (closeness, food, shelter, etc.). Families that function in nonabusive ways seem to be able to accept that change and stress are a part of life. An emotional rule in these families is that violence is not permitted in the family. The working parts (as described in Chapter 2) of nonabusing families work to the family's benefit, rather than their detriment.

The therapist must become aware of and help the family deal with interactional patterns that may lead to continued abuse, even when other features in the family change. For instance, as mentioned in Chapter 2, when children behave in a provoking way or as a scapegoat, they increase the danger to themselves through their actions. These patterns need to be changed if the family is to function without abuse. Since hiding and caretaking patterns are actually physical safeguards for the child, they may need to be maintained until the child's safety is insured.

Family therapy is a useful and constructive treatment approach for child abuse and neglect. A skillful family therapist can meet the individual needs of the family members and deal with dependency issues while working with the entire family group. Sometimes, however, only the parent(s) are singled out for therapy.

Marital Therapy

A great proportion of abusive parents have marital difficulties. Marital therapy may be the treatment modality of choice when the parents are aware of and willing to work on the difficulties and frustrations in their marriage. When parents are able to increase their gratifications within the marriage, less stress and less propensity to physical violence or neglect exist in the family. "Marital therapy is contraindicated in cases where the parents are very dependent and emotionally needy; they are likely to compete for the therapist's attention and will probably not accomplish much." (Lauer et al., p. 59.)

Marital therapy can be of primary importance to the child, not only in changing the parents' abusive patterns, but in helping to create a more positive home environment. If the parents are able to get more of their needs and wants met from one another in a positive fashion, the home is more likely to be a place of joy and nurturance and the child will benefit from this change.

Group Therapy

Group therapy is most frequently used as an accompaniment to other forms of therapy (one-to-one, family, or marital). The Justices state that group therapy is more advantageous than individual therapy for those who abuse their children because abusive parents are isolated people who lack a trust in others. The group helps them have different and positive experiences with other people. (Justice and Justice, p. 112.) If parents begin to ventilate pent-up feelings, discuss these feelings with others, and feel accepted by the other people, they may begin to establish the trust that they have never had before. People often form friendships in groups that can be helpful in their day to day lives. "Acceptance, new friends, trust, and the feeling that their opinions and ideas matter to others—all these new experiences greatly enhance a parent's self-image." (Justice and Justice, p. 112.)

Common goals for group work with parents include: (1) promoting changes that will ensure the safety of the child; (2) teaching people problem-solving skills; (3) promoting the couple's satisfaction with life and their emotional well-being.

The group leader usually conducts individual sessions with parents before the parents enter the group so that the leader can establish a bond that will transfer over into the group. "Group therapy is appropriate for parents who are not severely disturbed, who are not extremely threatened by expressing their feelings, attitudes and problems to others and who are capable of verbal expression." (Lauer et al., p. 60.)

Preadolescents and adolescents can also benefit from group therapy.

Youth who have been abused may find solace in discovering that they are not alone in these experiences. In addition, a group can facilitate socialization, self-awareness, and development of sensitivity to others.

Psychodrama can be a very effective form of group therapy for abused or neglected adolescents. Psychodrama occurs within a group. Instead of talking about problems, participants are encouraged and guided in a process of acting out their problems in the midst of their emotional reality. Psychodrama is considered an action therapy.

Many times, youth, like adults, cannot talk about their feelings or their problems. Recreational or occupational therapy can be utilized as a method of encouraging these youth to work through their feelings and actually reach resolution to problems. Sports, games, and projects such as leather work, ceramics, etc. are used as the medium to conduct recreational and occupational therapy.

Groups of youth who have been sexually abused offer a special kind of support to youth who are trying to deal with these problems. Such a group can help the youth develop healthy, positive attitudes toward sex and put sex into a developmental and psychological perspective.

Groups help youth gain support from others, find new friends, and gain self-acceptance. Groups can sometimes promote more rapid changes in youth than individual treatment because of the positive peer pressure in the group. Groups of youth must be led by skillful leaders because the potential for negative peer pressure also exists within the group.

Play Therapy

Play therapy is based on the premise that play is the child's natural medium for self-expression. Children are given the opportunity to play out their feelings and problems, just as adults are encouraged to talk out their feelings. Play therapy may take a directive or nondirective form. In directive play therapy, the therapist takes responsibility for guiding and interpreting for the child. In nondirective therapy, the therapist leaves the responsibility and direction with the child.

The therapist and the child engage in play therapy in a room that is commonly referred to as a play room. The child uses toys in the room to enact certain feelings and problems. The therapist assists the child in working out problems through the medium of play. The child learns to resolve conflicts and fears. Children who have low self-esteem, depression, or are extremely aggressive toward others, or who are severe behavior management problems can benefit from play therapy.

"Increasingly, research on abused and neglected children suggests that the child plays more than a passive role in abuse." (Friedrich and Boriskin,

p. 580.) "Special" children seem to produce more parental stress. Children who have developed the interactional pattern of being a scapegoat, provoking, caretaking, and hiding (mentioned in Chapter 2), those who are born prematurely, who are physically handicapped and frequently ill, mentally retarded, those who are perceived by the parent as different or bad, and children who seem to have physical abnormalities and behavioral styles that the parent finds unusual or problematic are all children who are considered high risk for parental abuse. (Friedrich and Boriskin, p. 581.) Special children are not the sole contributors to child abuse. Often these children work out some of their own frustrations by using play therapy to decrease danger to themselves and others.

Across the Modalities

Three major approaches are necessary for treatment, both when working with the child and with the parent or family.

1. Be critical in a positive way. Neither condone nor condemn the abusive behavior. (Zaphiris)
2. Be noncompetitive for the child. The parents need to be reassured that you are not trying to take their child away from them. Sometimes, if the child is already in an out-of-home placement, the parents fear that they will lose the emotional connection they have to their child through the process of the therapy. They are particularly afraid that the therapist may replace the parents in the eyes of the child.
3. Answer the parents' dependency needs.

> Professional training has often admonished against developing inappropriate dependency in clients. Such parents must be accepted as the emotionally starved infants they truly are, not in a demeaning way, but as an honest appraisal of what is necessary for them to grow to emotional adulthood and thrive. (Alexander, p. 292.)

The therapist must acknowledge the parent's original deprivation and help the parents meet these early needs before moving on to another stage. During this time, the parent probably will become very dependent on the therapist. This dependency is not inappropriate nor induced by the therapist for the therapist's own needs. Sometimes the therapist may need to do concrete things for the client (for example, make dental appointments and arrange for child care) that support the parent's need for dependency upon the therapist during this time. Lay therapists can be particularly helpful with this process.

   The child's age and developmental level, role within the family, verbal accessibility, ego strengths, level of social interaction and any physically handicapping condition all need to be considered in determining treatment goals and selecting modalities for working with children. (McQuiston and Kempe, p. 382.) For example, during infancy, the child needs to have a constant, nurturing parent figure. This is the primary treatment goal for the young child who has been abused. The infant and young child needs sensory stimulation, stimulation of language skills, introduction to play and development of play skills, improvement of fine and gross motor skills, introduction to safety issues, and reinforcement to build self-help skills.

   A therapeutic nursery may be the treatment of choice for a preschool child. The child may need help in dealing with extremes of behavior, poor language skills, gross and fine motor skills, pseudo-adult role-reversal behavior with adults and peers, poor impulse control, disturbed integrative process of thought, and indiscriminate affection with adults. Some children may require one-to-one play therapy to help them overcome the problems associated with the abuse. Working with the family is critical.

   Play therapy is the treatment of choice for school-age children (up to age 12 years of age). However, involving the parents may be difficult or negative. "Because so few of these referrals receive cooperation and follow-through by the parents, there have been experiments in incorporating psychotherapy in a special school program for some of these children who cannot function in a regular classroom." (McQuiston and Kempe, p. 386.)

   Treatment of adolescents may result from their acting out behavior, school failure, delinquency, or running away. The treatment of choice during this period of development is family therapy supported by either group or individual therapy for the adolescent.

   Regardless of the modality of therapy used in a formalized therapy process or in a community outreach service, it is important to assess the outcome and the response of the children and the adults to the treatment.

RESPONSE TO TREATMENT

One study of 51 abusive families suggested that the possibility of differentiating parents who responded to services from those who did not could be made on the basis of three aspects: (1) the number of abusers in the family, (2) the number of children abused, and (3) whether or not a contract was involved in the initial reunification plan. (Yates et al., p. 7.) If there was more than one abuser in the family, the probability of successful outcome to treatment was greater. ". . . when both parents are cited, an often crucial obstacle to change is circumvented: the couple must share responsibility and are presented a common goal. There is no 'bad' person to be blamed, disparaged, or disowned." (Yates et al., p. 7.) This study suggests that the severity of the abuse itself did not predict the outcome of treatment. The existence of a reunification plan was helpful to the successful outcome of treatment. Parents who had abused several children were not likely to respond favorably to treatment, much less acknowledge allegations or be willing to change or want reunification.

Treatment must also be considered from the standpoint of its harmful effects. Therapeutic procedures carry some risk of harm. (Lauer et al., p. 59.) Within the field of medicine, this is an unassailable fact. Methods must be found to ensure that the pain and trauma of help is less than the pain and trauma of the conditions for which the treatment is suggested.

If the child's separation from the child's parents is inevitable, it is crucial to help the child by anticipating the loss. Any kind of loss (parents, foster parents, or hospital staff) can be traumatic for the child. The child can be helped to modify the stress associated with the loss if the child can help negotiate an appropriate termination. It is important to help the child deal with the resulting feelings of guilt, anger, sadness, and ambivalence and allow the child a place to express these natural feelings. There is no "good" time for separation.

Sometimes an unforeseen harmful effect of treatment comes in the form of helper "burnout." "Faced with the family's lack of initiative and limited prognosis, and the slow balance of justice and rights in the courts, the worker's optimism can easily turn to cynical pessimism and their enthusiasm to impatience," (Ryan and Walters, p. 34.) Burnout creates a disruption in services to the clients, and adds a further stumbling block to successful outcomes. It may bring harm to clients. The case management system can and must foster the development of active teams of helpers who can talk to and encourage one another in the difficult task of confronting these seemingly insolvable problems.

Treatment Outcomes

Assessing whether treatment has been "successful" can be just as elusive and difficult as defining certain types of child abuse and neglect. Expectations for positive outcomes need to be realistic. A Berkeley study noted that expectation for success is no higher than 40% to 50% (Shapiro, p. 12.) Studies that report high success rates often have biased subject selection processes. None of the studies thus far have been conclusive. Many of the findings appear contradictory. People working with these families report their own limited success.

Parents charged with abuse and neglect are not candidates for quick change. Many of these parents require long-term treatment and long-term support in order to achieve any measure of success. "Parents do cease to be abusive and neglectful but just what protective service workers and other professionals in the community can do to increase the rate of improvement, apart from "staying with" the family for a substantial period of time, has yet to be clearly identified." (Shapiro, p. 12.) Staying with the family in a supportive way actually does not always occur, given the built-in difficulties of the social service support systems. Perhaps a goal of the system needs to be to increase the quality and quantity of support and treatment for these families.

Summary

This chapter focuses on the definitions of treatment. The first concern of treatment is safety of the child. Once this is accomplished, other concerns can be addressed. For treatment to begin, contact between helper and recipients of help must occur. Helpers must be self-aware and committed to working with people who may not seek, or accept help. Abusive families are often resistant clients.

All people have individual strengths. These must be discovered and worked with as a basis to psychological treatment. Individual treatment goals and plans need to be made that will use, expand, and strengthen the family's resources. The case management approach to treatment should be utilized in order to best coordinate and facilitate treatment resources. Goal setting is a crucial step in providing treatment. Goals for treatment vary with maltreatment categories.

A wide range of treatment modalities exist. The treatment modalities of individual, group, family, and play therapies were discussed. The case manager must consider the needs of the individual against the resources available in making treatment plans.

Response to treatment may relate to:

1. Number of abusers in the family.
2. Number of children abused.
3. Whether or not a contract was involved in the original reunification plan.

Treatment outcomes are difficult to assess. Studies relating to such outcomes have been unable to provide much guidance to people working with abusive and neglectful families. Clearly, working with these families is a difficult and emotionally depleting task with no guarantees.

BIBLIOGRAPHY

Alexander, Helen. Long-Term Treatment. In Kempe, C. Henry and Helfer, Ray E., Eds. *The Battered Child.* 3rd Ed. The University of Chicago Press, Chicago, 1980, pp. 288–296.

Besharov, Douglas. Visiting Scholar, Brookings Institute, Washington, D.C. Interviewed by Katherine Norgard on November 18, 1981.

Carroll, Claudia A. The Function of Protective Services in Child Abuse and Neglect. in Kempe, C. Henry and Helfer, Ray E., Eds. *The Battered Child*. 3rd Ed. The University of Chicago Press, Chicago, 1980, pp. 275–287.

Deitrich, Gay. National Center for Prevention and Treatment of Child Abuse and Neglect. Interviewed by Pamela D. Mayhall, November 3, 1981.

Fisher, Bruce, Berdie, Jane, Cook, JoAnn, and Day, Noel. *Adolescent Abuse and Neglect: Intervention Strategies*. U.S. Department of Health and Human Services, Office of Human Development Service, OHDS 80-30266, July 1980.

Fontana, Vincent J. *Maltreated Children*. Charles C. Thomas, Springfield, Illinois, 1971.

Fontana, Vincent J. *Somewhere a Child is Crying*. Macmillan Publishing Co., Inc., New York, 1973.

Friedrich, William N. and Boriskin, Jerry A. The Role of the Child in Abuse: A Review of the Literature. In *American Journal of Orthopsychiatry*. 46, 4, (October 1976) pp. 580–590.

Garbarino, James and Jacobson, Nancy. Youth Helping Youth in Cases of Maltreatment of Adolescents. *Child Welfare*. *LVII*, No. 8, (September/October 1978) pp. 505–510.

Hally, Carolyn, Polansky, Nancy F., and Plansky, Norman A. *Child Neglect: Mobilizing Services*. U.S. Department of Health and Human Services, OHDS 80-30257, May 1980.

Helfer, Mary Edna and Helfer, Ray E. Communicating in the Therapeutic Relationships: Concepts, Strategies and Skills. in Kempe, C. Henry and Helfer, Ray E. Eds. *The Battered Child*. 3rd Ed., The University of Chicago Press, Chicago, 1980, pp.117–127.

Helfer, Ray E. *The Diagnostic Process and Treatment Programs*. U.S. Department of Health, Education, and Welfare Office of Human Development/Office of Child Development/Children's Bureau. OHD 76-30069, undated.

Hinsie, Leland E. and Campbell, Robert Jean. *Psychiatric Dictionary*. Oxford University Press, New York, 1970.

Hyde, James, Morse, Abraham, Newberger, Eli, Reed, Robert. Family Advocacy: Implications for Treatment and Policy. In Maybanks, Sheila and Bryce, Marvin, *Home-Based Services for Children and Families*. Charles C. Thomas, Springfield, Illinois, 1979, pp. 177–193.

Justice, Blair and Justice, Rita. *The Abusing Family*. Human Sciences Press, New York, 1976.

Justice, Blair and Justice, Rita. *The Broken Taboo—Sex in the Family*. New York, Human Sciences Press, 1979.

Kempe, C. Henry and Helfer, Ray E. *The Battered Child*. The University of Chicago Press, Chicago, 1980.

Lauer, James W. Lourie, Ira S., Salus, Marsha K., and Broadhurst, Diane D. *The Role of Mental Health Professionals in the Prevention and Treatment of Child Abuse and Neglect*. National Center on Child Abuse and Neglect, U.S. Department of Health, Education, and Welfare. OHDS 79-30194, August 1979.

Levine, Theodore and McDaid, Elizabeth. Services to Children in Their Own

Homes: A Family-Based Approach. In Maybanks, Sheila and Bryce, Marvin, Eds. *Home-Based Services for Children and Families*. Charles C. Thomas, Springfield, Illinois, 1979.

Martin, Harold P. *Treatment for Abused and Neglected Children*. U.S.Department of Health, Education, and Welfare. OHDS 79-30 199, August 1979.

McQuiston, Mary and Kempe, Ruth S. Treatment of the Child. In Kempe, C. Henry, and Helfer, Ray E. Eds. *The Battered Child*. The University of Chicago Press, Chicago, 1980.

Mead, Jim. Executive Director, For Kids Sake. Brea, California. Interviewed by Pamela D. Mayhall, November 24, 1981.

O'Brien, Shirley. *Child Abuse: A Crying Shame*. Brigham Young University Press, Provo, Utah, 1980.

Polansky, Norman A, DeSzix, Christine, and Sharlin, Shlomo A. *Child Neglect: Understanding and Reaching the Parent*. Child Welfare League of America, New York, 1976.

Pollock, Carl and Steele, Brandt. A Therapeutic Approach to the Parents. In Kempe, C. Henry and Helfer, Ray E. *Helping the Battered Child and his Family*. Lippincott, Philadelphia, 1972, pp. 3–21.

Ryan, Gail, Walters, Elsie, and Alexander, Helen. *The Lay Person's Role in the Treatment of Child Abuse and Neglect*. The C. Henry Kempe National Center for Prevention and Treatment of Child Abuse and Neglect, Denver, 1981.

Satir, Virginia. *Making Contact*. Celestial Arts, Milbrae, California, 1976.

Schmitt, Barton D. The Battered Child Syndrome. *Pediatric Trauma*. Wiley Medical Publications, New York, 1978, pp. 177–216.

Scheurer, Susan and Bailey, Margaret M. Guidelines for Placing a Child in Foster Care. In Kempe, C. Henry and Helfer, Ray E., Eds. *The Battered Child*. 3rd Ed. The University of Chicago Press, Chicago, 1980, pp. 297–305.

Segal, Julius. *A Child's Journey* McGraw-Hill Book Company, New York, 1979.

Shapiro, Deborah. *Parents and Protectors: A Study in Child Abuse and Neglect*. Child Welfare League of America, New York, 1979.

Steele, Brandt. *Working with Abusive Parents from a Psychiatric Point of View*. U.S. Department of Health Education, and Welfare, OHD 76-30070, no publication date.

Stember, Clara Jo. Art Therapy: A New Use in the Diagnosis and Treatment of Sexually Abused Children. In *Sexual Abuse of Children: Selected Readings*. National Center on Child Abuse and Neglect, OHDS 78-30161, November 1980.

Thomas, Joyce N. Yes, You Can Help a Sexually Abused Child. In *RN*, (August 1980) pp. 23–29.

Tuszynski, Ann and Dowd, James. Home-Based Services to Protective Service Families. In Maybanks, Sheila and Bryuce, Marvin. *Home-Based Services for Children and Families*. Charles C. Thomas, Springfield, Illinois, 1979.

Webster, Noah. *Webster's New Twentiethh Century Dictionary*. 2nd Ed., William Collins Publishers, 1980.

Wechsler, Joseph, National Center for Child Abuse and Neglect. Interviewed by Pamela Mayhall, on October 29, 1981.

Yates, Alayne, Hull, James W., and Huebner, Robert. Child Abuse: Predicting Parental Response to Intervention. A study supported by a research grant from Loma Linda School of Medicine, California, undated, unpublished.

Zaphiris, Alex. Techniques of Individual Treatment. Produced and distributed by National Indian Child Abuse and Neglect Resource Center, Tulsa, Oklahoma, (Fall, 1980).

14

Child Abuse and Neglect: A Shared Responsibility

This chapter summarizes a perspective proposed by the authors, from which child abuse and neglect can be viewed and prevention, intervention, and treatment efforts can be made. It represents a determined optimism that is not shared by every researcher, practitioner, and observer. There is certainly sufficient evidence to show that, as a society, we do not take a consistent shared responsibility for child abuse and neglect. Nor do we agree on what they are or what should be done about them. Our helpfulness is not always helpful and the maze in which help is provided sometimes seems so incredibly complex and ambiguous that well-meaning helpers seem small and impotent in it. In such a context, something as optimistic as belief in positive change seems somehow out of place. Yet how else will such change ever occur?

In the view of the authors, the elements of positive change include but are not limited to belief in the possibility and desirability of change; the energy to act; the economic means to meet survival needs; caring, interpersonal connections; long-range supportive structure (such help takes time); competence. Competence is defined as having the required ability or qualities. The person and family being offered help will sometimes need to gain competence in basic social, work, interpersonal and/or parenting skills; the helper will need to offer the necessary competence to assist in achieving such an objective. The degree of which positive change occurs may rest in (1) how many of these elements the helper brings to the interaction, (2) how many of these elements the person being helped comes eventually to share, and (3) the quality of both.

There is no one to whom the responsibility for valuing children and families and preventing child abuse and neglect can be delegated. Responsibility for change belongs to everyone. It begins in assessing where we are and acting on our best knowledge in order to achieve and maintain change.

ASSESSING WHERE WE ARE

No Research Miracles

More research may be helpful (1) in defining categories of abuse and neglect more clearly; (2) in evaluating, at least in part, some specific treatment approaches; (3) in more clearly targeting some of the predisposing factors related to abuse and neglect; (4) in better clarifying the impact that official response has on the child and family. It may stimulate the improvement of treatment programs and encourage prevention. It is not likely, however, at least in the opinion of the authors, that research has any miracles, for example, that a direct cause and effect relationship between personality characteristics and abuse or neglect will be found or that a single solution or always successful treatment approach will be identified.

No Easy Solutions

There are no pills we can take to prevent or cure maltreatment. No surgery, even removal of the child or the parent from the home, guarantees long-term "cure." Since the problem is multifaceted and, in many ways, integral to our social structure, easy, all-encompassing solutions are rarely, if ever, available.

Constructive discipline and abusive punishment, and loving sensuality and abusive sexuality are, as Roland Summit suggests, separated by a thin, invisible line. Wisdom and ignorance, energy and inertia, hopefulness and hopelessness, and family function and dysfunction all operate on similar continuums. The dynamics of neglect express family tragedy and failure and sometimes a parent's effort, however inappropriate, to survive. Success rarely occurs in human experience without a measure of failure. No one seems to have a permanent corner on either failure or success.

All those who act on their feelings, lack impulse control, and confuse roles are not abusive parents. Many single parents, young parents, or people living in poverty and faced with multiple crises do not neglect or abuse their children. Many children who have been maltreated do not grow up to maltreat others, yet others who were not maltreated, at least not in any reportable definition of maltreatment, do grow up to maltreat others.

Issues of Time and Culture

Certainly child maltreatment relates to time and culture and is influenced by the priorities of the society and the unique interactions of a given child's family and environment. As we discussed in Chapter One, how children are valued and how they fit into the structure of our society and the family in which they live may, in subtle ways, help to predispose abuse and neglect. In a recent article in *U.S. News and World Report,* Alvin Sanoff and Jeannye Thornton state, "Today, when it can cost the average family almost $150,000 to see a child through the first 18 years of life, and more than $225,000 if the cost of a private-college education is included, many adults regard children as an economic liability." (p. 54.) Parents may be struggling with what seem to be competing priorities. Balancing two careers, finding time for themselves, finding time for the children, acquiring goods, services, and status are often all valued by parents. How much sacrifice of one is appropriate for another?

Children become more vulnerable as their families become more vulnerable through divorce, economic instability, and the added complexity and demands of single parenting. Data from the U.S. Departments of Labor, Commerce, and Health and Human Services combine to describe this vulnerability rather dramatically. In 1981, 19% of this nation's children were living with one parent and about 48% of women with children under 6 years of age were employed. In 1979, 597,800 children were born out-of-wedlock, an increase of 199,100 over the number born out of wedlock in 1970. (Sanoff and Thornton, pp. 54–55.) Census Bureau data indicates that almost half of the young children of full-time working mothers are cared for by agencies or by babysitters who are not family relatives. As jobless rates climb, particularly in some areas of the country, for some job markets and some age and ethnic groups, economic instability becomes a major vulnerability factor.

Other issues combine to place children at risk of abuse and neglect. We have discussed many of these issues: unrealistic expectations by parents of children; lack of parenting skills and knowledge of human development; lack of basic nurturing qualities on the part of parents; the mobility of families, which may increase isolation and disruption and make long-term treatment and support difficult to provide and on and on. Abuse and neglect are related to culture and time, factors of development, environment, personality, family systems, and response systems.

In the larger context of system, the authors take the position that every person shares in the responsibility for the existence of abuse and neglect in our society and for prevention and treatment. Every person has power to effect positive and negative change. Every person is also affected by the decisions of others.

Feelings of hopelessness and helplessness about child maltreatment are common. Such feelings seem to breed inertia. The inertia becomes a problem in itself for those who would be helpers, just as it does for abusing and neglecting families. If it is our hopelessness that we share with families who already feel hopeless, the change we effect may be to confirm their sense of being overwhelmed. Opportunities for change do occur both in formal and informal response. Such opportunities need to be recognized and acted upon or they are lost.

In the Formal Response System

System, program, and individual abuse and neglect within the response system is present in every state and probably in every jurisdiction. Policies, procedures, and practices are all part of problems and solutions. Our system of human services, regardless of the name it is given in a particular state or jurisdiction, is entangled in political process and tossed about by economic fluctuations. Many human service agencies seem to be involved in chronic management by crisis. Decisions are made from crisis to crisis with little opportunity for long-term planning and implementation. Either people and positions change so frequently that fragmentation is encouraged, or so infrequently that sensitivity and creativity are stifled.

Poor coordination and cooperation between agencies and individuals that provide services can create disuse and misuse of available resources. Well-meaning providers may be plagued with differences of opinion and philosophy while simultaneously feeling misunderstood, unappreciated, and overwhelmed. Working under these conditions can contribute to a person's low energy, reduced sensitivity, and heightened need for self-survival. The system providers sometimes have very similar problems to those they seek to help. If the basic life problem of self-esteem or survival is at issue, most energy is concentrated, however circuitously, on that problem. Little energy is left to be spent on other needs.

Blaming the system is easy. Legislators blame the governor (or other legislators who did not vote with them), workers blame the courts, the courts blame the welfare system or the individual worker. The abuser blames society and society blames the abuser. The worker blames the lack of resources. The resource providers blames the public or the federal government for lack of support. And on it goes.

Sometimes blaming becomes an excuse for inaction. Blaming parents, government, the economy, the agency administration, or the system as a vague sort of "thing" allows the blamer to be lulled into believing that others are responsible. Attaching blame seems not only to attach responsibility, but to relieve it as well. Since, by law, CPS is assigned the responsibility for protection and treatment of abused and neglected children and their families, is that agency or unit solely responsible for protecting children?

Even if the answer were "yes," it would also be "no." CPS is a part of a broader system that each one of us is a member of by choice and by default. We are responsible for its effectiveness and ineffectiveness, for the useful and useless laws that regulate it, and the abundance and dearth of resources which it offers and which are offered to supplement its services.

The Best That We Know

To act in helpful ways we first need

1. Belief in the possibility and desirability of change.
2. The energy to act.
3. The economic means to meet survival needs.
4. Caring interpersonal connections.
5. Long-term supportive structure.
6. Competency.

The degree to which positive change occurs may rest in three conditions.

1. How many of these elements the helper brings to the interaction.
2. How many of these elements the person being helped comes eventually to share.
3. The quality of both.

At A Policy Level

Policy makers practically define abuse and neglect; assign responsibility for response to various subsystems; determine staffing patterns; provide support for line workers with salaries, resources, training, and supervision. Every large agency seems to have bureaucratic and political issues. Money for human services has been reduced in recent years. In some agencies, in order for child protective services to receive new staff, long-term supervision staff must be reduced. The connection between the two in the long-term care of children and families seems to be ignored.

Helpful policy makers have at least indirect impact on all the elements of positive change. They directly influence three:

1. Providing economic means to meet survival needs, which actually

    requires the cooperation of the federal and state legislatures, agency policy makers, local administrators, and the community.

2.   Establishing long-term supportive structure, in part based on economic considerations and agency priorities. Decreased caseloads and increased resources are required if this is to be accomplished within the formal response system.

3.   Establishing hiring and training policies that will increase the competency of staff to work with the difficult and complex problems.

Policy makers could both indirectly and directly impact the elements of positive change through:

Priorities that are internally consistent.

Personal exchange of ideas on a regular basis between all levels of administration and staff.

An accent on the competence of an administrator rather than his/her politics.

Commitment of more staff to critical areas. An awareness that when one policy change is made in an agency, it effects other agency decisions and actions, and often the decisions and actions of other agencies that participate in the joint response effort.

Effective training in meaningful areas.

Consistency in management and support.

Sometimes a deliberate lack of active "management," so that effective caseworkers have the freedom to do it well.

At A Procedural Level

The elements of positive change are experienced and taught on an interpersonal, direct service level. Some of the ways that people working at this level in the formal response system (professionals, paraprofessionals, or volunteers) can use their knowledge of the system, themselves, and conditions of success to facilitate positive change include:

1.   Self-awareness and self-assessment.

2.   The development of strategies, inside and outside of the system, to reenergize and maintain a balanced perspective.

3.   Understanding systems theory as it applies to families and to the formal response system and subsystems. Such an understanding makes it possible to use system dynamics to help children and families. Understanding possible system weaknesses and strengths

and family and individual weaknesses and strengths increases personal skill in manipulating systems. Manipulation can be a very positive action.

4. Reparenting takes time and energy. Helping children become invulnerable requires establishing a caring connection. Resilience and stubbornness are critical tools of helpers.

5. System supports must be developed for those who work in these exhausting, stress-provoking circumstances. Often such supports are best established cooperatively among staff members.

6. Children do not understand as adults, nor do they have the potency of adults. Agency members may know that a long-term plan exists, but children, in a very short time, can get lost in the system. Consistent attention to the child and an effective tracking system are critical, no matter what other help is being offered to the family.

7. Many individuals and jurisdictions act, however unconsciously, upon negative myths by labeling abusing and neglecting parents and their children. ''Only a Mexican'' and ''Another Black Kid'' combine the effects of negative labeling with the added burden of prejudice. Working to remove such labeling and the effects of such prejudice is critical to helping the child.

8. Reaching out to young parents early may help to encourage change. Although young parents appear to be more likely to abuse or neglect, they may also be more willing to risk change. Developing programs for young single parents that include a follow up component may offer new skills to the parent and protection to the child.

9. When families are consumed by emotional pain, they do not make positive connections. It becomes the responsibility of the helper to work toward easing the pain and to tend to emergency issues. The helper may need to reach out, and to continue reaching out until the helping connection is made.

10. In order to step outside expectations and preconceived notions and labels (whether from the helper or the client), sometimes doing the unusual or the unexpected is necessary. As long as it is done respectfully, the unusual or the unexpected can open a person for change, permit a new perspective, and increase energy. The absence of criticism in itself may be ''unexpected.''

11. Again, every intervention creates some change, however minimal. It is the helper's responsibility to be aware of possible outcomes of intervention strategies and to assure insofar as possible that intervention does not add harm.

12. It is easy to be lulled into inaction. The very nature of the problems associated with maltreatment and with the response to it are discouraging. If success is elusive its definition may need to be reviewed. Success is possible; positive change can be achieved, but success must be defined in achievable minute steps. Success encourages success.

13. Chronic stress, that series of crises that continues to bombard the family and which, as a group, seem insolvable, must be made solvable. The solutions and the method must be learned, and, at least, eventually, owned, by the family.

14. Often family members involved in abuse or neglect have extreme difficulty in forming meaningful relationships with other family members and with persons outside the family. Helping may mean, to a large extent, building relationships and teaching relationship building.

15. Abuse and neglect are not a single problem. Within these categories are many other subcategories. The better the helper understands the differences in these categories and subcategories, the more likely the elements of positive change will exist and help can be effective.

A PERSONAL COMMITMENT TO INDIVIDUAL ACTION

Hope for children lies in personal responsibility for action. Direct help that is offered occurs on a local level, on a person to person basis, or it does not occur at all. Law and agency policy can make help more available and more probable. Reforms in these areas underwrite success. Reforms come only with the commitment of individuals who insist upon change. Law and agency policy can facilitate or complicate the helping process, but both are legislators of, not givers of help.

In the best system, the helper has the resources and power to achieve therapeutic goals. In a best system, effective helpers do not become overburdened and emotionally depleted victims. Still, it is possible, even in a best system, that help may not be extended to an abusing family. Services are delivered by people. If the helping person is inadequate to the task, services cannot be provided, even in the best of systems. On the other hand, in the most inadequate system, where resources are limited and the power assigned to the staff is inconsistent at best, help may be extended to a family because of the dedication and perseverance of a person in a helping position.

Hope for children and abusing and neglecting parents rests with the people whose lives touch theirs, whether those people are working in the system as professionals, paraprofessionals, or volunteers or outside the system as friends, neighbors, and family members.

In fact, the greatest opportunity for change may exist in informal response to abuse and neglect. If the concept of shared responsibility is taken seriously, maltreatment of children will be decreased, even in an economic environment that fosters maltreatment and a time in which formal social service resources and options are reduced.

Prevention Of Abuse and Neglect

Primary prevention of abuse and neglect, the action which compared to others costs less, offers more, and has no negative side effects, is the responsibility of all individuals. Primary prevention is one of three types of prevention: primary, secondary, and tertiary. Primary prevention reaches out to at risk individuals and families before abuse or neglect occurs. Secondary prevention is the early identification and treatment of child abuse and neglect. Its goal is to help the family or individual improve as soon as possible. Tertiary prevention is more difficult to comprehend as prevention. The family is, at this point, more involved and more encapsulated in the formal response system. In a sense, tertiary prevention is rehabilitation. Perhaps, as Gilbert suggests, secondary and tertiary prevention are treatment masked as prevention. (p. 293.) They are preventative, however, in the sense that if they are successful further abuse and neglect within the family does not occur.

TOUCHING LIVES

One of the difficult parts of preventing child abuse and neglect is in conceptualizing what a person who is not involved in the formal response system can do or how to use the elements discussed as an untrained, concerned citizen. It is easy enough to say "be a resource," but how to be a resource may be the better question. There are many possibilities, some direct and some very subtle and indirect.

Be a Helper

Most social service agencies have more time-consuming digital tasks to complete than they have staff to complete it. Some of the tasks routinely assigned to staff could be handled by volunteers, allowing the professional staff to provide more services to families. Some volunteers may also be involved in direct service to families.

Support A Belief in Change

Caseworkers are assigned to work with and help families who are sometimes seen as being beyond help. Their clients are often resistant to the caseworkers' efforts. They may believe that they cannot be helped. When the belief is mutual and shared by the public, it is the greatest of tragedies. Failure is supported and success is subtly undermined. In a sense, the energy that could be persistently used to achieve positive change is divided against itself. Believing in change and recognizing it where it occurs, even in small ways, helps to refute the circular negative process.

Support the Helpers

In child welfare, caseworkers have an awesome task. They are assigned cases that often seem to have no hope for successful outcomes. They are often inadequate to the task of helping because they are inexperienced, may not have the appropriate education or training, or because adequate supervision and support are not available to help them relate to the problems. They are faced daily with bureaucratic stumbling blocks and are spotlighted by the media for their mismanagement of difficult or seemingly impossible situations.

Trying creative, imaginative strategies seems absurd when set against the apparent realities of the system and the odds against change in resistant, issue-laden families. Survival may be defined by the helper as, "have no expectations" and "ride the tide of this organizational schizophrenia."

Caseworkers may begin to perceive themselves negatively. Those who believe in change may leave the organization. Working in these circumstances might be seen as a useful, temporary field experience in which to sharpen skills and gain work experience leading toward other professional positions.

Staying is more difficult. The person who stays is actually more at risk and, at the same time, is the person who, as an advocate within the system, might be able to make the system work more effectively for the child and family. This person has a greater opportunity to form interagency and intra-agency resource alliances. Time and experience can increase the depth and skill which the caseworker brings to the job; time and experience can also increase the emotional weight of the job and the possibility of stereotyping clients.

Valuing and assisting the assigned helper can generate new energy and perspectives. This may be accomplished at a personal level or on a broader community level. Appreciation and recognition for effort and skill is meaningful if it is honest and it costs very little to provide.

Influencing Social Change

Most recent literature in child abuse and neglect argues that this area is of critical importance if support for families, in general, and protection of children, in particular, is to occur. Among the suggestions:

> Teach parenting skills to children throughout their elementary and high school education as an integral part of the education process.
>
> Give *all* new parents, each time they are new parents, help in bonding with the child, and adjusting to the new challenges of parenting.
>
> Value children in society as our most important product and share in the responsibility for their care.

These suggestions and other similar ones do not target the abusing family or the abused or neglected child. They reach out to the total population and are what the Justices' call nonspecific strategies. Winning support for them, especially reaching out to every new parent, is difficult.

Making a Prevention Connection

Individuals and families that make healthy connections with other people are less likely to abuse or neglect their children. Connections provide outlets for frustration; resources in stressful, painful times; alternative perspectives; new ways of looking at problems and solutions; encouragement and energy; increased self-esteem and assurance; subtle models for changing behavior; and perhaps, most importantly, permission to join with others, not to be isolated from them, and practice in building relationships. Obviously not every connection will provide all of these elements. Without the beginning connection, these elements have no foundation to grow on. Prevention connections refrain from negative labeling. They accent and build on strengths. They are not structured as treatment in the sense that it is discussed in Chapter 13. Prevention connections are treatment, however, in the sense that they may also be helpful and healing to the participants.

Everyone can make prevention connections. Opportunities may come at strange times and places. Where people meet, they begin to connect. Standing together in a food stamp or unemployment line, whittling sticks on a park bench, attending the same parenting class, shopping at the same market, using the same day care service or bus route, working the same job, and living in the same neighborhood, all provide opportunities to reach out positively to someone else.

PREVENTION IS AN ATTITUDE

Labeling Contamination

Labeling is often disabling. If we knowingly or unknowingly label those who abuse or neglect or those who are abused or neglected as different, bad, or inadequate, we may disable the possibility of prevention or change. Helping relationships can be contaminated by labeling. Projects that are designed to "help the unfortunate" may actually increase the distance between the we's and they's and underwrite the "unfortunate's" feelings of inadequacy.

Separating "Them" from "Us"

Prevention requires a concentration on joining rather than separating. Its focus is upon building bridges between the "we" and "they" rather than separating "them" from the "rest of us." It requires a respectful approach and an accent on similarities rather than differences.

The Problems with Rescuing

The best resource we have to offer a person in a situation of high risk is ourselves, not as rescuers, but as energizers and facilitators of change. Rescuing implies saving a person from danger. In the act of rescue alone, the rescued learns no new skills, neither how to avoid danger, nor how to get out of danger without being rescued. The rescued may be grateful, but also may feel impotent and embarrassed. There are times that saving from danger may be necessary, but only as a first step to change.

Energizers and facilitators of change approach from a clear perspective. They offer to share the load, relieving the person who is overburdened until he or she is more powerful. The attitude of prevention includes respect and an accent on partnership.

Prevention: A Comment

Prevention of child abuse and neglect presupposes that we can identify factors that contribute or predispose to situations of abuse and neglect. Categories of high risk factors vary with different types of abuse and neglect, but they often include: (1) high risk parents, usually characterized by immaturity, youth, excessive use of alcohol or other drugs, isolation, lack of parenting skills, and difficulty in forming and maintaining functional relationships with others; (2) high risk children, usually noted as those who are born prematurely or with low birth weight, babies born out-of-wedlock, and/or children who are difficult to manage or who seem to be characteristically mismatched with their parents; (3) high risk environments, which are characterized by underemployment, unemployment, chronic change, and/or a lack of a sense of community; (4) dysfunctional family systems on all three levels of family definition, which may foster family violence in general.

Awareness of high risk factors is a first step to preventing abuse and neglect. The key question, however, is how to reach out to families who are at risk without being intrusive and labeling the family as "preabusive." The label itself may contribute to the problem. The dilemma can be resolved without fanfare and informally through individual action.

Prevention Resources

Many prevention resources both within and outside the system already exist and some have been discussed in various contexts throughout this book. The National Center for Child Abuse and Neglect, National American Indian Court Judges Association, American Humane Association, Child Welfare League of America, Parents Anonymous, and Parents United are among these resources. They can suggest others, both on a national and local basis. The National Committee for Child Abuse Prevention is a privately supported organization that supports a volunteer network and involves citizens in prevention. For Kid's Sake, directed by Jim Mead in Brea, California, offers public information programs, a hotline, in-service training programs, and positive parent programs.

For prevention to be broadly based, voluntary and religious groups must be involved on a local basis. Private business organizations need to offer their support to prevention programs. Existing resources of schools, preschools, colleges, universities, and the public media need to be utilized more effectively in prevention efforts. Prevention will be most broadly based as individuals see themselves as prevention resources.

If we truly wish to prevent maltreatment of children, we will have to take the time personally to make caring connections with others, both children and adults.

Summary

In the view of the authors, child abuse and neglect are a shared responsibility of those within and outside the formal responses system. There is no one to whom the responsibility can be delegated. It belongs to everyone.

In order for positive change to occur, the elements of belief in the possibility and desirability of change; energy to act; economic means to meet survival needs; caring, interpersonal connections; long-range supportive structure; and competence must be present. The degree to which positive change occurs may rest in how many of these elements the helper brings to the interaction, how many of these elements the person helped eventually comes to share, and the quality of both.

Opportunity for change exists in the formal response system and outside that system. Perhaps the greatest opportunity for change is in informal prevention connections. Personal action to alleviate factors or the impact of factors that might contribute to abuse or neglect will improve the quality of life for the children and ourselves.

BIBLIOGRAPHY

Gilbert, Neil. Policy Issues in Primary Prevention. *Social Work.* *27,* 4, (July 1982) pp. 293–297.

Justice, Blair and Justice, Rita. *The Abusing Family.* Human Sciences Press, New York, 1976.

Justice, Blair and Justice, Rita. *The Broken Taboo.* Human Sciences Press, New York,, 1979.

Sanoff, Alvin P. and Thornton, Jeannye. Our Neglected Kids. *U.S. News and World Report.* (August 9, 1982) pp. 54–58.

Schneider, Carol, Helfer, Ray E., Hoffmeister, James K. Screening for the Potential to Abuse: A Review. In *The Battered Child,* 3rd Ed., Kempe, Henry C. and Helfer, Ray E. (Eds.). The University of Chicago Press, Chicago, Ill., 1980, pp. 420–430.

Epilogue

Each of us experiences the moment with only the benefit of the encapsulation of the past. Youth are new at being young and are experiencing it for the very first time. In much the same way, every new moment of parenting is new to parents. The encapsulation of the past may not always offer all that is needed in the present. Sometimes a caring connection from someone outside the family unit can offer guidance and support important to every parent and youth, especially in moments of most difficult passage.

Appendix 1

Intervention and Protection of Children: A
Historical Perspective

Period	Dates	Events and Perspective
Antiquity (to 4th Century A.D.) Power to the Father	Hammurabic Code, 2270 B.C. Sumarian Codes, 1750 B.C.	Father's authority affirmed. Problems between child and parent observed even in this early period. Infanticide practiced in many cultures.
	Rome, 450 B.C., A.D. 4	Modification of father's authority. Infanticide equated with murder.
Medieval (4th–13th Century). Power to the Church and State	400 A.D.–1300s (Continent)	Feudalism dominant institution in England. The church (Roman Catholic) is the major relief agency. The Church attached penance for overlaying and scalding and provided for foundlings. Censure is provided for death of a child by a mother's hands or refusal of the mother to nurse.
	529	Laws of Justinian. Establishment of orphan homes.
	787	First foundling hospital in Milan established by Datheus, archpriest.
	1224	Statutes of Winchester (a secular court) penalized women for keeping infants in

Period	Dates	Events and Perspective
		bed with them. By 1300, considerable law governing apprenticeships. Bishop of Bamburg forbade killing girl babies. Royal courts of Henry I assumed authority when child killed by anyone other than parent.
	1348	Black Death in England increased the number of dependent children.
Renaissance (14th–17th Century) From Feudalism to Family Groups. Secular Authority and Jurisdiction	1400s–1500s (Continent)	Antibreast feeding reaches its peak in Europe. Wet nursing is popular.
	1500s	Montaigne and Erasmus discouraged use of violence in child rearing and brought positive attention to the handicapped. Rousseau, as a humanitarian, encouraged a new respect for children and their rights. This period saw a shift from feudalism and communal living to a focus on family groups and a child-centered philosophy.
	1509	Henry III on the throne of England; presided over beginnings of the English Reformation; broke off from the church of Rome and established secular authority and jurisdiction.
	1535	Laws imposed punishment of the poor, especially vagrants. Children, ages 5–14, begging in the streets were assigned to work in husbandry, labor, or other crafts.
	1555	First Bridewell (a workhouse) established in London.
	1562	Under Elizabeth I, statute of artificers, which gave government regulating control over apprentices.
	1563	First compulsory tax for relief of poor; made government responsible for caring for poor.
	1572	Legislated overseers of the poor.

Period	Dates	Events and Perspective
	1590s	Severe economic depression, famine, and unemployment.
	1597	Almshouses established for the genuinely unemployed.
	Late 1500s	Laws more stringent through modifications.
	1601	Elizabethan Poor Laws. Law of land for 150 years and influences U.S. laws as well. Local communities (and families) responsible for poor. Provides for placing out of children.
	1619–1620 (American Colonies)	Virginia Company of London recruits in almshouses for children for the New World.
	1670s	Office of Tithing established in Massachusetts to supervise behavior of families.
(18th–19th Century) Training and Guidance Doctrine of *Parens Patriae* General Improvement of Child Care. Power of Institutions and Charities	1700s (England)	Increase and much concern regarding vagrant, delinquent and destitute children and youth in England. Much literature of this time provides statement regarding lack of humane treatment of children.
	1720–1751 (England)	Removal of Gin restrictions in England creates a "Ginepidemic." Birth rates drop, deaths of young children increase, children born weak (Fetal Alcohol Syndrome). (TenBensel, p. I–6.) Training begins for inmates of all ages in making goods. Invention of pediatrics influences general improvement in child care.
	1729 (England/Colonies)	School for poor girls and orphans is established by Ursuline Nuns, in New Orleans, Louisiana
	1736	First almshouse built in New York City.

Period	Dates	Events and Perspective
	1751	Gin Controls reinstituted.
	1756	Marine Society apprentices vagrant and delinquent boys to sea service on warships (England).
	1758	Sir John Fielding establishes Home of Refuge for Orphan Girls to "rescue them" from prostitution.
	1788 (England and U.S.)	New York State legalized indentures entered into by minors with consent of parents or guardians.
	1790s	Private charity groups begin to emerge to champion protection of children.
	1800s	Public conscience regarding neglected, handicapped, schools for deaf, blind, mentally retarded increases.
	1815	Problems relating to organized gangs in England increase.
	1817	New York City Society for Prevention of Pauperism established to "save juvenile offenders from vice and poverty."
	1834	England. Royal Commission recommends segregation of children from adults in mixed workhouses.
	1843	New York Association for Improving Conditions of the Poor founded in New York Juvenile Asylum, 1851. In 1854, an offshoot of this group formed New York Children's Aid Society led by Charles Loring Brace. One of his innovations: to send children out west with families.
	1850s	Juvenile crime in London reaches extreme proportions.
	1863	Massachusetts State Board of Charities established to supervise all state institutions.
	1866	Society for Prevention of Cruelty to Animals is founded.
	1871	New York State Medical Society supports

Period	Dates	Events and Perspective
		Foundling Asylums "The right of every newborn to be protected and supported." Mary Ellen, an abused child is protected by Society for the Prevention of Cruelty to Animals. Charity worker, Etta Angell Wheeler.
	1838–1900	Various legal challenges made to the practice of removing children from home without due process. Most outcomes support doctrine of *parens patriae*, the state as the protective parent.
	1874	Society for Prevention of Cruelty to Children, (a social agency with police powers; focus to remove child and punish parents).White slavery question raised.
	1875	New York State forbids that children be placed with adults in almshouses for more than 60 days.
	1880	Thirty-three societies for protection of children in the U.S.
	1882	New York State Medical Society, Abraham Jacobi, President. Committee formed to cooperate with SPCC in formulating legislation to improve child labor laws. Child Labor Laws. The "mother image" child savers: Jane Addams, Louise Bowen, Julia Lathrop.
	1889	Michigan Law addresses the "ill-treated child."
	1890s	Beginning of "social work" intervention with more family support.
1900–1950's (20th Century) Power to the Juvenile Court Federal Responsibility; The "Discovery of Child Abuse"	1899	First Juvenile Court, Chicago, Illinois. Heralded as the most important social institution to grow out of the efforts of the "social workers" of the nineteenth century. Institutionalization of children decreases. Child protection agencies exist in England, France, Germany, Italy, U.S., and other civilized countries.

Period	Dates	Events and Perspective
	1907	L.A. Police Department specialized in juvenile affairs. By 1910, had a separate juvenile bureau.
	1910	Mann Act white slave traffic act prohibits transporting by women across state lines for immoral purposes.
	1917	Juvenile Court legislation exists in all but three states.
	1925	Dr. John Caffey, radiologist, head of Babies hospital x-ray department, New York, notes unexplained x-ray manifestations in bones of some children and the belief that parents might be responsible.
	1930s	Depression.
	1935	Social Security Act helps to alleviate destitution.
	1938	Federal Juvenile Delinquency Act. Fair Labor Standards Act.
	1940–1950s	Period of large detention facilities.
	1945	Juvenile/Family Courts exist in all states.
	1946	Caffey publishes paper called "Multiple Fractures in the Long Bones of Infants Suffering from Chronic Subdural Hematoma." Attracts pediatric attention.
	1951–1958	Henry C. Kempe and staff study all different features of child abuse and link it to pediatrics.
	1957	Sweden first recognized child abuse as a pediatric problem. Swedish National Board of Health issues regulations, counseling, and research insttute.
	1950s	Exploring various intervention strategies with youth are popular.
	1956–1960s	Work camps and job camps for youth are accented.

Period	Dates	Events and Perspective
1960's – Present Children's Rights: A Shifting Balance of Power	1961	Multidisciplinary conference entitled "The Battered-Child Syndrome." Chairman of Program committee of American Academy of Pediatric, Henry C. Kempe.
	1962	Children's Bureau provides grants for study of child abuse. American Humane Society carries out surveys, issues publications, and convenes a national symposia regarding child abuse. Result of conference: a model child abuse law, eventually adopted by every state (1967).
	1960s	Time of dramatic legal, social, and procedural change regarding juveniles. In *Re Gault* and other cases revolutionize juvenile justice procedures. Beginning of increased legalistic focus of juvenile justice system. Social welfare intervention more professional. More medical intervention Therapeutic focus. In 1969, Jerome Miller begins closing Massachusetts institutions. Since 1960s, all U.S., Virgin Island, and Guam enact laws to protect children if parents fail to meet minimum standard of care. Reporting of child abuse by health professionals increases.
	1966	Study by the National Society for Prevention of Cruelty to Children sets in motion Denver House, in honor of Kempe.
	1970s	Los Angeles Police Department establishes desk for abused children.
	1974	First battered child unit: physical and sexual abuse. Juvenile Justice and Delinquency Prevention Act of 1974.
	1974	Child Abuse Prevention and Treatment Act PL93-247.
	1979	*Parham* decision (U.S. Supreme Court) clarification of parents' rights.

Period	Dates	Events and Perspective
	1979	International Year of the Child.
	1980	National Concern: Child Abuse and Neglect.
	1981	Year of the Disabled.
	1981–1983	Concern for a balancing of rights.
		Redefinition of Abuse/Neglect Standards of Proof in dependency matters.

Appendix 2

Jess: A Case Study

Jess and Marlene were married two years ago. Their courtship had been a stormy one. Jess was on the rebound from another relationship when he met Marlene. Jess, at 24, had never been married and was not sure whether he ever wanted to be. Marlene, age 20, had lost both of her parents when she was five years old and had grown up with grandparents and other relatives. Marlene's only family was her brother who was five years older.

After Jess and Marlene had been dating for about three months, Marlene announced to Jess that she was pregnant. Her announcement coincided with the reappearance of Jess' former girlfriend. Jess was in a quandry. Marlene, a devout Catholic, was emphatic that she did not want an abortion. Jess cared for Marlene, but he was not sure that he wanted to marry her.

Jess could not turn to his parents for advice. Jess had grown up with his grandmother and his brother during his teenage years. Jess had voluntarily moved in with his grandmother when he was 14-years-old.

One evening, when Jess' father was away on a business trip, his mother had climbed into bed with him. Jess could tell that she had been drinking. She began fondling him. Jess was very embarrassed. However, his mother usually ignored him. The attention and closeness seemed nice. Jess had never had any sexual experiences with anyone before that night. He quickly became physically aroused at his mother's soft touching. Before he knew what had happened, his mother was on top of him and he was inside of her. Later that evening, Jess' mother climbed out of his bed and went down the hall to her own bedroom. Several days later, when Jess' dad returned, Jess felt even more upset and confused. He worried that his dad would find out what had happened.

Nothing was said about the event. Several weeks later when Jess' father again was away for a period of time, the situation was repeated. Again, Jess felt very strange and guilty. The experience had been pleasurable, but Jess knew it was wrong. Jess and his mother never talked about these experiences.

When Jess was given the opportunity to live with his grandmother in another town, he quickly chose to go. It was the perfect way to get out of the difficult situation with his mother. When Jess returned home at age 17, just before going into the military, he noticed that his parents' relationship seemed very strained. Jess' mother never approached Jess again and he and his mother never talked about these events.

Jess decided to marry Marlene and have their child. At first, the couple was very close. In fact, they were so close that Jess told Marlene about what had happened with his mother. Marlene was stunned. She did not want to visit Jess' mother after that.

Marlene and Jess' baby was born prematurely. Mary, their baby, had to stay at the hospital for two months after her birth. She was a beautiful baby and both Jess and Marlene doted over her. Once, in the midst of a fight between himself and Marlene, Jess shouted at Marlene that she wasn't as good in bed as his mother had been. From that moment on, Marlene was very uncomfortable leaving Mary alone with Jess. She had read a magazine article that said that if a person had been sexually abused there was a great likelihood that the person would sexually abuse his own children.

The relationship between Jess and Marlene became more and more strained. Finally, their pediatrician sent them for some marriage counseling.

This situation highlights the long-term impact of sexual abuse. Jess had never had the opportunity to vent any of his feelings surrounding the events between him and his mother. At times during the ensuing years, Jess often wondered if he was weird. His brother, three years younger than Jess, seemed safe from his mother's sexual attacks. Jess used to wonder, ''why me?''

Jess grew up in a family that was strained by his father's absence and marital problems. There seemed to be a rule in Jess' family that it was not OK to talk about problems openly. When Jess' father and mother had a disagreement, rather than attempting to solve it, Jess' father would leave and Jess' mother would sit at home with her loneliness. During these times, before Jess' mother began sexually abusing him, Jess would try to console his mother. He always felt impotent in these situations because he did not seem to be able to say or do anything that made his mother feel any better about her problems. Later, one thing he did feel good about in his sexual experiences with his mother was that he seemed to please her and to take her mind off her problems with her husband.

As an adult, ten years after the first sexual contact with his mother, Jess still felt guilty about the experiences. Sometimes when he was having sex with his wife, the confusion would seem greatest. Jess wondered whether he would ever be able to forget those events which had happened so long ago.

Jess lived in a family that had blurred roles. At a time when Jess was experiencing his own budding sexuality, he needed to have clear guidance and reassurance from the adults in his life.

Fortunately, Jess and his wife were able to improve their marital relationship with the assistance of a social worker who provided counseling for them and helped them learn the skills they needed to have a satisfying and joyful marriage and to parent their daughter, Mary. In addition, Jess opted to have his own personal therapy to deal with the old and confusing issues between him and his mother. This case is one with a good outcome largely because Jess and Marlene sought help in solving their problems.

Appendix 3

The Care and Feeding of a Child Protection Team

GETTING STARTED

Who will begin? Who will be the leader who can call together the targeted group and expect good attendance? Who has energy, humor, organizational skills, and the respect of the group?

> *Calling the Strategy Sessions.* Determining the when, where, who, what, how, and why involves strategy. The place must be convenient, central, and conducive to a positive meeting; the time must consider the schedules of those invited; who is coming and who is inviting must encourage attendance; how the invitation is worded will make a difference; why must be expressed in a way that all will believe they are important (which they are) and that they have a contribution to make (which they do).

> *Who Should Be Present?* Who will be willing to work toward some mutual goals? Who in the target agencies know better than others the problems and solutions? The group needs to include representatives of all critical agencies, but it needs to be small enough to remain personalized and to maintain a spirit of creativity.

> *Education as Innovation.* The first meeting must have an interesting, informative, educational component that helps to inform all people present about the common problem to be faced.

> *In An Atmosphere of Mutual Respect.* Each person contributes to the atmosphere of mutual respect. Attention must be given to establishing the group as a group. This is an important time, the beginnings of identity.

Defining the Problem Together. Defining the problem is critical to problem solving. As a group activity it will help to define a group as a team.

Whose Problem Is It? The whole problem needs to be defined in a way that belongs to all group members. If it is not defined as a group problem it will not be solved as a group problem. This process helps to define responsibility and commitment.

What Does Each Member Have To Contribute? Each member can discuss his role in relation to the problem and what can be contributed from that role to the problem's solution. This also helps to define responsibility and commitment.

What Does Each Member Need? The role of each member requires some stipulation or perspective. For example, the police investigation culminates in some type of report. Investigations by police must be made and evidence collected in such a way that the evidence will be admissible in court. The whole group must appreciate the needs of its individual member agencies. Forms that are developed and procedures that are established must take this into account.

What Are The Possible Solutions? The group will need to explore as broad a range of options as possible. Brainstorming options may help to accomplish this goal. The action of brainstorming also helps to encourage individuals in the group to expand resources.

Which Would Be Most Satisfactory? This question is determined in an interdisciplinary way by the members of the group, each representing his/her own discipline. It is best expressed in goals and objectives. This is a practical way for group members to come to consensus in developing a plan.

What Will Each Member Contribute To The Solution From Their Respective Disciplines? This step is a search for resources. What resources does each agency member bring? How can these contribute to the solution? Again, commitment from individual members is required.

Group Housekeeping. Who will the leader be? What will be the organizational structure? If there are problems, how will they be approached? Authority issues may be solved in this context and a framework set for resolving any future issues that may arise. A clearly established structure will provide some assurance to group members that no one and no one's opinion will be discounted.

Confidentiality. This is an important issue and must be dealt with explicitly in a group. A review of state guidelines and local agency policy is a start. Some group guidelines can be set within the available legal structure.

The Action Contract. What will be done, now, next week, regularly, and on specific occasions. Making decisions about action is easier than acting. Scheduling when tasks are to be completed helps to make them a reality.

The Action in Action. Implementation of the contract is one of the very important steps in this process.

The Feedback Process: Self Evaluation. "What is" versus "what had been expected." The group needs to evaluate its own policies and procedures on a regular basis. How effectively is the group functioning? What changes need to be made?

The Energy Store. The group as a support system for its members can help to nurture them and restore their energy. Working with abusing families and with the agencies that are designated to respond is energy depleting and sometimes discouraging. The support of peers in a caring group may do much to make the group members effective.

Education and Training. Training on topics relative to the group should be interdisciplinary and on-going. This team can and should provide training within the community in individual agencies, among agencies, and for other community groups.

Appendix 4
Improving Your Skill in Interviewing

Considerations Before Beginning An Interview With A Child

Who Should Be Present? Parents may or may not be present at the interview. It may be helpful to some children, however, to have a supportive and trusted adult present during the interview.

Where Should The Interview Take Place? Every situation is individual as is every child. Where a child is interviewed and the circumstances of that interview must be determined in terms of the needs of the child and his/her circumstances.

Consider the Comfort of the Child. It is important that the interviewer begin "where the child is." The child may be hurt, in physical pain, afraid, and/or hysterical. Taking the time to care for the child first and considering his comfort will contribute to a positive outcome for the interview.

The Attitude of the Interviewer. The attitude of the interviewer toward the child is very important. Children can be very sensitive readers of nonverbal clues, even though they are not always accurate in their reading. Confusion, anger, frustration, or accusation on your part will be transmitted quickly to the child.

A review of Chapter 2, "In the Context of Family," will be helpful to a person interviewing children. In a broad sense, children respond within their stage of development. It is easy for an adult interviewer to use terms and concepts that a young child does not understand or understands differently than the interviewer. Every family has its own terminology, especially relating to anatomical parts and sexual behavior. Very young children do not have an accurate concept of time and distance. Their discussion of when an event occurred may be inaccurate, unless it can be tied to some other event that they recall. (Sexual Assault Center.)

A Calm Approach

Whether interviewing a child or adult, a pleasant, soft spoken, nonjudgmental approach will be calming and reassuring to the person being interviewed.

BE A CHILD

For a moment, be a child. Walk in the child's shoes. Remember that you have more power than he[1] does and you are bigger. From his point of view, you must want something from him or you would not be talking to him. Maybe he has done something wrong and you will punish him? Or maybe you're just asking him to talk about private things. You, this outsider, whom he never met before, wants him to tell about the most personal things in his life. What are you going to do with this bomb he is about to drop. Who will you tell? What will happen to him? To his family? Will he have any control over his life, over his story, once he has told it to you?

Providing A Positive Context

Providing Protection. The child needs to know that it is safe to discuss very private matters with the interviewer. Safety may be defined both in terms of personal danger and in the control of who knows and when they know what he has to say. The setting needs to be private. The child may be very worried about the fact that what is said can be heard through a window or door or by someone eavesdropping or passing by in the hall. Safety will have to exist not only during the interview, but after it as well. The interviewer must be trustworthy. The child needs to be told what will happen to the information shared.

Providing Permission. The child needs to know that he has permission to say whatever needs to be said without judgment of him or judgment of the parents. The interviewer will need to confirm that the child made the best decision when deciding to discuss family matters with the interviewer. The child's family, since it belongs to the child, cannot be terrible. If the family is terrible, the child is terrible too.

Providing Potency. The child needs to believe that interviewer is powerful enough to provide safety and strong enough to allow the child to depend on him.

Providing Pacing. The child needs to be able to tell what needs to be said at his own pace and in his own way. Pressure should not be applied to tell what the child is not ready to say, nor to present it in a particular way or time frame.

Providing Humanity. The child needs to believe that the interviewer is a caring

---

[1]For convenience the child is referred to as "he."

person. Feeling the interviewer's concern is important. Concern, however, is not to be interpreted as pity or anger.

Within the limits of the child's age and understanding, be honest about why you need the interview. Allow the child, if very young, to play games or to be "busy" as you observe the child's behavior.

INTERVIEWING PARENTS

Special Issues in Interviewing Adults

Parents will need to be informed of their legal rights. They need to know who the interviewer is and his authority for being there. They have a right to know allegations but not the name of the person who made the report.

Parents will probably be resistant. Why not? The investigator is an intruder, not only uninvited but under suspicious and frightening circumstances. Any time a person's power over his life and family appears to be threatened, that person will work to regain that control.

Although some adversary nature will remain in the relationship during the interview, the interviewer often can increase or decrease the antagonism and intensity of the negative feelings by her own actions. The sample approaches suggest some pitfalls and the insert, "Interviewing Parents," provides some positive suggestions for successful interviews.

SAMPLE APPROACH #1. DOUBLE TALK

"I just came by to check with you, Mr. and Mrs. Jones, about a report our agency received. I'm sure the report is unfounded. There is always the possibility that Jimmy might need to be placed outside your home. Of course, that is unlikely but . . ."

SAMPLE APPROACH #2. THE POOR CHILD

"I am very worried about Janice. Why does she have bruises on her arms and legs? You know, if you can't take proper care of her, the court will make other arrangements. She's only three years old. We really have to protect her."

SAMPLE APPROACH #3. FAILURE TO COMMUNICATE

"Based on this preliminary investigation and the medical finding of the pediatrician, a dependency petition will be filed in Joseph's behalf alleging that he is an abused child and in need of the protection of the court. An adjudicatory hearing will be scheduled for June 3rd. You will be subpoenaed to attend."

INTERVIEWING PARENTS

- Show that you are worthy of their trust. Be honest and straightforward. If you engage in double talk, the parents will be even more certain that you are not to be trusted.
- Allow parents to express their feelings and do not discount their feelings or their opinions. If they have difficulty expressing feelings or if they attempt to deny all feelings, acknowledge how difficult it can be to express feelings to someone that you do not know very well.
- Respond to feelings, not to the content. "You are a spy for the welfare department. Get out of my house!" is a statement of fear, frustration, and desperation. "You" only happen to be the person toward whom it is said.
- Be objective and supportive, not judgemental. Encourage the parent(s) to express their "side" without centering on the "poor child." If your only concern appears to be for the child, then, from the point of view of the parents, you are not concerned, nor do you understand their plight. Centering on the poor child will also infer that you are being judgemental of them.
- Parents, too, have difficulty with the fact that we are sometimes not speaking a shared language. In addition to terminology that the parents may find foreign to them, the language itself may be a problem. Parents, whose first language is not English, may find communication, especially of feelings, very difficult in a foreign language. If you do not speak their native language, take someone with you who does.

DEVELOPING EFFECTIVE INTERVIEWING TECHNIQUES

An interview has a beginning, a middle, and an end. The following outline of an interview is, of necessity, generalized, but it will serve to illustrate the structure of an interview and positive use of the structure in investigating allegations of abuse or neglect.

Structuring An Interview

I. Before the Interview Begins
   A. Self-Knowledge
   This is the time for self-introspection. You should understand what you bring of yourself to the interview. Why you? What are your prejudices and your fears? What feelings are you taking with you to the inerview?
   B. The Facts and Allegations
   Commit the facts and allegations to memory before you visit with the family so that you will not need to refer frequently to notes. Know your information accurately and completely.
   C. Goal Setting
   Be clear about the purpose of the interview. Be prepared to share the purpose with the family.

  D. The Interview Environment

  Where will the interview be conducted? How will the setting affect the goals? How can you facilitate your goals through your influence over the setting of the interview?

II. Beginning the Interview

  A. Establishing a Relationship

  First of all, be on time for the interview and be respectful of the person being interviewed. It is necessary to begin where the client is, with his/her concerns, feelings, and understanding of the problem. State why you are there in a positive, clear way. State your concern regarding the family, and specifically, the parents. Be trustworthy, firm, and reassuring.

  B. Commitment and Flexibility

  Take cues from the family about how to proceed. Avoid increasing danger to anyone. Remain committed and clear, but calm and respectful. If the family refuses to talk with you, be understanding of their concern. If necessary, leave. A negative confrontation or a shouting match will be helpful to no one. In all circumstances, assure that the child is safe.

III. Data Gathering and Analysis

  A. The Time and Scope of the Interview

  The interview needs to be relatively short, so that intrusion into the family is limited. Maintain control of the interview and keep the conversation logical. This does not mean that the person should not be allowed to express feelings. Feelings, including anger, need to be expressed and acknowledged. It is important to maintain a logical structure to the interview, because emotion and tension are high.

  B. The Relevance of Irrelevance

  Listen, even if much of what you hear at first appears to be irrelevant to the quetions you wish to ask. It is important to learn what the person being interviewed feels is important. You may learn how a person organizes her thoughts, how she interacts with others, the content and structure of her family life, and other very important data.

  Reality is what *is* and *is not* said and what *is* and *is not* observed. These data are important to understanding the family and the environment. Attempt to observe without being obtrusive.

  C. Sorting and Tracking of Information

  Be sure that you clearly understand the information you have received. Double check if you are unclear about the meaning of a statement. If necessary, review the important points that the person is making. If reference is made to something that requires further explanation but you do not want to change the direction of the interview at the time it is mentioned, make a mental note and return to the topic at a later time.

IV. Closing the Interview

  A. Tying Loose Ends Together

  Summarize what you have heard and observed in terms of your concern for the family and child. It may be necessary to state and restate important information. Often, in a crisis, accessing information is blocked. Even though everyone is listening to what is said, people in crisis may have difficulty organizing it into useful, remembered information. Keep all parties informed of your evaluation, if you have made one.

B. What Will Happen Next

Explain what will happen next in terms that the person being interviewed can understand. Answer any questions regarding the process that you can. Repeat important information. Conclude the interview with a plan intact. Limits must be set and realistic expectations must be agreed upon at the close of the interview. Make no promises that you cannot keep. Be as clear as you can about what is to happen next.

C. Repeat Reassurances

Reassure the family or child that you are aware of their concern for their needs and their child's needs and you wish to help. Reassure the child and family that any disclosure that has been made is right. If possible, point out some of the strengths that you have observed. (See also Garrett; Benjamin; Sexual Assault Center.)

THE ART OF ASKING QUESTIONS

Questions are a part of interviewing. How those questions are asked make a major difference in the information obtained, the interaction betwen interviewer and person interviewed, and the closure that is possible.

Some helpful hints in asking questions include:

1. Use open-ended rather than closed questions. For example, do not ask questions that can be answered yes or no. If you want to know from a child, "Did your father hit you?", a better question might be, "How did you get the bruise on your cheek?" If you are asking the question of an adult, the question might be, "How did Joe get the bruise on his cheek?"

   Even this sort of question may be too direct for a child who is frightened or feeling guilty. It is possible to ask more general questions which eventually will lead more comfortably back to the issue. An example: "Would you tell me about your day?" An even more indirect question may be necessary with a child. "Will you be an easy going or a strict father/mother when you have children?"

2. Avoid "Why" questions as a general rule. William Glasser, author of *Reality Therapy* and other books, suggests that such questions imply the need for the statement of an excuse for some behavior. With children an even more important reason exists for not using such questions. "Why" did you or "why" didn't you or "why" don't you all imply that the child "should have" done something different. Why questions require a defense, an attack, or a withdrawal. None of these will be helpful in the interview.

3. Use "I" statements rather than "You" statements. "You" statements may appear accusatory. "I" statements are more neutral and acceptable. "You didn't answer that question clearly" sounds like an accusation. "I didn't understand your answer. Would you talk more about the subject?" connotes respect and interest.

Appendix 5

Helpful Hints for Witnesses

RESOLVING SOME OF THE ISSUES AHEAD OF TIME

If you are called on to testify in a dependency matter:

1. Keep accurate records. Instant recall of all pertinent facts is unlikely without records.
2. Review notes, but do not memorize them as a speech.
3. Dress appropriately for court. A businesslike approach, both in dress and in attitude is best.
4. Talk with the attorney who is calling you to testify before the hearing. Determine what sort of questions might be asked. If you are an expert witness and your field is very technical, explain some of the technical details to the attorney. The attorney will then be able to ask appropriate questions that will permit you to explain important facts to the court.
5. If you are employed and attending the court hearing voluntarily might present a hardship for you on the job, ask that you be subpoenaed to attend. Employers are bound to honor the command of the court without penalizing you.

RESPONDING TO QUESTIONS ASKED

1. Know your facts. If there are details you feel you may forget, jot them down.
2. Do not be afraid to share your concerns regarding the child's welfare with the court.

3. Speak in a clear tone of voice loud enough for all to hear easily.
4. Avoid mistakes, but if they are made, offer to correct them as soon as you become aware of them.
5. Tell the court when you are estimating something rather than saying it is absolutely such and such.
6. Avoid losing your temper. Be courteous to all participants in the case.
7. Be brief and responsible in your answers. Do not attempt to give testimony not called for by the questions put to you.
8. Listen carefully to the question. Do not answer it unless you are sure you understand it.
9. Tell the truth.
10. Answer positively rather than doubtfully.
11. Do not be rushed. Take your time.
12. Stop talking when there is an objection.

Index